INTERACTIONS IN THE WORLD ECONOMY

INTERACTIONS IN THE WORLD ECONOMY

Perspectives from International Economic History

Edited by
Carl-Ludwig Holtfrerich

NEW YORK UNIVERSITY PRESS
Washington Square, New York

First published in the USA in 1989 by
NEW YORK UNIVERSITY PRESS
Washington Square
New York, NY 10003

Copyright © 1989 by Carl-Ludwig Holtfrerich
All rights reserved
Manufactured in Great Britain

Library of Congress Cataloging-in-Publication Data

Interactions in the world economy: perspectives from international
  economic history / edited by Carl-Ludwig Holtfrerich.
    p. cm.
  Includes bibliographical references.
  ISBN 0-8147-3465-0
  1. International trade. 2. Economic development. 3. Economic
history. I. Holtfrerich, Carl-Ludwig.
HF1379.I55   1989
382'.09'03—dc20   89-39490
                                                                CIP

Festschrift
in honour of
Wolfram Fischer

Results of a symposium at Berlin on 6–7 May 1988
organised by Hartmut Kaelble,
Heinrich Volkmann, and Carl-Ludwig Holtfrerich
on the occasion of his sixtieth birthday

Wolfram Fischer

CONTENTS

Contributors   xiii

1 Introduction: The Evolution of World Trade, 1720 to the Present   1
Carl-Ludwig Holtfrerich

World trade and its structure   1
Determinants of world trade   10
The present contributions to the discussion of world trade issues   23
Notes   26
References   27

PART I   Theoretical Perspectives   31

2 Theoretical Issues Concerning the History of International Trade and Economic Development   33
Gerald M. Meier

Classical trade theory and growth   34
Development through trade: a 'nineteenth-century variety'   41
Development through trade: a 'twentieth-century variety'   48
Concluding remarks   54
Notes   55
References   56

PART II Pre-Industrial and Early Industrial Trade　　59

3 The China Seas and the World Economy between the Sixteenth and Nineteenth Centuries: The Changing Structures of Trade　　61
Peter W. Klein

Introduction	61
The China Seas, Europe and Japan	64
The East China Sea	66
The South China Sea	70
The arrival of the Europeans	73
The Dutch East India Company	77
The English East India Company and other traders	82
The Chinese junk trade	85
Conclusion	86
References	87

4 Opportunity and Risk in Atlantic Trade during the French Revolution　　90
François Crouzet

The Codman house and French inflation	91
Atlantic trade during the Anglo-French War	100
The perils of passage	108
The problem of information	116
Profits and loss	124
The end of the story	135
Notes	137
References	149

PART III The Modern Process of Technological and Financial Innovation in Europe Until 1913　　151

5 Some Thoughts on Economic Hegemony: Europe in the Nineteenth-Century World Economy　　153
David S. Landes

The roots of European trading and dominance	154
The nineteenth century and new technology	158

The twentieth century and its problems	161
Conclusion	165
Notes	166
References	166

6 British Coal on Continental Markets, 1850–1913   168
Rainer Fremdling

Introduction	168
British coal exports	169
France	174
The Netherlands	176
Northern Germany	178
Conclusion	186
Notes	186
References	188

7 The Growth of International Banking to 1914   191
Rondo Cameron

Banks: the first multinationals	191
The era of merchant banking	194
The rise of joint stock banks	197
International banking in its prime, 1870–1914	204
Conclusions	216
Notes	217
References	217

PART IV Aspects of Growth and Stagnation in the World Economy during the Twentieth Century   221

8 World Economic Performance Since 1870   223
Angus Maddison

The long-term record	223
Phases of growth	228
Conclusions	233
Appendix	233
References	237

9 Europe and the World Economy During the Inter-war Period   239
Herman Van der Wee and Erik Buyst

Introduction	239
The aftermath of the First World War (1918–25)	239
Misleading stability (1925–9)	245
The Great Depression (1929–39)	249
Conclusion	257
References	258

10 Motives for Currency Convertibility: The Pound and the Deutschmark, 1950–5   260
Alan S. Milward

'Operation Robot' and the 'Collective Approach'	261
A replacement for Bretton Woods?	265
Approach to the Federal Republic	268
The smaller European countries	271
US policy	273
Britain's falling reserves	274
British and German exports	275
The advantages and disadvantages of convertibility	278
Conclusion	282
Notes	283
References	284

PART V The Centre and the Periphery of the Twentieth-Century World Economy   285

11 The United States and the World Economy in the Twentieth Century   287
Charles P. Kindleberger

Goods markets	292
Foreign exchange	298
Capital flows	303
Coordination of macro-economic policy	307
The lender of last resort	310
References	312

CONTENTS xi

12 Hard Times: Latin America in the 1930s and 1980s 314
Albert Fishlow

Introduction 314
Origins of the decline 316
Adjustment of the balance-of-payments disequilibrium 321
Foreign capital 324
Effects of reduced debt service 330
Debt relief in historical perspective 334
Notes 335
References 336

13 Newly Industrialising Countries in the World Economy: NICs, SICs, NECs, EPZs or TEs? 338
Detlef Lorenz

Introduction 338
Just successful developing countries? 339
G-4 and the Asian NICs respectively 341
NICs and NECs or identifying the NICs in the new international division of labour 343
Emulating a model of a sequence of stages? 347
A closer look at NICs splitting up in 'hinterland' relationships 349
The constraint of being a transitional economy (TE) 354
Dangerous generalisations versus NICs revisited 359
Open research questions 360
Notes 361
References 363

Index 367

CONTRIBUTORS

Erik Buyst, born in 1960, is a research assistant at Leuven University. He has published several articles on the economic, social and political history of Belgium.

Rondo Cameron, born in 1925, is William Rand Kenan, Jr, University Professor at Emory University, Atlanta, Georgia. He is a past-president of the Economic History Association (USA) and is currently vice-president of the International Economic History Association. He served as editor of the *Journal of Economic History* from 1975 to 1981. His most recent publication is *A Concise Economic History of the World from Paleolithic Times to the Present* (Oxford University Press, 1989).

François Crouzet, born in Monts-sur-Guesnes, France in 1922, is Professor of History at the University of Paris-Sorbonne. Among his publications are: *Capital Formation in the Industrial Revolution* (1972), *L'Economie de la Grande-Bretagne Victorienne* (1978), *Britain and France: Ten Centuries* (ed. with F. Bedarida and D. Johnson, 1980) and numerous articles on the history and economic history of Great Britain.

Albert Fishlow is Professor of Economics at the University of California at Berkeley. He first joined the faculty there in 1961 upon completion of PhD studies at Harvard. During 1978–83 he was Professor of Economics and Director of the Center for International and Area Studies at Yale University. He has served as Deputy Assistant Secretary of State for Inter-American Affairs in 1975–6 and has been a member of many public task forces related to Latin American affairs. He is currently co-editor of the *Journal of Development Economics*. His research includes numerous books and articles that have addressed issues in American and Latin American economic history, Brazilian development strategy, economic relations between industrialised and developing countries, and the problem of developing country debt.

Rainer Fremdling, born in 1944, received his PhD at the University of Münster in 1974, where he was lecturer in economic history from 1970 to 1981. From 1981 to 1987 he worked as assistant professor at the Free University of Berlin. Since October 1987 he has held the chair of economic and social history at the University of Groningen. His research also pursued abroad (Philadelphia 1975–6, Oxford 1978–9, Leuven 1979 and Paris 1979), has concentrated on the industrialisation process in Germany and western Europe. Among his publications are two monographs: *Eisenbahnen und deutsches Wirtschaftswachstum, 1840–1879* (2nd edn, Dortmund 1985) and *Technologischer Wandel und internationaler Handel im 18. und 19. Jahrhundert. Die Eisenindustrien in Grossbritannien, Belgien, Frankreich und Deutschland* (Berlin 1986).

Carl-Ludwig Holtfrerich, born in 1942, is Professor of Economics and Economic History at the Free University of Berlin. He also taught at the University of Frankfurt (1980–3). He was a visiting professor at Oxford in 1982 and has done research on issues in international, financial and trade relations several times in the United States, especially in 1975/6 as a J.F. Kennedy Memorial Fellow at Harvard University and in 1982/3 as a fellow of the W. Wilson International Center for Scholars in Washington, DC. Among his publications are: *The German Inflation 1914–1923: Causes and Effects in International Perspective* (Berlin/New York: de Gruyter, 1986) and (with H.O. Schötz) *Vom Weltgläubiger zum Weltschuldner: Erklärungsansätze zur historischen Entwicklung und Struktur der internationalen Vermögensposition der USA* (Frankfurt: Knapp, 1988).

Charles P. Kindleberger was born in New York City in 1910. After having received degrees from the University of Pennsylvania and Columbia University he served in governmental and quasi-governmental positions, including military service, from 1936 to

1948 when he was appointed to a teaching position in economics at the Massachussetts Institute of Technology (MIT) from which he is now emeritus. He has written some twenty books and numerous articles on international economics, international finance and economic history, especially on Europe and the United States.

Peter W. Klein, born in 1931 in Vienna, has been Professor of Early Modern History at the State University of Leiden since 1985. Between 1965 and 1985 he was Professor of Economic and Social History at Erasmus University, Rotterdam. In addition to his membership in several academic associations, Klein is acting president of the Dutch Historical Society. Among his publications are: *Quantitative Aspects of the Amsterdam Rye Trade during the Seventeenth Century and the Economic History of Europe* (1978) and several other books in Dutch.

David S. Landes, born in 1924, is Professor of Economics at Harvard University. He is the author of *Revolution in Time: Clocks and the Making of the Modern World* (1983), which was recently issued in a revised and enlarged French edition, *L'heure qu'il est: les horloges, la mesure du temps et la formation du monde moderne* (1987). Landes has also written articles on social time and the links between time measurement and science. He is currently writing a book on *The West and the Rest: Why Are We So Rich and They So Poor?*.

Detlef Lorenz is currently Professor of International Economics at the Department of Economics, Free University of Berlin. He has been a British Council Research Associate, and recently a Visiting Fellow at the Institute of Southeast Asian Studies (ISEAS), Singapore, as well as a Professional Associate of the East–West Center, Honolulu, Hawaii. Professor Lorenz has written many articles on issues of international trade theory and policy. The current focus of his research is on neo-protectionism, newly industrialising economies (NICs) and problems of regionalisation in the world economy. Recent publications have included: *International Divison of Labour or Closer Cooperation? A Look at ASEAN–EC Economic Relations; Intra-Regional Trade and Pacific Cooperation: Problems and Prospects,* and *A GATT for the Mercantilists?*

Angus Maddison, born in Newcastle-upon-Tyne, England in 1926, is currently Professor of Economics at the University of Groningen, Netherlands. Between 1958 and 1978 he held several positions with OEEC and OECD. Maddison's main fields of interest are comparative economic studies, productivity and growth, and economic history. His book publications include: *Economic Performance and Policy in Europe 1913–1970* (1976), *Phases of Capitalist Development* (1982) and *Unemployment: The European Perspective* (ed., 1982).

Gerald M. Meier, born in 1923, is Professor of International Economics and Policy Analysis at Stanford University. Prior to coming to Stanford in 1963 he was Professor of Economics at Wesleyan University, and he had taught at Williams College, Yale University and the University of Oxford. Meier is the author of a number of books in international economics and economic development. These include: *International Economics: Theory of Policy* (1980), *Leading Issues in Development Economics* (4th edn, 1984), *Pioneers in Development* (1984–6), and *Financing of Asian Development* (1986). In addition, Meier has been General Editor of the *Economic Development Series*. Meier has also been a consultant to the World Bank.

Alan S. Milward, born in 1935, is Professor of Economic History at the London School of Economics and Political Science. He was formerly Professor of Contemporary History at the European University Institute, Professor of European Studies at the University of Manchester, and Associate Professor of Economics at Stanford University. Among his publications are: *War, Economy and Society, 1939–1945* (1977) and *The Reconstruction of Western Europe, 1945–1951* (1984).

Herman Van der Wee, born in 1928, is Professor of Social and Economic History at Leuven University and has taught at several other Belgian and foreign universities. He is president of the International Economic History Association. His publications include *The Growth of the Antwerp Market and the European Economy (Fourteenth–Sixteenth Centuries)* (1963) and *Prosperity and Upheaval: The World Economy 1945–1980* (1986).

1 · INTRODUCTION: THE EVOLUTION OF WORLD TRADE, 1720 TO THE PRESENT

Carl-Ludwig Holtfrerich

A broad subject like the one circumscribed by the title of this book is always in need of some concise basic information which may serve as the spine that provides shape and contours to the flesh of the more lively discussion of specific issues to follow. As a point of departure and as a frame of reference for the varied aspects of the discussion contained in the individual chapters of this book, I have chosen to present the broad trends in world trade growth and in its structural development since the eighteenth century as well as some standard explanations for these developments. I will briefly summarise the different contributions to the book at the end of this chapter.

WORLD TRADE AND ITS STRUCTURE

Overall volume since 1720

Statistics on the volume (and value) of world trade have been regularly collected and published by the United Nations since it came into existence in 1945. For the inter-war period the League of Nations performed similar functions, albeit less comprehensively. Although statistics on foreign trade were collected by most countries much earlier than any other macro-economic statistics, they become less complete and reliable the further back we go in time, especially when aggregated on to a more encompassing

Table 1.1 Growth rates of the volume of world trade and world industrial/manufacturing production, 1705/20–1985 (annual average in per cent)

	World trade	World industry
1705–85	–	1.50
1720–80	1.10	–
1780–1830	1.37	2.60
1820–40	2.81	2.90
1840–60	4.84	3.50
1860–70	5.53	2.90
1870–1900	3.24	3.70
1900–13	3.75	4.20
1913–29	0.72	2.70
1929–38	−1.15	2.00
1938–48	0.00	4.10
1948–71	7.27	5.60
1971–4	8.31	6.84
1974–80	4.15	3.60
1980–6	2.94	2.65

Sources: Rostow (1978: 67); GATT (1976: 4); GATT (1982): Table A1 of Appendix; GATT (1987: 155).

regional or world-wide level. While pre-First-World-War time series on the development of world trade are all estimates, their reliability diminishes considerably as we move backwards to 1720. Walt Rostow (1978: 663–9) discusses in detail the quality of the data and has compiled different previous estimates for different sub-periods into a volume index of world trade from 1720 to 1971 (for other estimates see Maddison, Chapter 8 in this volume). He has done the same for a volume index of industrial or manufacturing production (Rostow 1978: 659–62). I will not repeat his discussion on methods and sources, but I will present his figures on the average annual growth rates of world trade and – for comparison – world industrial production, extending both series into the mid-1980s on the basis of United Nations statistics (see Table 1.1).

Table 1.1 reveals that the growth of world trade lagged behind the growth of manufacturing production well into the early stages of industrialisation. While the pace of industrial growth accelerated after 1780, when Great Britain entered the industrial revolution, world trade growth remained moderate until the period of major trade disturbances came to a close. That period began with the boycott of British goods by American colonists, lasted through the War of Independence and the French Revolutionary Wars, and ended with the Napoleonic Wars in 1815.

From 1820 to 1840 both the trade and the industrial growth rates approached 3 per cent per annum. During the following three decades, world trade grew at around 5 per cent per annum which was not only far higher than ever before and for a long time thereafter, but also much higher than industrial production. From 1870 to 1913 the trade volume fell behind production growth again. This led Werner Sombart, who had observed the same trends in national relationships of domestic production and foreign trade growth, to formulate his 'historical law' of the 'declining importance of international trade' (Haberler 1964: 11; Sombart 1919: 368–76), which was to be empirically disproved after the Second World War by an unforeseen growth in intra-industry international trade.

The period from 1913 to 1948 was marked by the First World War, its consequences on monetary and trade relations, by a brief recovery of international trade growth in the second half of the 1920s followed by the greatest economic collapse ever, by policies of autarky and bilateralism in the 1930s, and finally by the Second World War. While despite interruptions industrial production kept moving ahead overall, world trade fluctuated wildly around a no-growth trend during that period.

As if to make up for its previous laggardly pace, world trade growth broke all records during the quarter-century after 1948 and even outpaced the growth of industrial production, itself at record levels.

After 1974 the rates of increase in the volume of world trade as well as world manufacturing production returned to the level of nineteenth-century growth rates. As in the period 1840–70, trade outpaced production in the 1970s and 1980s. Both periods share a liberal world trade regime, the prior period, however, exhibiting an increasing trend toward liberalisation, the recent one showing a decreasing tendency, mainly due to the spreading of the so-called neo-protectionist practices.

In the two-and-a-half centuries we have examined, world industrial production grew on the whole much faster than world trade. Even if we disregard the early industrial age and include the two major periods of world trade liberalisation, world industrial production on average grew 3.78 per cent per annum versus 3.55 per cent per annum for world trade from 1840 to 1971 (Rostow 1978: 662, 669). Of course, we get a different picture when we compare the growth of world trade with that of total world production. Maddison in his contribution to this volume presents and discusses statistics on real GNP (gross national product) growth since 1870 for the five biggest OECD (Organisation for Economic Cooperation and Development) and the five biggest non-OECD countries. Their weighted average annual growth rate of real GDP (gross domestic product) amounted to 2.7 per cent from 1870 to 1987, while the volume of world trade showed an annual average growth rate of 3.1 per cent from 1870 to 1971 (Rostow 1978: 669) and a rate of 4.48 per cent from 1971 to 1986. That is markedly higher than the economic growth of the ten-country sample comprising 68 per cent of world production. This is due to the fact that industrial growth, of course, outpaced the growth of primary production practically all the time and production in the tertiary sector most of the time.

Regional structure since 1720

Historical data on the regional structure of world trade are presented in Table 1.2. My critical remarks in the previous section on the reliability of the estimates on the volume of world trade are equally true for the data on regional structure. The broad trends, however, should be accurately reflected.

Europe dominated throughout the whole period.[1] It is clear from Table 1.2 that West European countries, with the exception of Great Britain, most likely France with its mercantilistic policy and Holland with its successful merchants, gained about the same six percentage points that India lost from 1720 to 1780.[2] Then came Great Britain around 1780, the 'first industrial nation' that embarked upon what Kuznets called 'modern economic growth'. By the time of the Napoleonic Wars – with their consequences for the international trade (and production) structure (Crouzet 1964: 567–88) – Britain reached the all-time high of one third of world trade, mainly at the expense of other European countries. After peace had returned in 1815, Great Britain's share in world trade hovered at around a quarter of the total before a steady decline began after 1870. Western continental Europe had lost out to

INTRODUCTION 5

Table 1.2 Regional structure of world trade, 1720–1985 (in per cent)

	Western Europe		Rest of Europe				America		Asia			
Year	Great Britain, France, Italy, Germany, Switzerland, Holland, Belgium, Scandinavia	Of which Great Britain only	Spain, Portugal, Austrian Empire, Turkish Empire, Russia and other Eastern Europe	Of which Spain only	Of which Eastern Europe (until 1901–5 Russia) only	Total Europe	North America (until 1889, USA only)	Latin America	Total	Of which India only	Other	Total world
1720	42	13	27	12	9	69	—	12	—	11	8	100
1750	45	13	27	10	10	72	—	11	—	7	9	99
1780	48	12	26	10	9	74	2	11	—	5	8	100
1800	61	33	16	3	9	77	2	7	—	3	7	99
1820	61	27	15	3	6	76	5	8	—	3	8	101
1830	61	24	16	3	7	77	6	8	—	3	7	101
1840	60	25	14	2	5	74	5	8	—	2	9	101
1850	57	22	12	1	5	69	7	8	—	3	9	99
1860	58	25	11	2	3	69	7	8	—	4	11	99
1870	58	25	14	2	5	72	9	6	—	3	12	101
1880	59	23	12	2	4	71	8	6	—	4	11	101
1889	58	22	11	2	3	69	10	5	—	4	11	100
1891–5	56	18	9	2	3	65	12	5	—	4	13	100
1901–5	55	16	10	2	4	65	13	—	—	4	23	100
1913	50	16	14	1	13	64	14	8	9	—	22	101
1928	41	14	10	2	8	51	18	9	13	—	6	101
1938	40	14	7	<0.5	6	47	13	7	17	—	10	100
1948	35	12	6	1	5	41	22	12	13	2.2	16	101
1958	37	9	11	1	9	48	19	9	14	2.6	11	100
1963	40	8	13	1	11	53	17	7	14	1.4	10	99
1971	42	7	11	1	9	53	18	6	15	1.3	9	100
1979	39	6	12	1	8	52	15	5	20	0.6	8	100
1986	38	5	13	1	9	52	18	4	20	0.5	6	100

Britain only as long as the Napoleonic Wars and the trade blockades connected with it lasted, but Spain and the other countries listed under 'Rest of Europe' lost out permanently. As Spain (and Portugal) had given way to Great Britain with the beginning of the nineteenth century, so had their colonies in Latin America given way to the United States.

From 1870 to 1913 Europe as a whole lost world market shares, while North America gained.[3] But inside Europe Great Britain lost in percentage points even more than Europe as a whole, which indicates that other European countries, especially Germany, gained in world market shares at the expense of Great Britain (Kindleberger 1975a). On the eve of the First World War, two countries were rivals to be the potential 'heir to Empire', to borrow an expression from Parrini's (1969) book on US foreign economic policy after the First World War. When he placed the rise of the United States and the decline of Great Britain into a broader historical perspective in 1900, Brooks Adams had correctly seen Germany as the only rival of the United States for a world leadership role (Adams 1900/1947: 193).

The First World War, the inter-war period, and the Second World War led to a severe decline in Europe's share of world trade, from which it only partially recovered during the reconstruction-related 'economic miracles' that lasted into the 1960s (Jánossy 1971). Until 1948 North and Latin America, as well as countries on the periphery of the world economy in Asia and other continents, had been increasing their supply to markets which had formerly been served by European producers. These were the decades in which industrialisation spread to the Third World, which due to its own 'demographic transition' with continuing high birth rates but diminishing death rates, experienced a population explosion even more pronounced than that of Europe from the late eighteenth century to the First World War (Fischer 1979a: 74–6). The resulting change in the distribution of world population in the twentieth century also contributes to the explanation of Europe's diminished role in world trade (Fischer 1980: 14–17).

Commodity and price structure since 1870

Post-World War Two time series for these variables are published by various international organisations (GATT, IMF, UN and

OECD). Historical statistics for the commodity structure of world trade have been presented by Yates (1959) back to 1913, by Baldwin (1958) back to 1900 and by Hilgerdt (1945) back to the 1870s. In conjunction with the current GATT (General Agreement on Tariffs and Trade) statistics on international trade, these data show that it wasn't until after the Second World War that manufactured goods became quantitatively more important in international trade than primary products.[4] In fact, the share of primary products in total world trade remained almost constant at around 63 per cent from the second half of the 1870s to the second half of the 1930s (Yates 1959: 37). Within the primary product commodity group, however, substantial changes also occurred during that period, namely the declining importance of food relative to mineral raw materials (Fischer 1985a: 27; 1979b: 15).

Kindleberger (1956) studied the terms of trade of industrial European countries in world trade as far back as 1870. Morgan (1959/60) added data on non-European countries' terms of trade to the collection. Hilgerdt (1945: 18) also pushed his analysis of the terms of trade between manufactured goods and primary products back to the 1870s (cp. Rostow 1978: 98). For the earlier part of the nineteenth century there are data on the terms of trade as well as the commodity structure for Great Britain (Imlah 1958) and for the United States (Heffer 1986; cf. also Kenwood and Lougheed 1983: 169). A recent critical discussion of historical terms-of-trade data and their relevance for the relationship between industrialised and Third World countries (for the Singer–Prebisch thesis) is supplied by Foreman-Peck (1983: 110–12) and by Fischer (1979b: 22–6).

Price data, such as the terms of trade, have historically fluctuated strongly with the business cycle. Hilgerdt (1945) was interested in the analysis of long-term cycles and the relationship between the commodity and price structures of world trade. He originally presented the data contained in Figure 1.1 that were updated to cover the post-Second World War period also.

Figure 1.1 is the result of calculations with indexes (1913 = 100). Its A-line, therefore, does not indicate the commodity structure of world trade itself, but only movements in the commodity structure. More exactly it shows the relative size of changes in world trade of manufactured goods versus those in primary goods. It displays the inverse relationship between movements in the terms

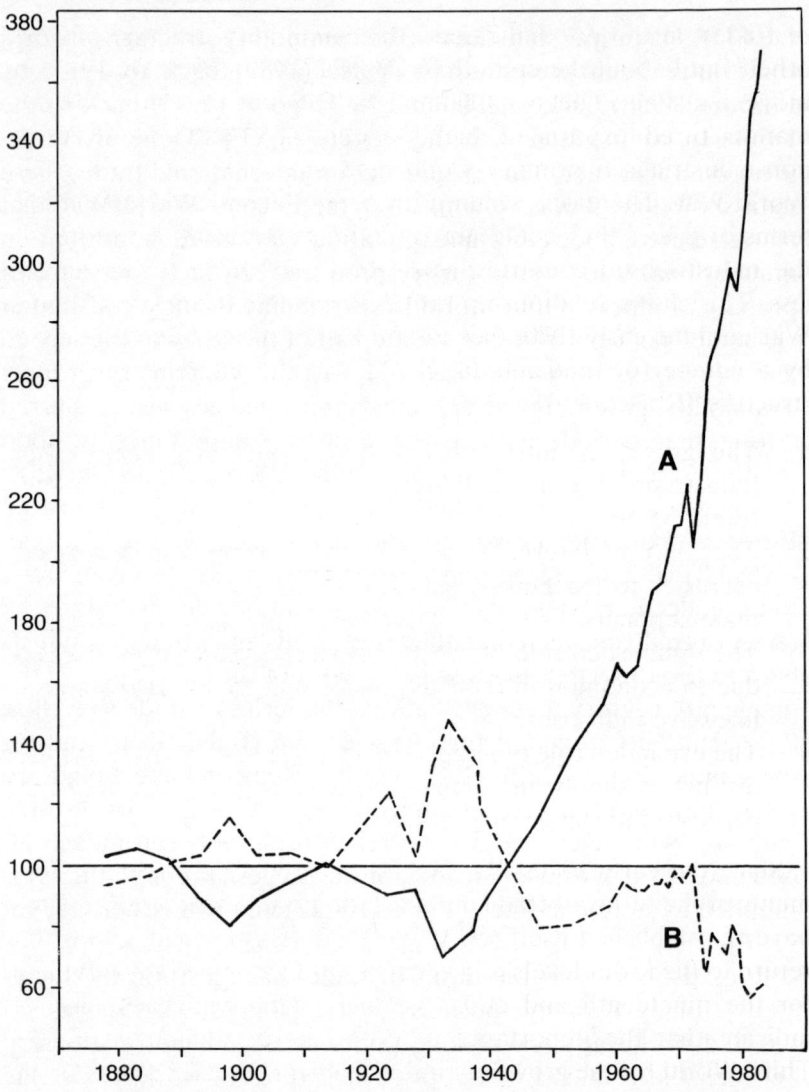

A = Quantum index of world trade in manufactured goods as percentage of that in primary goods.
B = Price index of manufactured goods as percentage of that for primary goods.

Figure 1.1 Relative price movements and world trade, 1876–1980 (1913 = 100). *Sources*: Rostow (1978: 98); United Nations (1985, 1986): Tables 14 each.

of trade, on the one hand, and the commodity structure on the other, until about the end of the Second World War. The inverse movements have been explained by the fact that most of the manufactured exports of highly industrial countries flowed to non-industrialised primary-producer countries up to the Second World War. Therefore, when primary producers faced favourable terms of trade, they could absorb more manufactured exports of the industrialised countries; and when they were unfavourable, less. This classic relationship broke down after the Second World War until the early 1970s (see Figure 1.1). This has been explained by a number of fundamental changes in the international trade structure (Rostow 1978: 98):

1. The growth in intra-industry trade which has made other industrialised countries their own best customers for manufactured exports.
2. The shift in international grain trade from less-developed countries to the United States, Canada and Australia as the main suppliers.
3. The diminished role of raw materials in industrial production due to economies in their use and a shift to less raw-material intensive industries.
4. The expanded role of mineral oil in international trade and the distinctive supply and demand behaviour in this market compared to the classic markets in primary products.

Since the early 1970s, the inverse relationship between movements in the terms of trade and the commodity structure seems to have re-established itself (cf. Figure 1.1). This coincides with the return to the lower levels of growth in production and trade typical for the nineteenth and early twentieth century. This seems to indicate that the importance of economic developments in the Third World for the growth of industrial exports and production in developed countries was interrupted only as long as extraordinary opportunities for investment and economic growth related to economic reconstruction needs existed in Europe and Japan. The first oil shock of 1973–4 might therefore be interpreted as the result of the realisation on the part of the supplier countries that the well-being of the industrial world was again hooked in the pre-war traditional way to that of primary commodity-producing countries on the periphery.

DETERMINANTS OF WORLD TRADE

The development of world trade since the eighteenth century can best be understood as a long-term process towards the integration of markets. It is true that there were interruptions, distortions, and at times reversions in this process, because the costs of integration seemed to outweigh the benefits when viewed from a narrow, statusquo and short-term perspective and, therefore, national governments sometimes (as in the 1930s) tried to hinder or reverse the process. But the attraction to entrepreneurial and consumer interests alike of exploiting new economic opportunities constituted a strong and powerful element in the long run, while modern democratic political systems remained flexible enough to overcome periods of stagnation or even retrogression in the process of world market integration. Only when the political process was dominated by rigid and strong ideologies, such as the nationalistic and antimodernist ones in inter-war European countries and Japan in the 1930s or the anticapitalistic ideology in socialist countries, did countries endure extended periods of success in denying the economic benefits of integration into world markets. But at present even the socialist countries no longer seem able to resist the lure of the efficiency gains from liberalising and integrating their markets internally and externally.

Some main factors that contributed to the progressive long-term integration of world markets and thus to the growth of world trade were innovations in the following fields:

1. Technological and organisational progress in primary production, industry and trade.
2. Fiscal innovations with consequences for trade barriers.
3. The technological and economic revolution in transport and communication.
4. The financial innovations in international monetary and credit relations.
5. Innovations in legal systems and international law.

I will briefly discuss each of these fields in the following section.

Industrial growth and increasing returns to scale

The prime mover behind the growth of international trade since the eighteenth century was the continuously innovative process of industrialisation and modern economic growth (Landes 1965; Kuznets 1966). As Wolfram Fischer (1978: 678) has pointed out, countries in Europe developed this economic dynamism because of a competitive environment forged by a superior private business culture and political and social decentralisation. Fischer (1981b: 37–46) has taken issue with the view that the impoverishment of Third World countries was a precondition for Europe's rise to industrial predominance. As David Landes concludes in his contribution to this volume, Europe's commerical pre-eminence in the nineteenth century 'was not the expression of superior power but of superior performance'. Economic behaviour was oriented towards the continuous exploitation of economic opportunities rather than towards one-time gains through pillage and rapine. Technological breakthroughs in agriculture and industry opened investment opportunities, especially after the late eighteenth century. Production became increasingly more capital-intensive. The proportion of fixed costs to variable costs grew accordingly. Minimising production costs per unit of output not only required the full utilisation of production capacities, but also larger scales of production. This meant that the expansion of markets nationally and internationally became crucial for the expansion of production with increasing returns to scale. Adam Smith had already seen this in 1776, when he made the famous description of the production of pins the point of departure for his trail-blazing book on the *Wealth of Nations*. Examples of how technological innovation and increasing returns to scale propelled industries into leading positions in world trade – often with fatal consequences for rival, but less efficient, producers – are: the growth of the British cotton textile industry and of the German and American iron and steel industries in the early and later parts of the nineteenth century, respectively, and of the Japanese car industry in the recent decades of the twentieth century.

Capital mobilisation and the effective allocation of capital not only nationally, but also internationally by banks and other financial intermediaries, became a prerequisite for industrial growth. As Cameron makes clear in his contribution to this volume, the financial sector cannot only be regarded as the first multinational enterprise arriving on the scene long before industrialisation, but it also produced a whole series of financial innovations when they were most needed to supply the funds for growth in the nineteenth century.

Industrialisation took place in Europe and the United States in the late eighteenth and nineteenth centuries. This clearly left its imprint on their share of world trade (cp. Table 1.2). When industrialisation took hold of other countries on other continents in the twentieth century, with the First World War giving a special boost to this process, they increased their world trade share at the expense of Europe.

The progressive utilisation of energy supplies as well as of raw materials plays a key role in industrial growth. In the nineteenth century, for instance, cotton needed for the textile industry in England and coal for steam engines, for the iron and steel furnaces and for heating the homes of a growing urban population, needed to be moved from the sites where they could be naturally produced or extracted to the industrial and urban centres where they were used. On the way, they increasingly crossed national borders, as did manufactured products which were delivered in exchange for primary products.

Trade barriers

As Wolfram Fischer (1987) has pointed out, there have been world-wide swings between protectionism and free trade since the late eighteenth century, even though individual countries sometimes or even persistently deviated from the general trend due to special geographic or economic conditions (like being a city state or an international trade and financial centre). It is the broad trend in which either higher or lower trade barriers contribute to the retardation or the fostering of the growth of world trade.

The mercantilistic policies prevalent in eighteenth-century Europe and its overseas dominions compartmentalised world trade and provided for strong protection of national primary producers and manufacturers against foreign competition. In 1776 in his *Wealth of Nations* Adam Smith denounced the mercantilistic practices of government intervention, regulation and excessive taxation. He pleaded for *laissez-faire* principles also in international trade in order to increase competition, the degree of international division of labour, productivity and thereby the real national product available for distribution to the different social classes and for consumption by the general population.

What we know about the history of trade barriers since Adam

Smith's attack on mercantilism is based mainly on the European and transatlantic experience. But as these two continents dominated world trade during the last two centuries, their general orientation towards free trade or protectionism is representative.

Mercantilist practices, including the maintenance of high barriers to trade between nation-states and often of customs duties and tolls in domestic commerce, weakened in the late eighteenth century, although 'no dramatic changes took place' (Fischer 1987: 22). Fremdling (1988: 28) reports on a trade treaty between Britain and France in 1786 aiming at freer trade. But the wars in the wake of the French Revolution interrupted this trend. Trade was severely hampered not only by the continental blockade, but by high-tariff policies as well. During and after the end of the Napoleonic Wars, high customs rates served not only trade purposes, but fiscal needs as well. Government war debts had to be serviced and repaid. In the early 1820s the average tariff exceeded 60 per cent *ad valorem* (Fischer 1987: 22). In the United States the average rate of duty reached around 50 per cent in the second half of the 1820s (US Bureau of the Census 1975: 88).

Great Britain initiated a long-term swing towards free trade in the 1820s (Fischer 1987: 23; Kindleberger 1975b). It culminated in Peel's policy in the 1840s to lower tariff rates in Britain to only 5 per cent for raw materials; to 12 per cent for intermediate goods; to a maximum of 20 per cent for finished goods; and finally to repeal the Navigation Act and the Corn Laws, which placed restrictions on foreign shipping in Britain's external trade and on the importation of grain, respectively. It is noteworthy that Britain initiated and pursued this policy without a quid pro quo attitude toward its foreign trading partners (see Bhagwati and Douglas 1987: 113–15). The conviction that the domestic economy would benefit from even unilateral trade liberalisation was the driving motive behind British policy during that period.

An international programme developed in the 1850s and 1860s which came close to a multilateral trade policy. Its cornerstone was the Cobden–Chevalier Treaty between Britain and France in 1860, reducing tariffs on goods important in trade between the two countries. A multilateral touch was given to it by a most-favoured-nation clause. On the basis of this principle, France, i.e. the government of Napoleon III, pursued its policy of international trade liberalisation by mutual agreement and covered almost all of western Europe (including Prussia and the German *Zollverein*) with a network of bilateral trade treaties (Fisher 1987: 24).

In the United States the rise of the Republican Party in the second half of the 1850s and the presidential election victory of Abraham Lincoln, the first Republican in the White House, heralded the age in which Northern industrial interests would prevail over Southern agricultural interests in Washington. The Civil War broke out over this issue of domestic power relationships and also finally settled it. With the dominance of the Republicans and thereby of industrial interests in Congress, came the highly protective tariff policy of the United States that lasted well into the 1930s (Ratner 1972: 28–53).

While Britain stayed the course of free trade well into the twentieth century, continental Europe swung back to a protectionist orientation after the Franco-German War of 1870–1 and the onset of the so-called Great Depression of 1873 to 1896. In the newly formed German Reich and in France, industrial and agrarian interests were able to gain influence on customs policy through the new or expanded power of the national parliament. The late 1880s and early 1890s were even marked by trade wars with tariff retaliation between, among others, France and Italy, France and Switzerland, Germany and Russia, and Germany and Canada (Fischer 1987: 24).

The First World War marked the beginning of yet another swing towards protectionism despite the relatively high protective level already reached in the decades before. The modest attempt of the Democratic Wilson administration to lower US customs duties somewhat in 1913 was reverted when the Republicans gained control of the White House again in 1921. In spite of the position the United States had attained as the world's most competitive industrial country, as well as the world's number-one creditor nation, the Republican Party failed to adjust its old-time religion of protecting, that is subsidising, domestic producers. In 1930 it came out with the notorious Smoot–Hawley Tariff Act that set the stage for world-wide *sauve-qui-peut* measures leading to the disintegration and regionalisation of world trade for the rest of the inter-war period (Jones 1934).

Great Britain, who had already turned away somewhat from her free-trade policy during the First World War continued to do so cautiously in the 1920s, and raised duties in 1932 as a reaction to both the American measure of 1930 and to the deepening world depression. At the same time, she introduced preferences in trade with Commonwealth countries.

It was again a Democratic administration in the United States that initiated the Reciprocal Trade Agreements Act of 1934, empowering the President to reduce tariff rates by up to 50 per cent on the basis of bilateral trade agreements which contained reciprocal concessions and the unconditional most-favoured-nation clause. A number of such agreements, especially with Latin American countries, Canada, Great Britain, France, Belgium, the Netherlands, Switzerland, Czechoslovakia and Scandinavian countries were reached before the Second World War interrupted the process (Holtfrerich 1987: 34). But the Act of 1934, periodically extended by the Congress, achieved its full importance for world-wide trade relations in the post-war period. It became the legal foundation for the American government's participation in the GATT in 1948, after the Congress in Washington had refused to ratify the charter of the ITO (International Trade Organization) and had thereby blocked the creation of a supranational organisation, in its power similar to the International Monetary Fund, to oversee the operation of a multilateral trade and tariff structure. The success of the GATT in reducing quotas and tariffs mainly for manufactured products is too well known to be recounted again here. But the dramatic post-war swing towards free trade has lost momentum considerably, since a 'new' protectionism established itself and grew in the 1970s along with further liberalisation measures in the GATT. It consists mainly of OMAs (orderly marketing agreements) and VERs (voluntary export restraints), i.e. restrictions by the exporting country, and of often ingeniously designed non-tariff barriers. The recent southern expansion of the European Community and the free trade zones formed by the United States with Israel and Canada (and in the future perhaps with Mexico, Japan and other East Asian countries) might be seen as symptoms of a new regionalisation of world trade, especially when viewed in conjunction with the 'new' protectionism. But it all depends on whether relations between these free trade areas and the internal European market will be developed in the spirit of the GATT or of the 'new' protectionism.

Transportation and communication costs

The reduction of transportation and communication costs affects international trade and the integration of world markets in much the same way as the lowering of trade barriers. With the spreading of the industrial modes of production came new modes of transport and communication, which were so highly efficient that nineteenth-century developments in these areas have been dubbed the 'revolution in transport' (Woytinsky *et al.* 1955: 306). The list of crucial innovations in transport and communication infrastructure starts with road and canal building, most visible in Europe and the United States in the first decades of the nineteenth century. Then came the 'iron horse', the railroad, with tremendous growth rates from the 1840s to the end of the nineteenth century (data for individual countries and the world as a whole from 1840 to 1888 in Rostow 1978: 152). At the same time the steam engine also revolutionised water transportation. Rates for domestic and international transport fell in the course of the nineteenth century, most noticeably during the so-called Great Depression from 1873 to 1896, with dramatic consequences for European agriculture which was facing increasing pressure from American competition (for freight rate data see Fischer and Nordvik 1986: 537–8). The stimulus of falling freight rates, strongly reinforced by the opening of the Suez Canal in 1869, rapidly drew Third World countries into the growing network of world trade during the last third to quarter of the nineteenth century (Lewis 1970: 13; Latham 1978: 26–32).

The telegraph also came into use around 1840 and speeded up the transmission of commercial information. Between 1850 and 1880 the telegraph network reached global dimensions. In 1866 the North Atlantic cable was put into use and within the next ten years all continents were linked by the telegraph. Commercial data or dispatches originating in London reached trading places on foreign continents in two or three days from then on, instead of two weeks (New York and Montreal) to up to nine or ten weeks (Sidney and Yokohama) by surface mail (Ahvenainen 1986: 507). Innovations in transport and communication that became important for the integration of markets in the twentieth century include: the telephone, the automobile, the aircraft, the radio, and the most modern means of telecommunication, including satellites.

Monetary relations

Nonbarter international trade relations require some sort of internationally accepted means of payment. It is no coincidence, therefore, that the nineteenth century not only brought about a unification of monetary standards on the national level and in regional monetary unions, but also showed a remarkable trend towards the formation of a common monetary standard world-wide, namely the gold standard (Kenwood and Lougheed 1983: 116–32; Foreman-Peck 1983: 67–93, 160–85). Traditionally, not only full-value gold and silver coins, but debased coins and even uncovered paper money were commonly used in different proportions. Governments often used their power to issue debased coins or treasury notes as legal tender in order to collect seignorage revenues for their fiscal needs. But international traders needed a reliable payment standard free from the danger of such government manipulations. A full metallic-value monetary standard would restrict government interference with the value of the currency. Gold and silver coins, mostly on a parity of metal weight stipulated by the government – in practice bimetallic standards – were widely in use in pre-industrial Europe. Because of their diversity, they served international trading and payment purposes often according to their metal weight.

Great Britain, the leading industrial country, had early on developed rules for the organisation of her monetary system, but was still practising a bimetallic standard when the international turmoil caused by the Napoleonic Wars disrupted monetary conditions and forced Britain to suspend the convertibility of Bank of England notes into gold (or silver). This bank restriction period lasted from 1797 to 1821. When the period ended, the minting of the one-pound sterling gold sovereign, thereafter Britain's basic monetary unit, had been authorised, the free coinage of silver had been suspended, a two-pound sterling limit on the legal-tender status of silver coins was in place, and restrictions on the melting of coin and the export of coin and bullion had been repealed (Yeager 1976: 295). Britain had fully adopted the gold standard.

France and the United States kept on practising their bimetallic standards. France promoted the concept of international monetary standardisation by forming the Latin Monetary Union in 1865 with Belgium, Switzerland, Italy and later, Greece. At that time Germany, the Netherlands, Scandinavia and the Orient (most notably India) still practised a pure silver standard. Russia, the Austrian Empire, and the United States were then on an inconvertible paper standard due to war-related fiscal problems.

Around 1850 gold was discovered in California and Australia, and its exploitation changed the relative scarcity of gold to silver. This, in practice, increased the circulation of gold in countries on a bimetallic standard.

Germany decided to use French reparation payments after the Franco-German War of 1870–1 to introduce the gold standard in Germany, mainly with a view to stabilising monetary relations with the British currency – then the dominant transaction currency in the world. The demonetisation of silver in Germany, the exploitation of newly discovered silver ores in Nevada in the face of restrictions on the free coinage of silver in the United States (since 1873) led to a situation in which European countries almost competed to achieve the earliest possible demonetisation of silver. In the United States silver mine interests and debt-ridden farmers, hard hit by the collapse of agricultural prices during the Great Depression of 1873–96, fought an extended political battle to avoid the adoption of a pure gold standard but were finally defeated in the election of 1896. New gold supplies in the Yukon area and in South Africa facilitated the transition. The US Gold Standard Act of 1900 marked the end of a period in which the gold standard had in fact been gradually adopted world-wide, including oriental countries such as India and Japan, but with the notable exceptions of China (which remained on the silver standard) and several Latin American countries with inconvertible paper standards.

Although exchange rates between the currencies of gold standard countries could vary between the so-called gold points, and although these were sometimes manipulated to avoid the consequences of a gold drain or inflow on the domestic credit situation, the gold standard tended to create a situation in which the participating countries were *de facto* linked by a common currency, managed by the Bank of England as the international lender of last resort at the centre of international trade and finance in London. Yeager (1976: 308) sums up the results: 'By and large, people were freer from government regulation – freer to transact any honourable business as they saw fit, to make investments, to transfer funds, to travel without formality – than in any age of history before or since.'

Wolfram Fischer (1975: 299), however, points out that this system, due to the shortage of gold in relation to the growing volume of world trade, would have impeded international trade, if not for the development of credit and banking, including central banking. To make his point clear he asserts: 'The huge expansion of world trade and of the national products of the most important countries has not come about on account of, but in spite of the gold standard.' He therefore prefers to call the pre-First World War monetary system a 'gold credit standard'. He also observes that the US Treasury with a quarter of the world monetary gold reserves was already before the First World War much better equipped with this metal than the Bank of England, yet American foreign trade was still largely financed on the London money market (Fischer 1981a: 166–8). This contributed to stabilising the role of the Bank of England as the world central bank in practice.

August 1914 shattered this almost ideal monetary basis for the world-wide integration of markets. The First World War started off a period which lasted until after the Second World War, in which world trade tended to stagnate or to decline (cf. Table 1.1). Monetary disruptions of all sorts occurred and the depreciation of currencies often pressured other countries into protecting their domestic markets by tariff and non-tariff barriers, which in turn contributed to the weakening of foreign currencies. A vicious circle between disruptions in international monetary and trade relations thus emerged, especially in the first few years of floating exchange rates after the First World War (and in the years of the Great Depression in the 1930s). Contemporaries were aware of these reinforcing injurious trends and, therefore, a world-wide attempt was made to restore an international gold standard with fixed exchange rates. The stabilisation of hyperinflationary European currencies, such as the Austrian and the Hungarian crown, the German mark and the Polish zloty in the first half of the 1920s, and of the more moderately depreciated European currencies, such as the British pound, the French and Belgian francs and the Italian lira in the second half of the 1920s, restored a system of fixed exchange rates under a gold exchange standard, with the US dollar assuming some of the functions that the pound sterling had performed alone in the pre-war period.

The strain that the world depression exerted on the system shortly after it had been restored was too much for it to survive. Germany restricted convertibility and introduced exchange controls in July/August 1931. In September Great Britain left the gold standard and let the pound depreciate on the foreign exchange markets. Twenty-five countries followed Great Britain's example, mainly those in the empire and other important trading partners in Scandinavia, Eastern Europe and overseas (Kindleberger 1986: 159). The United States held out until the new Roosevelt administration devalued the dollar in 1933, and the gold bloc countries with France at the helm heroically weathered the storm until 1936, when the Tripartite Monetary Agreement between Britain, the United States and France allowed for an overdue depreciation of the French franc with the assurance that the United States and Britain would not engage in competitive exchange depreciation.

All in all, the monetary system had been transformed into a non-system in the sense that internationally respected rules for the conduct of monetary and exchange rate policies were absent, and individual countries acted according to a *sauve qui peut* mentality in currency exchange matters just as they did in trade policy matters. As Kindleberger again points out in his contribution to this volume, there was no international lender of last resort who was willing and able to carry responsibility for the system as a whole, a role that Britain had played before 1914, but that she was no longer able to play after the First World War. The United States, which had the power to do so, declined to fill the vacant leadership role.

Lessons were drawn from the disastrous international currency experience of the inter-war period. Ragnar Nurkse (1944 and 1946) judged speculative international capital movements to be primarily destabilising and therefore recommended principally fixed exchange rates which were to be defended by cooperation of central banks. The United States, even more powerful than before because of the Second World War, was finally ready to assume responsibility for the international system. The Bretton Woods monetary system, a gold–dollar standard with fixed but adjustable exchange rates, was shaped primarily according to the American *White* plan rather than the British *Keynes* plan.

On the back of this system and in conjunction with trade

liberalisation, world trade showed unprecedented growth until the Nixon administration closed the gold window in 1971 and floating exchange rates were generally adopted in 1973 (cf. Table 1.1). When European countries had managed to restore fully or at least to increase the degree of currency convertibility in the 1950s (cf. Milward's contribution to this volume, Chapter 10), international capital movements started to flow again on a massive scale. Currencies that were considered over- or undervalued were heavily attacked by such flows, and central banks that were obliged to defend the exchange rate parities came under such heavy pressure that they lost control of money and credit policies targeted at domestic requirements. Thus, the very success of the Bretton Woods system in restoring external convertibility of member-country currencies undermined the stability of the system. Under the pre-First World War classic gold standard, full convertibility of each currency into gold (or gold-convertible foreign exchange) at pre-determined parities was a necessary condition for the smooth operation of the fixed exchange rate monetary system. But at that time, prices and wages were flexible, and large variations up and down provided the necessary adjustments when the internal or external balance was threatened. In the Bretton Woods era, in contrast, prices and wages showed downward rigidity, and as a legacy of the Great Depression, national stabilisation policies had been adopted to adjust the economy when internal balance, especially full employment, was threatened. Some autonomy in domestic stabilisation policy could peacefully coexist with fixed (but adjustable) exchange rates in the Bretton Woods era, as long as currency convertibility and thus international capital movements were still restricted. But with convertibility fully restored, the system was overdetermined and – when finally forced to make a choice and to eliminate one of the three elements (fixed exchange rates, full external convertibility, and national autonomy in stabilisation policy) – the participating countries finally agreed to remove the fixity of exchange rates in 1973.

In contrast to Nurkse, advocates of flexible exchange rates, prominent among them Milton Friedman, assumed that speculative international capital movements were stabilising, not destabilising. The experience with the floating exchange rate system has not quite substantiated this view. The variation not only in nominal, but in real exchange rates has been much greater than anticipated, and the independence of domestic monetary policy from foreign influences through the free floating of exchange rates has been much less than was expected and hoped for.

It is, therefore, probably not a coincidence that the 'new' protectionism started spreading in 1973, when the floating exchange rate system had been adopted. Economic history has demonstrated time and again that competitive pressures emanating from exchange rate depreciation breed the demand for more protection of the domestic market.

Legal security

Wolfram Fischer (1975) especially has paid attention to the progressive unification of economic and commercial law during the growth of the world economy and of world trade in the nineteenth century up to the First World War. It is true that European influence and dominance in overseas parts of the world – first by Spain and Portugal – had been spreading since the fifteenth century (Woodruff 1967: 19). But the industrial revolution in Europe beginning in the second half of the eighteenth century changed and strengthened the European position in the world economy. Overseas territories not only grew into the role of suppliers of raw materials for feeding the fast-growing industrial machinery of Europe. They also provided markets on which the growing output of industrial goods could be offered and sold. As trade relations intensified, the need for harmonising the legal systems for the conduct of such affairs grew. Sometimes it came about under pressure from the advanced countries, as when Japan was forcefully opened up to American and European trade and shipping in the mid-nineteenth century. In many cases, however, the European technical, economic, political and legal norms and customs were adopted voluntarily overseas in the hope for material advancement and some of the dynamism of European development. This is true for Japan after its forceful opening and for Latin American states. When the latter became independent of Spanish rule in the nineteenth century, they substituted more and more of their old-fashioned Spanish legal tradition for the modern elements of French legal codes (Napoleon's *Code Civil* and *Code de Commerce*), in some cases even of German and Swiss commerical law.

Above all, two European law systems competed in the nineteenth century the world over: Anglo-Saxon common law, on the one hand, and continental Europe's Roman law tradition on the other. What counts in this context is that the European principles of commercial, financial, credit, bankruptcy, inheritance, maritime and civics law were widely adopted the world over, at least in as much as European and world trade affairs were concerned. A most striking example of this are the so-called unequal treaties with China in the 1840s, in which the Europeans were granted exterritorial status in China in order to pursue their business on European terms. As Fischer (1975: 293) has summarised: 'The adoption of European legal principles over large parts of the inhabited earth constitutes the most general element of order for the economic exchange in the pre-First World War world.'

The advancement in legal security also found expression in the fact that the number of multilateral treaties increased considerably during the hundred years from the Vienna Congress of 1815 to the First World War. As Fischer (1975: 295) reports, only twelve such treaties were concluded from 1815 to 1850, but forty-six in the period 1851–80 and 129 in 1881–1910. Not all of them–but most–had economic implications, such as accords on weights and measures, customs classifications and conventions, maritime signals, laws on rules for the international use of the telegraph or telephone, on international offices, the agreement on the founding of the Universal Postal Union in 1875, and international law agreements, including those on courts of arbitration. Business and commercial interests were a major driving force behind these developments (see also Sartorius von Waltershausen 1931: 470–90).

THE PRESENT CONTRIBUTIONS TO THE DISCUSSION OF WORLD TRADE ISSUES

Theoretical issues to which the usual textbooks are devoted of course play a prominent part in explaining world trade developments as well. In Part I of this volume Gerald Meier surveys the theoretical literature on international trade and its relation to development economics. He discusses what seems to be an ever-present question since modern economic growth began with industrialisation: '... should the nation abandon comparative advantage and relinquish the gains from trade the better to secure the gains from growth?'

The following, more empirical contributions to the discussion of the international economy contained in this volume can naturally only touch upon a few aspects of the wider field of the development of world trade over the last three centuries.

Peter Klein's chapter reaches back far beyond the age of industrialisation. It is an interpretation of trade developments in and with the China seas, using Fernand Braudel's concept of maritime space which defines and shapes interconnections, structures, and common features of civilisations, societies, states and economies. Klein takes his reader into a distant part of the world from a European perspective, a world in itself with its own power relationships, and – as Table 1.2 indicates for Asia – with trade shares that had not yet suffered under European industrial expansion. Klein analyses the trade between the China sea world and Europe and comes to the conclusion that the basis of European trading links with that part of the world was shaky and weak, and that its influence on the region's economy was marginal until European industrialisation during the nineteenth century. What helped to establish European economic hegemony in East Asia then were not the structural ties established during pre-industrial times, but rather a sort of revolutionary breakdown of the pre-industrial structure of exchange relations.

François Crouzet's chapter, especially rich in original research, contributes to the discussion on the beginning of the expanded role of the United States in world trade. He draws on historical records of a New England merchant firm, the house of John and Richard Codman, to present a case-study of how the economic and financial disruptions of the French Revolution as well as the wars in Europe during the decade afterwards helped to project American merchants to more prominence in transatlantic trade.

David Landes traces the roots of Europe's growing nineteenth-century hegemony in the world economy. He points to what distinguished Europe from other parts of the world since the fifteenth century: her capability constantly to adapt new technologies and to pursue an active policy of expansion and domination of the world outside with a view to continuous exploitation of economic opportunities instead of pillage and rapine. Landes explains Europe's growing advantage in the nineteenth century by the production-cost-reducing effects of industrial modes of production and the trade-cost-reducing effects of new and better modes of transportation and of other services ('transaction cost').

The subsequent chapters by Rainer Fremdling and Rondo Cameron are devoted in more detail to pre-First World War transportation and transaction cost developments. Fremdling investigates the effects of transport price reductions on market shares of British coal in continental Europe. Cameron discusses the role of international banks – 'the first multinational business firms' – in international trade finance, on the one hand, and as instruments of material progress, international diffusion of technology and economic growth in general, on the other.

Angus Maddison's detailed quantitative presentation leads the way into the twentieth century and up to the present. He compares the long-term economic growth performance of the five biggest OECD (i.e. advanced) economies and the five biggest non-OECD economies (Brazil, China, India, Mexico and the USSR) from 1870 to 1987, which together account for about half of world trade. Among other things, he notes that there was no convergence in income levels between the two groups over the period as a whole; that the United States emerged as the number-one country in terms of real national income per capita around 1890; and – consistent with my Table 1.2 – that the share of the rich countries in world trade was lower in 1985 than in 1870.

The essay by Herman Van der Wee and Erik Buyst surveys the conglomerate of domestic monetary, employment, and growth problems and the international debt, trade, and exchange rate problems during the troubled inter-war period. While countries resorted to nationally-oriented palliatives to their employment and growth problems after the deepening of the Great Depression in the early 1930s, the fabric of international trade and monetary relations did not recover from the fatal blows that the Depression had dealt to the gold standard and to what was left of liberal attitudes in trade policy until after the Second World War.

Alan Milward's chapter takes us into the post-1945 period. On the basis of new archival sources, he discusses the struggle to restore the currency convertibility of two key currencies in Europe, the British pound and the German mark as an essential part of freeing world trade from financial and commercial restrictions in the 1950s. The study reveals the underlying conflict in policy orientation between regional European arrangements like the EPU (European Payments Union) and the wider transatlantic perspective aimed at currency convertibility *vis-à-vis* the US dollar. In Germany policy decisions seem to have been made with regard to the interests of manufacturing and exporting industries, while in Britain policy was shaped primarily with a view to the financial sector of the City of London.

Charles Kindleberger presents a framework for defining and timing the rise and decline of US leadership in the world economy during the twentieth – the 'American' – century. He discusses the leadership function in terms of commercial policy, responsibility for the maintenance of the international monetary system and of a flow of capital from the rich countries to the poor, coordination of macro-economic policies and lender of last resort in financial crises. In each of these areas he traces US policies throughout the twentieth century and finds that US leadership in the world reached its apogee in the first decade after 1945, and that it has dangerously degenerated in the last twenty years.

Albert Fishlow compares the difficulties of Latin American countries, that is regions on the periphery of the world economy, during the debt crises of the 1930s and of the 1980s and draws lessons from the earlier experience for coping with the present crisis.

Finally, Detlef Lorenz draws attention to the spectacular performance of another set of countries on the periphery, the NICs (newly industrialising countries) and to the conditions and factors that contributed to their increasing role in world trade during the last two decades.

NOTES

1. For the geographical structure of European foreign trade since 1800 see Bairoch (1974: 557–608). Summary tables for the crucial decades from 1850 to 1914 are given in Fischer (1985b: 168–70).
2. For more details on international trade in this period cp. Sartorius von Waltershausen (1931: 14–24).
3. During this period fears in Europe, especially in Great Britain, of world-wide aggressive competition by US producers were great and

resembled similar anxieties about Japanese competition in recent decades (cf. Stead 1902/1972: 7). On the non-marginal role of the periphery (Third World) in nineteenth-century world trade see Hanson (1980).
4. For the commodity structure of manufactured articles alone see Maizels (1963: 162–87).

REFERENCES

Adams, Brooks (1900/1947), *America's Economic Supremacy*, 1947 reprint of 1900 original edition, New York/London: Harper.
Ahvenainen, Jorma (1986), 'Telegraphs, trade and policy: the role of the international telegraphs in the years 1870–1914', in Wolfram Fischer, R. Marvin McInnis and Jürgen Schneider (eds), *The Emergence of a World Economy 1500–1914*, Part II: 1850–1914, Wiesbaden: Steiner, pp. 505–18.
Bairoch, Paul (1974), 'Geographical structure and trade balance of European foreign trade from 1800 to 1970', *Journal of European Economic History*, vol. 3, pp. 557–608.
Baldwin, Robert E. (1958), 'The commodity composition of trade: selected industrial countries, 1900–1954', *Review of Economics and Statistics*, vol. 40, pp. 50–68.
Bhagwati, Jagdish N. and Douglas A. Irwin (1987), 'The return of the reciprocitarians: US trade policy today', *World Economy*, vol. 10, pp. 109–30.
Crouzet, François (1964), 'Wars, blockade and economic change in Europe, 1792–1815', *Journal of Economic History*, vol. 24, pp. 567–88.
Fischer, Lewis R. and Helge W. Nordvik (1986), 'Maritime transport and the integration of the North Atlantic economy, 1850–1914', in Wolfram Fischer, R. Marvin McInnis and Jürgen Schneider (eds), *The Emergence of a World Economy 1500–1914*. Part II: 1850–1914, Wiesbaden: Steiner, pp. 519–44.
Fischer, Wolfram (1975), 'Die Ordnung der Weltwirtschaft vor dem Ersten Weltkrieg: die Funktion von europäischem Recht, zwischenstaatlichen Verträgen und Goldstandard beim Ausbau des internationalen Wirtschaftsverkehrs', *Zeitschrift für Wirtschafts- und Sozialwissenschaften*, pp. 289–304.
Fischer, Wolfram (1978), 'Die Rohstoffversorgung der europäischen Wirtschaft in historischer Perspektive, in Jürgen Schneider (ed.), *Wirtschaftskräfte und Wirtschaftswege*, vol. IV: Übersee und allgemeine Wirtschaftsgeschichte. Festschrift für Hermann Kellenbenz, Stuttgart: Klett-Cotta, pp. 675–93.
Fischer, Wolfram (1979a), 'Die Weltwirtschaft im 20. Jahrhundert', *Historische Zeitschrift*, vol. 229, pp. 54–84.
Fischer, Wolfram (1979b), *Die Weltwirtschaft im 20. Jahrhundert*, Göt-

tingen: Vandenhoeck & Ruprecht.
Fischer, Wolfram (1980), *Weltwirtschaftliche Rahmenbedingungen für die ökonomische und politische Entwicklung Europas 1919–1939*, Wiesbaden: Steiner.
Fischer, Wolfram (1981a), 'Internationale Wirtschaftsbeziehungen und Währungsordnung vor dem Ersten Weltkrieg (1870–1914)', in H. Kellenbenz (ed.), *Weltwirtschaftliche und währungspolitische Probleme seit dem Ausgang des Mittelalters*, Stuttgart/New York: G. Fischer, pp. 163–9.
Fischer, Wolfram (1981b), 'Ein Kommentar zu Hans-Heinrich Nolte "Wie Europa reich wurde und die Dritte Welt arm blieb"', *Geschichte in Wissenschaft und Unterricht*, vol. 32, pp. 37–46.
Fischer, Wolfram (1985a), 'Die Entwicklung der Weltwirtschaft seit 1945 im historischen Vergleich', in H. Giersch (ed.), *Probleme und Perspektiven der weltwirtschaftlichen Entwicklung*, Berlin: Duncker & Humblot, pp. 19–38.
Fischer, Wolfram (1985b), 'Wirtschaft und Gesellschaft Europas 1850–1914', in W. Fischer (ed.): *Handbuch der europäischen Wirtschafts- und Sozialgeschichte*, vol. 5, Stuttgart/New York: Klett-Cotta, pp. 1–207.
Fischer, Wolfram (1987), 'Swings between protection and free trade in history', in Herbert Giersch (ed.), *Free Trade in the World Economy. Towards an Opening of Markets*, Tübingen: Mohr, pp. 20–32.
Foreman-Peck, James (1983), *A History of the World Economy. International Economic Relations Since 1850*, Hemel Hempstead: Harvester Wheatsheaf.
Fremdling, Rainer (1988), 'Die Zoll- und Handelspolitik Grossbritanniens, Frankreichs und Deutschlands vom späten 18. Jahrhundert bis zum Ersten Weltkrieg', in Hans Pohl (ed.), *Wettbewerbsbeschränkungen auf internationalen Märkten*, Stuttgart: Steiner, pp. 25–62.
GATT (1976, 1982, and 1987), *International Trade* 1975–6, 1981–2, and 1986–7, Geneva: General Agreement on Tariffs and Trade.
Haberler, Gottfried (1964), 'Integration and growth of the world economy in historical perspective', *American Economic Review*, vol. 54, no. 2, Part 1, pp. 1–22.
Hanson II, John R. (1980), *Trade in Transition. Exports from the Third World, 1840–1900*, New York: Academic Press.
Heffer, Jean (1986), 'Les termes de l'échange Américains, 1860–1900', in Wolfram Fischer, R. Marvin McInnis and Jürgen Schneider (eds), *The Emergence of a World Economy 1500–1914*, Part II: 1850–1914, Wiesbaden: Steiner, pp. 54–71.
Hilgerdt, Folke (1945), *Industrialization and Foreign Trade*. ed. by the League of Nations, Economic, Financial and Transit Department, Geneva: League of Nations.
Holtfrerich, Carl-Ludwig (1987), 'The Roosevelts and foreign trade. Foreign economic policies under Theodore and Franklin Roosevelt', in Cornelis A. van Minnen (ed.), *The Roosevelts: Nationalism, Democracy and Internationalism*, Middelburg, Netherlands: Roosevelt Study Center.

Imlah, Albert H. (1958), *Economic Elements in the Pax Britannica*, Cambridge, Mass.: Harvard University Press.
Jánossy, Ferenc (1971), *The End of the Economic Miracle. Appearance and Reality in Economic Development*, White Plains, NY: International Arts and Science Press.
Jones, Joseph M., Jr (1934), *Tariff Retaliation: Repercussions of the Hawley-Smoot Bill*, Philadelphia: University of Pennsylvania Press.
Kenwood, Albert G. and A.L. Lougheed (1983), *The Growth of the International Economy 1820–1980. An Introductory Text*, London: Allen & Unwin.
Kindleberger, Charles P. (1956), *The Terms of Trade. A European Case Study*, New York: The Technology Press of Massachusetts Institute of Technology and John Wiley & Sons.
Kindleberger, Charles P. (1975a), 'Germany's overtaking of England, 1806–1914', *Weltwirtschaftliches Archiv*, vol. 111, pp. 253–81, pp. 477–504.
Kindleberger, Charles P. (1975b), 'The rise of free trade in Western Europe', 1820–1875', *Journal of Economic History*, vol. 35, pp. 20–55.
Kindleberger, Charles P. (1986), *The World in Depression 1929–1939*, revised and enlarged edition, Berkeley: University of California Press.
Kuznets, Simon (1966), *Modern Economic Growth. Rate, Structure, and Spread*, New Haven: Yale University Press.
Landes, David S. (1965), 'Technological change and development in Western Europe, 1750–1914', in H.J. Habakkuk and M. Postan (eds): *Cambridge Economic History of Europe*, vol. VI: 'The Industrial Revolution and after: incomes, population and technological change', Cambridge: Cambridge University Press, pp. 274–601.
Latham, Anthony J.H. (1978), *The International Economy and the Underdeveloped World 1865–1914*, London: Croom Helm.
Lewis, W. Arthur (ed.) (1970), *Tropical Development 1880–1913. Studies in Economic Progress*, London: Allen & Unwin.
Maizels, Alfred (1963), *Industrial Growth and World Trade. An Empirical Study of Trends in Production, Consumption and Trade in Manufactures from 1899–1959*, Cambridge: Cambridge University Press.
Morgan, Theodore (1959/60), 'The long-run terms of trade between agriculture and manufacturing', *Economic Development and Cultural Change*, vol. 8, pp. 1–23.
Nurkse, Ragnar (1944), *International Currency Experience: Lessons of the Interwar Period*, ed. by the League of Nations, Princeton, NJ: League of Nations.
Nurkse, Ragnar (1946), *The Course and Control of Inflation. A Review of Monetary Experience in Europe After World War I*, ed. by the League of Nations, Geneva: League of Nations.
Parrini, Carl P. (1969), *Heir to Empire. United States Economic Diplomacy, 1916–1923*, Pittsburgh: University of Pittsburgh Press.
Ratner, Sidney (1972), *The Tariff in American History*, New York: van Nostrand.
Rostow, Walt W. (1978) *The World Economy. History and Prospect,*

Austin/London: University of Texas Press.
Sartorius von Waltershausen, August (1931), *Die Entstehung der Weltwirtschaft. Geschichte des zwischenstaatlichen Wirtschaftslebens vom letzten Viertel des achtzehnten Jahrhunderts bis 1914*, Jena, East Germany: G. Fischer.
Sombart, Werner (1919), *Die deutsche Volkswirtschaft im neunzehnten Jahrhundert und im Anfang des 20. Jahrhunderts*, 4th edn, Berlin: Bondi.
Stead, William T. (1902/1972), *The Americanisation of the World or The Trend of the Twentieth Century*, 1972 reprint of 1902 original edition, New York/London: Garland.
United Nations (1985 and 1986), *Statistical Yearbook 1982 and 1983–4* (33rd and 34th issue), *New York: United Nations*.
UNCTAD (1988), *Handbook of International Trade and Development Statistics 1987 – Supplement*, New York: United Nations.
US Bureau of the Census (1975), *Historical Statistics of the United States. Colonial Times to 1970*. Washington DC: Government Printing Office.
Woodruff, William (1967), *Impact of Western Man. A Study of Europe's Role in the World Economy 1750–1960*, New York: St. Martin's Press.
Woytinsky, Wladimir S. and E.S. Woytinsky (1955), *World Commerce and Governments. Trends and Outlook*, New York: Twentieth Century Fund.
Yates, P. Lamartine (1959), *Forty Years of Foreign Trade. A Statistical Handbook with Special Reference to Primary Products and Under-Developed Countries*. London: Allen & Unwin.
Yeager, Leland B. (1976), *International Monetary Relations: Theory, History and Policy*, 2nd edn, New York: Harper & Row.

PART I

THEORETICAL PERSPECTIVES

2 · THEORETICAL ISSUES CONCERNING THE HISTORY OF INTERNATIONAL TRADE AND ECONOMIC DEVELOPMENT

Gerald M. Meier

Analyses of the contribution of international trade to economic development display a curious tension between pessimistic and optimistic conclusions. If a nation follows its comparative advantage and realises the gains from trade will it also be on its optimal development path? Or, in contrast, should the nation abandon comparative advantage and relinquish the gains from trade the better to secure the gains from growth? Theoretical perspectives on this issue can come from classical trade theory, neo-classical trade theory and recent theories of international trade. Historical perspectives can be derived from even before the industrial revolution; subsequent chapters will illuminate the historical experience of a number of countries. This chapter focuses on the theoretical issues, with concentration on the pessimistic–optimistic strand in the history of thought.

A colleague's *Festschrift* is a stimulating occasion for one's own retrospection, and perhaps a bit of autobiography can sharpen the central issue that I want to discuss. When I first studied international trade in the early 1950s at Harvard with Professor Gottfried Haberler, the theory of international trade theory took resources, technology and tastes as given. The following year at the University of Oxford, Hla Myint introduced me to problems of economic development, and I studied the macro-dynamic models of Roy Harrod and John Hicks. I then read the pioneering works of Ragnar Nurkse and Arthur Lewis. Both Nurkse and Lewis were pessimistic about the power of international trade to act as an 'engine of growth' (in D.H. Robertson's phrase) (Robertson 1949: 501) for the late-developing nations of Asia, Africa and Latin America. And Harrod and Hicks were stressing the importance of dating variables that are changing. The problem for me thus became how to relate the great tradition of Ricardo, Marshall and Edgeworth on comparative advantage and the static gains from trade with the development issues raised by Nurkse and Lewis and with the dynamic theory introduced by Harrod and Hicks.

I want to pursue that problem again here. I shall, however, offer a necessarily highly-condensed statement of the relationship between international trade and economic development from different theoretical perspectives, and I shall concentrate on only these limited issues in trade-pessimism theory: the stimulus from exports in an open dualistic economy, and import-substituting industrialisation versus export promotion strategies.

CLASSICAL TRADE THEORY AND GROWTH

Extremely simple but justly celebrated, Ricardo's model of England and Portugal and cloth and wine establishes a basis for international specialisation according to comparative differences in real cost. In his two-country two-commodity one-factor (labour) model, Ricardo demonstrated that under conditions of free trade, a country will specialise in the production and export of those commodities for which its costs are comparatively lowest, and will import commodities it can produce only at high relative cost. The cost of 'indirectly producing' imports through specialisation on exports is less than if the country directly produced the importables at home. In following its comparative advantage, each country maximises output (imports) per unit of input (exports). The welfare result, according to Ricardo, is that 'the extension of foreign trade ... will very powerfully contribute to increase the mass of commodities, and therefore, the sum of enjoyments.' (Ricardo 1817: ch. VII) And these gains from trade will accrue to each trading nation: trade is symmetrically beneficial. We would now phrase Ricardo's conclusion on the merits of free trade in terms of an increase in real national income attained by an optimal allocation of resources on a world-wide basis – the attainment of Pareto international efficiency, with trade as a positive sum game.

Perhaps of even more significance for developing countries are two earlier versions of trade theory in classical thought – a 'vent for surplus' theory and a dynamic 'productivity' theory.[1] These two theories are clearly expressed in Adam Smith's *Wealth of Nations*:

> Between whatever places foreign trade is carried on, they all of them derive two distinct benefits from it. It carries out that surplus part of the produce of their land and labour for which there is no demand among them, and brings back in return for it something else for which there is a demand. It gives a value to their superfluities, by exchanging them for something else, which may satisfy a part of their wants, and increase their enjoyments. By means of it the narrowness of the home market does not hinder the division of labour in any particular branch of art or manufacture from being carried to the highest perfection. By opening a more extensive market for whatever part of the produce of their labour may exceed the home consumption, it encourages them to improve its productive powers, and to augment its annual produce to the utmost, and thereby to increase the real revenue and wealth of society. (Smith 1776/1937: 413)

Smith's 'vent for surplus' theory of international trade contrasts with Ricardo's comparative cost theory in two ways. The comparative cost theory assumes that a nation's resources are given and fully employed before the nation enters into international trade. After being opened to trade, the country faces a new set of relative prices on world markets, and reallocates its given resources more efficiently between expansion of export production and contraction of domestic production. In contrast, according to the vent for surplus theory, the country enters into international trade with surplus productive capacity over domestic consumption requirements. The function of international trade then is not to reallocate given resources but rather to provide the new effective demand for the output of surplus resources that would have remained unutilised without trade. Export production can thus be increased without reducing domestic production; exports become a virtually costless means of acquiring imports and expanding domestic activity. This was how Smith used the theory to support free trade.

J.S. Mill thought this theory crude and 'a surviving relic of the mercantile theory' (Mill 1848: 579). Modern economists may also consider it crude because of its deficiencies in technical analysis. The theory, however, has helped to illuminate some historical episodes of nineteenth-century development. Myint, for instance, has applied the theory to the opening up of the primary exporting countries in Southeast Asia, Latin America, and Africa during the nineteenth century. When brought into world markets in the nineteenth century, these underdeveloped countries began with a sparse population in relation to natural resources. At this time the economies were essentially subsistence economies and a well-developed price mechanism and high degree of factor mobility did not exist to equilibrate away the disproportion between land and labour. As Myint observes, given the genuine historical setting of an isolated economy, the initial disproportion between its resources, techniques, tastes and population showed itself in the form of surplus productive capacity.

Once the opening-up process got into its stride, the export production of these countries expanded very rapidly along a typical growth curve, rising very sharply to begin with and tapering off afterwards. Peasant export production of a traditional crop (for example rice in Southeast Asia) expanded by using underemployed labour and by bringing more land under cultivation using the traditional methods of cultivation. Even where new peasant export crops were introduced (for example palm oil and ground nut exports in West Africa), they could be produced by fairly simple methods that involved no radical change from the traditional techniques of agricultural production. While peasant export crops expanded by extension of cultivation using the traditional methods of production, the mining and plantation sectors of the economy expanded through the inflow of cheap labour from India and China, improvement of transport and communications by Western enterprise and the discovery of new mineral resources (the 'unlocking of the tropics' in Professor L.C.A. Knowles' phrase). Rather than making a given volume of resources more productive, these external influences increased the total volume of resources that could be drawn into export production.

Myint concludes that

instead of a process of economic growth based on continuous improvements in skills, more productive recombinations of factors and increasing returns, the nineteenth-century expansion of international trade in the underdeveloped countries seems to approximate to a simpler process based on constant returns and fairly rigid combinations of factors. Such a process of expansion could continue smoothly only if it could feed on additional supplies of factors in the required proportions. (Myint 1958: 317–20)

Some similarities to the Smithian vent for surplus theory also exist in the staple theory (Caves 1965: 103) and in Lewis's dual sector model of development with unlimited supplies of labour (Lewis 1954).[2]

The term 'staple' designates a raw material or resource-intensive commodity occupying a dominant position in the country's exports. It has a structural similarity to the vent for surplus view in so far as 'surplus' resources initially exist and are subsequently exported. It also has some affinity with Lewis's model when the surplus to be vented through trade is one of labour and not natural resources.

The staple theory postulates that with the discovery of a primary product in which the country has a comparative advantage, or with an increase in the demand for its comparative advantage commodity, there is an expansion of a resource-based export commodity; this in turn induces higher rates of growth of aggregate and per capita income. Previously idle or undiscovered resources are brought into use, creating a return to these resources and being consistent with venting a surplus through trade. The export of a primary product also has effects on the rest of the economy through diminishing underemployment or unemployment, inducing a higher rate of domestic saving and investment, attracting an inflow of factor inputs into the expanding export sector and establishing linkages with other sectors of the economy. Although the rise in exports is induced by greater demand, there are supply responses within the economy that increase the productivity of the exporting economy.

The staple theory also has some relation to Rostow's leading-sector analysis in so far as the staple-export sector may be the leading sector of the economy, growing more rapidly and propelling the rest of the economy along with its growth. In

Rostow's analysis, however, a primary-producing sector can be a leading sector only if it also involves processing of the primary product.

Since the pioneering studies of Harold Innis,[3] the staple theory of economic growth has often been used to relate the pace of development in Canada to Canada's resource intensive exports (Watkins 1963). It has also been applied to several other countries. Although it should not be interpreted as a general theory about the growth of export-oriented economies, it does have illuminating applications to the case of a new country. It is significant in relating a country's development not only to its export revenue, but also to the spread effects of its export sector – i.e., the impact of export activity on the domestic economy and society.

This emphasis on spread effects brings us back to our more general question of the contribution of international trade to the pace and pattern of a country's development and to the policy implications regarding alternative trade regimes.

Lewis's dual sector model provides some relationships that should be considered. Lewis analyses the process of economic expansion in a dual economy composed of a 'capitalist' sector and a 'non-capitalist' sector. The capitalist sector is defined as that part of the economy using reproducible capital, paying capitalists for the use thereof, and employing wage labour for profit-making purposes. The subsistence sector is the part of the economy that does not use reproducible capital and does not hire labour for profit – the indigenous traditional sector or the self-employment sector. In this sector, output per head is much lower than in the capitalist sector; given the available techniques, the marginal productivity of labour in agricultural production is very low and possibly zero as a limiting case. As a result of institutional arrangements, such as the family farm or communal holdings of land, members of the farm labour force consume essentially the average product of the farm's output even though the marginal product of some farm labourers may be well below the average product. The fundamental relationship between the two sectors is that when the capitalist sector expands, it draws labour from the reservoir in the non-capitalist sector. Labour is 'unlimited' in the sense that when the capitalist sector offers additional employment opportunities at the existing wage rate, the numbers willing to work at the existing wage will be greater than the demand: the supply curve of labour is infinitely elastic at the ruling wage.

Lewis's account of how he postulated this fundamental relationship is of interest. He states that he was concerned with what were the sources of capital formation in a developing economy. It was clear to him that in the nineteenth century the bulk of finance for Europe came from a rising share of profits in the national income.

> And what caused this rise in the share of profits? Neo-classical economics was no help. Keynes' model provided for the profit share to rise in a cyclical upswing. The evidence showed, however, that profits share and the saving share were more or less constant in the long run after 1870, in both Britain and the United States. What we were getting from the neo-classicists ... were demonstrations of how to combine long run savings constancy with short run savings volatility. This was of no use to us, since what we were trying to understand was a long term rise in the savings propensity.
> As I was walking down a road in Bangkok one morning in August 1952, it suddenly occurred to me that all one needed to do was to drop the assumption – then usually (but not necessarily) made by neo-classical macroeconomists – that the supply of labor was fixed. Assume instead that it was infinitely elastic, add that productivity was increasing in the capitalist sector, and one got a rising profits share. It also occurred to me that this model would solve another problem that had bothered me since undergraduate days: What determined the relative prices of steel and coffee? I had been taught that marginal utility was the answer to this question. But this answer made no sense to me. If, however, one assumed an infinite elasticity of labor in terms of food to the coffee industry, and an infinite elasticity also in terms of food to the steel industry, then the factoral terms of trade between steel and coffee were fixed, and marginal utility was out the window. So in three minutes I had solved two of my problems with one change of assumptions. (Lewis 1984: 132–3)

Thus Lewis made the driving force in the system the reinvestment of the surplus in the capitalist sector. As the capitalist sector expands, and the wage–price ratio remains constant, the share of profits in national income increases. And since the major source of savings is profits, savings and capital formation also increase as a proportion of the national income. Barring a hitch in the process, the capitalist sector can expand until the absorption of surplus labour is complete and the supply function of labour becomes less than perfectly elastic. Capital accumulation has then caught up with the excess supply of labour; beyond this point, real wages no longer remain constant but instead rise as capital formation occurs, so that the share of profits in the national income will not necessarily continue to increase and investment will no longer necessarily grow, relative to the national income. What is essential for savings to rise as a fraction of national income is that the internal terms of trade between agriculture and industry do not turn against the modern capitalist industrial sector: if real wages rise, profits will fall and so will savings.

We may now relate Ricardo to Lewis. Ricardo did not formulate his model as mere abstraction, but wanted to provide a persuasive case for free trade in order to secure repeal of the Corn Laws. He wanted this policy outcome, however, not simply because it would reduce the price of food and so increase 'the sum of enjoyments' – the static gain from trade – but because it would also redistribute income from landowners, who absorb their rents in luxury consumption, to capitalists who save and invest (Ricardo 1815; Findlay 1984a). The growth of England would thereby accelerate.

But while Ricardo showed the dynamic gain to England (E), does it necessarily follow that Portugal (P) would also have dynamic gains from trade that would accelerate its development? Ricardo demonstrated that the static gains from trade are symmetric for E and P, but would this also provide to P as much of the gains from growth as would P's departure from free trade in favour of an interventionist trade regime?

Critics of orthodox trade theory have long argued that the relations between a P and an E are actually asymmetric in character so that the gains from trade are unequally divided between Ricardo's primary producing P and industrial E, or that trade may make a primary producing P actually worse off, or that the northern E at the centre of the world economy underdevelops the southern P on the periphery.[4] These assertions have been amply criticised elsewhere on both theoretical and empirical grounds (Meier 1989: ch. 5). At this point I want to evaluate only the argument that the strategy of import-substituting industrialisation would provide more dynamic gains than export promotion (where by 'export promotion' is meant a neutral trade regime that does not bias the allocation of resources towards either importables or exportables).

THEORETICAL ISSUES 41

DEVELOPMENT THROUGH TRADE: A 'NINETEENTH-CENTURY VARIETY'

It has been asked whether the nineteenth-century experience of growth in the 'regions of recent settlement' and in underdeveloped primary producing countries conforms to the hypothesis that the expansion of nineteenth-century trade served as an 'engine of growth' – that growth was induced by export demand.

Resource intensive exports rose from the temperate countries of overseas settlement and also from tropical countries during the last quarter of the nineteenth century. But there were differential effects among the countries from the standpoint of their pattern and pace of economic development. From his interpretation of the evidence, Kravis concluded that it

> does not support any simple generalisations about the dominant role of trade in the success stories of nineteenth-century growth. Export expansion did not serve in the nineteenth century to differentiate successful from unsuccessful countries. Growth where it occurred was mainly the consequence of favorable internal factors, and external demand represented and added stimulus which varied in importance from country to country and period to period. A more warranted metaphor that would be more generally applicable would be to describe trade expansion as a handmaiden of successful growth rather than as an autonomous engine of growth. (Kravis 1970: 850)

Kravis goes on to state that

> This is not, of course, to deny that it is helpful to a developing country to have a strong external demand for a commodity that it can advantageously produce – such as cotton, wheat, oil or coffee. It is to deny that the presence of such a demand is a necessary or sufficient condition for growth or even for trade to play a helpful role in growth. It is to say that trade is one among many factors affecting growth, and that it is unlikely to be the dominant variable in many instances. (Kravis 1970: 869)

This is an eminently sensible but rather empty conclusion. It would be more significant to spell out the combination of conditions under which trade might or might not act as an engine of growth – the conditions under which the stimulus from exports would provide such strong spread effects that it can be said that growth is export-led.

To formulate the theory underlying such a statement we may

find it useful to return to Smith and his productivity theory of trade. This theory follows from Smith's famous dictum that 'the division of labour is limited by the extent of the market.' The productivity theory thus links development to international trade by interpreting trade as a dynamic force based on economies of scale. By widening the extent of the market and the scope of the division of labour, trade may raise the skill and dexterity of labour, encourage technical innovations, overcome technical indivisibilities and generally enable the trading country to enjoy increasing returns and economic development. (Myint 1958: 20; Smith 1776/1937: book I, chs II and III; Young 1928).

We can now add that as increasing returns are realised, an expansion of demand from abroad will not only increase output but also lower price. This, in turn, will raise real income and so provide more savings for investment, leading to further economies of scale in an expanding 'virtuous circle' of greater investment and higher productivity (Findlay 1984b: 24).

John Stuart Mill also presented elements of a productivity theory. Trade, according to comparative advantage, results in a 'more efficient employment of the productive forces of the world', and this is to be considered the 'direct economical advantage of foreign trade. But there are, besides, indirect effects, which must be counted as benefits of a high order.' One of the most significant 'indirect' benefits, according to Mill, is

> the tendency of every extension of the market to improve the processes of production. A country which produces for a larger market than its own, can introduce a more extended division of labour, can make greater use of machinery, and is more likely to make inventions and improvements in the processes of production. (Mill 1848: vol. II, book III, ch. XVII, sec. 5)

Another important result 'principally applicable to an early state of industrial advancement', is that

> the opening of a foreign trade, by making [people] acquainted with new objects, or tempting them by the easier acquisition of things which they had not previously thought attainable, sometimes works a sort of industrial revolution in a country whose resources were previously undeveloped for want of energy and ambition in the people: inducing those who were satisfied with scanty comforts and little work, to work harder for the gratification of their new tastes, and even to save, and accumulate capital, for the still more complete

satisfaction of those tastes at a future time. (Mill 1848: vol. II, book III, ch. XVII, sec. 5)

Mill also recognised what we would now term the 'educative effect' (Myint 1971: 255; Lockwood 1963: 320–34) of an open economy:

> It is hardly possible to overrate the value in the present low state of human improvement, of placing human beings in contact with persons dissimilar to themselves, and with modes of thought and action unlike those with which they are familiar ... Such communication has always been and is peculiarly in the present age, one of the primary sources of progress. (Mill 1848: vol. II, book III, ch. XVII, sec. 5)

Further, Mill stated that trade benefits the less-developed countries through

> the introduction of foreign arts, which raises the returns derivable from additional capital to a rate corresponding to the low strength of accumulation; and the importation of foreign capital, which renders the increase of production no longer exclusively dependent on the thrift or providence of the inhabitants themselves, while it places before them a stimulating example, and by instilling new ideas and breaking the chain of habit, if not by improving the actual condition of the population, tends to create in them new wants, increased ambition, and greater thought for the future. (Mill 1848: vol. I, book I, ch. XIII, sec. 1)

The indirect benefits of trade on development are therefore of three kinds: (a) those that widen the extent of the market, induce innovations and increase productivity; (b) those that increase savings and capital accumulation; and (c) those that have an educative effect in instilling new wants and tastes and in transferring technology, skills and entrepreneurship. This emphasis is on the supply side of the development process – the opportunity that trade gives a poor country to remove domestic shortages, to overcome the diseconomies of the small size of its domestic market and to accelerate the 'learning rate' of its economy.

A modern analysis of the effects of trade on the rate of growth has been offered by Corden (Corden 1971). Instead of the 'demand-promoted' model of the staple theory, Corden analyses a 'supply-motored' model that emphasises growth in factor supplies and productivity. After a country is opened to world trade, five different effects may be distinguished. First is the 'impact effect' corresponding to the static gain from trade: current real income is raised. Then there may be the 'capital-accumulation effect': an increase in capital accumulation results when parts of the static gain are invested. This amounts to a transfer of real income from the present to the future instead of an increase in present consumption. Third may be the 'substitution effect'. This may result from a possible fall in the relative price of investment goods to consumption goods if investment goods are import-intensive. This would lead to an increase in the ratio of investment to consumption and an increase in the rate of growth. The fourth possibility is an 'income-distribution effect': there will be a shift in income towards the factors that are used intensively in the production of exports. If the savings propensities differ between sectors or factors, this will have an effect on the overall savings propensity and hence on capital accumulation. Finally, there is the 'factor-weight effect'. This considers the relative productivity of capital and labour and recognises that if the rate of growth of output is a weighted average of capital and labour growth rates (with a constant returns-to-scale aggregate production function), then if exports rise, and exports use the faster-growing factor of production, the rate of growth of exports will rise more rapidly. These effects are all cumulative, and intensify the increase in real income over time as a result of opening a country to foreign trade.

This positive view of trade and development thus emphasises the direct gain that comes from international specialisation plus the additional support to a country's development through a number of spread effects within the domestic economy.

From the foregoing insights we may now offer a more general analysis of the development-through-trade model. For the model to produce a success story, the export sector cannot remain an enclave, separate from the rest of the economy, but instead an integrated process must be established. To explain the differential performance records among the primary producing countries in the nineteenth century, we should therefore focus on the varying strength of the export stimuli in different countries according to the nature of their export base, and on the different response mechanisms within the exporting countries. The strength of the potential for development-through-trade will differ according to the strength of the forces in the integrative process that combines the stimuli and carry-over effects.[5]

Different export commodities will provide different stimuli, according to the technological characteristics of their production (Baldwin 1963; Baldwin 1956). The nature of the export-goods production function (namely, the technical relationship between physical inputs of the factors of production and the resultant physical output) has a close bearing on the extent of other secondary changes elsewhere in the economy beyond the primary increase in export output. With the use of different combinations of inputs to produce different types of export commodities, there will be different rates of learning and different linkage effects. For instance, the degree to which the various exports are processed is highly significant in determining external economies associated with the learning process: the processing of primary-product exports by modern methods is likely to benefit other activities through the spread of technical knowledge, training of labour, demonstration of new production techniques that might be adapted elsewhere in the economy, and the acquisition of organisational and supervisory skills.

In contrast, growth of the export sector will have a negligible carry-over if its techniques of production are the same as those already in use in other sectors, or if its expansion occurs by a simple widening of production without any change in production functions (recall Myint's application of the vent-for-surplus theory to nineteenth century exports). If the introduction or expansion of export crops involves simple methods of production that do not differ markedly from the traditional techniques already used in subsistence agriculture, the stimulus to development will clearly be less than if the growth in exports entailed the introduction of new skills and more productive recombinations of factors of production. More favourable linkages may stem from exports that required skilled labour than from those using unskilled labour. The influence of skill requirements may operate in various ways: greater incentives for capital formation may be provided through education; on-the-job training in the export sector may be disseminated at little real cost through the movement of workers into other sectors or occupations; skilled workers may be a source of entrepreneurship; skilled workers may save more of their wage incomes than unskilled workers (Caves 1971). The level of entrepreneurial skill induced by the development of an export is also highly significant. The level will be expanded if the development of the export commodity offers sufficient challenge and instils abilities usable in other sectors, but is not so high as to require the importing of a transient class of skilled managerial labour.

Although the processing of a primary product provides forward linkages in the sense that the output of one sector becomes an input for another sector, it is also important to have backward linkages. When some exports grow, they provide a strong stimulus for expansion in the input-supplying industries elsewhere in the economy. These backward linkages may be in agriculture or in other industries (Hirschman 1958: ch. 6).

Beyond this, the nature of the production function of the export commodity will also determine the distribution of income and, in turn, the pattern of local demand and impact on local employment. The use of different factor combinations affects the distribution of income in the sense that the relative shares of profits, wages, interest and rent will vary according to the factor intensity of the export production and the nature of its organisation – whether it is mining, plantation agriculture or peasant farming. If the internal distribution of the export income favours groups with a higher propensity to consume domestic goods than to import, the resultant distribution of income will be more effective in raising the demand for home-produced products; and to the extent that these home-produced products are labour-intensive, there will be more of an impact on employment. In contrast, if income is distributed to those who have a higher propensity to import, the leakage through consumption of imported goods will be greater. If income increments go to those who are likely to save large portions, the export sector may also make a greater contribution to the financing of growth in other sectors.

If export supply depends on foreign investment, such as in plantations and mines in contrast with peasant crops, this may then lead to an outward flow of profits instead of providing profit income for local reinvestment. But this is only part of the impact of the foreign investment. For a full appraisal, it would be necessary to consider all the benefits and costs of the foreign investment. And these too will vary according to the nature of the export sector in which the foreign investment occurs.

Finally, the repercussions from exports will also differ according to the degree of fluctuation in export proceeds. Disruptions in the flow of foreign-exchange receipts make the development process discontinuous; the greater the degree of instability, the more difficult it is to maintain steady employment, because there will be disturbing effects on real income, government revenue, capital formation, resource allocation and the capacity to import according to the degree of amplitude of fluctuation in foreign-exchange receipts. To the extent that different exports vary in their degree of fluctuation, and in revenue earned and retained at home their repercussions on the domestic economy will also differ. Depending on the various characteristics of the country's export, we may thus infer how the strength of the integrative process, in terms of the stimulus from exports, will differ among countries.

In summary, we would normally expect the stimulating forces of the integrative process to be stronger under the following conditions: the higher is the growth rate of the export sector, the greater is the direct impact of the export sector on employment and personal income; the more the expansion of exports has a 'learning effect' in terms of increasing productivity and instilling new skills, the more the export sector is supplied through domestic inputs instead of imports; the more the distribution of export income favours those with a marginal propensity to consume domestic goods instead of imports, the more productive is the investment resulting from any saving of export income; the more extensive are the externalities and linkages connected with the export sector, the more stable are the export receipts that are retained at home.

The differential strength of the stimulus from exports is, however, only half the story. After analysing the character of a country's export base, we must go on to examine the strength of the response or diffusion mechanism within the domestic economy for evidence of how receptive the domestic economy is to the stimulus from exports. The strength of the integrative process, in terms of the response mechanism to the export stimulus, will depend on the extent of market imperfections in the domestic economy and also on non-economic barriers in the general environment. The integrative forces are stronger under the following conditions: the more developed is the infrastructure of the economy, the more market institutions are developed; the more extensive the development of human resources, the less are the price distortions that affect resource allocation; and the greater is the capacity to bear risks. Under such conditions there will be a more extensive carry-over from the foreign trade sector to other sectors in the economy.

In sum, the effects of a strong integrative process will be the following: (a) an acceleration in the learning rate of the economy; (b) an enrichment of the economic and social infrastructure (transportation, public services, health, education); (c) an expansion of the supply of entrepreneurship (and a managerial and administrative class); and (d) a mobilisation of a larger surplus above consumption in the form of taxation and saving. These effects constitute the country's development foundations. Once these foundations are laid, the country's economy can be more readily transformed through diversification in primary production and the service industries, new commodity exports, and industrialisation via import substitution and export substitution beyond traditional primary products. If, however, there is a lack of carry-over to domestic sectors, trade will not promote development; but the lack of carry-over may be because of domestic impediments that cut short the stimulus, and not because of the character of international trade.

This type of analysis might be applied to a typology based on the economic organisation of the country's export base – distinguishing whether the exports were foodstuffs, industrial raw materials, or minerals, and whether the organisation of export production was characterised by peasant production, estates or plantations, or mines.[6]

DEVELOPMENT THROUGH TRADE: A 'TWENTIETH-CENTURY VARIETY'

The twentieth century provides quite a different historical context from the nineteenth for the question whether the gains from trade merge with the gains from growth. In the twentieth century there was much more exploitation of import substitution (beginning in the 1930s in Latin America and the 1950s in Asia and Africa), and there was the emergence of the NICs that experienced development-through-trade based on their exports of manufactures embodying surplus labour (especially the East Asian NICs).

Arguments for import substitution stem from various forms of export pessimism – a belief that exports do not provide a sufficiently strong development function and that ISI (import-substituting industrialisation) will provide stronger dynamic gains for a country's development.[7]

Most prominent among ISI arguments is that of infant industry protection. The case for infant industry protection has often been argued by proponents as diverse as Alexander Hamilton, Friedrich List, Gunnar Myrdal, Raul Prebisch and members of the dependency school. Normative trade theory does provide some justification for protection of an industry that may offer a potential comparative advantage – but only under limited conditions. If correctly stated, the case rests on a very narrow theoretical foundation. In modern times the nature and scope of the infant industry argument has been refined by the theory of domestic distortions and the application of welfare economics. It has also been delimited by considering the benefits and costs of alternative policy instruments – a subsidy, tariff, or quantitative restriction – in the context of a hierarchy of policy-making.

The essence of the infant industry argument rests on 'dynamic learning effects' so that the economy's production possibility frontier (transformation curve) shifts outwards over time, and an industry that is not currently competitive may achieve comparative advantage after a temporary period of protection. Properly stated, the following conditions are necessary for infant industry protection: (a) irreversible technological external economies are generated that cannot be captured by the protected industry; (b) the protection is limited in time; and (c) the protection allows the industry to generate a sufficient decrease in economic costs so that the initial excess costs of the industry will be repaid with an economic rate of return equal to that earned on other investments.

If condition (a) is not fulfilled, the private market should be able to yield an efficient allocation unless capital markets are imperfect or there is imperfect information so that risks are overestimated. Infant industry protection is justified not by the fact that there are losses until the infant grows up – but by the fact of external economies associated with the learning process so that there is underproduction from the social point of view. Condition (b) guarantees that the industry is not protected from infancy to geriatric or even senile stages. And condition (c) guarantees that the expected benefit must be sufficiently great to offset, in present value terms, the current costs of the policy required to produce the benefit.

If free trade is not optimal because of the presence of externalities and the possibility of lower costs over time, what then are the optimal policy instruments for protecting the infant industry? The normative theory of international trade policy has established that the first best policy would be a production subsidy aimed at the source of the distortion. This would be preferable to a tariff, which would lead to a by-product consumption distortion. Although the tariff could restore equality between the marginal rate of domestic transformation and the marginal rate of transformation through foreign trade, it also would drive a wedge between the marginal rate of substitution in consumption and that of transformation. A tariff, in turn, would be preferable to a quantitative restriction which would yield quota profits instead of customs revenue, and would entail the cost of rent-seeking if there are import licenses.

The infant industry argument is also sometimes generalised to an 'infant economy' argument in which it is claimed that the entire industrial sector must go through an infancy stage, that the learning by each firm generates benefits for the whole sector and that by their mutual expansion all firms will enjoy a reduction in their production costs. Such a belief may underlie a broad import substitution strategy with a uniform rate of effective protection to all manufacturing activities. But import substitution strategies beyond the first easy stage are likely to prove excessively costly in developing countries, and their adverse effects on agricultural development and on export promotion limit the rates of development.

In contrast to import substitution, it should be recognised that an export industry may also be an infant industry. Free trade may fail to bring about socially optimal levels of knowledge and factor endowment in new export industries. Policy interventions are then justified. Another possibility is that actual consumption experiences may be required to learn about an export commodity's qualities, but each firm's efforts at overcoming foreign buyer resistance benefit not only itself but also all other firms that try to sell the same product in the same new market. The social returns of investments in market cultivation exceed the private returns, and subsidisation is then justified (Mayer 1984). The higher rates of economic growth enjoyed by many countries that promote exports suggest that it is possible that the infant industry proponents are correct in their basic argument that there is a period of learning and of relatively high costs, and that an export promotion strategy is a more efficient way of developing an efficient, low-cost industrial structure.

In opposition to the earlier claim that ISI would yield the greater dynamic benefits, the actual experience with inward-looking strategies and outward-looking strategies demonstrates the superior development performance of countries that followed export promotion. (Balassa 1978; Bhagwati 1988; Feder 1983; Michaely 1977).

Why should various indicators of development – real GNP, real per capita income, employment, income distribution, non-monetary indicators – be superior in countries that follow export promotion instead of import substitution? Neo-classical trade theory, based on the static gains from trade, can provide only a part of the answer. For what must be explained is not merely the neo-classical once-over change to a higher level of real income as a result of following comparative advantage. More significantly, it is necessary to explain the higher rate of growth in income over time. And to do this, we must return to implications of the productivity theory of trade and to other explanatory variables.

In terms of favourable effects on resource allocation an export-oriented industrialisation strategy may result in not simply a once for all improvement in allocation according to the country's comparative advantage in international trade, but more importantly in the realisation of dynamic benefits. While a reallocation of resources in conformity with comparative advantage can raise the level of income, the dynamic gains are significant in increasing the rate of growth in income.

There may be increased capacity-utilisation of plant, realisation of economies of scale, the creation of employment through export of labour intensive products, a multiplier effect that gives rise to increased demand for intermediate inputs and increased demand by consumers, and an increase in total factor productivity. Marginal factor productivities in export-oriented industries also tend to be significantly higher than in the non-export-oriented industries. The difference seems to derive, in part, from intersectoral beneficial externalities generated by the export sector.

Most important may be a realisation of dynamic efficiency in the sense of a fall in the incremental capital-output ratio, the realisation of 'X efficiency', the extension of informational efficiency, enjoyment of external economies, and realisation of Verdoon effects. Considering the latter, there is evidence that the faster export output grows, the faster is the growth in productivity. This is because of economies of scale, higher investment embodying capital of a more productive vintage, and a faster pace of innovation in products and processes.

More generally, dynamic efficiency may be interpreted as a reduction in what Myint terms 'organisational dualism' (Myint 1985). Myint interprets a developing country as being within its production possibility curve on a lower curve – its production feasibility curve. Even if one could remove all the policy-induced distortions, a substratum of 'natural' dualism would still exist in factor markets, goods markets, and in the administration and fiscal system because of institutional features and the costs of transactions, transportation, information and administration. Given the incomplete state of development of its domestic organisational framework, the country is within its production possibility frontier and the gap between the production possibility curve and the production feasibility curve is not uniform, but is slanted against an increase in output of the traditional sector. This is because the frictions and the costs of overcoming them are not uniformly distributed. These frictional costs are higher within the unorganised traditional sector and in the transactions between the traditional and the modern sectors and are lower within the modern sector and in the transactions between the modern sector and the outside world.

The incompletely developed organisational framework of a developing country can be improved or repressed by appropriate or inappropriate trade policies. By overcoming indivisibilities and filling in the gaps in the organisational framework of the traditional sector, the expansion of exports may be able to shift the production feasibility curve upward. In moving from a position on the production feasibility curve to the production possibility curve, a developing country gains much more than simply a once-over change to comparative advantage. Beyond this, organisational dualism is reduced in the sense of a reduction in the costs of transactions, transportation, information and administration.

The improved effectiveness of the domestic economic organisation allows the developing country to take advantage of available external economic opportunities in the form of international trade, foreign investment, technological adaptation and ideas from abroad. There is institutional adaptation to realise the potential comparative advantage in trade. The mutual interaction between economic policies and economic institutions results in improvement of the organisation of production, more effective incentives, and a strengthening of markets. Dynamic efficiency is realised as diseconomies of a small economy are overcome, the transformation capacity of the economy widens, and the learning rate of the economy accelerates. The integrative process that we discussed above (pages 44–8) is stronger in terms of stimulus and diffusion from the export sector.

Whereas proponents of the old export pessimism could criticise neo-classical trade theory and assert that the dynamic gains from ISI would outweigh the possible static costs of protection, it is more likely that the dynamic gains are far superior for export promotion. The case for development through trade can actually be expressed in stronger terms than in its neo-classical version.

A dynamic theory of comparative advantage is also part of the explanation. The H–O (Heckscher–Ohlin) theory of trade explains comparative advantage in terms of the differences in relative factor endowments among countries. A dynamic theory of comparative advantage can be formulated by allowing for changes in factor endowments, technology, and tastes over time (Meier 1963: ch. 2).[8] Such a theory suggests that in the course of its development a country accumulates more capital and experiences improvements in skill and technological progress. As these changes occur, the country's comparative advantage changes from an initial comparative advantage in natural resource-intensive exports through other stages of comparative advantage in exports that are successively unskilled-labour intensive, skilled-labour intensive, capital intensive, and knowledge intensive. (Balassa 1981: essay 6). The progression nullifies the constraint of foreign demand for a given export from a given country. As a country progresses through the stages of comparative advantage, another country can then replace the exports previously produced by the country that has graduated along the comparative advantage scale.[9] Export possibilities are not constrained by external factors but rather depend on supply conditions. Again, for each country, the dynamic gains from trade remain pronounced.

If theory is useful for retrodiction as well as prediction, then a history of a country's trade and development might be written in terms of changing factor endowments.[10] Initially the less-developed country is capital scarce (low ratio of physical capital to labour). But we might then distinguish two different sequences according to degree of 'land scarcity'. If the country is initially 'land abundant', the high land–labour ratio will give a relatively high wage level, and the country's comparative advantage will be in land-intensive primary exports. In accordance with our previously mentioned typology, we may consider countries that initially are predominantly peasant export economies, or plantation export economies, or mixed. We are then back to the 'vent for surplus' theory and the nineteenth-century variety of trade-through-development with differential effects according to the integrative process.

Alternatively, if the country is initially 'land scarce' but experiences rapid population growth, it must then escape the Malthusian sequence of diminishing returns in agriculture, high rents and low wages. The country might do this by exporting labour-intensive manufactures, gradually proceeding to higher stages of comparative advantage. In conformity with the Ricardian principle and the Lewis model (pages 38–40 above), the country may also succeed in raising productivity in agriculture and thereby keep domestic labour costs in manufacturing low. We are then back to the productivity theory of trade and the dynamic gains of the twentieth-century variety of development-through-trade.

Although we have focused only on international trade in goods, there may, of course, also be international movement of factors. International capital movements, foreign direct investment, technology transfer, and migration of labour may all play a role in enriching the story of changing comparative advantage and the development function of trade. To add these elements here, however, would make the story too long for present purposes.

CONCLUDING REMARKS

This has been a short chapter on a vast subject – and hence necessarily selective and superficial. As theory, it has been interested in general phenomena and general tendencies in normal development (Hicks 1969: ch. 1). But its usefulness must depend on what it can contribute to the writing of particular analytical histories of development experience.

We have had in mind the less-developed countries that are small open dualistic economies. They must overcome diseconomies of small size while achieving structural transformation. The question of the development function of trade is therefore important, and it is desirable to sort out the range of views regarding potential gains from trade and the relation to the gains from growth. In doing this, we have gone beyond neo-classical trade theory to the vent for surplus and productivity theories and to recognition of organisational dualism. We have then sketched conditions under which the development-through-trade integrative process will be relatively strong, and we have distinguished a nineteenth-century variety of trade from a twentieth-century variety. In contrast to the often alleged dynamic gains of ISI, the twentieth-century variety of trade based on export promotion may often yield superior dynamic gains. Unlike classical and neo-classical trade theory that concentrates on the gains from trade from the viewpoint of importables and static efficiency, the development-through-trade model emphasises exportables and dynamic efficiency. Thus, the theoretical elements imply that when analytical histories are written trade may well be found to have been an engine of growth or at least a handmaiden of growth.

NOTES

1. For more detailed exposition, see Myint (1958). The term 'vent for surplus' was first used by John H. Williams.
2. In Myint's analysis, as given above, the staple and unlimited labour models are combined.
3. Watkins (1963). There is also a close relation of the staple thesis to Hirschman's linkage approach (see Hirschman 1977).
4. Findlay designates the Ricardian model as being symmetric in the sense that the economies of E and P are qualitatively similar but only differ in the quantitative dimensions. By asymmetric relations, Findlay refers to North–South models that postulate qualitative differences as well as qualitative differences among the economies.
5. The following paragraphs are adapted from Meier (1975: 435–7).
6. Such an application was made for cocoa exports during the nineteenth century from the Gold Coast, palm products from Nigeria, and copper exports from Northern Rhodesia (Meier 1975).

7. Three versions of elasticity pessimism became prominent in the 1950s: Nurkse's inward-looking balanced growth, Rosenstein-Rodan's argument for coordinated investment in a balanced growth pattern, and Mahalanobis's case for heavy sector ISI (Bhagwati 1984: 199–200).
8. Changes in factor endowments and technical progress shift the production possibility frontier. These changes together with changes in the structure of demand will shift the reciprocal demand curves, thereby changing the volume of trade, its composition and the terms of trade.
9. Compare the progression of Japan, Asian NICs, and ASEAN (Association of Southeast Asian Nations) countries.
10. To do this, we must depart from a 2x2x1 Ricardian model to a 3-factor, 2-sector model as presented by Jones (1971: ch. 1). The approach that we sketch below is applied in detail in a forthcoming volume by Lal and Myint.

REFERENCES

Balassa, Bela (1978), 'Exports and economic growth: further evidence', *Journal of Development Economics*, vol. 5, June, pp. 181–9.

Balassa, Bela (1981), *The Newly Industrialized Countries in the World Economy*, London: Pergamon Press.

Baldwin, Robert E. (1956), 'Patterns of development in newly settled regions', *The Manchester School of Economic and Social Studies*, vol. 24, May, pp. 161–79.

Baldwin, Robert E. (1963), 'Export technology and development from a subsistence level', *Economic Journal*, vol. 73, March, pp. 80–92.

Bhagwati, Jagdish (1984), 'Comment on Raul Prebisch', in Gerald M. Meier and Dudley Seers (eds), *Pioneers in Development*, New York: Oxford University Press, pp. 197–204.

Bhagwati, Jagdish (1988), 'Export-promoting trade strategy: issues and evidence', *World Bank Research Observer*, vol. 3, no. 1, pp. 27–57.

Caves, Richard E. (1965), '"Vent for surplus" models of trade and growth', in Robert Baldwin *et al.* (eds), *Trade, Growth and the Balance of Payments*, Amsterdam: North-Holland

Caves, Richard E. (1971), 'Export-led growth and the new economic history', in Jagdish Bhagwati, Ronald W. Jones, Robert A. Mundell and Jaroslav Vanek (eds), *Trade, Balance of Payments and Growth. Papers in International Economics in Honor of Charles P. Kindleberger*, Amsterdam: North-Holland, pp. 403–42.

Corden, W. Max (1971), 'The effects of trade on the rate of growth', in Jagdish Bhagwati *et al.*, *Trade, Balance of Payments and Growth*, Amsterdam: North-Holland, pp. 117–43.

Feder, G. (1983), 'On exports and economic growth', *Journal of Development Economics*, vol. 12, April, pp. 59–73.

Findlay, Ronald (1984a), 'Growth and development in trade models', in

R.W. Jones and Peter Kenen (eds), *Handbook of International Economics*, vol. I, Amsterdam: Elsevier Science Publishers, pp. 185–91.

Findlay, Ronald (1984b), 'Trade and development: theory and Asian experience', *Asian Development Review*, vol. 2, no. 2, pp. 23–42.

Hicks, John (1969), *A Theory of History*, Oxford: Clarendon Press.

Hirschman, Albert O. (1958), *The Strategy of Economic Development*, New Haven: Yale University Press.

Hirschman, Albert O. (1977), 'A generalized linkage approach to development, with special reference to staples', in L. Manning Nash (ed.), *Essays on Economic Development and Cultural Change in Honor of Bert F. Hoselitz*, Chicago: University of Chicago Press, pp. 67–98.

Jones, R.W. (1971), 'A three-factor model in theory, trade, and history', in Jagdish Bhagwati *et al.* (eds), *Trade, Balance of Payments and Growth*. Amsterdam: North-Holland, pp. 3–21.

Kravis, Irvin B. (1970), 'Trade as a handmaiden of growth: similarities between the nineteenth and twentieth centuries', *Economic Journal*, vol. 80, pp. 850–72.

Lal, Deepak and Hla Myint (forthcoming), *Political Economy of Growth, Poverty, and Equity*.

Lewis, W. Arthur (1984), 'Development economics in the 1950s', in Gerald M. Meier and Dudley S. Seers (eds), *Pioneers in Development*, New York: Oxford University Press.

Lewis, W. Arthur (1954), 'Economic development with unlimited supplies of labor', *Manchester School*, vol. 21, pp. 139–91.

Lockwood, W.W. (1963), *Economic Development of Japan*, Princeton: Princeton University Press.

Mayer, W. (1984), 'The infant-export industry argument', *Canadian Journal of Economics*, vol. 17, May, pp. 249–69.

Meier, Gerald M. (1963), *International Trade and Development*, New York: Harper & Row.

Meier, Gerald M. (1975), 'External trade and internal development', in Peter Duignan and Louis Gann (eds), *Colonialism in Africa 1870–1960*, Cambridge: Cambridge University Press.

Meier, Gerald M. (1989), *Leading Issues in Economic Development*, 5th edn, New York: Oxford University Press.

Michaely, Michael (1977), 'Exports and growth: an empirical investigation', *Journal of Development Economics*, vol. 4, March, pp. 49–53.

Mill, John Stuart (1848), *Principles of Political Economy*, London: Parker.

Myint, Hla (1958), 'The "classical theory" of international trade and the underdeveloped countries', *Economic Journal*, vol. 68 (June), pp. 317–37.

Myint, Hla (1971), *Economic Theory and the Underdeveloped Countries*, New York: Oxford University Press.

Myint, Hla (1985), 'Organizational dualism and economic development', *Asian Development Review*, vol. 3, no. 1, pp. 24–43.

Ricardo, David (1815), *Essay on the Influence of a Low Price of Corn*

Upon the Profits of Stock, London: John Murray.
Ricardo, David (1817), *Principles of Political Economy and Taxation*, London: John Murray.
Robertson, D.H. (1949), 'The future of international trade', *Readings in the Theory of International Trade*, The American Economic Association, Philadelphia/Toronto: Blakiston, pp. 497–513.
Smith, Adam (1776/1937), *An Inquiry into the Nature and Causes of the Wealth of Nations*, Edwin Cannan (ed.), New York: Modern Library.
Watkins, Melville H. (1963), 'A staple theory of economic growth', *Canadian Journal of Economics and Political Science*, vol. 29, no. 2, pp. 141–58.
Young, Allyn (1928), 'Increasing returns and economic progress', *Economic Journal*, vol. 38, December, pp. 527–42.

PART II

PRE-INDUSTRIAL AND EARLY INDUSTRIAL TRADE

3 · THE CHINA SEAS AND THE WORLD ECONOMY BETWEEN THE SIXTEENTH AND NINETEENTH CENTURIES: THE CHANGING STRUCTURES OF TRADE

Peter W. Klein

INTRODUCTION

Since the publication of Fernand Braudel's book *La Méditerranée et le monde méditerranéen à l'époque de Philippe II* in 1949, economic historians have become used to the concept of maritime space as a significant object of historical enquiries. For Braudel the idea of space served as a source of explanation. In his view, space contained all important historical realities such as states, societies, civilisations and economies. The maritime space of a large inland sea such as the Mediterranean presented a more or less definite and intrinsic interconnection between ports, commerce and hinterland societies – in short a 'world' of its own. The peoples of this world were living and breathing with the same rhythms of time,

I would like to express my gratitude to Dr J.L. Blussé of the State University in Leiden, who introduced me to the fascinating history of the China seas. This chapter would have remained unwritten had I been unable to benefit from his wide knowledge and profound understanding. However, his views do not necessarily coincide with mine and he is not to be held responsible for the shortcomings of my chapter.

actually sharing a common destiny. Braudel's approach was so alluring that his concept of maritime space has been widened and stretched rather far beyond its original meaning. All kinds of seas – whether inland or not – and even oceans, have become objects of historical enquiry à la mode de Fernand Braudel. Apart from such areas as the Baltic, the North Sea, the Caribbean, the Atlantic and the Pacific it would seem that the Indian Ocean has recently enjoyed particular attention (Steensgaard 1985; Chaudhuri 1985; Arasaratnam 1986).

Although it is recognised that the unity of such a vast and open-ended maritime space as the Indian Ocean is 'less obvious' (Steensgaard 1985: 34), it is maintained that Braudel's triple analytical framework for the study of history – space, time, and structure – may very well support the study of Asian trade relations (Chaudhuri 1985: 2). If this is true for the Indian Ocean, with its many regional differentiations and variations and where it would be difficult to speak of any 'common destiny' whatsoever, it would certainly hold for the much more homegenous area of the China seas of East Asia. It is therefore no great surprise to learn from another of Braudel's publications that the Far East actually consisted of three different major parts: first the Arabic world of Islam between the Red Sea and the west coast of India, secondly the Indian world eastward of Cape Comorin and finally the Chinese world of East Asia (Braudel 1979: 417–21). And it is of course true that the territories and countries around the China seas have been closely corresponding to each other since time immemorial as far as their rice-growing economy, their polity, their social structure and their system of cultural values are concerned. As is also obvious, these similarities were partly the consequence of natural and geographical conditions and circumstances, and partly the effect of history, which had practically ensured the successive empires of China of their hegemony or dominance in the region. On the other hand it should not be overlooked that Southeast Asia at the border of the South China Sea had also been open to Indian and Arab influences. However this may have been, it would seem as if the maritime space of the China seas fits very well into the concept Braudel had applied to the Mediterranean world. It is therefore rather surprising that Braudel's example has not yet encouraged any following as far as the China seas are concerned.

Even so, it is not my intention to try to fill this gap now and for the time being I would just like to take it for granted that the regional space of the China seas is sufficiently distinct in order to consider it separately as a meaningful and consistent economic and historical unit. As far as I know until now the external trade of East Asia during early modern times has been exclusively studied in the form of separate national case studies of particular East Asian countries such as China, Japan, Korea, Siam, Malacca, the Philippines, Vietnam, Cambodia, etc. However necessary and useful such a fragmented and rather traditional approach may be, I would like to contend that it is a less workable method for understanding the role of long-distance trade in the shaping of the world economy. In this case there is certainly more to be learned from an overall view of a consistent regional space. What I would like to question in this chapter is to what extent and in what manner the East Asian economy had become integrated into the world market through the development of its long-distance trade with other areas before the second half of the nineteenth century. My contention is that Western technology, shipping and communication had by then only developed sufficiently for establishing an indissoluble direct bond between the world market and this secluded and almost inaccessible area, far from the main habitual and familiar shipping lanes. The China War of the 1840s and Japan's forced opening in the 1850s left no doubt about this. It was a contingency of an enormous significance and with many momentous consequences for the course of world history in the nineteenth and twentieth centuries.

But how did it come about? Was it really the logical and almost irrevocable outcome of the aggressive and continuous overseas expansion of capitalist Europe since late medieval times? So it appears to be in the eyes of such a leading historian as Immanuel Wallerstein who took his cue from none other than Fernand Braudel himself (Wallerstein 1974). But in their approach to the phenomenon of the European overseas expansion Braudel and Wallerstein applied themselves to a rather peculiar concept of the notion 'world economy'. However helpful their idea may be in some respects, it is also a very confusing one for in its omission of any reference to the global dimensions of space it is almost the opposite of the accepted thinking. In Braudel's words *'l'économie-monde'* must be distinguished from *l'économie mondiale*, which is indeed covering the whole of the earth. But *l'économie-monde* 'ne met en cause qu'un fragment de l'univers' (Braudel 1979: 12). One of the three main characteristics of *une économie-monde* is its actual confinement to more or less inflexible spatial limits. The other two hallmarks of such world economies are the polarisation between a centre and its environment and the hierarchisation of zones. *L'économie-monde* is a '*couche supérieure*' but also '*une économie d'ensemble*', actually '*un ensemble de multiple cohérents*'. Even so the matter is obviously not yet sufficiently confusing. Braudel thought it proper to add that any world economy is no simple economic entity. It also consists of social, political and cultural components.

As I have noted, Braudel perceived three different Asian world economies, operating next to each other during early modern times. But with the arrival of Vasco da Gama in Calicut on 27 May 1498 a fourth world economy had already entered the Asian scene (Braudel 1979: 420). It was the European world economy that was accomplishing a unique feat, which actually set it apart from Braudel's regional understanding of the concept 'world economy' itself. In fact, the European *économie-monde* had somehow or other succeeded in breaking through the spatial limits of its regional confinement. Indeed, it was now on its way to conquering the whole global space of the earth. Through the means of the forceful deployment of its long-distance trade, the European world economy penetrated slowly but continuously into the domain of other 'worlds', more or less devouring them in the course of its progress. The Portuguese, the Dutch, the English, the French and a few others disposed only of very small means. They encountered enormous problems and difficulties in the Asian environment: an environment that was unknown and completely strange to them, physically, socially, culturally. '*Ils ne devraient pas réussir et pourtant ils réussissent*'; they should not have succeeded and yet they succeeded ...

THE CHINA SEAS, EUROPE AND JAPAN

But did they really succeed as far as the maritime space of the China seas is concerned? It is my contention that they did not. At least not until after the middle of the nineteenth century when conditions had become quite different from those that had determined the structure and development of long-distance trade in pre-industrial times. In the meantime the European advance into the area had proceeded not continuously but intermittently, suffering many setbacks. It was held in check until far into the eighteenth century. As a consequence, Europeans never came near to domination or control of the region's economy. If there was any success, it was due rather less to domination than to adaptation to the political and economic conditions of the trading system in the maritime space of the China seas and its relations with other Asian areas. As I will try to show, the maritime space of the China seas under pre-industrial conditions did not correspond very closely to the idea of a simple polarised regional entity of hierarchical zones. The region's economic networks and trade patterns were actually conditioned by more or less sweeping changes of the power relations within the area itself, which caused a considerable upheaval during the sixteenth century.

This state of affairs continued until the third quarter of the seventeenth century when a new regional balance was established. During the preceding era of chaos and anarchy the Portuguese and the Dutch had succeeded in gaining a more or less substantial share in the region's internal and external trade. It would be quite wrong, however, to consider this accomplishment as evidence of the subordination of the maritime space of the China seas to any European centre. During the eighteenth century the new regional balance of power more or less restored the traditional pattern of trade relations into which various newcomers were absorbed. It is not yet quite clear who profited most from the new conditions but it is likely that the mercantile economy of the maritime provinces of Fukien and Kwangtung in the southwest of China, the Dutch entrepôt trade at Batavia and finally the English country trade from India gained most. But in the end the Dutch were losing as well, just as the Portuguese and the Japanese had lost before them. The composition of the region's export trade also experienced substantial change. To begin with, the Portuguese and the Dutch – like the Chinese and the Japanese at the same time – had been mainly trading in silks and precious metals, including copper. Then during the eighteenth century commercial interests focused ever more strongly on tea. But when all is said and done, none of these commodities can be taken to have been a strong enough bond for linking the whole of the region's economy to any single process of price formation in the world market, whether central or not. And price formation is of course the only yardstick available to the economist for measuring the extent and the workings of any market, the world economy's market included.

THE EAST CHINA SEA

Since I have now revealed my overall views on the matter, it is about time to start substantiating them. Let me begin by indicating briefly the main characteristic features of the maritime space in question. It is actually made up of two different seas – the East China Sea to the north and the South China Sea to the south. The area takes the form of an hour-glass shaped inland sea connecting tropical and non-tropical regions. At the western side it is rimmed in by the continent of Asia and on the eastern side by a string of islands fanning out from Japan in the north to the Indonesian archipelago in the south. Contrary to the space of the Indian Ocean where the Islam and Indian civilisations have exerted an enormous influence from the cultural point of view, most nations and countries around the China seas have been living under the unifying emanation of China, even though the civilisations of Arabia and India had also reached out far into Southeast Asia. The exit from or entry into the China seas could be effected through various routes. One of them led over the narrow Kra isthmus of the Malay peninsula, another through the Straits of Malacca. The latter was favoured by the Portuguese even though it could take up to nearly three years to make the return journey from Goa in India via Macao in China to Nagasaki in Japan and back again (Boxer 1969: 63; Boxer 1959). This long duration was due to the delays caused by the need to wait for the proper monsoon winds at crucial ports like Malacca. The Dutch later preferred the passage through the Sunda Straits. Their shipping to and from Nagasaki was nevertheless also restricted to only one set of seasonal voyages a year. As a rule ships had to leave Batavia in the months of May and June in order to be able to return in October and November. It would therefore be no great surprise to learn that the European performance in the shallow and dangerous East China Sea, where navigation was very tricky, had remained negligible. And Nagasaki was, indeed, the only port in the East China Sea ever to become of any significance to European trade. Nevertheless during the century between 1580 and 1680 Nagasaki was a main centre of regional and inter-regional trade and European commercial enterprise held a substantial share in its volume.

However, during the last quarter of the seventeenth century the Dutch trade in Nagasaki declined to about 15 or 20 per cent of the maximum it had attained only two or three decades earlier. It should be noted that this rise and decline actually occurred under conditions that had put Dutch trade in Japan in a very privileged position. Thanks to Japan's foreign policy since 1639 the Dutch only had to take Chinese competition into account. From the beginning of the 1690s Dutch trade in Nagasaki remained at more or less the same low levels. At the same time, trade in the East China Sea continued to flourish. During the eighteenth century Japanese exports of precious metals over the isle of Tsushima into Korea and China actually surpassed the amounts of silver that had earlier been carried away from Nagasaki by the Chinese and Dutch (Tashiro 1986; Tashiro 1976). As the internal trade in the area of the East China Sea continued, European penetration was actually reversed. In fact, European trade never managed to gain a foothold in either the north of China or the Korean peninsula. Now even the Dutch had to withdraw almost completely from the East China Sea. It was not only their Japanese trade that suffered. After having taken possession of Formosa in 1624, the Dutch had to abandon the island in 1662. In the end, the island was annexed by China in 1684 and the Dutch had not only lost an entrepôt for trading and a suitable naval base but also a centre of growing importance for sugar production, which might have considerably strengthened their commercial standing in the region (Campbell 1903). It was not to be, however, and the East China Sea closed like an oyster, leaving only a small trickle of trade with the outside world.

It would be quite wrong to maintain that the seclusion of this part of the maritime space of the China seas had been caused by the xenophobic policy instituted by Japan during the 1630s. Actually, the English and Spanish had already left the country during the 1620s, the first voluntarily, the latter involuntarily. The interdiction of overseas trade to Japanese commercial enterprise itself between 1633 and 1635 and the expulsion of the Portuguese in 1639 are generally taken as evidence of the so-called closing of the country. But as a matter of fact the country still remained open at that time. The Chinese and the Dutch were actually encouraged to carry on. Between 1633 and the first half of the 1660s the Dutch East India Company's exports from and imports into Japan reached their apex. During pre-industrial times it was never again equalled, let alone surpassed. Dutch trade with Japan began to deteriorate only when the accelerating growth of the Japanese economy in the later parts of the seventeenth century caused a declining need for the main Dutch imports, particularly silkware and other textiles. The very same growth also gave rise to the domestic monetary demand for precious metals which the Dutch and Chinese – and the Portuguese and Japanese before them as well – had been exporting in large quantities. During the second half of the seventeenth century, however, the output from mining decreased as a consequence of inadequate technology.

The acceleration of economic growth in Japan that had already been noticeable earlier in the seventeenth century, had been implemented in its turn by the very fundamental transformation of the region's polity and social structure during the century of chaos between 1550 and 1650. To begin with, Japan had been torn up by civil war. Japanese society only came to settle down during the first three or four decades of Tokugawa rule, which had been instituted in 1600. As domestic pacification proceeded, the nation's foreign policy posed some very fundamental problems as well. These problems had come to light as a side issue of the civil war during the sixteenth century. The conditions of war had allowed Japanese traders or pirates to infringe even more than usual on the tributary system that constituted the traditional trade pattern between Japan and China. The Ming regime in China, which was itself running into the protracted strife that would finally lead to its downfall in 1644, retaliated in 1557 by putting a ban on all official relations with Japan. Expelled from the Chinese world system, Japan had now become the outcast of East Asia. Japan's military invasions of China's vassal, Korea, at the end of the sixteenth century prevented any chance of re-establishing the former system of international relations with China as its recognised centre of harmonious domination.

It took another century before the traditional stability was regained in the form of an alternative establishment of international relations. But at the end of the seventeenth century the Tokugawa regime succeeded in manoeuvering Japan into the centre of a regional system of international diplomacy of its own making. The system included a concoction of tributary trade relations. The various forms of tribute served the traditional purpose of properly distinguishing between partners of unequal standing. Official equivalence was accorded only to the Kingdom of Korea. Next came the subordinate Ryukyu isles. The Dutch were taken to represent the western barbarians and therefore enjoyed an even more humble diplomatic status, but this was still higher than the one allotted to the Chinese, who had no official status whatsoever, although their trade to Nagasaki was recognised and allowed. It is evident that the Japanese East Asian 'world-system' had been modelled on the Chinese system of Confucian hierarchy. It is true that the Japanese structure of international diplomacy only related to regional dimensions and that it comprised only a few components but it was nevertheless quite effective in its operation and actually contributed substantially to a considerable change of the global power relations.

From about 1680 the international anarchy that had been dominating the scene in the East China Sea became part of the past. In its place came a balanced system of two interlocking but nevertheless self-contained polities. After the fall of the Ming in 1644 the Ching succeeded in restoring the domestic order of China during the third quarter of the seventeenth century, just as the Tokugawa regime had restored order in Japan. With China and Japan as strong and stable centres, there was little or no room for further European penetration into the East China Sea. As the protracted age of anarchy and chaos in East Asia came to its end, the chances for the European outsiders to strengthen their economic or political position decreased accordingly. There was not much that they could do about this. For the conditions under which their penetration had been possible during the preceding era had been drastically changed.

The change had dramatic consequences for the Dutch especially, not only in the region itself but in the whole of the Asian market. Their trade in the China seas had actually been one of the main pillars supporting the complicated and extensive network of intra-Asian trade which had become the Dutch East India Company's most rewarding source of profit during the seventeenth century. Through its trade to the China seas the Company had been able to acquire the large amounts of bullion needed for servicing other Asian markets. And as less bullion became available, the company was forced to reorganise the whole structure of its enterprise. During the eighteenth century the Company was forced to expand its bilateral European–Asian exchange relations at the expense of developing its multilateral intra-Asian trade. In the meantime and for the time being, the East China Sea saw the re-establishment of its traditional self as it more or less retired from the world market. In Fernand Braudel's terms of reference this would signify nothing less than the disconnection of what he understood to be '*le temps du monde*', the world's rhythm of structural historical change.

THE SOUTH CHINA SEA

I would like to turn now to the penetration of European trade into the other part of the hour-glass, the South China Sea – so much nearer to the well-worn trading networks of the Indian Ocean. The external maritime economic relations of the region had been integrated since time immemorial into the traditional pattern of Asian trade (Simkin 1968). As a rule, shipping and commerce depended on the portages of the Malaysian peninsula as a centre of trans-shipment and entrepôt trade for connecting East Asia to the economies in the Indian Ocean. Since early times, however, merchants and mariners from India, Arabia, Persia and other parts of South Asia had entered more or less regularly into the South China Sea as well (Meilink-Roelofsz 1962: 14). East and Southeast Asians in their turn ventured into the Indian Ocean. At the beginning of the sixteenth century the cosmopolitan city-port of Malacca had become the central market for South and East Asia. Since its rise a century earlier, it had not only attracted merchants from trading economies in the Indian Ocean and the Indonesian archipelago, but also hundreds of Chinese colonists. As a matter of fact, even the Celestial Court of China and its mandarins were less prone to perennial introspection than their notorious reputation of neglecting shipping and trading would let one believe. The naval expeditions far into the Indian Ocean during the early Ming period between 1405 and 1433 can be taken as evidence of commercial expansion. The extension of the Chinese tributary system of foreign and overseas trade to the states of Southeast Asia also contradicts the idea that official China kept close to an anticommercial and antimerchant tradition. Chinese policy in these matters was actually founded on rational logic requiring strict control of overseas trade by the state (Curtin 1984: 124–5). The tributary system of foreign trade was only partly successful, however, and private merchants always remained indispensable (Chaudhuri 1985: 13). Unofficial Chinese enterprise had therefore also held a substantial share in the external trade of the South China Sea. According to some authorities the Chinese before the ninth century had already undertaken long voyages westwards right past the Malay Peninsula and as far as the Persian Gulf (Meilink-Roelofsz 1962: 15).

The growth of the maritime trade of China during the next centuries had led to a great number of Chinese overseas commercial settlements. In the first half of the sixteenth century they had spread over all the major seaports in the South China Sea from Indo-China, Malaysia and Siam over the arc of islands from Sumatra in the west to Timor in the southeast and to the Philippines in the north. At that time a well-organised network of Chinese intermediaries had actually succeeded in controlling and dominating the regional trade of the South China Sea. The Chinese connected their system of interlocking trade diasporas through two main divisions or shipping routes (Blussé 1988; Curtin 1984: 167). One was the western route along the mainland of Southeast Asia from Annam (i.e. Vietnam) southwards to Cambodia, Siam and Malaya. The eastern coastal route connected the province of Fukien via the Philippines with the Indonesian archipelago. To begin with, the latter had also included the link with the Ryukyu islands and Japan in the East China Sea, but this connection was broken off in 1557 when China renounced its diplomatic relations with Japan. Smuggling and unofficial trade between the countries continued, of course. Chinese and Japanese merchants now also relied on the opportunity of trading with each other in the seaports of the South China Sea. It was actually one of the reasons why the Japanese during the sixteenth century, following the example of the Chinese, in their turn established mercantile settlements in the main maritime markets of Southeast Asia, notably in Vietnam, Makassar, Siam and the Philippines. They were preceded by enterprising mariners from the Ryukyu islands who had already penetrated into the South China Sea as early as the end of the fifteenth century.

Recapitulating for a moment, I would like to conclude that the state of affairs in the South China Sea in the sixteenth century had become much more complicated than the situation in the north, in the East China Sea. In the latter the regulation of the internal political and economic affairs was left to a relatively small number of regional powers. The maritime economy of Southeast Asia, however, had always been linked more closely to the world of shipping and trading in the Indian Ocean. Its products had reached even the European market since Roman times at the latest. As a consequence, the area had been very much subject to the dynamic factors of historical change. Since the earliest times it was a melting pot of different cultures, which emanated from civilisations as far away as India, Arabia and China. In the sixteenth century trade in the South China Sea had emerged as a dynamic but well-ordered business of a cosmopolitan community of merchants.

But however great the influence of maritime China in the area may have been at that time, it was never anything like that of the power of the Europeans. As John E. Wills pointed out, the classic example of the European pattern is to be found in the Mediterranean, which was so brilliantly pictured by Fernand Braudel (Wills 1979: 208–10). In that area, power centres facing a relatively closed maritime space sought to profit from their relations with each other through trading, piracy, plunder and raiding in order to force better conditions of trade and colonisation. The centripetal interaction of profit and power was reinforced by two political cultures, European and Muslim, mutually strengthening each other in continuous struggles. The Mediterranean environment had fostered a competitive system from the times of the city states of Greece and Rome, a system that had regained its vigour in Renaissance Italy.

By contrast, the South China Sea offered only meagre opportunities for such an interaction between profit and power. Apart from the attempts of commercial city-states to control the Straits of Malacca or the Sunda Straits – as the medieval kingdom of

Srivijaya had temporarily succeeded in doing earlier – there were, to be sure, a number of other maritime centres of commerce and shipping. However, as centres of naval power they were only of very minor significance. The South China coast confronted an open ocean. Ports and other destinations were widely dispersed over a very extensive area. Most conflicts between the states originated from disputes about land frontiers. China itself always had to be on guard against dangers from North and Central Asia. The kingdoms of Tonkin, Annam, Champa and Quinam in Vietnam, Cambodia and Ayuthaya in Siam were more or less contiuously entangled in land wars (Hall 1964).

The position of the Philippines was even more marginal than that of Japan and the Ryukyus. The latter were, nevertheless, potential partners of maritime South China for a game of profit and power interaction. However, as I tried to indicate before, the game came to nothing through the establishment of peaceful coexistence in the East China Sea of the Chinese and Japanese world systems. The political traditions conditioned by the Chinese pattern of political control and bureaucratic administration actually reinforced the geographical imperatives of the China seas, which precluded the rise and development of what we now may call the Mediterranean model of profit-and-power relations.

THE ARRIVAL OF THE EUROPEANS

At the middle of the sixteenth century it appeared that the complicated and dynamic state of affairs in the China seas was rapidly becoming even more complicated and dynamic. The South China Sea at that time was not only penetrated by the newcomers from Japan and the Ryukyus but, as of course we all know, by newcomers from Europe as well. The Portuguese were the first to arrive. In 1511 they conquered Malacca, taking control of the main connecting link between the Indian Ocean and the China seas. In 1557 they were allowed to establish a trading post in Macao. After having already arrived in Japan during the 1540s, they founded another of their main trade settlements in Nagasaki in 1580. The Spaniards also moved into the China seas after establishing their Asian headquarters in Manila in 1571. The Dutch and the English arrived on the scene at the beginning of the seventeenth century and it seemed as if the French and maybe the Danes and the Swedes would soon follow.

The European penetration into the maritime space of East Asia may be taken as a token of discontinuity in the sense that something was happening that had never happened before. But, however impressive and spectacular the European achievement may have been, it is doubtful whether its immediate consequences in the sixteenth and seventeenth centuries were really so momentous as they were later generally believed to be in the nineteenth and twentieth centuries. Quite apart from the obvious fact that the European intervention could hardly make an impression on the continental, mainly rural subsistence economies of the peoples of East and Southeast Asia, its effects on maritime commerce and shipping had to remain rather minimal as well. Asian maritime trade generally, and East Asian trade and shipping too, had already been well developed into a smoothly operating system. Its networks could be penetrated to some extent. And as the Portuguese were the first to discover to their profit, they were relatively easily exploited through the deployment of naval power in the ways that the Europeans had become accustomed to. As a matter of fact, the Portuguese had taken their cue from Venetian and Genovese advisers, who were not only quite familiar with Mediterranean practices but who also fitted well into the military tradition of the Portuguese feudal aristocracy. However, it had to be an exploitation not without proper prudence and restraint for fear of killing the goose that laid the golden egg (Steensgaard 1972).

In the meantime, the structures of Asian exchange relations were not quickly or easily improved upon. So Portugal, as the initial main European agent in the China seas during the second half of the sixteenth century, simply had to be satisfied with adapting itself to the requirements and conditions of the time and the place. In this particular region its naval power was of small avail. Any method of aggressive exploitation was out of the question. Even the conquest of Malacca was less of a success than the Portuguese had hoped it to be: it never gave them the trade monopoly they had looked for; its original rulers had escaped and they actually succeeded in establishing the evasive kingdom of Johor, constantly threatening the economic position of Portuguese Malacca (Andaya 1975: 20–3). Before the century had closed the

Portuguese had to launch no less than nine major military campaigns against Johor. And as the ally of the Dutch, Johor rose to a new prosperity after the Portuguese had been forced to surrender Malacca to the Dutch in 1641.

The Portuguese empire in the Far East was actually more idea than fact. Betwen 1500 and 1634 only 470 Portuguese ships made it back from the East, less than four a year. Almost a third of the outgoing vessels had been lost at sea. At the same time the Portuguese had to participate in intra-Asian trade on much the same terms as Asian traders. In the China seas they had to compete with a variety of traders from all sorts of countries and places. They never even succeeded in monopolising the traffic in pepper and spices that not only gave substance to their trade with Europe but was also part of their intra-Asian trade, including the one in the China seas. Apart from that, the Portuguese involvement in the maritime trade in the China seas was linked to four markets: India, China, Japan and Manila. The main profit seems to have resulted from setting up a triangular trade between India, China and Japan. Once a year a great *nao* of about 800–1,000 tons left Goa for Macao where Indian products such as cotton and calico textiles were exchanged for silk and gold. They were used to obtain silver in Japan. Silver, being more worth in China than in Japan, was accordingly brought to China where it was used for buying gold which in its turn was more in demand in India than in China (Boxer 1948: 5–8).

It was a rather cumbersome but very profitable enterprise. It was also the main enticement that was going to attract their Dutch competitors into the China seas in the first quarter of the seventeenth century. The very great profits reaped by the Portuguese from this enterprise were due to the political situation in East Asia, following the institution of the Chinese trade embargo against Japan in 1557. There was also the coincidence of the discovery of large silver, copper and gold deposits in Japan which proved to be especially favourable for the Portuguese. Even under these conditions their position was less secure than it seemed. Their position in the Japanese market was actually already eroded before the arrival of the English and Dutch with the resurgence of trade by the Chinese, the emergence of Japanese and, to a much lesser degree, Spanish competition (Souza 1986: 46–70). During the 1590s, however, the position of the Portuguese in the China seas was temporarily fortified by the Manila trade. Since the 1570s, Spanish silver had found its way across the Pacific into the Philippines where it was used to purchase Chinese silks. The stream of silver gradually turned into 'a roaring river' (Souza 1986: 65) and the Portuguese profited. They were not the only ones, however. In this branch of Southeast Asian trade also, the Chinese proved to be their main and often superior competitors. The last quarter of the sixteenth century and the first three or four decades of the seventeenth century were actually an age of growth and rising prosperity for Asian maritime enterprise in the region of the Chinese seas.

The maritime expansion of China after 1570 quite outside the framework of the tribute system has by now become a well-substantiated fact (Blussé 1986: ch. VI). It was soon to be followed by the remarkable rise and development of Japanese overseas commercial enterprise. Between 1604 and 1635 no less than 355 officially recorded ships sailed from Japan to destinations in Southeast Asia. During the 1620s Japanese-based maritime enterprise actually controlled the overseas trade of Siam in its main market, Ayutthaya (Smith 1977). The Japanese–Siamese trade continued with ups and downs until the end of the seventeenth century, notwithstanding Japan's closed door policies (Seiichi 1963). The spectacular expansion of the Asian maritime enterprise in the China seas at the end of the sixteenth century and the first quarter of the seventeenth century outshone the achievement of the Europeans. Even the annual share of the Portuguese in the very rewarding and important exports of silver from Japan gave evidence of the extreme uncertainty. Between 1600 and 1620 it ranged from nil to less than 10 per cent. Its average rose dramatically to 37 per cent during the 1630s, obviously because of the ban on the overseas activities of the Japanese themselves (Souza 1986: 54–8). However, the Portuguese were soon forced to give up in their turn.

It is evident that the European penetration into the maritime space of the China seas was still far from getting a stranglehold on the region's economy. Rather, the commercial activities of the Europeans probably contributed to the extension of the market as the framework of the tribute system lost some of its weight as a factor of exchange relations. But the Europeans had no objection to adapting themselves to official gift exchanging or similar tribute arrangements wherever and whenever this was possible or necessary. In short, they tried to adjust themselves as best as they could to whatever circumstances appeared to be most profitable.

Adjustment was necessarily a matter of trial and error. It required organising decision-making in the face of the alien and uncertain conditions of the Asian environment. Decisions had to be taken on poor information, which was only available in bits and pieces which more often than not arrived too late anyway. In these circumstances adaptation actually contained, perhaps, even a greater risk than one usually associates with the act of innovation in modern times.

THE DUTCH EAST INDIA COMPANY

The entry of the Dutch into the China seas is a case in point. After having accidentally arrived for the first time in Japan in 1600 and after their first visit to the China coast a year later, it took them about four decades of pondering on ways and means before they succeeded in establishing a profitable trade in the China seas. Even so, they had not reached the goal that they had set themselves from the beginning. Unlike the Portuguese, they failed to establish any direct connection with the destination they desired most: the silk market of China. Not until 1729 did the Dutch begin to send ships directly to Canton and the main objective then was the tea trade, not silk (Jörg 1982).

During the first quarter of the seventeenth century the Dutch East India Company had used its naval force several times in order to coerce its way into China. After suffering a final defeat at Macao the Dutch were driven to conduct their trade outside the territory of China. In 1624 they were persuaded to establish a trading post in Formosa and at the same time Chinese junks acquired permission to sail to this island with the cargoes the Dutch wanted. A status quo had been arrived at with the Chinese government. But the arrangement was not quite as satisfactory as the Dutch had expected it to be. The silver market in Manila continued to attract more of the Chinese silk exports than the Dutch were prepared to accept. Realising, however, that the use of force was of no avail, the Dutch had to wait until after the fall of the Ming empire in 1644. Between 1653 and 1690, however, they unleashed all the diplomatic energy they could muster, sending no less than eleven official embassies either to the Imperial Court in Peking or to local rulers in the maritime provinces of China (Wills 1974; Wills 1984). But these embassies were out of contact for years on end and brought about nothing but frustration for their Dutch masters.

The Dutch persistency requires explanation. It is to be found in the information about Asian trade which they had at their disposal right from the very beginnings. It seemed to leave no doubt whatsoever that the journey to the Far East was worth the effort because of no more than two separate sources of profit: spices from the spice islands and silk from China. Considering the lack of means at its disposal, the Dutch East India Company found itself in a dilemma: how to employ its capital and manpower for optimal results? Obviously, some very fundamental choices had to be made. It took the company almost a quarter of a century before it had even found a more or less satisfying organisation for making the proper decisions in Asia. The creation of the office of governor-general in 1611 and the foundation of Batavia as a central naval base and commercial entrepôt in 1619 were important steps in this direction. They contributed significantly to the company's control of the spice trade but the effort actually restricted the forces for penetrating directly into the China seas.

But the trade with China, the mysterious Cathay, remained a much-desired goal because of the enormous gains that were anticipated from it. The Dutch, moreover, soon realised what chances they were missing as long as they could not follow the Portuguese example of exporting Chinese silks into Japan in return for the much-required silver. With this silver, the Dutch would be able to take part in all sorts of profitable intra-Asian exchange relations covering a much wider variety of products than silk and spices only. At first, the company had not particularly wanted intra-Asian trade; the initial deliberations and calculations which decided upon the tactics and strategies of the Dutch enterprise in Asia did not consider the possibility of inter-country trade within Asia. The perennial shortage of bullion caused by the deficit on the Dutch balance of trade with Asia also seemed to condemn to failure any attempt in that direction. Nevertheless, Asian country trade actually became the company's most profitable source of income during the seventeenth century – much more important than the importation of spices and silk into Europe.

The company's success in this area of activities was to a large extent due to its exports of precious metals and copper from Japan. In fact, it was Japan and not China that became the main centre of the Dutch activities in the China seas in the seventeenth century. The exports of precious metals from Japan could only be secured, however, if the proper import commodities were available. To start with, the Dutch had great trouble in acquiring them. As they failed to obtain silk directly from China they turned first to Patani – a centre of trade in northeastern Malaya – and Siam (Terpstra 1938; Smith 1977).

But Patani soon proved to be a disappointment. The company's office that had been opened there in 1608 was already closed by 1622. Patani was of small importance as a silk market; so was Siam. But from this country the company obtained large quantities of hides, a commodity which was very much in demand in Japan and which was soon supplied by Formosa as well. In this way, Siam actually became part of the Dutch trading network in the China seas. Its importance to the Dutch varied according to the development of their relations with Japan. In Siam itself they never obtained control of the country's overseas trade. Having arrived in Ayutthaya at the beginning of the seventeenth century, the Dutch East India Company was quick to profit from the political conditions in Siam, which was still engaged in a process of reconstruction after a long period of Burmese domination and exploitation. The trade privileges which were granted to the company did not prevent, however, stiff competition from, among others, Chinese, Japanese, Malaysian and Muslim traders. But the King's monopolising trade factory in Ayutthaya, which actually controlled the bulk of imports and exports, was their main opponent. During the seventeenth century the Dutch interest in Siam changed many times, but the import and export markets of Siam were limited and the Dutch never considered them to be of major importance. Their interest gradually declined, especially after 1680. In the meantime the Siamese commerce and, in fact, the Siamese economy had remained quite unaffected by European trade. During the seventeenth century no important structural economic change occurred there (Smith 1977: 113).

When all is said and done it is evident that by the early 1630s the Dutch had still not solved the problem of acquiring sufficient quantities of silk for importation into Japan (Klein 1986). Even the establishment of the Dutch trading station in Formosa had been of small avail. But the situation changed dramatically in the middle of the 1630s. Suddenly the Dutch succeeded in obtaining large quantities of silk from Vietnam, first from Quinam and after 1637 mainly from Tonkin. It is probable that a substantial quantity of this silk had not been produced locally. It may have first been imported into Vietnam from China by Chinese or Vietnamese silk merchants. However this may have been, thanks to its newly established connection with Vietnam the Dutch East India Company suddenly increased its silk imports into Japan by no less than some 300 per cent between 1635 and 1637. Their silver exports from this country rose accordingly. The company owed its success to some extent to its cooperation with Japanese traders who had settled earlier in the main Vietnamese centres of export, but were now banned from any business with their home country.

The boom in the Dutch–Tonkinese silk trade marked the beginnings of the spectacular development of the company's trade with Japan, reaching its peak between 1640 and the end of the 1660s. It was the time when an annual average of ten to twelve Company ships was sent out to Japan. The number represents 15 to 20 per cent of the merchant navy the Company had permanently stationed in Asia at a time when a total of about twenty Company ships per annum were leaving from Holland for destinations in the Far East. During this period the company exported an annual average of more than 1.5 million guilders of silver from Japan. About half of it was used for procuring silk for the Japanese market. The other half found its way over Batavia into the various channels of the Company's network of intra-Asian trade.

The success of the Company's Vietnamese silk trade was a very temporary one, however. During the second part of the 1650s the Tonkinese silk market fell into decline, just as the silk market of Quinam had already collapsed earlier. The reasons for this decline are not very clear. It is likely, however, that wars and all sorts of domestic troubles in Vietnam were at least partly to blame. During the seventeenth century Tonkin and Quinam were continuously engaged in fighting and the Dutch East India Company went to great trouble to avoid being involved. The silk-road from China into Vietnam was disrupted. A change in demographic conditions and property rights in Vietnam led to the extension of rice growing at the cost of the domestic sericulture.

In the end the Company decided to shut down its trading station in Hanoi where it had been operating for sixty years. It was not a difficult decision to take. As a matter of fact the Company had already found an alternative to its Vietnamese silk trade in the 1640s. Partly backed by its supply of Japanese precious metals, the Company had succeeded in obtaining silk from Bengal. At the same time Batavia proved to be more of a commercial attraction to Chinese silk merchants than Formosa. The Chinese junk trade began to ship increasing quantities of silk from China towards Batavia from where it was partly re-exported to Nagasaki. Between 1641 and 1654 half of the Dutch silk imports into Japan had come from Vietnam. But between 1655 and 1668 this figure had already declined to 19 per cent. At the same time the re-export of Bengal and China silk from Batavia to Japan had already risen to 67 per cent of the Company's total silk imports into that country. Since the Company's own trading with Bengal and the Chinese junk trade had obviously succeeded in keeping the Company's stock in Batavia well supplied with silk, the need for a direct access to the silk markets of China seems to have been considerably less urgent than before. It became even less pressing when Japan, for domestic economic reasons, began to put gradually increasing restrictions on the export of precious metals – first of silver in 1668, then of gold in the 1680s and finally even of copper in the 1690s. The Japanese demand for foreign silk declined accordingly. Small wonder then that in about 1690 the Company finally desisted from the forceful diplomatic efforts by means of which it had once hoped to obtain a substantial share in the China trade. The Company even omitted to avail itself of the opportunity for trade when the Ching empire finally proceeded to open Chinese ports after the conclusion of the civil wars in 1685 (Furber 1983: 126).

It is just as obvious that the eclipse of Japan as a substantial source of bullion had very adverse consequences for the Dutch East India Company. Its position in the Asian inter-country trade received a severe blow from which it never recovered. During the eighteenth century the Company had to withdraw from its profitable network of multilateral intra-Asian trade, concentrating its efforts ever more strongly on the bilateral exchange between

Europe and Asia. During the seventeenth century there had never been a moment when the Company would have come anywhere near controlling shipping and commerce in the China seas, however vital this would have been to its trading position in Asian markets. As a matter of fact, its profitable venture into the China seas only succeeded thanks to its careful adaptation to the region's economic and political conditions of the moment. These regional conditions were certainly not the product of any centralised world economy or hierachical world market. They were rather structurally defined by the complicated dynamics of a changing variety of domestic factors in the countries which themselves bordered on the China seas.

THE ENGLISH EAST INDIA COMPANY AND OTHER TRADERS

This is certainly not to say, however, that external factors were so insignificant that they merit no attention whatsoever. Quite the reverse. The European enterprise in the China seas of the sixteenth and seventeenth centuries was not only unprecedented but also very spectacular in itself. Until the last quarter of the seventeenth century this enterprise had been mainly the business of the Portuguese and the Dutch. Things began to change, however, with the expansion of English commerce in the second half of the century.

Its first thrust from Surat in India right towards Manila in the Philippines was already made in the 1640s (Quiason 1966). It was unsuccessful to begin with, but in time, the Madras–Manila trade became one of the important branches of the English inter-country trade in Asia. Like the Portuguese and the Dutch before them, the English were strongly attracted by the region's silver trade. This time, however, the magnet was American and not Asian silver. By entering into the so-called *Manilha trade* the English actually followed the lead that had been taken long before them by the junk trade from China. The basic pattern of this Sino-Philippine trade had been established as early as the 1570s when it was based on the exports of silks and other luxuries from China to Manila. The commodities concerned were re-exported to Acapulco in Mexico, from where large amounts of specie were shipped towards

Asian markets. By establishing considerable exports of Indian calicoes and other *piece goods* to Manila, the English succeeded in more or less following suit in the 1670s. As a consequence, the trade pattern in the South China Sea was substantially altered. Indian cotton materials became – next to silk – the second major item of Asian exports into America.

But during the eighteenth century the English did not succeed in ousting their Chinese competitors from first place. The outflow of Manila silver to China was greater in quantity and value than that to India. This characteristic trend was still evident up to 1810 when the value of Manila silver shipped to India still fell behind silver exports to China (Quiason 1966: 79). It must also be realised that even by the middle of the eighteenth century the Manila market had not yet fallen under European domination or control. The Manila trading community consisted of a colourful mixture of nationalities, Spanish Mestizos, Chinese, Armenians and Tagalogs amongst them (Quiason 1966: 93).

It has been maintained that the penetration of the English in the Manila market during the eighteenth century contributed greatly to their ultimate commercial primacy in Manila in the nineteenth century (Quiason 1966: 3). But this opinion seems to be mainly based on hindsight. As far as can be ascertained, it is very uncertain to what degree the matter had already been decided upon in the eighteenth century. It has also been maintained that the Manila trade of the seventeenth and eighteenth centuries represented already '*une conjoncture dominée par les rythmes européens et américains de l'économie atlantique*' (Chaunu 1966). But these words of Pierre Chaunu are hardly confirmed by the quantitative evidence he himself had produced. His figures show that the Manila trade continued to be dominated by the Chinese right to the end of the eighteenth century. The trade with New Spain, which had severely declined during the second half of the seventeenth century, only partly recovered afterwards. And Manila's country trade with India only achieved the same level as its China trade as late as the 1790s. These were developments that did not coincide at all with any European or Atlantic economic rhythm. Dermigny was therefore probably more correct when recording that '*la conjoncture extrême-orientale présente . . . un caractère particulier*' (Dermigny 1964: 139).

The second English thrust into the China seas, actually occurring at the same time as the first one, was perhaps of greater consequence. It actually restored China in the place of Japan as the region's main centre of European maritime enterprise. This time, however, it was neither silk or silver that attracted the principal interest, but tea. The regular trade between the English East India Company and China did not effectively begin until the last quarter of the seventeenth century (Morse 1975). Between 1676 and 1698 twelve English voyages to Amoy took place, but the results were not very satisfactory. The arrival of English India-based traders in the South China Sea from the late 1690s onwards, however, marked the beginnings of a new mercantile era (Blussé 1988: 3). Over the next 150 years this country trade gradually developed into a formidable challenge to the existing traditional political and economic institutions which were regulating the maritime commerce of the China seas. The change was not apparent, however, during the greater part of the eighteenth century.

In fact, institutional change may have affected European commerce and shipping to an even greater extent, as it became obvious that the heyday of the big European trading company was passing by. The era of free private trade was beginning. During the fifty years from 1690 to 1740 the Dutch East India Company's country trading had already been subject to a sharp drop. Maybe it was partly replaced by Dutch private trade in the form of smuggling.

The English East India Company and a number of smaller European companies at first also took their share from the Dutch. During the first decades of the eighteenth century a number of European trading posts was established in China's official port of entry, Canton and the city soon became the main centre for European trade in the China seas. But as the century proceeded, free and private country trade expanded all over the seas of Asia, particularly after 1740. And the main stimulus to this country trading was the expansion of the China trade (Dermigny 1964: 137-141). British country merchants, being relatively free from restrictions of the English East India Company, gave the best performance. British country tonnage to the South China Sea had already risen from about 3,000 tons in 1719-20 to maybe even 9,000 tons twenty years later (Furber 1983: 274). It was not until after the middle of the eighteenth century, however, that British trade in the China seas really surged ahead. It was the time when the English East India Company's tea trade and British private, free country trade were stimulating each other vigorously. During the last quarter of the eighteenth century the British expanding China trade became fortified by the spectacular rise of opium imports from Calcutta. This relatively new merchandise was now soon replacing Indian piece goods as a main commodity of intra-Asian trade. During this period the net annual profits of the English East India Company actually doubled (Furber 1983: 176).

But nevertheless, the change in the commodity structure of trade was to have adverse effects on the Company's position. Before the century had closed, the Company had already run into serious financial troubles. Like its Dutch predecessor before, it had failed to suppress the illegal operations of its own servants but this may have been the least of its worries. The clandestine trade ventures of British private country traders, hiding under the disguise of various foreign flags, probably gave more trouble. It was precisely this expansion of private British trade which in the nineteenth century would finally triumph over the old order in the China seas.

THE CHINESE JUNK TRADE

During the eighteenth century the Chinese system of tribute trade with the outside world had continued in theory, if not in practice (Curtin 1984: 242). Actually, it had been a legal fiction for a very long time. But now the vast majority of trade went through other channels, even Canton, the official port of entry for overseas trade. Here, the foreign trade with Europeans was monopolised on the Chinese side by a licensed group of merchants who were collectively responsible to the Imperial officials. Thanks to this monopoly, these *hong* merchants were in a strong position, at least in theory. But at the beginning of the eighteenth century Europeans still held only a very minor share of the overseas trade of China. Just as before, the main share was taken by the Chinese junk trade itself. In fact, European commerce in the maritime space of the China seas suffered a substantial loss through the shrinking of the Dutch East India Company's intra-Asian trading network between 1690 and 1740. It would be quite wrong to assume that the decline of the Dutch trade was compensated at once by the commercial enterprise of other Europeans. Instead, the Chinese junk trade, emanating from the southeast coast of China, experienced a phase of unparalleled growth and expansion between 1680 and 1740. After the penetration into the China seas, first by Portuguese and then by Dutch power and commerce, the region now experienced an interlude of declining European influence and rising internal economic strength. To begin with, the Dutch Company's trade with Japan was largely taken over by the Chinese. Their junk trade to Nagasaki rose threefold between 1680 and 1720. According to Dermigny, the Chinese had now become masters of the copper market which had been so crucial to the Dutch (Dermigny 1964: 141).

However, the Chinese junk trade to Japan detoriated in the 1720s, when it was its turn to be hit by the restrictive economic policies of Japan. In the meantime, the Chinese junk trade to Manila also experienced its heyday. It continued its expansion right into the 1740s, when it finally stabilised under the influence of the development of the British country trade. The Chinese junk trade to Batavia also finally reached its maximum during a phase of spectacular development between 1690 and 1740 (Blussé 1986: 121). It was not until after 1740 – the year of the great massacre of the Chinese in Batavia – that stagnation and decline set in. Contrary to what historians have maintained formerly, the massacre, however repulsive, was no more than an incident. Rather, the decline of the Chinese junk trade with Batavia was due to the structural change of intra-Asian trade relations under the gradual emergence of the commercial supremacy of the British informal empire. As the Dutch came under the increasing pressure of this empire they took all sorts of exclusive policies, including the fragmentation of the Chinese trade. It is one of the ironies of history that the centralised control of the so-called European world economy of the nineteenth century was only established after the crumbling of the structure of exchange relations from which Asian as well as European maritime commercial enterprise had been profiting for about three centuries.

CONCLUSION

The European penetration into the maritime space of the China seas during the sixteenth and seventeenth centuries had only been possible thanks to the peculiar development of the domestic and regional power relations in the area itself. Its influence on the region's economy had been marginal. Its commercial effects on the world economy had only been temporary, restricting themselves mainly to its consequences for the establishment of a rather weak and limited European trading network in Asia. After the region had regained a new balance of power in about 1680, its internal maritime trade experienced a new era of growth within a well-established framework of traditional institutions. This trade and its institutions were gradually eroded during the later part of the eighteenth century. At the same time, however, the institutions by means of which European commerce had made its entry into the China seas, also fell prey to disintegration. The establishment of the European economic hegemony during the nineteenth century found no base in what had happened during pre-industrial times. Rather, its foundation depended on revolutionary structural change, producing entirely new conditions and circumstances.

REFERENCES

Andaya, Leonhard Y. (1975), *The Kingdom of Johor 1641–1728*, Kuala Lumpur/London: Oxford University Press.
Arasaratnam, Sinnapah (1986), *Merchants, Companies and Commerce on the Coromandel Coast 1650–1740*, Delhi/New York: Oxford University Press.
Blussé van Oud-Alblas, Leonhard J. (1986), *Strange Company. Chinese Settlers, Mestizo Women and the Dutch in VOC Batavia*, Dordrecht/Riverton: Foris Publications.
Blussé van Oud-Alblas, Leonhard J. (1988), *No Boats to China. The Dutch East India Company and the South China Sea Trade, 1635–1690*, unpublished paper.
Boxer, Charles R. (1948), *Fidalgos in the Far East*, The Hague: Martinus Nijhoff.
Boxer, Charles R. (1959), *The Great Ship From Amacon: Annals of Macao and the Old Japan Trade, 1555–1640*, Lisbon: Centro de Estudos Historicos Ultramarinos.
Boxer, Charles R. (1969), *The Portugese Seaborne Empire 1415–1825*, New York: Alfred A. Knopf.
Braudel, Fernand (1979), *Civilisation matérielle, économie et capitalisme, XVe-XVIIIe siècle. Tome 3: Le temps du monde*, Paris: Armand Colin.
Campbell, William (1903), *Formosa under the Dutch*, London: K. Paul, Trench, Trubner & Co.
Chaudhuri, K.N. (1985), *Trade and Civilisation in the Indian Ocean. An*

Economic History from the Rise of Islam to 1750, Cambridge/New York: Cambridge University Press.
Chaunu, Pierre (1966), *Les Philippines et le Pacifique des Ibériques, XVIe-XVIIe-XVIIIe siècles. Construction graphiques*, Paris: SEVPEN.
Curtin, Philip D. (1984), *Cross-Cultural Trade in World History*. Cambridge/New York: Cambridge University Press.
Dermigny, Louis (1964), *La Chine et l'Occident. Le Commerce à Canton au XVIIIe siècle, 1739–1833*. Tome 1, Paris: SEVPEN.
Furber, Holden (1983), *Rival Empires of Trade in the Orient, 1600–1800*, Minneapolis: University of Minnesota Press.
Hall, Daniel G.E. (1964), *A History of South-East Asia*, 2nd edn, part 1, London: MacMillan.
Jörg, C.J.A. (1982), *Porcelain and the Dutch China Trade*, The Hague: Martinus Nijhoff.
Klein, P.W. (1986), 'De Tonkinees-Japanse zijdehandel van de Verenigde Oostindische Compagnie en het inter-Aziatische verkeer in de 17e eeuw', in W. Frijhoff and M. Hiemstra (eds), *Bewogen en Bewegen. De historicus in het spanningsveld tussen economie en cultuur*. Tilburg: H. Gianotten.
Meilink-Roelofsz, Marie A.P. (1962), *Asian Trade and European Influence in the Indonesian Archipelago between 1500 and 1630*, The Hague: Martinus Nijhoff.
Morse, H.B. (1975), *Chronicles of the East India Company Trading to China, 1635–1834*, Taipei: Oxford University Press.
Quiason, Serafin D. (1966), *English 'Country Trade' with the Philippines, 1644–1765*, Quezon City: University of the Philippines Press.
Seiichi, Iwao (1963), 'Reopening of the diplomatic and commercial relations between Japan and Siam during the Tokugawa Period', *Acta Asiatica*, vol. 4, pp. 1–18.
Simkin, Colin G.F. (1968), *The Traditional Trade of Asia*, London/New York: Oxford University Press.
Smith, George V. (1977), *The Dutch in Seventeenth-Century Thailand*, Detroit: Cellar Bookshop.
Souza, G.B. (1986), *The Survival of Empire. Portugese Trade and Society in China and the South Chinese Sea, 1630–1754*. Cambridge/New York: Cambridge University Press.
Steensgaard, Niels (1972), *Carracks, Caravans and Companies: The Structural Crisis in the European-Asian Trade in the Early Seventeeth Century*, Lund: Studentlitteratur.
Steensgaard, Niels (1985), 'The Indian Ocean network and the emerging world economy c.1500–c.1750', *Rapports I. Grands thèmes, méthodologie, sections chronologiques (I)*. Comité international des sciences historiques, XVIe Congrès international des sciences historiques, Stuttgart.
Tashiro, Kazui (1976), 'Tsushima Han's Korean trade, 1684–1710', *Acta Asiatica*, vol. 30, pp. 85–105.
Tashiro, Kazui (1986), 'Coinage and exports of silver during the Tokugawa era', in Akira Hayani (ed.), *Preconditions to Industrialization in*

Japan, mimeograph, Ninth International Economic History Congress, Bern, 24–29 August.

Terpstra, H. (1938), *De factorij des Oost-Indische Compagnie te Patani*, The Hague: Martinus Nijhoff.

Wallerstein, Immanuel M. (1974), *The Modern World-System. Capitalist Agriculture and the Origins of the European World Economy in the Sixteenth Century*, New York: Academic Press.

Wills, John E. Jr (1974), *Pepper, Guns and Parleys. The Dutch East India Company and China 1662–1681*, Cambridge Mass.: Harvard University Press.

Wills, John E. Jr (1979), 'Maritime China from Wang Chich to Shih Lang', in Jonathan D. Spence and John E. Wills (eds), *From Ming to Ch'ing. Conquest, Region, and Continuity in Seventeenth-Century China*, New Haven/London: Yale University Press.

Wills, John E. Jr (1984): *Embassies and Illusions. Dutch and Portugese Envoys to K'ang-hsi, 1666–1687*, Cambridge: Council on East Asian Studies.

4 · OPPORTUNITY AND RISK IN ATLANTIC TRADE DURING THE FRENCH REVOLUTION

François Crouzet

> Les Américains sont poussés à conquérir les mers comme les Romains à conquérir le monde.
>
> Alexis de Tocqueville[1]

During most of the eighteenth century the pattern of trade across the Atlantic was rather simple: it was basically made up of direct, but separate traffics between European colonial powers and their possessions in America; the 'triangular' trades were the only exceptions to this rule, which reflected – *inter alia* – the prevalence of the 'old colonial system'. The emergence of the United States, i.e. of an independent power on the western side of the Ocean, which was at liberty to trade with most other countries, started a process of change. Eventually, after Brazil and most Spanish colonies had also been emancipated, a new and much more complex Atlantic was created; it was characterised by the crisscrossing of multifarious trade routes – though the commercial and maritime ascendancy of Britain was a strong factor of polarisation.

In this process, the wars of the French Revolution and Empire played a significant role, as they gave a sharp stimulus to the foreign trade and navigation of the United States, to which they opened many ports and many routes which had been formerly closed to Americans. From 1793 to 1807, even up to 1812, American ships, thanks to their neutral status, were *les rouliers des mers*, to use the expression which Colbert had applied to the seventeenth-century Dutch, the general carriers on the seas of the world.

The emergence of new patterns in Atlantic trade, and in particular the mixture of opportunities and dangers which European wars brought to American merchants, is the theme of this chapter; but it will be examined during the 1790s, and at the micro-economic level, from the vantage point of a New England merchant firm, the house of John and Richard Codman, thanks to a collection of records which, despite serious gaps, contains a wealth of interesting data. This approach may seem too microscopic, but it throws some light on the concrete and daily problems which merchants had to face.[2]

THE CODMAN HOUSE AND FRENCH INFLATION

Unlike several well-known merchants of his time, who were recent immigrants, John Codman III (1755–1803) was a fifth-generation American descended from an Englishman who had come over in 1637. His grandfather and his father had been shipmasters and merchants in Charlestown, opposite Boston. He was apprenticed to a merchant in the latter city, then set up in business in 1781 in partnership with William Smith, son of his former master; this firm, of Codman and Smith, lasted up to 1790. Then, on 1 May 1791, John went into partnership with his younger brother, Richard (1762–1806), under the name of John and Richard Codman. As Richard went to Europe in 1793 and stayed there to represent the firm, John, who anyhow owned two-thirds of the capital, was in control in Boston.[3] The Codmans were both merchants and shipowners; they owned four to six ships (depending upon the years), the cargoes of which were generally for their own account; none the less, they also took freight for other merchants and some of their own goods were carried on ships which did not belong to them.

Few documents about the activities of Codman and Smith have survived, but they show that their trading pattern was roughly the traditional one, which Yankee merchants had followed in the eighteenth century. They sent foodstuffs – especially dried cod, grain, flour – to the West Indies,[4] to Madeira, to Portugal and Spain; and they imported sugar, molasses, wine (madeira, port, sherry), currants, capers, olive oil, salt, etc. (B8, f89; B15, f191, 196, 198; B16, f213; B17, f220). However, there was a gradual widening of horizons, though some ventures were isolated instances, such as the ship which was sent to the west coast of Africa (possibly for slaves) in 1784, and the interest which John Codman had in two American ships, *President Washington* and *Governor Bowdoin*, which were dispatched to Canton in 1790. They returned, loaded with tea and textiles, early in 1793: the former went to Boston and the latter to Hamburg.[5] Indeed, the new openings were mostly in northern and western Europe, where, before independence, American ships had been forbidden to go.

There is evidence that Codman and Smith had trade relations with England in 1783, with Holland in 1785[6] and with Russia in 1788.[7] Trade with the latter was to be the most regular and stable among the speculations which the Codmans undertook. Actually, the United States needed, particularly because of the rise of their merchant marine and their shipbuilding industry, increasing quantities of some Russian goods, mostly iron (in bars and hoops), sail cloth and hemp;[8] so the number of American ships which cleared from St Petersburg rose from four in 1784 to thirty in 1793 and eighty-four in 1803, and the United States became Russia's second-best customer.[9] The Codmans had an honourable share in this growing trade. Every spring two of their ships arrived in St Petersburg, generally after having landed a cargo of American produce (for which there was no market in Russia) at some Continental port further west; they loaded Russian goods and sailed directly to Boston, where they arrived in the autumn. The Russian exporters were paid by bills which they drew on the Codmans' correspondents in Europe – at first in Amsterdam and later on in London.[10]

The Boston house also started to trade with France; there are indices of some traffic in 1788 (B6, f171; B35, f58), but the earliest unquestionable document is a bill of lading dated 13 July 1789 for the shipment to Rouen of $74\frac{1}{2}$ tons of whale oil on the brig *Rambler*; three more similar shipments were made in late 1789 and early 1790.[11] These cargoes of oil were consigned to the famous merchant and banking house of Rouen and Paris of Le Couteulx et Cie[12] and the Codman papers contain a bundle of letters from this house, written between January 1790 and early 1793,[13] as well as some from another well-known Paris merchant, Pierre Le Roy d'Allarde.[14] These letters are quite interesting, because they reveal the problems which French merchants, who were engaged in foreign trade, were facing during those early years of the Revolutionary period, especially because of the inflation resulting from the issues of *assignats* (the first of which had been authorised in December 1789). Their interest is enhanced by the fact that both Pierre d'Allarde and Jean-Barthélémy Le Couteulx de Canteleu, the head of Le Couteulx, were involved in politics, as members of the Constituent Assembly.[15]

The French rate of exchange had started to fall early in 1789, well before the issuing of *assignats* was contemplated, and the aggravation of its fall by their introduction was slow; however, in November 1790, the *livre* weakened and the rate on London fell to 16 per cent below par (Bouchary 1937: 51, 53, 55–7, 59–60). This was worrying for importers who had to make remittances abroad. On 22 November 1790 Horcholle, the manager of Le Couteulx in Rouen, asked John Codman 'in all circumstances to draw on France as much as possible, till the exchange on London recovers its current price, because we repeat to you that we lose now 15 per cent on the said exchange' (normally, the French house would have sent bills on London to the correspondent of Codman in England). Alternatively, Horcholle asked to 'make the term of credit the longer . . . to give us the opportunity of seeing a favourable alteration in the exchange'. This was wishful thinking, of course, but the interesting point is that it seems to have been quite sincere, in good faith: Horcholle – and likely many French merchants – did not realise that increasing issues of *assignats* made depreciation, both internal and external, of the currency inevitable. One month later, on 22 December 1790, Horcholle sent a large order for spermaceti oil and wrote that Codman could draw on Le Couteulx in London for the whole amount, 'as we flatter ourselves that the Exchange will take its regular course before the time of payment is due' (B14, f178).

The hoped for 'favourable alteration' did not take place – though there was no further depreciation before the spring of 1791, and on 6 February 1791 Le Couteulx had to ask for delay in paying 27, 723 *livres* which were due on a cargo of whale oil; they wanted J. Codman's London correspondent, Lane Son and Fraser, 'to defer the most they can to draw for the balance, because the exchange is very disadvantageous to you in this moment and which may change in a minute, since our new Constitution is strengthened in spite of the aristocrats who are gone into foreign parts to discredit it, and to strain their useless endeavours for the re-establishment of their quondam Privileges; but which they must renounce absolutely'.[16] Le Couteulx wrote, to the same effect, to Lane Son and Fraser; the latter sent the following comments – somewhat ironic and condescending – to J. Codman: 'They (Le Couteulx) lament the heavy loss which will ensue by the low state of the Exchange' between Paris and London and ask the English house to 'forbear' their drafts for some time; 'being assured it cannot remain so long and extolling at the same time the most admirable constitution they have adopted; and which we suppose it to effect the look'd for rise in the Exchange, as we permit Mons' Le Couteulx to know the Affairs of his own country better than we do, and conscious if we draw now the loss must be heavy.' Lane Son and Fraser wrote that they would presently refrain from drawing, though, in their view, 'The prospect for some time hence [is] no ways flattering if we may judge from the past' as the exchange of France had continuously fallen since June 1790.[17] However, on 2 April, they announced that they had waited for one month and that the exchange had not improved, 'or in the opinion of Mercantile People here would shortly'[18] therefore they had drawn on Le Couteulx for 25,000 *livres*.

This delay had worried John Codman, and on 13 May 1791 his London correspondent wrote reassuringly that the house of Le Couteulx 'are in as great reputation and credit as any house in France. They are sanguine in the good effects of their Revolution and perhaps it may be so, tho' it may not be so early as they flatter themselves it will. When they wrote us that exchange would very soon be more favourable, it was the opinion of the generality of our negociators that it would be some time first.'[19] That a powerful house such as Le Couteulx had to beg for delays from much smaller foreign firms and that they were condescendingly granted is a good illustration of the humiliations which inflation brings to the denizens of countries in which it prevails.

As for Le Couteulx, after believing – or pretending – at first that depreciation would only be temporary, they had to make a change of policy when actually it aggravated. In November and December 1790 they had ordered John Codman to buy and ship as much spermaceti oil as he could obtain, plus a cargo of potashes. Now, on 19 March 1791, they cancelled these orders. They wrote later that 'the loss of exchange which is greater and greater since our last made us renounce absolutely all speculation (on their own account) while the present crisis continues'; American goods had become so expensive in France, 'both from the unfavourable exchange and the additional price of fret, that no profit can be made of them' (B14, f178, 179).

At the same time, Le Couteulx imagined a new scheme – which, obviously, had been germinating for some time. When American independence had been achieved, many French administrators and businessmen had dreamed of capturing the American market; indeed, France had exported a good deal to the United States during the war years, but as soon as peace had been restored, the British reconquered their former markets and, for simple reasons which do not need to be recalled here, exports by France to her transatlantic ally were insignificant. So Le Couteulx came upon the idea of developing the export of French goods to the United States, in order to be able to continue their imports of American goods without suffering from the depreciation of the French currency. In December 1790 they had written to John Codman: 'We ask whether it is possible to take French goods in exchange for yours. This is the only means of nourishing our commerce. Therefore write to us upon the subject.' In February 1790 they added: 'We observe with great pain that all your vessels come to this country loaded and return empty', so that French people were discouraged from buying American goods; and on 19 March 1791: 'We repeat again that at this hour more than ever, America should demand goods made in France if she design to sell this country any of her produce.'

On 19 April 1791 Le Couteulx wrote that the only way which was left open was barter ('*echange de marchandises*'). They proposed to John Codman a joint venture, on joint account, in which he would buy and ship whale oil, whale bones, potashes and pearlashes and receive in payment brandies, silks and any merchandise which would command a ready sale in America; the details of the scheme would have to be worked out, but the Rouen house was asking for samples of the wool and silk fabrics which the United States were importing from Britain in order to have them imitated in France (unlike many French exporters, they had regard for the habits and tastes of potential customers!). John Codman's answer to this proposal is unknown, but is unlikely to have been positive. Anyhow, Le Couteulx did not insist and in October 1791,

Horcholle wrote: 'For the present the great advance in the price of goods renders the idea (of a joint account) impossible.'[20]

However, from July 1791 onwards and up to late 1792, Le Couteulx and d'Allarde – who suddenly comes into the picture – made several shipments of miscellaneous goods, which were consigned to J. and R. Codman in Boston (B14, f179; B15, f184; B17, f219). D'Allarde was very keen from the start and his shipment on the *Cato*, from Le Havre in July 1791, was larger than that of the other house; if the venture was successful, he wrote, he intended to develop this trade as much as possible and contemplated buying in Boston one or two ships. Le Couteulx was more reserved at first, but when it was learned that the goods sent on the *Cato* were selling with profits ranging from 15 to 66 per cent, they became much interested and in December 1791 they asked John Codman to draw a list of assorted goods, for about 100,000 *livres*, which would be shipped in the spring of 1792, possibly as a joint venture with d'Allarde and the Codmans.[21] They wrote that they were ready to have in Boston a warehouse which would be continually supplied with French goods. Anyhow, the shipments of 1791 by the two houses, on five different vessels, from Le Havre, had a total value close to 150,000 *livres*, and possibly higher (B17, f219).

It has been often maintained that the depreciation of the *assignats*, which accelerated from the autumn of 1791 and reached 50 per cent in March 1792, stimulated French exports in 1791 and 1792 (Lefebvre 1951: 171; Bouchary 1937: 63–4). But in the present case, the main stimulus did not come from French goods becoming cheaper for foreign buyers. Actually, d'Allarde was to write in May 1792: 'Our manufactured goods are at enormous prices ... Everything must be paid in ready money and one can not get as much merchandise as one wants, because the workmen have gone to the war.' And in August 1792 Le Couteulx wrote that they had not shipped some goods which Codman had asked for, because their prices had risen 30 to 40 per cent: 'if the increase is not proportionate with you, it will be better not to send anything'.[22] The real factor may have been that some merchants, like Le Couteulx, discovered that they had to export in order to be able to carry on their imports, or that they tried to balance the fall in their imports by increased exports.

Advice from two Americans who were in France was resorted to for selecting the goods to be exported, the range of which was very wide. The main items were silks, woollens, lace, ribbons, gloves, wallpaper, window glass and mirrors, but there were also hats and shoes, fans and dolls, clocks and watches, hair powder and perfumery, plus some of the knick-knacks and fancy articles which were later to be called 'Paris goods'. Special mention must be made of statuettes and busts of Franklin, La Fayette and Washington (500 busts of the latter; the profiles of the three heroes, in Sèvres china, were also on six-and-a-half dozen snuffboxes), of twenty-four groups of Voltaire and Rousseau disputing and of sixteen copies of Diana and Apollo by Houdon (B2, f26; B3, f36, 37; B15, f184). Moreover, in the spring of 1792, d'Allarde sent the *Marie-Antoinette* from Marseilles to Boston and Le Couteulx the *Marie-Françoise* and *Les trois frères* from Sète; these three small French vessels had cargoes of wines and brandies, plus some perfumery on the former.[23]

At last, therefore, some French goods penetrated the American market; this is confirmed by customs statistics, which show exports from France to the United States reaching 3,373,000 *livres* in 1792, while they had been only 1,242,000 in 1789 (none the less, the balance of trade between the two countries remained very unfavourable to France) (Kutz 1986: 254, table 7). On 23 October 1791 Horcholle wrote: 'We learn with great pleasure that the merchandise of France is getting into estimation with you ... '; still he complained that goods had to be sold on credit in Boston and asked Codman to make it as short as possible and to guarantee payment (the inability of French exporters to grant long credit, like the British, had been a cause of their failure on the American market). Actually some of these imports had to be disposed of by auction, at no profit (B14, f179).

On the other hand, the fast rise in prices in France[24] brought about a change in the import policy of French merchants. On 14 December 1791, Horcholle gave an order to Codman for two cargoes of whale oil without any upper price limit, since demand for it was very strong in France, and he authorised them to 'purchase continually everything that is cheap', especially whale oil and potash, on condition that they not draw bills on France and accepted payment from the sale of French goods that had been or would be consigned to them (B14, f179). This can be interpreted as a flight into real assets in order to offset the depreciation of money, but there is no sign that Le Couteulx and d'Allarde were trying to export capital, a charge which has often been made against French merchants, both by contemporaries and by later historians. Actually, during 1792 the two French houses were unceasingly pressing Codman to sell without any delay the goods they received and to remit immediately the sales' proceeds either in American produce, or in good bills of exchange on London or Amsterdam, 'in order to gain by the exchange what we lose on the other side', as Le Couteulx wrote on 13 May 1792;[25] and also 'for the reason that paying everything here in ready money, our funds must return promptly to us in order to be again employed'. D'Allarde wrote that 'Your quick remittances are absolutely necessary to support my consignments to you' and he even suggested to Codman 'to remit at least one half of the amount of invoice immediately on arrival of the goods'. Le Couteulx would have liked an advance or a remittance to be made after each sale, but as Codman's answer was negative, he told them to order only goods which could be sold shortly after arrival (B15, f181, 182, 186, 187).

To the disturbances which inflation brought to business – and of which the Codman papers give some revealing glimpses – were added during 1792 the 'Second French Revolution' and the beginnings of war – which France declared on Austria on 20 April. 'You know not the situation in this country at present', wrote d'Allarde on 9 March 1792.[26] And the outbreak of war alarmed merchants; on 23 April Le Couteulx wrote that there would be insecurity at sea; he asked Codman to stop at once all shipments and to 'remit our funds in bills on London'. On 13 May they sent more detailed instructions: shipments ought to be made on American ships and on American account only; the two French ships from Sète would be sent home on ballast, unless cargoes for Portugal or Spain could be found for them; as for the goods imported from France, they were to be sold on arrival 'at any price', and the proceeds used to get 'all the good paper' on London, Hamburg and other foreign *places*. D'Allarde gave the same kind of instructions; but, though, according to him, 'it is not improbable that this war will become very general' (25 April), he told Codman to send 'new orders for more (goods), which shall be complied with'. Indeed, by 2 June, Le Couteulx had become more optimistic, as they wrote that they would risk serious losses 'if the exchange happened to improve, as it must occur sooner or later'.[27]

Strangely enough – but possibly out of caution – the letters written by the French merchants during the summer and autumn of 1792 make almost no reference either to the war or to politics, especially the overthrow of the King.[28] Only Le Couteulx alluded, on 3 September, to 'everything which has happened in France since our shipments'. They went on to say that it was impossible to authorise Codman to buy American produce and 'to draw on us like in quiet times when the variation in exchanges was only 1 or 2 per cent'. Le Couteulx wished to wait for a more steady period to transact business in the usual ways; meanwhile, Codman had to speed up the sale of French goods and to send returns in oil, potashes or bills on London, without waiting for payment for those sales to have been made (B15, f183; Bouchary 1937: 67).

Despite this increasingly turbulent environment, the trade of the Codmans with France was kept up, nay, increased during 1792. For the first time they sent tobacco to France – 55 hogsheads (hhd) on their ship *Catherine*, which landed them plus other goods in Le Havre while on her way to Russia. Another novelty was the French ships that sailed to America from the Mediterranean with wine and brandy, and which were mentioned earlier in this chapter. As for shipments of French manufactures consigned to the Codmans, there were at least three of them, the *Ceres*, that sailed from Le Havre in April 1792, carried 136,649 *livres* of goods sent by Le Couteulx and 93,830 *livres* shipped by d'Allarde. From 24 April 1792 to 5 June 1793 the net sales by Codman for the account of Le Couteulx amounted to £9,472; and from 21 July 1792 to 25 February 1793, those for the account of d'Allarde were £7,879 (B3, f36, 37; B15, f181, 185). So a modest, but genuine breakthrough on the American market was confirmed. Still, remittances remained a problem: on 18 September d'Allarde complained: 'Exchange has now taken such a turn that I lose 25 per cent on above £3,000' which he had not yet received; 'it has injured me that much'.[29] And there was the unceasing rise of French prices: on 12 September Le Couteulx had written that no shipment would be prepared for 1793 if Codman had not stated 'whether our new prices can be suitable with you'. None the less, an amazing confidence in the future appears in a letter from d'Allarde of 3 November 1792: 'I have an idea to establish a manufactory of soap alongside of my Distillery. So that it would be necessary to keep me advised of the low price of whale oil, potash' (B15, f180, 187, 188).

However, on 20 December 1792 one of d'Allarde's clerks wrote that it was 'very probable that war with Great Britain and Holland will break out this winter or spring'[30] so it would be wise for any shipment on d'Allarde's account to be 'in your name [Codman's], adding a mark particular to distinguish them and always in American Bottoms. Dont mention anything of this kind in the Invoices, Bills [of] lading, letters with the goods. Let all be simply and clearly in your name'.[31] Then, on 24 January 1793 d'Allarde asked that a cargo of salt meat, which he had ordered in September 1792, be sent in the name of a merchant of New York, to whom he had sold it 'and during the war', he concluded, '[I] mean to cease all American business' (B15, f189). Indeed, relations between the Codmans and the houses of Le Couteulx and d'Allarde came to an end when the Anglo-French war broke out.[32] This confirms the view that the turning – or breaking – point for French sea-borne trade, and possibly for the French economy as a whole, came in 1793 and not 1789. During the early years of the Revolution, France, which was the second Atlantic power, had suffered increasing economic difficulties, but businessmen had tried to fight on, as it appears from the pages which precede. But 'maritime war' and the dirigist policy of the Montagnards caused an economic collapse. None the less, the Codmans continued to trade with France, but this was restricted to the export of American merchandise.

ATLANTIC TRADE DURING THE ANGLO-FRENCH WAR

The first consequence for the Codmans of war breaking out between England and France was the failure of their London correspondent, the respectable house of Lane Son and Fraser. On 26 February 1793 John Lane wrote to John Codman: 'The scarcity of money that took place almost immediately after it was known that a war with France was inevitable has born so hard upon us, as to oblige us to stop payment; whether the house will go on or a bankruptcy issue is uncertain.' However, he requested Codman 'not [to] engage your business from us', as he was hoping his firm would be 'enabled to carry on some business in a short time'. But the next day he had to confess: 'I find our house will not be able to arrange their affairs so as to enable them to fulfil their engagements.' Still, the London firm seems to have done its best to prevent embarrassment for the Codmans: eventually, on 22 May 1793, an agreement was concluded between the assignees of the Lane and Fraser estate on one side, John and Thomas Amory, of London, and Richard Codman – who had recently arrived from Boston, on the other; the former accepted that the Codman property would not be attached, and they handed over to the Amorys a set of bills for £8,586 which belonged to the Codmans.[33]

To take the place of their unfortunate 'friends', Richard Codman made arrangements with the great merchant-banking house of John and Francis Baring and Co., who, as they wrote to Boston, accepted 'to transact your business here'.[34] However, he had to deposit in their hands one hundred shares of the Bank of the United States, 'as a collateral security for advances that we are about making for your account'. Actually, these shares were sold on 23 July at the price of £111 each, for a net amount of £10,831, which Baring credited to the account of John and Richard Codman.[35]

Baring was eventually the largest of the London houses which played a crucial role in the trade of the United States, not only with Britain, but with Europe at large, as they supplied American merchants with both services and finance. They transmitted instructions to their ship captains, whom they also advised and helped if they had difficulties; they had their ships and cargoes insured with London underwriters.[36] The main role, however, was financial: Baring (like Lane and Fraser earlier) accepted and paid bills of exchange drawn on them by the Boston house, by its suppliers in Europe, by its captains in foreign ports; and vice versa they cashed bills which were remitted to them by the Codmans or by the latter's debtors – on whom they drew in other instances. It was also through the intermediation of Baring and their like that the proceeds of cargoes from America, which had been sold in Europe, were used to pay for exports of British goods to the United States. Altogether those London firms made up a clearing-house for American trade, which thanks to them enjoyed a multilateral system of settlements with its various trading partners, and was freed from the shackles which heavy favourable or unfavourable (according to cases) balances of trade might have created (Hidy 1949: 21–22, 49).

The house of Baring was one of the City's pillars and it had close connections with HM's government. So there is irony in the fact that it assisted J. and R. Codman in some trading ventures to the land of the Jacobin terrorists.

In August 1793 the ship *Enterprise*, of 280 tons, which had been chartered by the Codmans, sailed from Alexandria (Virginia), with a cargo of 467 had of tobacco (worth £4,535).[37] She arrived in October at Le Havre, where she was joined by the *Catherine*, a ship belonging to the Codmans, which carried tobacco, whale and spermaceti oil. Richard Codman was on the spot to look after the cargoes. During the summer of 1793 he had travelled from London to Amsterdam and Hamburg; in the latter place he had bought the ship *Governor Bowdoin*, on which he had sailed to Le Havre.[38] The difficulty for him – and for the captains of other American ships which had come to the port – was the question of the *maximum*; they claimed that the sale of their cargoes would bring a large loss if it was made at the official prices; they also demanded that payments be made in specie or in bills of exchange of foreign countries. Eventually, the matter was referred to Paris, to the Committee of Public Safety itself, which, on 15 November 1793, authorised the *Commission des subsistances* to buy the cargoes of the twelve American ships which were at Le Havre and to pay them in specie (for a total price of 1.8 million *livres*). This practice, of paying in specie and bullion for the import of 'essential' goods by neutral ships, was frequent under the system of strict control of foreign trade which prevailed during the Terror. The rationale – which was stated in the *arrêté* of 15 November – was to prevent further deterioration in the French rate of exchange and depreciation of the *assignats*, which the drawing of bills of exchange on abroad for large sums would have caused; it would have 'jeopardised the credit and dignity' of the French Republic and brought about further rises in the prices of imported goods (Aulard 1889: 430; Caron 1925: 35, 44). As for paying in French goods, foreigners would have to be persuaded to accept them; moreover, at a time of shortages, the *sans-culottes* might have opposed exports, which, moreover, would have given a chance to disaffected merchants to send capital abroad.

Anyhow, on 26 November 1793 Richard Codman wrote from Le Havre to Baring that he had completed the sale of the two cargoes to the French Commissary; payment would be one-quarter in bills, three-quarters in specie, which might be exported; both the selling prices and the rates of conversion into coins and drafts were said to be advantageous. Richard sent at the same time bills on Hamburg and London for £3,034. Baring was worried: 'we cannot but entertain great doubts of all bills drawn from France'; but on 1 January 1794, they wrote that all those bills had been accepted.[39]

However, the conveyance of the specie took some more time, partly because of an embargo on sailings by American ships from French ports. On 30 January 1794 Richard Codman wrote that he would sail the next day from Le Havre for England, on the *Catherine*, bringing 'one parcel of French crowns'. By the end of February, he had not arrived, and Baring wrote to Boston: 'You may ... well conceive how anxiously we are expecting to hear from Mr. Richard Codman.' However, at the end of March, *Catherine* arrived in London; she carried $38,132\frac{1}{2}$ ounces (1,186 kg) of silver (mainly in 'old' and 'new' *écus*), which were sold on 29 March for a net price of £9,298 (B16, f201; B2, f127).

This was the Codmans' only venture to France during the Terror, but there was another example, after 9 Thermidor, of payment in specie – no wonder, as the depreciation of the *assignats* accelerated.[40] In August 1794 the Codman ship *Commerce* sailed from Richmond (Virginia), with 385 hhd of tobacco. She went to Le Havre, where her cargo was sold in November against bills of exchange and precious metals. In December she arrived in London, with gold and silver ingots, plus 2,400 gold *louis*, which sold for £5,139. In February 1795 she left London with a new cargo of tobacco, which she carried again to Le Havre, whence she sailed for St Petersburg. Meanwhile, in January 1795 two other American ships – *John and Jane* and *Betsy* – had brought to London the balance, in bullion and specie, of the first cargo on *Commerce*, which gave a total net product of £14,131. This suggests a large profit, as the cost FOB of the tobacco at Richmond had only been £5,460.[41] The Codman papers thus supply evidence – though on a modest scale – of the way in which the precious metals which France lost during her hyperinflation went straight to England.

Subsequently, however, payments from France were once more by bills of exchange. In 1795 J. Codman made three shipments to French ports: the brig *Leonard*, loaded with tobacco, and the ship *Thetis*, with cotton and rice, went to Le Havre, while the *Minerva* carried to Bordeaux a cargo of cod; but the market was not good and part of the fish had to be re-exported – on the *Mary* to Bilbao and on the *Robert* to Lisbon, while the *Minerva* was sailing to the

Baltic.[42] The destination of the ships that followed was Dunkirk, which was a convenient port of call on the way to Russia; two Codman ships went there in 1796: the *Catherine*, which carried mainly whale oil, and the *Minerva*, with tobacco from Norfolk. In 1797 there was only the *Thetis*, also with tobacco, from Richmond.[43] Indeed she was the last ship belonging to the Codmans that sailed to a French port, owing to the growing tension between France and the United States from late 1796 onwards, which resulted in 1798 in a 'quasi-war' between the two countries, during which Congress imposed an embargo upon trading with France. This trade had been mostly the carrying of American produce to France; however, there are a few cases of French goods being imported by the Codmans; in September 1793, 160 boxes of glass were shipped from Le Havre to Boston, on the *Hannah*, for their account; in 1795 Richard Codman sent to his brother seven bales of black silk lace, plus pots of ointment, gloves, ribbons and feathers (B17, f220, 222, 223; B3, f29). It is rather amazing to see such goods being exported across the Atlantic shortly after the end of the Terror and in the midst of war, and these shipments, though for a modest amount, are of more than anecdotal interest as evidence of a swift recovery in French production of luxuries and of some demand for the latter in the United States.[44]

Despite the quasi-war, Richard Codman stayed in Paris, but his brother redirected his trade to the north, i.e. mainly to the Hanseatic towns; as a matter of fact, after the conquest of Holland by the French, Hamburg was becoming the foremost mart, the leading commercial and financial centre of northern Europe (exports from the United States to 'Germany' rose from 9.6 million $ in 1797 to 14.6 in 1798 and 17.9 in 1799).[45] Moreover, while his export trade had formerly been confined to American produce,[46] J. Codman went, like many of his fellow-Americans, into the re-export from the United States of colonial produce. This was connected with adventures to the Dutch East Indies. In June 1795 the Dutch East India Company freighted one ship belonging to the Codmans, the *Abigail*; she sailed on ballast from Rotterdam to Batavia, which she reached in the spring of 1796. From there she took a cargo of sugar, coffee, pepper, tin and japanwood, and the officers of the Dutch company made the captain sign false bills of lading, according to which the cargo was neutral property, belonging and consigned to Parish and Co., of Hamburg. On her way to

Europe (actually Amsterdam) the *Abigail* was taken by the British privateer *Henry* in October 1796 and brought into Jamaica. The local court of the Admiralty ordered the confiscation of the cargo and the release of the ship.[47]

John Codman had better luck in his next venture into the 'carrying trade' of the Dutch colonies, which had become more attractive than traffic with the West Indies. The ship *Minerva* went to Batavia in 1797 and returned to Boston in March 1798 with a cargo of Java coffee. This safe arrival was a pleasant surprise for the Barings, who had heard in April 1798 that the ship had been captured and sent to Cape Town; they wrote, after learning that she was safe, that they would not have insured such a risk for a premium of 50 per cent.[48] However, the coffee was not re-exported to northern Europe on the *Minerva*; possibly to minimise risks, it was divided into several separate shipments but still they did not escape some misadventures.[49]

Shortly after the *Minerva's* arrival, John Codman shipped 15 tons of coffee on the *John Jay*, consigned to Thomas T. Cremer, of Rotterdam. When the ship, however, arrived off the Dutch coast, she was hailed by an English warship, who forbade her to enter the port of Texel. The captain was frightened, he wrongly inferred that all Dutch ports were blockaded and he therefore sailed on to Copenhagen (which he reached in May 1798), where the market for coffee was not good. Still Cremer was happy to know the ship was safe: 'Upon no account I would venture it att [sic] sea again hither, it swarms with French privateers', inasmuch as she did not carry certificates of origin for her cargo. The latter was sold by auction in Copenhagen in July by Ryberg and Co., the Danish house which had a quasi-monopoly of dealings with Americans.[50] Eventually, the proceeds – £1,920 – were remitted to Baring in February 1799. Cremer stated that, if the sale had taken place in Rotterdam, it would have brought £2,300, but he may have been biased, as he added: 'So that I dont see but loss to our Friends to pass our country'.[51]

A second shipment, of 22 tons of Java coffee, was made in August 1798 for the account of Frederick Delius, a merchant of Bremen with whom J. Codman had done business before,[52] on the brig *Apollo*. For unknown reasons, she went to Hamburg, not to Bremen. Delius, who was confidently expecting '50 per cent net profit', was disappointed and asked Caspar Voght to send the coffee immediately to Bremen. There followed a wrangle, which shows the rivalry between the two Hanseatic cities. Voght wrote that the coffee was of very inferior quality (damaged beans, a damp smell...) and ought to be sold in Hamburg. Delius complained that 'the sample had been a little worsted (which we may always expect from Hambro)' by adding some gravel; there was also disagreement over the weight, which 'proves the jealousy of a Hambro merchant and the extent this may carry his manoeuvres for to darken our advantages'. Eventually the coffee was sent overland to Bremen and sold there in October 1798, at a good price, wrote Delius, but not as good as the one which it would have fetched one month earlier, as there had been large imports in the meantime.[53]

The next shipment was 25 tons of coffee, on the *Superb*, which sailed from Boston in October 1798 and arrived in Hamburg in December. The sale of the cargo, which was for the account of the Codmans, was entrusted to Beeldemaker and Co., which was actually a newly opened branch of Rocquette, Beeldemaker and Co., of Rotterdam. The latter had written in August 1798 that, under existing circumstances, they could not advise American ships to come to Holland. 'In our opinion the safest plan is to come north about to Hambro'; according to prices on the two places, cargoes would be either sold in the latter port, or sent to Rotterdam on 'small vessels thro land'. Thanks to their extensive connections, from Brabant to Switzerland, and to the strong demand for colonial produce, they vouched that 'brilliant speculations are to be made'.[54] Actually, the unloading of the *Superb* had just started, when a 'cruel deception' occurred – the river froze[55] and the cargo had to be carried on sledges over the frozen Elbe, which was quite expensive. None the less, the coffee was sold at a good price (shortly before the market crashed in Hamburg) and altogether the venture had 'a favourable issue' (B3, f32; B13, f169, 170, 171; B19, f265).

On the other hand, Rotterdam was the destination of the brig *Mahala Winsor*, which sailed from Boston in February 1799 with about 40 tons of Java coffee for the account of John Codman. She arrived on 28 March and the cargo was quickly sold. She sailed again for Boston, early in May, with over 200 pipes of gin and a large quantity of linen, but on the same day, she was captured by the British – who were taking every ship coming in or from Dutch ports – and sent into Yarmouth (B3, f32; B13, f166, 170, 171; B19, f265).

To sum up, from March 1798 to February 1799, John Codman made four shipments of coffee to northern Europe (most of it, if not all, having been brought from Java by the *Minerva*).[56] The total weight of the three first cargoes was 137,654 lb, i.e. 62.6 metric tons; the last shipment was about 40 tons, so that the overall figure was just over 100 metric tons. The invoice price of the coffee is known only for the first two cargoes; if it is assumed that the average price per lb. was the same for the two others, the total value FOB would be 48,500 dollars. As to the net proceeds of sales, a rough estimate, from the inadequate evidence which is available, would give a total equivalent of 89,000 dollars. This can give no idea of the profits, as freight, insurance, commission and other charges, which are unknown, ought to be taken into account. Moreover, two shipments were for the account of J. Codman and two for the account of his correspondents in Rotterdam and Bremen.[57] None the less, one is entitled to assume – and it fits with remarks made at the time, which have been quoted earlier – that both J. Codman and his continental friends made handsome profits on the coffee from Java.[58] Luckily, they had completed their sales before the 'dreadful revolutions ... in the mercantile world' and the many bankruptcies in the Hanseatic towns and elsewhere, which took place during the summer and autumn of 1799.

There was a last adventure by the Codmans to northern Europe, but it had an unhappy end. Their ship, *Abigail*, sailed from Boston in the autumn of 1799. She called at Plymouth and then made for Bremen, where her cargo was consigned to F. Delius, but on 28 January 1800 she was wrecked at the mouth of the Weser. The crew was saved, but the cargo was lost. John Codman wrote to his wife that the vessel was 'tolerably well insured', but that it would have been better if the insurance had been for a larger sum. 'However', he concluded, 'I do not know but it is as well for me as if she had arrived safe.'[59] This unfortunate voyage is the last one from the United States of which there is some evidence in the Codman papers, and it is likely to have actually been the last, because in 1800 John Codman was trying to retire from business and he arrived in England in July in order to settle his European affairs. None of his ships went to Russia that year,[60] and trade with southern Europe, which had never been important to the Codmans, had been given up earlier.[61] This retreat may have been a wise decision, as foreign commerce had become a 'miserable pursuit' for American merchants, and the Olivers of Baltimore have been praised by Stuart W. Bruchey, for their caution and foresight in restricting their operations in 1799–1801 (Bruchey 1956: 202–3, 206, 214, 223).

THE PERILS OF PASSAGE

The 'adventures' to northern Europe, which have been sketched, illustrate some of the chances and risks which American trade had to face. Perils of the deep, like the loss of the *Abigail*, were not, of course, specific to the period under consideration, but they must not be overlooked. In January 1799, the *Thetis* arrived in London from Charleston with serious damage resulting from bad weather: she had sailed in winter in order to arrive in St Petersburg as early as possible after the opening of navigation. Actually, she had to enter dry dock in London and to be repaired at great expense; she sailed again in late April 1799, but the convoy she had joined was detained off Yarmouth for some time by adverse winds.[62] There were also, for some Americans, problems in dealing with foreigners. In September 1794 Captain Hammond complained from Amsterdam of delays in the unloading of his cargo: 'There is no hurrying business here as in America' (B12, f163). More serious for American ships during the early years of independence, was the danger of attack by pirates from Barbary. On 9 May 1793 William Codman, captain of the *Catherine*, which was to sail from Falmouth to Cadiz, asked that his person be insured against the risk of capture by the Algerians – which he rated very high – and to be allowed to draw on Amory in London for £450 if he was taken. Six months later, on 6 November, Baring wrote that Portugal having made a treaty with Algiers, four Algerian frigates and five chebecks had put to sea in order to attack American ships, and therefore insurance premiums of the latter had risen. Actually, on 9 December, the captain of the *Governor Bowdoin* wrote from St Ubes that eleven American ships had been taken off the Portuguese coast and he complained of a 'very distressing situation'. This was alleviated in January 1794, as the Portuguese government arranged an escorted convoy for American ships, but for some months, American captains were reluctant to sail for Portugal or Spain. However, treaties with the Barbary powers were to put an end to those 'depredations'.[63]

In wartime, however, neutral merchant ships were liable to be captured by the belligerents and there was, for Americans, an additional risk. On 9 May 1793, William Codman wrote from Falmouth: 'The press gang has just been on board and taken two of my people', the cabin boy and a sailor; he was not sorry, as they had never 'earned their salt on board', but feared that his other seamen would refuse to proceed as the crew was incomplete (B12, f163). Actually, the Codmans suffered from seizures by both the British and the French. It has been already mentioned that the *Abigail* was taken in 1796, while on her way from Batavia to Holland, by an English privateer and sent into Jamaica; the cargo was confiscated, the ship released, but there was protracted litigation about the freight. As for the *Elisabeth*, she was an American brig, which an agent of John Codman, W. Tudor, bought in Bordeaux during the summer of 1799. She was to go to Charleston, via a Spanish or Portuguese port where she was loaded with wines, worth 43,528 *livres*. The money had been supplied by Richard Codman, from Paris, but did belong to John. The *Elisabeth* was taken by a British ship and sent to Plymouth, because of some irregularity in her papers. John Codman tried to get the support of the American government to have the ship released, but a difficulty arose – at the time when she had taken her cargo, American citizens were forbidden by law to trade with France, so that the British could claim they had taken a ship which was breaking American law. When John Codman arrived in England in July 1800, he made renewed attempts to have his ship released, but eventually, in August, he accepted a compromise with the captors – because he feared that the name of his brother Richard, who had long resided in Paris, might crop up if the case came before the court of Admiralty. He paid £200, about one tenth of the cargo's value, and all costs; he wrote that, if he had not been in England, he would have lost everything, and he complained of the trouble and expense. The *Elisabeth* was then sent to Rotterdam, where ship and cargo were sold by auction, at a poor price (B3, f33; B14, f174, 175, 176; B19, f257; B20, f288; B118).

During the quasi-war with France the main danger for American ships came from French privateers, and the letters which John Codman received from Europe in 1798 abound with references to this threat – many of them alarming (see below, pp. 120–2). And in May 1798 one of the Codman ships, the *Thetis*, was captured by the French privateer *Le Brave*; but she was soon retaken by a British frigate, to whom salvage had to be paid. Likewise, in the spring of 1800 the *Minerva*, which was returning to the United States, was captured by a French ship and retaken by the British. On the other hand, in 1799 these same two ships, who were going to Russia, took advantage of the British convoys to the Baltic, as French privateers were cruising off Norway. The captain of the *Minerva* wrote boldly on 8 May that he intended to 'keep the ship in readiness to defend ourselves against any that their [*sic*] is the least chance of opposing'; he also planned to return by the Northern route.[64]

Eventually, none of the ships and none of the cargoes belonging to the firm of Codman were condemned and confiscated (B13, f167; B14, f171, 174). None the less, captures, even when they were followed by releases, caused delays and expenses against which there was no insurance; likewise, when action by a belligerent power prevented the conclusion of a trading venture as planned. The case of the *John Jay*, which, in 1798, was prevented by a British cruiser from entering Rotterdam and had to go to Copenhagen instead, has already been mentioned. In June 1795 the *Commerce* arrived in St Petersburg, but she was not authorised to take a cargo as she had come from a French port, Le Havre, at a time when the Russian government did not allow any intercourse whatever with France. She had to leave on ballast after waiting for one month; she then went to Copenhagen, where she took a cargo of hemp and Swedish iron, but she was far from fully loaded and her voyage was unprofitable. As for the *Minerva*, which was coming from Bordeaux, her captain was informed of the problem when he called at Copenhagen by a letter from the Codmans' St Petersburg correspondent. The latter made some recommendations on the way to evade the Russian ruling, but Captain Clement was frightened, did not dare to go to St Petersburg and took a cargo in Copenhagen; the cargo was larger than the *Commerce*'s, but still its sale did not make any profit. John Codman wrote later: 'It added not a little to our chagrin to observe that our friends in St Petersburg had never written us a line on the subject', and when the *Commerce* went back to the Russian capital in 1796, she had to load the 'old hemp' of 1795 and storage expenses were charged (B3, f30, 31; B12, f164; B16, f207, 209, 210; below, Table 4.1).[65]

The Codman papers supply therefore some examples of the tribulations which neutral trade suffered; on the other hand, they also show how neutrals succeeded in getting round obstacles which the belligerents imposed. This is a well-known story, but it is not uninteresting to observe some concrete instances.

To start with, there is the simple, but vital problem of corresponding. It has been seen that Richard Codman went from London to Hamburg during the summer of 1793 and then sailed to Le Havre on the *Governor Bowdoin*; he stayed in France up to March 1794, when he travelled to London on the *Catherine*; he went back to France in the autumn of 1794 and henceforth lived in Paris. There is no evidence that he had any difficulty, even during his first stay, which happened to be during the Terror, in exchanging letters with his 'friends' in England, especially J. and F. Baring. Many letters were sent via Hamburg, and quite quickly: one letter from a merchant in the Hanseatic town to Richard Codman, 'from Boston, Havre-Marat' (this was the name which the Montagnards had given to the *Havre-de-Grâce*), which was dated 23 December 1793, was delivered on 6 January 1794 (B12, f163). It appears that some at least of such letters were sent via Switzerland; on 24 March 1795, Thomas Amory, who was about to leave Paris for London and Boston, gave instructions to Richard Codman:

> When you write to Hamburg or Copenhagen, put your letters under cover to Daniel Merian, Basle, *en Suisse*, and desire him to charge the postage to Ryberg and Co. (in Copenhagen) for my account. When you have occasion to write me, direct Mr Payne, Boston, America, and put your letter under cover to Thos. Boulton Jr, n° 46 Threadneedle Street, London. Also write under cover Rucker and Wortman (house in Hamburg) enclosed to Merian, Basle. (B20, f293)

However, it is obvious that some mail was sent direct across the Channel, on smugglers' or fishermen's boats. On 27 August 1793 Thomas Amory – who was then in London – mentioned, in a letter to Richard Codman (addressed '*chez* Homberg and Homberg frères', Le Havre) that he had intended to write via Dunkirk, but he had learned that the latter port was besieged by the British army, so he was sending his letter via Amsterdam, and a copy via

Bordeaux (B12, f163). On 2 December 1793 the house of Baring received a letter from Richard Codman in Le Havre, which, bearing the date 26 November, could not have come other than directly by sea (B15, f200). There is also a letter of 4 September 1794, which was sent from London to Richard Codman, 'poste restante. Brighton', and which bears, on its back, these French words: *'point d'occasion pour la France'* (B12, f164). As for Richard Codman, he wrote to Baring on 3 February 1797 that, by getting in touch with Messrs Moreland and 'mentioning the name of M. Perregaux, you will have an opportunity of writing me immediately if you wish it' – which shows that J.F. Perregaux, a leading Paris banker, had a permanent arrangement for fast correspondence with London (Baring Mss. HO. OS. 24).

Early in the war the British government had taken a number of measures intended to cripple the trade of France. Its interdicts intimidated some merchants, for instance G.C. Fox and Sons, of Falmouth, who, in September 1793 refused to convey to the captain of the *Enterprise*, which had called at their port, the order to go to Le Havre, as they thought this was 'in opposition to the wishes of our government, which we cannot do' (B12, f163). However, the house of Baring was not so peculiar. On 9 April 1794 they wrote to John Codman that a recent Act forbade the payment of any draft for, or on account of, any person who had been in France since 1 January 1794; Richard Codman was one of them and the prohibition extended to the firm of J. and R. Codman, of which he was a partner. But Baring added that henceforth payments would be 'made by us for your (John Codman's) sole account and you will please to correspond with us in your own name only'; they regretted the 'difficulties which at present exist and harass trade without answering any good purpose'. Three months later, in July 1794, a proclamation authorised the payment of bills to American citizens who had sojourned in France, except 'drafts passed for any goods knowing the same to be intended for France'. Owing to this clause, in 1795 Baring refused a number of drafts which were on account of a cargo from Norfolk to Le Havre, but they asked the Amorys 'to interfere for your honour'. Likewise, as an Act of Parliament had forbidden British subjects to insure ships and cargoes which were bound for France; on 24 April 1795 Baring declined to arrange an insurance for the *Minerva*, which was to sail from Falmouth to

Bordeaux, but they informed Caspar Voght in Hamburg 'we doubt not he will take care to cover your property' (B16, f202, 203, 206).

Not surprisingly, there are a number of allusions to the use of false papers by neutral ships. On 23 June 1795 Porter, Brown and Wilson wrote from St Petersburg to Captain Clement, of the *Minerva*, about evading the Russian ban against ships coming from France:

> Your best method of proceeding would be to clear out from Copenhagen and to report at Cronstadtz [sic] in the mate's name, suffering him to appear as Captain, you appearing as a passenger. In this case it would be proper to leave the ship's logbook and all papers relative to the preceding voyage at Copenhagen and to put into the hands of Messrs de Conninck and Co. any letters you may have for us, to be forwarded by the first ship. (B16, f209)

Later, on 31 July 1800, Rocqquette, Beeldemaker and Co. advised John Codman – in case the latter sent a ship to them – to give Emden – a Prussian and therefore neutral port – as its avowed destination: 'For providence sake ... sham papers could be made but as if bound for Emden [sic], where if necessitated to go in; in such a case the goods can be forwarded by inland navigation with little expense to our port' (Rotterdam). Actually, several American ships, with cargoes of colonial produce, went to Emden in 1799 and 1800, when access to Dutch ports was difficult'.[66] Likewise, during the 'quasi-war' the port of St Sebastian, in Spain close to the French border, suddenly became busy: on 7 March 1799, a house there, Widow Bermingham and Son, wrote that several American ships had recently arrived with cargoes of colonial produce, for the account of merchants in Bordeaux. 'The locality of our place situated in the Frontier of France facilitates in the present circumstances of interruption of trade between your states and their Republick [sic], the circulation of such goods that comes from your ports; we are at hand to provide both Spain and France' – and also to supply French or Spanish brandy (this firm had just made two shipments of brandy which had come from Bayonne). From Bordeaux, Strobel and Martini confirmed, on 11 April 1799, that produce intended for France had arrived in northern Spanish ports, to the point that tobacco was 'dull' on the Bordeaux market and that the prices of all West Indian produce had fallen; but they added that such speculations would be unprofitable, because of import duties and enormous transport costs. However, this traffic was still going strong during the early months of 1800 (B13, f170; B14, f171; B19, f252).

Thanks to such subterfuges and also, of course, to good shipbuilding, to the enterprise of merchants and shipowners and to the seamanship of captains and crews, from 1793 onward American ships became *les rouliers des mers*. This reconstitution of the successive voyages by some of the ships which belonged to the Codmans supplies a good illustration.

In 1793 the *Commerce* sailed from Boston to St Petersburg and back; in 1794 she went from Boston to Richmond and then to Le Havre, loaded with tobacco; later she carried to London the proceeds, in specie, of her cargo. Early in 1795 she brought from London to Le Havre another cargo of tobacco and then sailed to St Petersburg. As seen earlier, she was not admitted, went to Copenhagen where she took an incomplete cargo, and returned to Boston. In 1796 she went from Charleston to Bremen with some indigo, then to Russia and back home. Next time the ship is heard of, in May 1798, she was abandoned in the docks of Liverpool, stripped of her stores and part of her rigging; the local correspondent of the Codmans had her repaired, found a captain and a crew, sent her to Philadelphia with a cargo; in March 1799 she brought some goods to Newry and went back to the United States with some coal, loaded at Liverpool.[67]

As for the *Catherine*, in 1792 she carried to Le Havre a cargo of tobacco and whale oil, then sailed to St Petersburg and returned to America. In May 1793 she arrived in Falmouth with a cargo of wheat, which had shifted; she was sent to Cadiz and, being 'disappointed in a freight', sailed to Boston with a ballast of salt and some 'superior sherry wine'. Shortly after arriving, she left again for Le Havre with tobacco and whale oil; they were sold for specie, which she carried to London in March 1794; then she sailed to St Petersburg and back to Boston. In April 1795 she was in London, about to sail for New York with a full cargo on freight; and in 1796 she carried American goods to Dunkirk (B5, f58; B6, f70; B12, f163; B17, f220; B19, f257; B20, f289, 293).

During the summer of 1793 there had been plans to send the brig *Minerva* from Virginia to Le Havre with tobacco, but they were cancelled and eventually she sailed from Alexandria in February 1794 with a cargo of wheat which was intended for Lisbon. The captain had orders to call at Falmouth, for instructions, because of the danger from Algerian pirates. When the *Minerva* arrived in England, Richard Codman took control and sold the cargo, which was to be delivered at St Sebastian, the purchaser running all risks – this was quite a profitable transaction.[68] From St Sebastian, the *Minerva* sailed to St Petersburg – where she arrived in July – and back to Boston. In 1795 she was to go to Lisbon with fish, but eventually was sent to Bordeaux; she sailed for St Petersburg but did not go further than Copenhagen, as we have seen, where she loaded iron, hemp and tallow. In 1796 she carried tobacco to Dunkirk and proceeded to St Petersburg. In 1797–8 she made the long journey to Batavia, bringing back a cargo of coffee, plus one pipe of 'London Particular Madeira'.[69] In 1799 she went once more to Russia, after a call in London for instructions and for landing some staves and potash. In 1800 she was captured by the French, then retaken by the British (B3, f30, 32; B6, f70; B12, f164; B15, f200; B16, f201, 203, 205, 209; B17, f225).

The career of other Codman ships was shorter, as far as we know. The *Governor Bowdoin* had also sailed to the Far East, but before she was bought, in a rather poor condition, by Richard Codman in Hamburg in July 1793. He travelled on her to Le Havre and she went to St Ubes, and from there to Alexandria, with a ballast of salt.[70] She departed in the autumn of 1794 with a cargo of tobacco and bound for Rotterdam, but when she arrived at the mouth of the Maas, in November, the French armies were about to enter Holland. The captain and the Dutch consignees decided that the ship would go to Hamburg, 'the critical situation of Holland not making it prudent for his cargo to be landed there'. However, the ship was unable to reach Hamburg, because of ice at the mouth of the Elbe; she stopped at Glückstadt, where the cargo was landed and stored (B6, f67; B12, f163; B16, f201, 204; Baring Mss: HO. OS. 14; Archives Nationales: F11 229, no. 114). As for the *Abigail*, it is known that she went to Russia in 1793 and to Amsterdam with tobacco late in 1794; she was freighted there by the Dutch East India Company, to go to Batavia and back. On her return journey, she was taken and sent to Jamaica. She was released, called at Havana and Charleston, and went to Europe. She arrived late in 1797 in Plymouth, where she was repaired. In April 1798 she was ready to sail to Hamburg and from there to St Ubes for salt. In December 1798 she was in Lisbon, and we know of her last voyage, from Boston to Bremen, when she was lost in the Weser on 28 January 1800 (B3, f28; B13, f169; Baring Mss: HC. OS. 14 and 15; HO. OS. 24).

THE PROBLEM OF INFORMATION

This disaster brings us back to the problem of incertitude and risk in oceanic trade in wartime (and in the age of sail), and to the related question of decision-making by merchants. A striking feature of the Codman collection is the mass of information which letters from abroad brought to a firm which was only medium-sized (it was, of course, completed from American or foreign newspapers and from chit-chat among businessmen). It dealt with market conditions, military and political developments, but it also included forecasts on future price movements and on the chances of peace or war; it was changing, kaleidoscopic and often contradictory, while difficulty was compounded by distance and slow communications. American exporters had to make their decisions on the basis of economic and political intelligence which was already obsolete when it reached them; when the ship which was dispatched following such intelligence arrived, off European coasts, weeks later, the *konjunktur* could have decisively changed. Captains were, of course, told to call at Falmouth or to drop anchor at the Downs, in order to obtain the most recent pieces of news and to ask for instructions from their principals' European correspondents, but this could only be a palliative.[71]

Two sets of letters in the Codman papers are quite instructive about the context in which American merchants had to make decisions and about the high degree of risk in which neutral traders operated. First, letters from J. and F. Baring to J. and R. Codman, written from July 1793 to November 1795, which contain regular comments on the political and economic situation – valuable as coming from such a prominent house; they deal mostly with the progress of the war between France and the coalition, and with Anglo-American relations. On several occasions the latter seemed close to breaking point, which would have been disastrous for American trade; on the other hand, the prospect of a protracted war between France and her enemies was not bad news from an American point of view.

On 3 July 1793 the Barings wrote: 'At present we are sorry to say there appears but little probability of the war being terminated this campaign; yet convulsion may arrise [sic] which may bring a sudden peace.' One month later, on 6 August, the prospects were better: 'Since the reduction of Mayence and Valenciennes, the prices of our funds have advanced and likewise those of America' (as the end of the war would cause a fall in interest rates). But, on 27 August, a different threat emerged, owing to the capture by the British of some American ships: 'our underwriters are become very timid of writing American ships', because of 'reports of some misunderstanding' between the two countries, 'which we hope will not be followed by any serious consequences; in the meantime the alarm is given and no insurance can be done but at an advanced premium'. 'Even the rumour of the chance' of a war with America had made American funds fall sharply, and if war actually would break out, they would become unsaleable. And the letter concluded: owing to the 'present precarious state of affairs in Europe ... tho' money is at present pretty abundant, there is no saying how long it will continue.' A few days later, on 4 September, the tone remained sombre: 'Public affairs are very gloomy, with a moral certainty of another campaign in Europe. We are full of apprehension that the harmony between our countries will be interrupted, for we cannot conceive that the expectations of America, however moderate they may be deemed on your side, can be submitted to by the allied powers in Europe.'[72]

At the end of 1793, on the other hand, Baring had become more optimistic as regards Anglo-American relations but less so about prospects in Europe. On 6 November they mentioned that American funds had risen in London.

> This we attribute to the political situation of Europe; an opinion that the intemperate conduct of Monsr Genet will cooperate with your executive government to preserve peace, and a desire that becomes rather more prevalent amongst individuals to invest a part of their property in the funds of America, to guard against the possibility of the *sans-culotte* system spreading its influence over a great part of Europe.

However, Baring's view was that such investment would be limited, as the large loans which the British government would soon require would absorb 'all the loose money in this country'. And on 4 December: 'Every preparation is making for another campaign, but with no better prospect of its being decisive than the last, except that all parties are heartily sick of the war.'[73]

However, Anglo-American relations were upset anew by the 'discovery' of the Order-in-Council of 6 November 1793, against neutral trade with French colonies. 'We have been much alarmed', wrote Baring on 1 January 1794. They were not reassured by the promise of 'explanations', which Lord Grenville had given to London merchants: 'As our Court have manifested this disposition to interfere with French produce although neutral property, we doubt much whether the exceptions to be admitted can be ascertained speedily – on which a reliance can be placed'; so insurance premiums had become extravagant and even 'cannot be quoted correctly'. This panic, however, was short-lived and came to an end when the new Order-in-Council of 8 January 1794 was published; on 11 January, Baring wrote: 'We are persuaded ... that the property *bona fide* American and coming direct from America will be protected' (B16, f201).

None the less, it was only after the arrival in England (June 1794) of John Jay that 'the fears of an interruption to the harmony' between England and the United States subsided. On 14 July 1794 Baring wrote: 'we feel great satisfaction in consequence of the temperate and judicious manner in which your government have conducted themselves, as we feel the most lively interest in the preservation of peace and harmony.' With 'such able and respectable men' as Jay and Pinckney in charge, negotiations were progressing: 'The ground will be cleared for a treaty ... on broad and liberal principles, which we are inclined to think may be accomplished'.[74]

Then came a blow from another quarter – the French victory at Fleurus. On 13 August Baring wrote:

> Our Exchanges have experienced lately a great revolution owing to the distress the commercial world would suffer should the French penetrate into Holland, of which great apprehension are entertained, as the union of the Allied powers is not such as the cause in which they are engaged demands. The fears of such an event have occasioned large quantities of Gold and Silver to be poured into this country, ... being principally for the purpose of being invested in your stocks.

So the shares of the Bank of the United States, which had fallen to £100–1 during the alarm of January 1794, had risen to £109.[75]

On the other hand, Anglo-American relations continued to improve and on 20 November 1794 Baring sent 'a few hasty lines . . . for the pleasure' to announce the signing of a treaty, 'on terms that we apprehend will be thoroughly satisfactory to yours [*sic*]'. However, as far as Continental affairs were concerned, they were rather defeatist; on 13 December 1794 they wrote that the loan by England to the Emperor – which was just being settled – 'baffles all hopes of peace and we are afraid we shall see another campaign'. And on 24 April 1795 they stated that the separate peace treaty between France and Prussia 'is thought to be the forerunner of a general peace which we most heartily wish' (B16, f204, 206).

A similar alternation of blowing hot and cold appears in the many letters which J. Codman received in 1798 and 1799 from merchants in a number of Continental ports, but mainly from Holland and the Hanseatic towns. On the one hand, they stress the favourable market conditions for colonial produce and advise the despatch of shipments (and some of them may have been instrumental in John Codman's decision to make the shipments of coffee which have been described); on the other, they contain alarming news and comments about French policy towards neutrals and the development of the 'quasi-war'.[76]

On 18 January 1798 F. Delius sent from Bremen a copy of the new French decree against British goods: 'It is as bad as it possibly can be made, so much that it may be call'd a declaration of war against *all* nations at sea'; a neutral ship could be confiscated if the captain or mate had a watch or a quadrant of English manufacture; 'shameful indeed for a nation to support her treasury by such means'. On the other hand, he represented that this decree would only push prices upwards, specially for coffee, as 'our demands for the supply of the upper parts of Germany, Switzerland, etc etc is daily increasing'; despite large imports, 'there is not much at hand . . . indeed as long as no general peace is restored in Europe prices can not decline'. Any cargo of sugar and coffee, which would arrive safely in European ports would obtain high profits. Delius was therefore recommending a large joint venture – to send quickly a ship of 200–250 tons, laden with good quality produce. He was willing to take an interest in it, but he recommended that the cargo be insured against all risks by 'safe underwriters' and to have certificates that it was not of English origin.[77]

Similar intelligence came from Holland. On 9 January 1798 Rocquette, Beeldemaker and Co. had written from Rotterdam that the prospects for the spring were excellent: 'All West India produce will fetch very high prices and our supplies are nothing in comparison to our wants.' On 26 January, according to another Rotterdam house, there was 'not any the least apprehension there [sic] relaxing from the present quotations unless a general peace should take place, of which at present there is not any appearance'. From Amsterdam, Wills and Co. were even more confident: 'Sugars, coffee, cotton and tobacco are generally scarce in Europe and above all in our place. Germany is almost destitute and France is but little better provisioned.' There was no danger of prices falling 'if the war should continue which there is too much fear of it .... If we have the happiness to obtain peace, the immense wants of Europe will render an immediate diminution almost impossible'.[78]

Likewise, on 26 March, W. Muir wrote from Hamburg: 'A general peace is unhappily not likely to take place soon', but the trade of Hamburg would not be molested too much as the Senate had agreed to make a loan to the French government, 'and for all the prohibitory acts against English goods, means are already used to have them conveyed to their usual markets'; stocks of colonial produce were low and prices could only rise. A few days later (6 April) Caspar Voght asserted that high prices would prevail as long as the 'present precarious circumstances exist'; American ships could be insured in London and Hamburg at a premium of 15 per cent, on condition that they sailed north (i.e. around Scotland), and several of them had already arrived, without trouble from French privateers. On 12 June, Muir wrote again that the market was very brisk: 'nothing remains at hand, and without peace (which seems yet distant)', prices were bound to go up, in as much as 'Holland (which had its trade obstructed by the British) is obliged to draw from us a large portion of her supplies, which France will be compelled to do likewise'.[79]

This last view was confirmed by letters from Holland. On 1 May Rocquette and Beeldemaker had maintained that 'harmony' would be restored between France and the United States, but afterwards they panicked: on 31 May, writing 'as real friends', they pressed not to send ships to Holland, they had received 'private information' and 'We are persuaded the crisis is approaching and circumstances are in our opinion so critical,[80] that we think it our duty to advise you to guard against it'. On 10 August they confirmed that, under existing circumstances, they could not any more advise American ships to come to Holland. They had therefore opened a branch in Hamburg: 'In our opinion the safest plan is to come north about to Hambro'; according to market conditions, cargoes would be either sold there or sent to Rotterdam by small vessels, safely, at low cost and no double commission, and they promised that 'brilliant speculations are to be made'.[81]

So trade was diverted to the Hanseatic towns, inasmuch as news from southern Europe had not been comforting: in February 1798 R. and J. Montgomery wrote from Alicante that the Court of Prizes at Aix-en-Provence had confirmed the condemnation of several American ships who had been brought into Carthagena; The fate of captured vessels depended upon the 'caprice' of the French authorities; none the less, this firm maintained that American ships 'properly abilitated', with papers in order, had nothing to fear. However, Jacob Dohrman and Co., of Lisbon, who had written on 10 March that there was 'not any opening whatever to a Prospect of a general peace however distant', and that French and Spanish privateers were harassing 'the little trade that can be carried on', told on 18 April of 'increasing depredations' by privateers; 'neutral navigation is at its last gasp... The French continue to act with despotic power by land and to keep England in perpetual alarm of an invasion which however most people now think will not be attempted' (B13, f166, 167).

During the second half of 1798, letters from northern Europe continued to stress the alluring market conditions and rising prices for West Indian and American produce. They also display a sharp rivalry between the merchants of the main ports, who were trying to attract shipments from America, so that the views they expressed about developments in Franco-American relations were not quite unselfish. From Bremen, F. Delius wrote on 14 July that the British were blockading Texel, so that his city would have to supply all the 'upper country' which used to buy in Holland, and he pressed his 'friends' to send him shipments. On 1 September another Bremen firm, Buckner and Thomas, pointed out that Bremen was nearer than Hamburg to the countries which were supplied from Holland before the war, and that imports in Hamburg 'are much more redundant than what comes to this city'. On 25 August a Hamburg house, Rucker and Wortman, recommended shipping on Hamburger or Danish ships, for which insurance was only 15 per cent,[82] while on American ships it had risen to 25 per cent, as relations between the United States and France were 'very like a state of war' and on 28 August W. Muir added: 'If hostilities take place (which is a thing very likely) between France and America ... this market must of consequence be much more resorted to than it has yet been.' On the other hand, on 16 September T.T. Cremer, of Rotterdam, was much more optimistic: 'Every mark is in favour of peace between you and France. So I flatter myself to be speedily able to manage your affairs without northerly assistance which I experience runs very high' (B13, f167, 168). Even from Bordeaux, on the 17th, Strobel and Martini wrote that there was a prospect of a friendly settlement between France and the United States; the first American ships to arrive after it had been concluded would find an excellent market. Indeed most letters of late 1798 stress that the French appear less hostile to the United States and do not make as many depredations on their trade as earlier on.[83] So, on 5 November 1798, Delius wrote to J. Codman that he was willing to take an interest in one or even several cargoes of sugar, coffee and cotton, to be sent from Boston at the beginning of 1799; he was sure that 'much money must be made on such expeditions early in the spring'. From Hamburg, Beeldemaker and Co. also pressed for shipments, as their market would be 'most advantageous in the spring'.[84]

However, on 18 January 1799 Edward Bromfield, an American who had come to Hamburg to supervise the Codmans' business there, wrote a rather alarmist letter: general war was to break out soon on the Continent, but Hamburg was likely to remain neutral, on condition of the payment of tribute 'now and then to the French liberators; it would not be politic in the latter to kill the goose which lays the golden eggs ... If the French arms continue their usual success what the Empire will become God only knows!'. On the other hand, Bromfield announced that several leading merchants and bankers in Paris and other large cities in France had failed or stopped payment, so that it was almost impossible to negotiate any commercial paper. And most Americans in France were about to leave. Then, in March 1799, prices of colonial produce, especially of coffee, started to fall because of heavy imports and an interruption of shipments to the interior of Germany – owing to the 'critical situation of that country' – and of a scarcity of money, which pushed the discount rate up to 10 or 11 per cent. Letters from Hamburg asserted that the fall was only temporary, that the trade of the city was bound to profit from the blockade of Dutch ports by the British, but actually there was an epidemic of bankruptcies in the Hanseatic towns and elsewhere during the summer and autumn of 1799.[85]

Still, hopeful views had come from Homberg and Homberg in Le Havre. They wrote on 13 April that they would not have broken their long silence 'had there been no favourable change in politics. But our Directory has of late adopted a milder system respecting neutral navigation', so that 'we shortly expect your shipping abound again here direct from America'. As 'our market is entirely exhausted of foreign goods', speculations on several articles would offer 'ample reward'. And they concluded: 'We are now more and more confirmed by the pacific steps of our government that harmony between the two countries will soon be re-established. The derangement occasioned by the sundry failures has ceased and confidence begins to revive again.'[86] Actually, more than a year elapsed before the Franco-American conflict was settled.

Far less optimistic was a letter written from Amsterdam, on 24 August 1799, by W. and J. Willinck. They described the crisis, which had spread from Hamburg to many places, including their own city, and which had resulted in general stagnation, forced sales, falling prices. British cruisers were taking all ships who tried to enter or leave Dutch ports and were harassing the navigation of Hamburg and Emden. Russia was threatening Denmark to oblige it to join the coalition against France, with whom the Hanseatic towns would also have to sever their relations. 'What the further intention of the Russian fleet combined with the armada in England will be, either against our coasts, Flandres or France, time will clear up. To our opinion we are at the eve of important affairs' (indeed, three days later, the British landed at the Helder) (B14, f172).

Still, it must have been in the autumn of 1799 that an understanding took place between John Codman and F. Delius for sending the *Abigail* to Bremen – a choice which may be connected with the Anglo-Russian expedition to Holland. After her loss,

Table 4.1 Ventures from Russia

Year	Ship	Proceeds of the cargoes' sales	Profits	Profits/sales (%)	Freight/sales (%)	Insurance/sales (%)
1793	Commerce	£14,342	£3,232	22.5	11.2	4.7
1794	Catherine	17,642	1,686	9.6	7.6	5.1
	Minerva	$62,149	$3,714	6.0	8.6	5.6
1795	Commerce	26,918	–	–	–	5.1
	Minerva	44,676	–	–	–	–
1796	Commerce	54,792	3,072	5.6	9.7	4.5
1797	Thetis	47,710	7,991	16.7	9.3	2.5[a]
1799	Thetis	52,629	5,121	9.7	5.7	–

Notes: Before 1795 accounts were kept in £ currency, which has been converted into US dollars at the rate of 3.33.
[a] This percentage is surprisingly low and might be an error.
Source: See note 87.

Delius wrote: 'This unfortunate event spoils all our projects' (he had been thinking of diverting the ship to France) (B20, f292). On 25 February 1800, a house in Leghorn, Webb, Holmes and Co., was to write: 'So much of the Prospects not only of this, but [of] every other Market in Europe, depends on Political events, that it is difficult to give an opinion' (B14, f177). The assemblage of quotations which precedes supports this generalisation and one can therefore feel sympathy for Delius, who had written, on 18 January 1798: 'I never feel more at my ease than at my desk fully engaged at my business; in the same time I must confess to you that I despise commerce when ever it interfears [*sic*] with ease and safety' (B13, f165).

PROFITS AND LOSS

Though war brought additional worries to merchants – even to neutral ones, it could also bring good profits. The books of J. and R. Codman have not been preserved, but a few extracts of accounts have survived: they include eight 'sales invoices' of adventures to (or rather from) Russia, which are summarised in Table 4.1.[87] They were profitable, except those of the *Commerce* and the *Minerva* in 1795, as both ships were not allowed to trade at St Petersburg and came back with incomplete cargoes which they

Table 4.2 Profits of J. and R. Codman (see Table 4.1 about the monetary units)

Year ending on 30 April	£ Currency	US Dollars
1793	3,818	12,717
1794	4,161	13,856
1795	2,225	7,408
1796	–	11,091
1797	–	26,199
1798	–	54,342

had loaded at Copenhagen.[88] The table shows that the ratio profits/sales varied greatly from year to year, with a minimum of 5.6 per cent and a maximum of 22.5 per cent; for the six profitable operations, total profits, at $36,275, were 11.2 per cent of total sales ($323,787). Moreover, the cargoes had travelled on ships belonging to the Codmans, the freight charges of which included some profit. It can be observed, in this respect, that freight makes up from 5.7 per cent to 11.2 per cent of sales, while the cost of insurance, despite wartime risks, is markedly smaller, fluctuating around 5 per cent.[89]

Fortunately, we can have a more general view of the profitability of the firm, thanks to a number of personal accounts between John Codman and the house, which mention the profits he received (B5, f58, 62; B6, f66, 70, 74; B7, f78, 82, 86). As he was entitled to two-thirds of profits, the total figure is easily calculated (see Table 4.2). There was a sharp fall of profits in the year 1794–5, followed by a good recovery and a very high figure for the year 1797–8. From remarks which have been made earlier, one can infer that 1798–9 – when several parcels of coffee were exported to northern Europe where market conditions were good – must have also been a profitable year. There are no data which would allow us to compare profits with the firm's capital or its turnover. One can only mention that copies of the 'Exchange accounts' have been found for three years (ending on 30 April); total figures on the credit side are as shown on Table 4.3.[90] These figures might imply a progress of the firm's activities, but this idea does not fit with data from J. and F. Baring's books, which have been used in Table 4.4, column 3: the average monthly figures of

Table 4.3 Credits on the exchange accounts of J. and R. Codman

1795	$104,459
1796	137,935
1797	180,881

Table 4.4 John and Richard Codman in account with John and Francis Baring & Co.

Date	1 Net liabilities (£)	2 Net change in indebtment since previous balance (£)	3 Gross liabilities: monthly average since last balance (£)
1794: 1 September	11,610	–	3,112 (since 1 July 1793)
1795: 23 April	12,944	+1,334	3,834
1796: 17 February	25,734	+12,790	3,595
1797: 1 January	33,581	+7,847	3,251
25 May	36,327	+2,746	4,127
1798: 22 May	49,490	+13,163	3,361
1799: 1 January	48,392	−1,098	–
30 June	33,976	−14,416	–
1800: 30 June	36,370	+2,394	–

Source: Baring Mss, Guildhall, 18325, vols. 7,8,9,10.

the Codmans transactions with Barings does not show any significant expansion from 1794 to 1798. Still, J. and R. Codman's profits do not compare unfavourably with those of Oliver Brothers, of Baltimore, which added up to $127,186 for the five years from April 1796 to April 1801.[91] But there were book profits, and the Baring ledgers, confirmed by other sources, reveal that the firm's good results were jeopardised by the extravagances of the junior partner.

It is clear from Table 4.4 that the Codmans' account with Barings showed a serious debit balance, from the first years of their relations.[92] One reason – and possibly *the* reason – was that Richard Codman, who had settled in Paris, retained for his own use – i.e. by buying property and living in a comfortable, even luxurious way – part of the proceeds from the cargoes which were sold in Europe, instead of remitting them to London.[93]

This situation worried the Barings. On 15 June 1795 they wrote that they were fully confident that the 'present depending balance of about £12,000 will be reimbursed us from assets in the hands of M. Caspar Voght'; so they would not hesitate to accept some new drafts for £10,000 which were announced. But early in September they wrote that they were anxiously waiting for letters from Richard Codman, 'as our advances to your House are at present very large' (B16, f206, 207).

Shortly afterwards, on 23 September, Alexander Baring, Sir Francis' second son (aged 21), sailed for America. This followed an offer to his father by William Bingham, of Philadelphia, to buy land in Maine (then part of Massachusetts); and in January 1796, Alexander, who had full powers from his father and from Hope and Co., bought the moiety of 1,225,000 acres in Maine.[94] The Barings and the Hopes had plans for large-scale speculations in the United States and there is strong evidence that they thought of using John Codman as an agent and correspondent.[95]

Anyhow, Alexander Baring visited him in Boston shortly after arriving, and his first letters – of December 1795 – were enthusiastic. John Codman

> is a very able respectable man and is very much esteemed here ... I have the highest opinion of him in every respect and think him perfectly suited for a confidential man if we need one. He has very considerable property which is calculated at about £50m sterling[96] and is himself very prudent. He permits his brother Richard to try some light speculations in France, but he is perfectly master of the principles on which they rest and of the extent to which he is willing to go in them.

Alexander Baring told his father that he had never met anybody who reasoned better about the principles of his business, which had been 'in a particularly prudent line' – except what he had allowed his brother to do. They had discussed at length Richard's speculations in France, which John had tried to discourage 'and only allows of to give his Brother a chance of coming forward'. John wished that Richard would come home in the spring of 1796; he was – or pretented to be – diffident about the enormous profits which Richard held out. And anyhow, wrote Alexander, he was 'so far easy in this business that if the whole of the capital in France was to sink, nobody can lose but himself, as his property here is more than double the amount'. Rather naively, Alexander believed that Richard, knowing that he was risking his brother's fortune, would be more cautious, and that there would be some profits, even though they could not be calculated before 'the whole is out of France'. He admitted that J. Codman was entitled to risk a limited sum, 'in availing of the advantage their situation affords, tho' I condemned several of his Brother's adventures', especially his purchases of land and estates in France, 'which are large'. And, while recommending caution, he expressed unbounded confidence in John Codman, (who was delighted): 'he is a man of much sensibility and delicacy on the score of credit and treatment and he feels with much gratitude that his Brother has exposed him to just remarks on your part which your liberality has saved him from'. He had no idea of the extent of Barings' engagements for his house; Richard would settle them; 'otherwise he will do it from here'. Meanwhile he offered to give as security some public stock, worth about £6,000; but Alexander Baring refused and assured his father that they were 'completely safe' (Baring Mss: DEP 85, Part V, vol. I, no. 15, 16).

However, the Codmans' debit balance, which had been stable for a year, increased anew and quite fast: in February 1796 it had almost doubled since April 1795; on 1 January 1797 it reached £33,581 (this was the period when Richard bought several *biens nationaux*). Moreover, John Codman had taken some bad bills on a New York house, which failed and divided very little, so that Baring, who had accepted them, suffered a loss. Alexander Baring admitted in November 1796 that there had been some 'mismanagement' by John Codman, but he added at once that it would be unfair to judge the latter on this misadventure; 'my opinion of Codman remains always the same. He is certainly prudent and a good merchant, tho' perhaps rather sharp when he acts as agent ... In general he is very quick and judicious in his speculations'. As for Richard, he was beginning 'to see his way clear in France and has really made something handsome. I am told he has nearly squared the house's account with you' – an amazing statement ....[97]

Actually, the Codmans' debit balance was to reach £49,490 by 22 May 1798. A letter from Richard Codman to J. and F. Baring, of 3 February 1798, has been preserved. He promised several remittances, for a total of £24,000, including the freight of the *Abigail* from Batavia (Baring answered that this was generally considered as 'desperate' and that anyhow there would be no decision for two years). 'It will not leave us much in arrears', Codman concluded, adding 'I have a very extensive property in this country and do not owe a farthing to any one in Europe but to you' (Baring Mss: V, I, no. 37).

The Barings answered on 6 April in a rather curt fashion; they described the situation as 'vexatious and distressing', the balance due by the Codmans being much larger than Richard appeared to think: £46,400, against which only small remittances could be expected. Then, on 15 May 1798 they wrote to John Codman that the situation was more threatening than ever, so that they were worried about Richard's affairs, 'which continue to press upon us in so heavy a manner as to render them extremely inconvenient from their duration and we must insist that steps are taken without delay for a very considerable reduction' (the balance stood at $47,959) (Baring Mss: HO. OS. 24). P.C. Labouchère also pressed Richard to give satisfaction to Baring; he answered on 15 June 1798 that the debt to Baring was only £35,000,[98] which would be covered by the coffee from Batavia which was on its way to Europe. Still, he was quite apologetic and added that he had enough assets, but chiefly in property and as 'such property not selling well at this moment', he was reluctant to part with it (Baring Mss: HO.OS. 24).

After this, Alexander Baring was ready to blame Richard severely but he remained loyal to his brother: 'John Codman is an honest man', he wrote on 20 January 1799 to one of his father's partners. Richard had sunk an enormous amount of money, which his brother's intelligence and industry had accumulated over the years. John had been kept 'in perfect ignorance' of Richard's doings, receiving only 'one occasional scrap of paper to keep up his expectations of an enormous fortune from France. I pity John sincerely'; he had to be respected for his readiness to pay the debts to Baring, 'for enabling his brother to ruin him'.[99] 'He can pay you in full', while retaining a decent property, asserted Alexander Baring.[100] He added, none the less, that, in case of 'misunderstandings' with Richard, 'you must stop short and hold fast for, though the brothers appear at variance, they will support each other, and you must make no reliance on liberality, for though John is honest, he will be more afraid of cheating himself than you' (Baring Mss: DEP 85³, VII, III, no. 79).

However, the Codmans' debit balance retrograded from

£48,392 on 1 January 1799 to £33,976 on 30 June. This resulted partly from the remittance to Barings of the proceeds from the coffee sales on the Continent – though Richard managed to intercept £6,500 from the cargo of the *Mahala Winsor*[101] – and partly from Baring having stopped most new credits to the firm of J. and R. Codman. Moreover, in May 1798, John had officially dissolved his partnership with Richard, because of the quasi-war with France; Baring opened a new account for him in July 1798, which became the truly active one. Still this account was at first in the red, but during 1800 it changed from an overdraft of £15,189 on 30 June to a credit of £16,368 on 30 December. During the three years which followed, large sums were credited, which seem to have been used to extinguish the deficit on the earlier account (Baring Mss: Guildhall, 18325, vol. 9, 10, also 18001, vol. 1). So disaster had been avoided. It remains to see how it had been courted.

Richard Codman had lived in Paris since the autumn of 1794. He was not content with just looking after the ships and cargoes which his brother was dispatching to Europe, and he had his fingers in several other pies, especially in property speculation. Actually, large quantities of *biens nationaux* – property which had been confiscated from the church and from the *émigrés* – were on the market and at low prices, especially for purchasers who, during this period of runaway inflation, had the command of foreign currency, specie or imported goods. Early in 1795 Thomas Amory, Richard's brother-in-law, who was leaving France and entrusting him with the disposal of various merchandise in Bordeaux and Le Havre, wrote: 'If you can meet a real good Estate in Land (or Houses and Land at P -) [Paris], you may interest me the proceeds of the above, and if [it] can [not] wait the disposal, draw for about £2,000 at as long sight as possible for B [aring] a/c J. and RC., but, should you prefer your draw on America, in the latter case only if extremely low, that is if 2 or 3 years' former rent will pay the cost.'[102] To acquire an estate at two or three years' purchase would have been indeed a bargain; it did not come off but Richard secured conditions which were both strange and favourable when, on 4 January 1796, he bought the *hôtel de Créqui*, rue d'Anjou-Honoré, a large and splendid private house, which had belonged to an *émigrée*, the marquise de Créqui, and which was on a prime site, close to the Place de la Concorde. The price was 4 million *livres* in *assignats*, or 25,000 *livres* in specie, but it was actually paid in kind, by 8,333 lbs of Pernambuco cotton, which was on board the ship *Thetis* in the port of Le Havre and which Richard undertook to deliver to the seller within two weeks.[103]

Previously, Richard had bought, in May 1795, the *château des Ternes*, a country house just outside Paris,[104] as well as three farms in the department of Eure-et-Loire[105] and an apartment building, rue de Bourgogne on the left bank. Then, in 1797, he acquired the *château de la Thuilerie*, another country house at Dammartin, 60 kilometres east of Paris. Moreover, Richard had work done on a large scale for repairing and renovating his two *châteaux* (including the planting of many trees in the park at *les Ternes*) and his *hôtel* – the latter was furnished lavishly. It is very likely, none the less, that he intended to resell most, if not all of those properties when prices of real estate would have recovered.[106] Richard also bought more than one hundred paintings – some of them through J.B.P. Lebrun, the husband of the talented painter, Mme Vigée-Lebrun – but he sent most of them to his brother (some are now preserved in the Codman house at Lincoln). They include no masterpiece, but their price was low.[107]

Richard also became a book collector, buying the complete works of various Greek, Latin and French writers, including Buffon, Condillac, Mably and Voltaire. A few of those books would have made proper Bostonians frown – especially the *Contes* by La Fontaine in the prestigious *édition des fermiers généraux* (for 5,500 *livres assignats*!), but the puritan streak re-emerged in Richard's subscription to a new edition of the Bible, decorated with 300 pictures.[108]

Richard Codman also speculated in stock – buying and selling French public funds – but the evidence, though definite, is meagre and no more can be said about this except that he had dealings with famous Paris bankers, such as J.F. Perregaux and J. Récamier.[109] We have more information, on the other hand, on two minor episodes which, however, show that Richard was not over-scrupulous in some matters and that he was involved in smuggling activities, which are openly discussed in several letters. In the summer and autumn of 1795, with the help of a fellow-Bostonian, Stephen Deblois, he shipped from Le Havre to Guernsey several parcels of cambrics, lace, gloves, fans, looking glasses, chinaware, etc., and also some champagne, which were obviously intended to be illegally introduced into England. Deblois rejoiced that Richard was 'determined not to be concerned in the smuggling any of these to England, which I was fearful was your plan', but on 25 November 1795 he wrote: 'I am exceedingly sorry that this speculation is likely to prove so unprofitable a business to you and me' (B20, f288, 292).

Another smuggling operation was to the United States. A brother-in-law of William Codman (brother of John and Richard), Francis Coffin, had come to Europe to finish his apprenticeship; when about to leave for home from Le Havre in the summer of 1800 he bought, with the help of Richard, an assortment of kid and silk gloves, of silk stockings, of fans, of cambrics and silks. These goods were packed in four or five 'small trunks; it will be much more convenient for *many reasons*'. Actually, the main reason was that they were to be loaded on shipboard 'in a cask called oats', 'without knowledge of the officers', and, naturally, to be landed in America 'without knowledge' of the Customs. Coffin envied a fellow passenger, one Mr Rand, who managed to get goods on board 'to the amount of 20,000 *livres* and nobody knows but that they are oats, potatoes and he will make 2,500 or 3,000 dollars'. At the last moment Richard sent a 'little box of lace', which was also put on board 'unknown to any soul'. The irony is that these two petty smugglers were sailing on the ship which was bringing home the American commissioners who had negotiated the treaty of Mortefontaine, and also that Coffin was much disappointed by this venture, which gave him a profit of 500–600 dollars only, as 'the cambricks and gloves are totally unsaleable here at any price', he wrote from New York on 1 April 1801 (B20, f288, 292). There is a conventional view about a great deal of unscrupulous speculation going on during the years of the Directory; obviously Richard Codman was not out of his depth in the Paris of the late 1790s, though most of his ventures do not seem to have been successful.

After a time, John Codman worried about his brother's activities in Paris; he would have preferred the proceeds of the cargoes he had sent to France to be invested in French goods for the American market, instead of being sunk in property, and he professed scepticism, as we have seen, about the fortune which Richard promised to make from *biens nationaux*. On 17 November 1797 he wrote to Baring: 'We have not heard from our Richard Codman for a long time, we thank you for mentioning you heard from him on the 6th September. We are perfectly tired of his continuance in that Country (France), and wish he was as much so' (Baring Mss: HC. OS. 14). Meanwhile, relations between the United States and France were deteriorating, so that on 1 May 1798 John officially dissolved the partnership with Richard. Some weeks later he pressed his brother to leave France, which, in his view, was behaving as badly as Britain towards the United States; Richard ought to understand that it was time to return to his country, if ever he intended to do so.[110]

This was to no avail. Richard is said to have been careless in money matters and 'extravagant' in his spending. He fell into debt and to sustain his high living, he had to sell his 'castles'. The *château des Ternes* was sold as early as June 1797 and as for the *hôtel de Créqui*, Richard sold it on 9 January 1800 to no less a person than Talleyrand, at the time minister of foreign affairs, for 110,000 francs cash (plus 19,569 for the furniture, silver, etc.). He retained the Dammartin estate, but it had been mortgaged (and eventually it was let out in 1801).[111]

Moreover, Richard became involved in an unsavoury affair. He was friendly with another American in Paris, William Vans, from Salem. A sea-captain, he had sold a cargo in Le Havre at a good profit during the Terror, and afterwards had traded from that port under the American flag – and had probably been involved in privateering. In 1794 he had married Céleste-Rosalie Gauvain, the daughter of a *havrais* shipowner. In January 1799 Vans, who was in debt, had to leave Paris; when he came back in August 1800 he found that Richard and Céleste-Rosalie were openly living together; also that a power of attorney which he had left to his wife had been used to sell the *hôtel* which he owned, and that, to boot, Richard had appropriated the money. Vans asked for a divorce and obtained it; he also claimed that Richard owed him 192,000 *livres* plus interest – for advances he had formerly received (for stock speculations) and for the sale of the *hôtel*. This started a lawsuit, which was to drag on, opposing Vans to the heirs of Richard and John Codman, and in American courts, up to 1837 (Bizardel 1980: 24, 31, 36; 1965: 72; 1975: 240–44)!

Richard was thus in serious trouble when his brother John – who had contemplated going to Europe in 1799 in order to clear up the position (Baring Mss: DEP 85, VII, VIII, no. 79) – landed in England in July 1800. He spent several months there, trying to settle some matters which were in abeyance, such as the case of the *Elisabeth*, and the freight and insurance which remained due after the capture and release of the *Abigail*. On 24 August he wrote to his wife: 'My affairs here are better than I expected ... If I have to pay all here and everywhere else without any aid from Richard, I can do it and have all my real estate left beside, and something else', altogether a 'handsome fortune'. On the other hand, he was told that Richard had lived 'in and about Paris in as great style as any of them in this country, that his establishment has been as handsome and expensive and his mistress as beautiful as any one's in Europe and that he himself is quite the accomplished man, the very man to enjoy life in fashion.' He added, some days later: 'The general opinion is that Richard has in habits and manners become so much of a frenchman' that there was little hope he would return home. John was somewhat proud that his brother was such a man of fashion, but he also found it 'unfair' that Richard had lived in luxury 'without property to support it', and actually by sponging on him.[112]

In October John left London and arrived in Paris, via Calais, on the 22nd. He then learned the worst from Richard, who confessed that nothing could be recovered from the 'advances and entrustments' which had been made to him except, at best, some 'remnants'. On 29 November 1800 John wrote to Sir Francis Baring:

> Although my B [rother's] affairs are of such a nature that I am in no way personally answerable, they are so situated that he cannot raise money from any property that he has to meet his engagements. The system he has pursued of making unnatural exertions to meet them has but increased the difficulty arising from want of punctuality in those that own him and the total impossibility of raising money by the sale of his Estates.[113]

John did his best to salvage something from the wreck, but on 30 December 1800 he wrote to his wife that Richard's debts were such that he (John) could not help him without unfair damage to his own family; a large part of his property had been consumed by Richard, and 'the engagements I am already under will occupy all my means'. After an unsuccessful attempt to settle the dispute with Vans,[114] John returned to England in February 1801. On 5 April he wrote to Sir Francis Baring:

> You will see that I conceive any new advances (to Richard) will be perfectly unavailing and it is necessary that I should decidedly say

that I cannot authorize them, in order that in future I may be released from that suspense which I have too long experienced. Beside I have every reason to think it is the only way to terminate my Brother's affairs in France. (Baring Mss: HO. OS. 24)

On 1 May 1801 John sailed from England and he was back in Boston in June.

Even before his journey to Europe, John Codman was 'quite tired of business' and of the anxieties it caused (he had worried enormously about the capture of American ships by the French), and in April 1800 he told his wife that he was determined to retire as soon as possible.[115] It has been mentioned above that the last trading operations by the house of Codman, for which we have evidence, took place in 1800 and John did not live to enjoy a long retirement for he died in 1803 at the age of forty-eight.[116]

Despite the losses which he had suffered because of Richard, John Codman left a 'handsome fortune': his house and some other property (on the Town dock) in Boston, and about $100,000 in stocks and shares (during the 1790s he had bought American funds, which had appreciated) (B19, f254; B118). Moreover, he had 'federalised' the house in Lincoln and renovated the surrounding estate, for which he was trustee on behalf of one of his sons, to whom they had been left by an uncle in 1790. He had been member of the House of Representatives of Massachusetts from 1796 to 1800 and State Senator from 1800 to his death. As for Richard, he lost his lawsuit with Vans, both in the court of first instance and in the Court of Appeal. Deprived of any property, he was declared a bankrupt and left Paris for good in 1802. He is said to have tried his luck in South America, before returning to Boston, where he died in 1806, at forty-four (Bizardel 1980: 37, 41; 1965: 72). John Codman had not become a millionnaire, like Stephen Girard, Alexander Brown, or Robert Oliver; but the others had a much longer career, and their brothers were unlike Richard.

THE END OF THE STORY

The story of Richard Codman, his *châteaux*, his Norman girl-friend, his high-living and his final discomfiture may look purely anecdotal, though it could have been used by some nineteenth-century moralist: the innocent Yankee abroad, falling prey to the guiles of corrupt Europe, to the lures of Paris under the Directory, which had lost the elegances of the *Ancien Régime* but none of its vices . . . . On the other hand, it has happened time and again that a firm has been brought to the brink by a junior partner's indiscretions, and we find here a good example of this process, and how it was compounded by distance and slow communications, which made it most difficult for the senior partner to exert control. The positive role of kinship in eighteenth-century business has been rightly stressed, but misplaced confidence in a close relative or natural reluctance to distrust him could have disastrous consequences. Still, Richard Codman was not a complete fool: he had a bright idea in purchasing *biens nationaux*, at obviously low prices; his mistake was to believe he would make quick gains, while such a speculation could only be profitable in the long run, when the French economy would have recovered.[117] And he was only one of many American merchants and adventurers who came to Europe during the Revolutionary wars, to take advantage of the opportunities which they opened up to enterprising traders.[118]

This chapter has stressed the difficulties and risks which seaborne trade encountered during those wars (and the situation was to be worse, though less chaotic, during the Napoleonic period). However, commerce also displayed a great deal of buoyancy, of resilience, of vitality which deserve to be emphasised. Americans were, of course, the first to take advantage of the new opportunities and the huge expansion of their maritime activities in wartime is well known. European merchants, however, were not slow to adapt and to carry on business, as best as they could, despite military operations, blockades, embargos, interdictions of all kinds, seizures of ships and goods. The Codman papers are rich, as it has been mentioned, in handwritten letters or printed circulars emanating from firms in many European ports, from Leghorn to Hamburg. Many of them are just offers to do business and did not result in any transaction, but they are interesting as proofs of the alacrity which European merchants were displaying to attract into their ports ships and cargoes from the United States (though some were honest enough to discourage shipments, when they would have been dangerous). Reading the Codman papers often leaves the feeling that businessmen were desperately trying to do 'business as usual', not only in the gathering storm, but even when hell had broken loose!

NOTES

1. I am grateful to my colleague, Professor Jeanne-Marie Santraud, for this quotation.
2. The *Codman Family Manuscripts Collection* is preserved at the Harrison Gray Otis House in Boston, the headquarters of the Society for the Preservation of New England Antiquities (SPNEA). In 1969, after the death of the last of the Codmans – a prominent Boston family – the Society came into the possession of a splendid eighteenth-century house at Lincoln, near Boston; a mass of old papers was discovered there, then deposited in the Society's library, classified and catalogued. This collection contains, *inter alia*, records of the house of J. and R. Codman, though they are far less complete and rich than the papers of other American merchants of the time (such as S. Girard and R. Oliver). They are mostly in-letters; there are no letter-books (the only letters by J. Codman which have survived – as copies which appear to have been typewritten in the early twentieth century – were sent to his wife during his European trip in 1800–1), and no ledgers – though a number of accounting documents have survived. I have found some valuable additional materials in the archives of Baring Brothers and Co. at the Guildhall Library and at their London office. The 'Brown Family Papers' in the John Carter Brown Library, Providence, Rhode Island contain some letters exchanged between John Codman, Richard Codman, John and Richard Codman, and Brown and Benson, merchants of Providence.

   I am most grateful to Professor Charles K. Warner, who revealed to me the existence of the Codman Collection and introduced me to the SPNEA, and to Mrs Ellie Reichlin, the Society's librarian, who has been extremely helpful and kind. Also to Baring Brothers and their archivist Dr M.J. Orbell.

   Old-Time New England, LXXI, no. 258, 1981, is a special number of the SPNEA's bulletin, which has articles written on the Codman family and the house at Lincoln, but not on the firm which is studied here. A preliminary and incomplete version of this study has been published in French: 'Deux négociants de Boston et le commerce avec l'Europe pendant la Révolution Française', *L'Atlantique et ses rivages (1500–1800)* (Bordeaux 1984, pp. 79–99).

   Almost all quotations of papers in the Codman Collection are from documents written in English or a sort of English (the writer has no responsibility for their grammatical and other mistakes – only for his own). The original spelling has been generally respected, but punctuation has been corrected to prevent misunderstandings.
3. According to Alexander Baring, writing in 1795, John Codman had 'made his fortune entirely himself'; he was the support of his whole family, having set up in business his younger brothers, Stephen in Boston and William (some time a sea captain) in New York, and

taken Richard into partnership, though he had no capital (Baring Mss: Dep. 85³, Part V, vol. I, no. 15, 16).

As a comparison, Stephen Girard's fleet at no one time consisted of more than six ships (McMaster 1918: vol. I, VI).

4. The Codman Mss contain *some* evidence (but not much) that the firm's trading with the West Indies continued during the 1790s, but we have no idea of its scale (B3, f33; B12, f160; B13, f170; B14, f171, 174; B17, f224; B19, f255).
5. (B8, f89; B10, f119, 120.) The interest of J. Codman in these two ships on their return journey was insured for £5,000.
6. The exports to Holland in 1785 were whale oil and logwood, imports were gin, iron, hemp and sundry goods.
7. Inference from B5, f54, but there is no doubt that two Codman ships went to Russia in 1790 (B2, f23; B4, f51).
8. J. Codman is said to have owned a cordage manufactory in Boston.
9. (Crosby 1965: 14–16, 18, 23–4, 42–3, 53, 56, 78, 93; Rasch 1965: 36–7, 40–2; B16, f212.) The number of ships fluctuated, of course, from year to year and fell back, for instance, in 1794 and 1800.
10. According to A. Baring, J. Codman and Thomas Russell (brother of John's first wife and the richest merchant in Boston) had a monopoly of the trade between Boston and Russia. He stressed it was a steady and safe trade in which a large amount of capital was needed (Baring Mss: Dep. 85³, Parts V, VII, vol. I, III, no. 16, 79). There were, however, some risks (B12, f163; B16, f201).

S. Girard sent one of his ships – the *Voltaire* – to St Petersburg, via Hamburg, for the first time in 1797 (McMaster 1918: I, 350).
11. (B10, f122; Archives Nationales: G5/142.) In 1790, Baudin et Rateau of St Martin de Ré sent to John Codman 15 pipes of brandy aboard *The Expedition* for a value of 8,010 *livres* (B17, f218).
12. In answer to the letter which announced that the partnership of John and Richard Codman had been set up, Le Couteulx offered 'our congratulations because our house which has been established in commerce for many centuries and desiring to continue it, whether by ourselves or our Heirs, we would be flattered to find the same principles in your house, in order to establish between our two houses a correspondence equally advantageous' (B14, f178). As a matter of fact, the Le Couteulx family was in trade in Rouen in the fifteenth century. They established their bank in Paris in 1670; at the end of the Old Regime their house was large and powerful with widespread interests in France and abroad. The main base of their fortune had been the supply to the Royal Mint of American silver imported via Cadiz and Rouen.
13. Actually, most of these letters were signed by the manager of the house in Rouen, Horcholle.
14. These d'Allarde letters start in July 1791.
15. D'Allard (1752–1809), a nobleman and ex-army officer, had become a merchant, banker and coal-owner. He is remembered for having

introduced the law of 2 March 1791, often called *loi Dallarde*, which abolished the guilds system and established *laissez-faire* in France. During the Terror, he emigrated to the United States and bought land in Virginia and Kentucky. He came back to Paris in the late 1790s, was active again as a banker, but he failed in 1803.

As for J.-B. Le Couteulx (1746–1818), he was a member of the Finance committee of the *Constituante* and tried to prevent excessive issues of *assignats*. He spent two million *livres* in vain attempts to save Louis XVI; he was jailed during the Terror and narrowly escaped the guillotine. Under the Directory, he was a prominent banker and active again in politics; he also bought real estate on a very large scale. He played a part in the preparation of the *coup* of brumaire and was *régent* (director) of the Bank of France from 1799 to 1804. Napoleon made him a senator and a count, Louis XVIII a peer (Bergeron 1978: 27–8, 59–60, 65, 88, 116, 273, 279, 301, 303, 311, 330; Bouchary 1937: 51, 53, 55–7, 59–60; Szamkiewicz 1974: 213–24).

16. (B14, f179.) Actually the drafting and voting of the 'Constitution of 1791' were not completed at that time.
17. Letter of 15 February 1791 (B15, f191). On February 19 they advised J. Codman not to speculate on his own account (in shipments to France), 'for the Exchange is against them (the French) in every commercial city in Europe at present and in our opinion must remain so for some time, tho' perhaps not quite so much as it is now' (this suggests that the true situation was not quite understood in London). The fall of the exchange rate from June 1790 to February 1791 had been 8 per cent.
18. Actually, a new fall of the exchange rate was starting (Bouchary 1937: 50–1, 136).
19. (B15, f192). On 23 May, Lane Son and Fraser added that Codman's loss would have been heavier if they had waited longer to draw, as the exchange had fallen again (indeed, May was a very bad month, and on 30 May, depreciation reached 25 per cent). (Bouchary 1937: 60–1).
20. (B14, f178, 179.) See also (National Archives: Bordeaux,1). In a letter of 25 September 1791 the American consul in Bordeaux regretted that French manufactures were little known in the United States; in his view, the two governments ought to take steps to stimulate trade on a reciprocal basis, for instance the sale in the United States of French wool and linen textiles. But both on 31 August and 27 December he stressed that shortage of specie, depreciation of *assignats*, high prices, fluctuations in exchange rates, political incertitude were hampering American trade with France.
21. (B15, f185.) Meanwhile, d'Allarde was preparing a parcel of goods, which was eventually shipped in April 1792.
22. (B15, f186.) D'Allarde was writing to a correspondent in Guadeloupe, announcing that he would have goods sent to him from New

England 'up to the time when the affairs of the Kingdom (France) will be restored upon a stable footing and when merchandise of one's choice will be available at reasonable prices'.

The last sentence from Le Couteulx shows a misunderstanding of the process of inflation and 'devaluation'.

23. (B19, f255, 263; B10, f122; B14, f179; B15, f180, 182, 183, 185, 187; B16, f21–3.) This project had been mentioned in the summer of 1791, but a bad crop, which drove up the prices of wines and brandies, delayed its implementation. The *Marie-Françoise* went to New York, the two other ships to Boston. They returned to France late in 1792 with cargoes of whale oil, tobacco and flour.

24. (B15, f184, 185.) Letters from d'Allarde; 17 November 1791: 'Every day there seems an augmentation'; 14 December: 'All kinds of goods here are about seven to eight per cent raised'; 3 March 1792: 'You will observe all kinds of goods rise here: but this is more the effect of international trouble than scarcity; but this must not hinder you from selling at the old rates, as things will soon return to their old standards' (this again shows a misunderstanding of the situation).

25. (B15, f181.) See also f185, letter from d'Allarde, 3 March 1792 (on that date the French exchange on London had fallen 46 per cent): 'In case Bills on London or Amsterdam should be scarce, ship dollars or gold and insure at Boston. The position of our exchanges offers such profits as determinates the above proposal.'

26. (B15, f185.) As for Lane Son and Fraser, they wrote on 15 March: 'The French affairs are in great disorder.' One minister had resigned and another was 'said to be in the custody of the people'. On 5 April they added that the exchange on Paris 'is so fluctuating that we cannot guess whether it will rise or fall next post' (B15, f195, 196). This was quite true: in March the rate on London fluctuated between 15 and 20.

27. (B15, f181, 186; McMaster 1918: I, 154–6.) Actually, exchange improved in May and June (Bouchary 1937: 65, 93).

28. On 22 August Le Couteulx wrote that no ship had been hitherto captured by the enemies of France (B15, f182).

29. Exchange on London had improved since March, but was 36 per cent below par.

30. From London, Lane Son and Fraser had warned Codman on 29 November 1792 that war might break out with France.

31. (B15, f188.) See also this postscript of the same date to a copy of an earlier letter: 'Give no possible hint on paper upon this subject which may be taken hold of in case of falling in the Enemy's hand.'

32. See B6, f67, for the settlement of the balance due by Codman to d'Allarde, which was completed in September 1794. However, Richard Codman had some dealings with d'Allarde in Paris in 1798.

33. (B15, f199.) On the other hand, the Amorys promised to pay within three years £5,253 which J. Codman owed to Lane and Fraser. Thomas Amory was the brother of John Codman's second wife.

34. (B15, f200.) These arrangements had been finalised before 3 July 1791.
35. (B2, f26; B12, f163; B16, f201; B20, f292; Baring Mss.: vol. 7, f380.) The shares (of $400 each) had been sent from Philadelphia to London in March 1793 'for the purpose of facilitating Mr. Codman raising a loan thereon.'
   Shortly afterwards, J. Codman proposed to Baring to buy more American stocks 'against drafts', but the latter declined, because of the rumours of war between England and the United States, which made those securities unsaleable.
36. J. Codman took out a number of insurance policies in the United States. Baring only insisted on the insurances which were necessary to cover their advances passing through their hands (B16, f203–5). However, they made some insurances themselves (Baring Mss, Guildhall, 18325, vol. 8).
37. A letter from Alexandria, dated 17 May 1793, had informed J. Codman that tobacco would fetch 'a great price' in France (B12, f160). One can mention also that Baudin et Rateau, of St Martin de Ré, had written on 23 June 1793 that a shipment, 'for our quarters', of grain, flour, lumber, whale or cod oil, fish, etc., with return in brandy, would be very profitable, as 'we are in want of every article', and the rate of exchange made French brandies inexpensive for foreign buyers. Anyhow, this French house was wanting to do business with Americans at this critical moment of quasi-civil war in France (B15, f199).
38. (B12, f163.) This ship had recently arrived from China.
39. (B15, f200; B16, f201, 204.) On 23 December 1793, the correspondent of the Codmans in Hamburg, C. Voght, sent to Richard congratulations for the success of his sales to the French authorities (B12, f163).
40. On 21 December 1794, Thomas Amory wrote from Paris, in connection with the arrival of the ship *Betsy* in Le Havre: 'I should much prefer selling for gold.' On 15 June 1795, he instructed R. Codman (about another cargo): 'Do not sell for paper unless you can at the same time (or previously) invest it in something solid' (B20, f293). And the captain of the *Minerva*, which arrived in Bordeaux in April 1795, had instructions to take specie in payment, if he could (B16, f206).
41. (B3, f28; B6, f67, f74; B16, f204, 205; B17, f221, Baring Mss.: vol. VIII, f410–11.) Two small 'parcels' (for £236 and £686) were received in April and June 1795 on the *Mary and Ann* and the *Harmony*. The ship *Betsy* belonged to Stephen Codman.
42. (B3, f28; B6, f72; B16, f204, 205, 206, 207; B17, f222.) At first, the *Minerva* was intended to go to Lisbon. Her cargo was worth £12–13,000.
43. (B3, f30; B7, f80, 85.) The net proceeds of the sale of those three cargoes was 838,182 *livres* (paper), which were remitted to J. Réca-

mier in Paris. In the spring of 1797, S. Girard decided not to send back to Bordeaux his ship, the *Liberty*, which had just arrived from that port, because of the tension with France. However, another of his ships went there and back early in 1798 (McMaster 1918: I, 327–8, 360).

44. In 1795 J. Codman was pressing his brother to ship such goods (Bizardel 1980: 37; B20, f293). See also B20, f293, T. Amory to R. Codman, 11 January 1796: 'Our sister Mrs. Codman will thank you to send her 6 French looking glasses with frames... to fit places between windows'; and B2, f18, letter from an American couple that wants to buy in Paris a table set in porcelain. In 1798, S. Girard imported furniture from Bordeaux (where he came from, of course) (McMaster 1918: I, 360).

45. Years ending 30 September (Crosby 1965: 78; Kutz 1986: 259, table 12). At the same time US exports to Holland collapsed. 110 American ships arrived in Hamburg during the second half of 1797, ninety-nine during the same period of 1798 (National Archives: Hamburg 1). In May 1798, the four ships of S. Girard were all at one time in Hamburg (McMaster 1918: 1, 380).

46. His first shipments to Hamburg in 1793 and 1794 were of tobacco; some indigo was sent in 1796 (B13, f163; B6, f175). See also notes 52 and 55.

47. (B2, f18; B19, f252, 257; Baring Mss.: HC. OS. 15.) The captain of the ship claimed his freight and expenses and appealed to the Lords of Appeals in Prize Causes, on the ground that the contract with the Dutch had been made before war had started between Britain and the Batavian Republic. In February 1800 the matter was said to be settled and taken out of court. The owner of the *Henry*, who was in Liverpool, accepted to pay £4,500, but in Jamaica. During his stay in England J. Codman went to Liverpool to look after this business.

48. (Baring Mss.: HO. OS. 24.) J. Codman had been preceded in the trade to Batavia by the Olivers whose *Maryland* returned to Baltimore in May 1797 with coffee and sugar (Bruchey 1956: 81, 178–9). According to Bruchey, price information (coffee was very cheap in Batavia) and the high cost of alternative ventures (French privateers made the West Indies dangerous) led Oliver to send two ships to Batavia in June and July 1797.

49. (Bruchey 1956: 26ff.) See below, pp. 118–24, on the information which J. Codman had received on market conditions. On the other hand, the Olivers made few shipments during 1798, because relations with France were deteriorating (Bruchey 1956: 187).

50. Rotterdam was considered as 'the best market in the North of Europe' for coffee. In April 1798 the Olivers re-exported there part of the cargo of the *Harmony*, which had returned in March from Java (Bruchey 1956: 188–9). On Ryberg, see Rasch 1956: 57.

51. (B3, f31, 32; B13, f167, 168; B17, f224.) Remittance to London was delayed by Cremer because of the fall of the pound on the exchange market.

52. At the very end of 1797 the ship *Sally* had arrived in Bremen from Boston with some sugar (see note 58) and 111 tons of whale oil. One half of the cargo was on the account of the Codmans, the other for Delius. In January 1798 the snow *Adventure* brought some more oil on the joint account of Codman and Delius. The oil, however, was of poor quality and Delius did not manage to sell it before the 'warm season'. He had to ship part of it to Amsterdam and he concluded on 30 October 1798 that it had been 'a losing speculation'. John Codman wanted a return cargo of linen on the *Sally*, but she went to Lisbon for salt. Later, Delius made a shipment to Codman of linen, looking glasses and Nuremberg toys (for £2,066). In July 1798 he mentioned that exports of linen from Bremen to the United States had greatly increased within four or five years. Presently seven ships were ready to sail for Baltimore with cargoes to be re-exported to the West Indies. Actually, in the autumn Baltimore was 'completely glutted with German Linens' (B3, f31; B13, f165, 167, 168; B17, f223; B19, f265; Bruchey 1956: 190).
53. (B3, f31; B13, f165, 168, 169; B17, f224.) There was a project of a return cargo of linen, but Delius gave it up, as large quantities had already been sent. There were no more shipments to Delius – except a very small one of sugar late in 1799, before the unfortunate voyage of the *Abigail* (see *infra*).
54. (B13, f168, 169.) The establishment of the new firm had been announced by a printed circular of 10 August 1798.
55. The same misfortune had happened four years earlier to the *Governor Bowdoin* at Glückstadt, and 'a jury bridge over the ice' had been built in order to unload the tobacco on board (Baring Mss, HC. OS. 14).
56. It seems that one more – rather small – shipment of coffee from the *Minerva* was made in August 1799 (or later) on account of J. Codman, but from London to Holland via Bremen or Emden. The coffee had been sold at auction by the East India Co. (so it looks like prize goods) and bought by Baring for J. Codman. It sold at a loss (Baring Mss, Guildhall, 18325, vol. 10, f370–1; B118).
57. Estimates from figures in B3, f32, f31; B13, f169; B14, f171; B17, f224; B19, f265.

The proceeds of sales are in different currencies, and the exact rate of exchange at the time of remittance is difficult to ascertain.
58. The 16 hhd of sugar per the *Sally*, invoiced $1,612 after drawback, were sold in Bremen in January 1798 for 2,963 Rix dollars (net price), i.e. US $3, 170 (B3, f31; B17, f223).
59. (B14, f174, 176; B20, f292; B118.) The cargo of the ship is not known.
60. Baring told the captain of the *Thetis* not to go to Russia, as prices of local goods were too high there. After arriving in England, J. Codman sent the ship back to America (B14, f175, 176; B118).
61. Some ships went to St Ubes to take salt back to America. In 1797 the ship *Mary* went to Lisbon and Cadiz with a cargo of staves and came

back in 1798 with sherry, salt, linens, part of the cargoes being for the account of the Codmans (B13, f165–7).

Later on, there was no answer to the entreaties of J. Dohrman and Co. of Lisbon, of some houses in Spain and of one in Marseille to send shipments (indeed some of the accompanying information was not encouraging: for instance, during the summer of 1799 the British were said to capture many ships which were going to Spain or leaving it) (B13, f167; B14, f175; B20, f292).

62. (B13, f169, 170; B14, f171.) On 23 December 1798, Captain Hammond wrote from Lisbon about the bad weather: 'Many ships wrecked on this coast as well as in the harbour.' S. Girard lost the *Modest* during a squall in the West Indies (1798) and the Olivers' *Harmony* foundered off Java (1799).

63. (B12, f163; B15, f200; B16, f201; B20, f288.) This was why the insurance on the *Minerva* (31 January 1794) was so high: 12 per cent from Alexandria to Lisbon or some other port outside the Straits; to return: 7 per cent if she unloaded in England; 6 per cent if she went to Holland or Ostend; 7 per cent if she sailed from the United States under convoy for the Peninsula and arrived there. Actually, she was sent to Falmouth to receive there instructions from Baring.

64. With the possible exception of the parcel of coffee mentioned in note 56.

65. See also note 88. The proceeds of the *Commerce*'s journey were $26,918; $1,166 were allotted 'to ship *Commerce* for ballance' [*sic*] so that the freight was only partially paid. The results were better for the *Minerva*: proceeds of $44,676 and 'balance' to the ship of $4,643.

66. (B3, f32; B13, f170; B14, f171, 172, 176; Bruchey 1956: 191.) In October 1798 the Olivers sent the *Nelly* to Emden with coffee, which was trans-shipped to Rotterdam.

67. (B3, f31, 32; B6, f74, 75; B13, f167, 168, 170; B16, f209, 210; B17, f223.) It seems that the captain had been jailed for debts.

68. This is the only export of wheat to Europe by Codman. Still, from August 1794 to July 1795 Baring stressed several times that prices were rising and would rise again (B16, f203, 204, 206).

The cargo had been insured for £3,000; the net proceeds from its sale were £4,902.

69. This is an example of the practice of sending wine to the East Indies and back so that it would age and mature. In 1795 J. Codman had already imported one pipe of madeira on a ship from Madras.

70. 8,485 bushels of salt were sold for £1,414, i.e. £930 net (duties of £419) which shows that such a ballast could pay most of the journey's costs: freight from Russia to Boston was £1,300 or 1,600 (B2, f27).

71. (Bruchey 1956: 142ff) has stressed this incertitude and chanciness in US trade during the wars. One can add that decision-making was complicated for American merchants by the fact that – unlike most traditional eighteenth-century traders – they were 'polyvalent', non-specialised. They were not restricted to one route (London or Bor-

deaux to the West Indies, for instance) and they had a wide choice both of ports to trade to and from and of goods to export and import. They could also send their ships 'tramping'.

72. (B12, f163; B15, f200.) T. Amory wrote from London to R. Codman on 27 August 1793: 'It's not impossible that ye English may force the Americans into a war, but it certainly will be against them.' On 19 July J. Parish, US consul to Hamburg, wrote that complete anarchy prevailed in France and the general opinion was that the war could not last much longer. But on 20 September he recanted: 'It is generally believed the present campaign. bloody as it is, will not decide the dispute' (National Archives: Hamburg 1).

73. (B15, f200.) The idea of a flight of capital to the United States reappears later. On 26 April 1795 Baring mentioned 'the end of the general alarm which induced the public to turn their thoughts to American stocks' (B16, f206). And on 1 June 1797 (admittedly a period of danger for England after the suspension of cash payments) Alexander Baring wrote to his father: 'I am fully convinced that serious convulsions in property in England are approaching and inevitable and I am as confident of the security of America for probably some centuries' (Baring Mss. DEP 85^3, Part VI, vol. II, no. 54).

74. (B16, f203.) Richard Codman, 'who feared much a rupture' between the two countries, had given orders for the *Catherine* and the *Minerva* to be insured for large sums, at 6 and 8 per cent premiums, on their way back from Russia.

75. (B16, f203.) US bank shares were to reach 114 after the signing of the Jay Treaty (19 November 1794), 123 one month later and 130 in February 1795. Baring wrote on 12 December 1794 that American stock would have been risen more 'was it not for the many favourable opportunities that now offer in investing money in this country' (i.e. government loans).

76. Disturbing news also came from relatives of J. Codman who happened to be in Europe. From Bristol, James Russell wrote on 24 February 1798: 'All appearances of peace are vanish'd and seemingly at a greater distance than ever. In short nothing but another revolution there [in France] can keep you of it [the war] longer than this summer ... You must make up your mind to have the depredations on your trade continued.' As for Francis Amory – Mrs Codman's brother – he had direct experience of those 'depredations': the ship on which he was travelling from Boston to Europe as a passenger was captured by a French privateer on 13 February 1798. He 'was under the painful necessity of throwing over board every paper I had for England', including a letter from John Codman to Baring (this was normal precaution in case of capture, but, if observed by the captors, it could be used in Court as a proof of 'intent to defraud'). On 3 May 1798 Francis Amory commented:' No paper whatever will protect American property from French captures ... everything looks so dark', and he recommended not to

re-export the cargo of the *Minerva* (his letter was received in Boston on 3 May). On 22 July James Russell was of a contrary opinion (B13, f166, f168).

77. (B13, f165.) Also (B13, f167) letter of 16 May: the demand for coffee 'from our upper country' is increasing.
78. (B13, f165–7.) On 23 March and 1 May Rocquette and B. repeated that the prices of colonial produce had risen and were unlikely to fall. Coffee was very scarce and the most advantageous article to send from the United States.
79. (B13, f166, 167.) Muir's are printed circulars. McMaster (1918: I, 358–9) also mentions that S. Girard received many letters written from various ports in early 1798, which 'gave most alluring accounts of trade conditions'.
80. This is likely to be an allusion to a French attempt to invade England, which many people expected any moment.
81. Also the letter of 1 June 1798 from T.T. Cremer of Rotterdam which has been quoted *supra*: he would not send a ship to a sea which 'swarms with French privateers'.
82. Prices were said to be so high that they gave a profit on goods which had been insured at premiums over 15 per cent.
83. (B13, f167–9.) But in April 1799 Strobel and Martini had to confess that all relations between France and the United States had been interrupted (B14, f171).
84. (B13, f169.) Delius mentioned about cotton: 'The constant demand of our inland manufactories are again increasing.' Beeldemaker pointed at the 'daily arrivals' of American ships which had come on the northern route.
85. (B13, f170; B14, f171.) On 13 May 1799 the Olivers wrote 'a prophetic letter'. 'The conduct of the French ... will probably occasion great changes in Europe and make trade very precarious. If the French take Hamburg, we will have no safe market in Europe for West India produce ... we would not like to engage in new operations until we see things differently' (Bruchey 1956: 193).
86. (B14, f171.) This letter had transited via Hamburg and Philadelphia.
87. B3, f29, 30, 31, 33, 34; B17, f225 give the complete and final results of these operations after their winding up. See (Bruchey 1956: 135–9) on the problem of determining profits.
88. Strangely, no loss was declared. As mentioned in note 65, the *Minerva* was credited $4,643 for her freight, which means that the operation almost broke even. With only $1,166 allotted to the *Commerce*, one can consider there was a loss.
89. The subject of insurance on the St Petersburg to Boston journey deserves a fuller study. Premiums rose, of course, because of the war. In 1794 and 1797 some policies were obtained at 8 or even 10 guineas per cent, against three per cent in 1792, but there are instances of 5 per cent in 1795 and 1796. Also, generally 2 per cent were to be returned if the ship sailed before 20 August or 15 September. On the other hand, J. Codman did insure the ship and

cargo for a round sum (he had no idea of the 'real' value of the goods on board). So we have used the actual cost of insurance (for instance $2,481 for the *Commerce* in 1796) and calculated its ratio to sales.
90. (B6, f70, 74; B7, f78.) If the balances due at the beginning of the year were deducted, the net figures would be: 1796 $98,658, 1797 $168,436. This fits with the failure of Russian ventures in 1795, which caused a decline in turnover.
91. (Bruchey 1956: 214–16.) True enough, the profits of Oliver and Thompson for 1793–5 (including the gains from ventures not concluded when the war broke out) were £111,898 Maryland currency. And later on, from 1804 to 1809, Oliver Bros. gained $1,360,000. But Bruchey (1956: 93, 341) writes: 'Some of it was water.'
92. As mentioned earlier, on 30 July, 1793, £10,381 had been credited to the Codmans after the sale of the Bank of the US shares. Without this 'deposit', the deficit would have been much larger. One can add that on 31 December 1794 J. Codman sent to Baring one certificate of a capital of $8,000 in the Union Bank of Massachusetts. He also authorised Baring to draw for $17,000 more. This was most likely in order to reduce his unfavourable balance. However, Baring declined to complete this transaction and eventually sent back the certificate in July 1795, 'because, as this Bank Stock is not understood here, we shall not be able to meet with a purchaser', inasmuch as there was then no demand for any American stocks (B16, f205, 206).
93. There may be other causes of a business nature of this deficit, but we have not been able to see them. Except the case in April 1794 of the silver imported from France by the *Catherine*: £4,000 of the proceeds were credited to J. and R. Codman, but £5,298 to John's account with Baring (B16, f201; Baring Mss, Guildhall, 18325, vol. 7).
94. (Hidy 1949: 28–9.) Alexander Baring was a partner in Hope and Co., which had 'withdrawn their house at Amsterdam in consequence of the present situation in Holland' (B16, f207). He stayed in the United States until 1803 and married a Bingham daughter.
95. In November 1795 Baring asked J. Codman to buy two cargoes of salt provisions and to send them to a house in Kingston, Jamaica, which would forward them to another in Port-au-Prince. 'You will accept the drafts of each house for our account to the amount of £50,000' (B16, f208). There is no evidence that this large transaction was carried out.
96. A. Baring added that there were in Boston two or three capitals of £80,000 to 100,000 and many from £20,000 to 50,000. So J. Codman was just below the top men. He owned real estate with an income of £50,000 currency from which he 'could live very handsomely' without doing business.
97. On 9 January 1797 A. Baring wrote: 'Codman I think very highly of, he is certainly since Russell's death the best man at Boston' (Baring Mss, DEP 85³, Part VI, vol. II, no. 43).
98. He alluded to an arrangement through which one Parker had bought in 1796 700,000 *livres* of French *rentes*, half of them for the Barings,

who as a consequence owed Richard £10,000 plus interest. But Parker had disappeared ...
99. A. Baring mentioned that John had had to pay at least $50,000 for Richard in Boston, 'for when I presume you (Baring) refused to paying for him he drew directly on America'.
100. He asked the London firm to let one or two Codman ships go to Russia, which shows that it had been contemplated not to grant the relevant credit.
101. T.T. Cremer had to accept, in May 1799, Richard's drafts for 30,000 florins (£6,500) on orders from William Tudor, John Codman's new agent in Europe. Richard promised to repay soon, but the debt was still standing in December 1800 (B14, f177).
102. (B20, f293.) Actually, Richard did not display much zeal in the sale of T. Amory's goods. The latter complained about it in October 1796 and again in June 1797.

W. Vans (see *infra*) also bought a good deal of land plus a *château* at Ablon (south of Paris) and a *hôtel*, 24, rue de l'Université in Paris (Bizardel 1965: 71).
103. (Bizardel 1965: 71; Bizardel 1980: 9, 11–13, 23; Pardailhé-Galabrun, Aubry and Charneau 1987: 474–5). The *hotel de Créqui*, which had been built in 1774, was a prestigious building of the same size and appearance as the *Petit Trianon* in Versailles. It was demolished in the nineteenth century. When Richard bought it, the *assignats* were on their last legs. They were demonetised on 19 February, 1796.

On the low prices of *biens nationaux* see Aftalion 1987: 138–9.
104. Nowadays in the seventeenth *arrondisement* north of Etoile. Part of it is still standing.
105. 105 km southwest of Paris.
106. (Bizardel 1965: 67–9; Bizardel 1980: 12–14.) According to a note in Richard's hand (B20, f290), the house in rue d'Anjou cost him 29,165 *livres* (specie). He spent 45,000 in repairs and 43,500 in furnishing, and he estimated the total cost at 141,323 *livres*. At *les Termes* the joiner's bill alone was 4,360,836 *livres* (paper). ($1 = 5 *livres* specie.)
107. Those purchases were made from 1794 to 1797. The first one – 80 paintings – cost £270. They were mostly works by minor Dutch and French artists, but Teniers, Greuze, Joseph Vernet were represented (Redmond 1981: 103–6; Bizardel 1965: 7, 15).
108. See invoices by booksellers in B20, f290.
109. (B20, f290, docs. 12, 19.) On 22 February 1796 Richard paid 6,696,700 *livres* (paper) for *rentes*. On 13 April 1798 he settled (for an unknown sum) his purchase of *rentes au grand livre*. According to Bizardel (1980: 44) Richard also speculated on *assignats*, bills of exchange and gold bullion.
110. (Bizardel 1980: 38–9.) James Russell, John's brother-in-law, was worried for Richard's safety, 'knowing the rascality of that Nation' (the French) (B13, f168).

111. (Bizardel 1980: 27, 34–5; Bizardel 1965: 70, 72.) On 22 March 1800 J. Récamier asked in pressing terms for a payment of a debt of 14,895 *livres*. Richard had pretended that he would get 20,000 *livres* through mortgaging a farm (B20, f288).
112. Copies of letters from John C. to his wife in B118.
113. (Baring Mss: HO. OS. 24.) Richard was so embarrassed that he was unable to supply money for John's expenses in Paris. John had to use the balance of the sale of the *Elizabeth* cargo in Holland.
114. (Bizardel 1980: 40–1.) This proposal (to hand over to Vans some property – especially La Thuilerie – and IOUs for a total of 199,000 frs) is proof that Vans' claims were not groundless. Vans refused.
115. (B118.) However, after having been courteously received by Sir Francis Baring – during his stay in England in August 1800 – John observed that Sir Francis knew that he (John) had been and *would be* a 'profitable customer'.
116. Poor health may have been also a reason for retiring. There are hints about illness in letters written during the European trip.
117. Morison (1961: 170–3) on the rush of young adventurers to France. Bergeron (1978: 86; B12, f163) contains a letter from an American who was trying to reach France during the critical summer of 1793 obviously hoping to find business opportunities there.
118. One or the other of Robert Oliver's brothers – John and Thomas – was in Europe almost continuously from 1796 to 1803, but neither of them succumbed to its blandishments (Bruchey 1956: 132).

REFERENCES

References to documents in the Codman collection are given as: B -, f -, for Box -, folder -. References to materials in the archives of Baring Bros. and Co. are given as: Baring Mss.

Aftalion, F. (1987), *L'économie de la Révolution française*, Paris: Hachette.
Archives Nationales, Documents from the, Paris.
Aulard, F.A. (1889), *Recueil des Actes du Comité de Salut Public*, vol. VIII. Paris: CTHS.
Bergeron, L. (1978), *Banquiers, négociants et manufacturiers parisiens du Directoire à l'Empire*, Paris: Mouton.
Bizardel, Y. (1965), 'Un acquéreur de biens nationaux: Richard Codman, de Boston', *Bulletin de la Société de l'Histoire de Paris et de l'Ile-de-France*, vol. 92, pp. 67–73.
Bizardel, Y. (1975), *The First Expatriates. Americans in Paris during the French Revolution*, New York: Holt, Rinehart and Winston.
Bizardel, Y. (1980), *Deux Yankees et trois demeueres parisiennes*, Paris: Clavrenil.
Bouchary, J. (1937) *Le marché des changes à Paris à la fin du XVIIIe siècle (1778–1800)*, Paris: CTHS.

Bruchey, S.W. (1956), *Robert Oliver, Merchant of Baltimore, 1783–1819*, Baltimore: Johns Hopkins Press.
Bruguière, M. (1969), *La Première Restauration et son budget*, Geneva: Droz.
Caron, P. (1925), *La Commission des subsistances de l'an II. Procès-verbaux et actes*, vol. I. Paris: CTHS.
Crosby, A.W. Jr. (1965), *America, Russia, Hemp, and Napoleon. American Trade with Russia and the Baltic, 1783–1812*, Columbus, Ohio: Ohio State University Press.
Hidy, R.W. (1949), *The House of Baring in American Trade and Finance. English Merchant Bankers at Work 1783–1861*, Cambridge, Mass: Harvard University Press.
Kutz, M. (1986), 'Aussenhandel und Krieg 1789–1817', in *The Emergence of a World Economy 1500–1914*, Part I, Fischer/McInnis/Schneider (eds) Wiesbaden: Franz Steiner Verlag.
Lefebvre, G. (1951), *La Révolution Française*, revised edition, Paris: Presses Universitaires de France.
McMaster, J.B. (1918), *The Life and Times of Stephen Girard, Mariner and Merchant*, 2 vols, Philadelphia: J.B. Lippincott Cy.
Morison, S.E. (1961), *The Maritime History of Massachusetts 1783–1860*, Boston/Cambridge: Houghton Mifflin/The Riverside Press.
National Archives, Department of State, *Consular Letters. Bordeaux, Hamburg*, Washington.
Pardailhé-Galabrun, A., Y. Aubry and R. Charneau (1987), 'Une contribution à l'histoire de l'habitat parisien. L'exemple de la rue d'Anjou', *Histoire, économie et société*, vol. 6, no. 4, pp. 469–84.
Rasch, A.A. (1965), 'American trade in the Baltic, 1783–1807'. *Scandinavian Economic History Review*, vol. 13, No. 1, pp. 31–64.
Redmond, E. (1981), 'The Codman collection of pictures', *Old-Time New England*, vol. 71, pp. 103–14.
Szamkiewicz, R. (1974), *Les régents et censeurs de la Banque de France nommés sous le Consulat et l'Empire*, Geneva: Droz.

PART III

THE MODERN PROCESS OF TECHNOLOGICAL AND FINANCIAL INNOVATION IN EUROPE UNTIL 1913

5 · SOME THOUGHTS ON ECONOMIC HEGEMONY: EUROPE IN THE NINETEENTH-CENTURY WORLD ECONOMY

David S. Landes

Let me begin with a disclaimer: this is not what I am doing these days. Still, it is a subject that fits directly into a larger project that I call, for want of a better working title, 'The West and the rest'. The name may be ethnocentric, but it sums up the historical problem: why are we become so rich and they so poor? It is a complex and difficult problem, as any policy-maker knows, but surely one major aspect of that divergence has been the changing economic relationship of Europe to the rest of the world.

To understand that relationship in a given period, in our case in the nineteenth century, one must, as every historian knows, look at the before and after. One must embed this particular time in time, and one should begin by considering that principal aspect and criterion of economic place, that measure of relative economic performance, namely trade – specifically the composition and volume of commodities exchanged between Europe and the rest of the world.

The general *why* of trade is well known. It rests, as Adam Smith was probably the first to point out (I say 'probably', because one never knows in matters of intellectual priority), on comparative advantage. This much misunderstood but simple idea does not refer to the advantage one economy may have over another (absolute or relative advantage), but rather to the advantage of one activity over another within a given economic unit, even for a single actor. All it says is, it pays to do what pays best.

Payment, of course, is a function of exchange. For this reason, it pays to produce more of a given commodity than one can use oneself – because one can exchange it for other things one needs and wants and that one makes or does less well.

Hence it pays to trade, even for countries whose techniques and costs are such that they have little or no relative or absolute advantage over other countries. At a minimum, they can, and will, sell (export) people (cf. the histories of the slave trade and of international migration).

Europe in the nineteenth century was the most active trading area of the world. It had long emerged from a stage when autarky was a condition imposed by circumstances and sought for the security it promised. Even in the most depressed centuries of the Middle Ages, some thready trade had persisted, and indeed an international institution such as the Church counted on its ability to maintain the supply of liturgical commodities over long distances. And from the tenth or eleventh century on improved security combined with reurbanisation and recommercialisation to restore and surpass the trade currents of antiquity in a Europe whose economy paradoxically profited from its political fragmentation.

This period of commercial rebirth and revolution was not to be taken for granted. There is a model, implicitly Smithian (the argument in Marc Bloch's *Société féodale* runs along similar lines), that says that once the burden of invasion and incursion was lifted, once internal security improved and people could get on with their natural propensity to pursue their comparative advantage, production and trade were bound to grow. And there is much truth in that.

THE ROOTS OF EUROPEAN TRADING AND DOMINANCE

Yet there was more. Europe, as region and civilisation, took a different path and diverged increasingly from the other, older, richer civilisations of the world (Islam, India, East Asia). The critical manifestation of this divergence, from an economic point of view, was the development of new technology, based in part on borrowing from outside or resurrecting long-abandoned ways, but going well beyond the inherited stock of techniques; and from a political point of view, the commitment to an active policy of expansion into and domination of the world outside expressed not only in the age-old manner of pillage and rapine but as a means of continuing exploitation.[1]

This divergence, I repeat, cannot be taken for granted as some kind of natural response to opportunity. One finds nothing like it elsewhere. Undoubtedly its roots are deep in European culture and the European psyche; and the study of this momentous transformation from ineptness to triumphant (and triumphalist) capability and from victim to aggressor is one of the greatest tasks and opportunities facing the historical profession.

By about 1500 the world had been turned upside down. The rest of the world did not know it yet, and Europeans had barely begun to comprehend the implications of the opening of the globe and of their superior power, that is, of their ability to mobilise, deliver, and use weapons of destruction. Even economic historians (than who no one is more learned and clever), hypnotised by static, would-be quantitative data on comparative income or product per head, have not understood what was going on, or rather, what had already happened. But listen to a Florentine resident of Lisbon, writing in 1499 about Portuguese intentions in the eastern seas:

> Should the King of Calicut not allow the Portuguese to trade in these countries, the Captain of the vessels is instructed to capture as many native craft as he can. In my opinion he will be able to capture as many as he chooses, for they are frail and so badly constructed that they can only sail before the wind. (Padfield 1979: 41)

Nor was it simply a question of having more manoeuvrable and seaworthy vessels. The Europeans had the firepower. The instructions to Pedro Cabral, commander of the second fleet dispatched to the eastern seas, thirty-three years old and already Admiral of the Indies, made it clear that power was in the barrel of the gun:

> If on the voyage you encounter any ships of Mecca and it appears to you that you are able to capture them you are to try to take them, but you are not to come to close quarters with them if you can avoid it, but only with your artillery are you to compel them to strike sail and launch their boats. (Padfield 1979: 43)

There is no better sign of technological superiority in arms than the ability to kill at a distance against adversaries who must close and resort to cold steel. *By 1500, Europeans could plant themselves anywhere on the face of the globe within reach of naval guns.* This advantage, moreover, could only grow: given the radical superiority of European science and applied science (their ability to learn and to know), the area of their domination was bound to widen, as it did.

The salient character of this domination, from an economic standpoint, is that it made possible and promoted a growing trade between Europe and the rest of the world. (It also made possible huge windfalls of pillage, but these are one-time gains, rapidly used up.) This trade combined what we may call normal exchange, based on comparative advantage, on the one hand, with newly created import flows of cultivated cash crops (plantation products, colonial wares) on the other. These latter commodities were often produced under compulsion, sometimes by Europeans using slave labour, sometimes by non-Europeans forced in one way or another to deliver the goods the Europeans wanted (thus the Dutch system of rice levies in Java). Compulsion of course entailed a continuing European presence or the cooperation of local intermediaries, political and economic, with European trading interests (formal and informal imperialism).

It should be emphasised that this period of European expansion occurred before that transformation of the European economy that we know as the Industrial Revolution, that is, before the gap in technologies and consequently in productivity and income became a gulf, and before the Europeans felt the special and growing resource needs of a modern industrial system. As a result, the trade relations between Europe and the rest of the world took on what *today* we might perceive as a strange character. For example one usually expects the exchange between rich and not-so-rich, powerful and weak, 'centre' and 'periphery', to be one of manufactures (normally articles of high value added) for primary products. But the Europe of the early modern period, at least before the mid-eighteenth century, produced little in the way of manufactures that might tempt markets abroad. Britain, for example, that infant workshop of the world, did its best to interest the Chinese and Indians in the woollens that sold so well at home and in older export markets; but they were ill-suited to warmer climes and scratchy by comparison with traditional silks and cottons and fine cashmeres. At that time the older civilisations of China and India were more advanced both for quality and price in such important branches as light textiles, ceramics (Europe did not know how to make porcelain until the 1720s), fine-laquered wooden objects and furniture, so that the opening of oceanic trade between Europe and Asia was followed by a surge of demand for Asian manufactures.

In addition, the Europeans bought primary products from outside – not the raw materials of industry, which Europeans already possessed in abundance and which cost in any event too much to transport over such long distances, but rather consumer goods of a special kind: condiments, tea, coffee, chocolate, tobacco, and above all sugar. These, be it noted, are all materials for ingestion; I do not say 'food' because they offer little or nothing in the way of nourishment and some of these (tobacco and sugar especially) are distinctly harmful. Why did Europeans want them? Because they couldn't help it. Because these commodities are in one way or another *habit-forming* stimulants (or in the case of tobacco, a stimulant–tranquillizer) and constitute collectively what I call the Big Fix. As a result, what began as costly novelties (sugar was originally sold by apothecaries) turned into necessities, even for the poor. (See, for example, the dietaries of English poor-houses in the late eighteenth century. People would give up bread sooner than tea with sugar.)

Together, manufactures and stimulants, these imports cost far more than Europe was able to pay for with commodity exports. The deficit was covered by bullion and specie, primarily by silver extracted from Spanish mines in the New World and exchanged for the goods and 'services' (including imperial government) of European powers. But Spanish bullion was only part of the story. Thanks to new research, we now know that for a time the Europeans were also able to settle accounts by means of a triangular exchange of Japanese metal for Chinese goods – until the Japanese decided that they could not afford the haemorrhage. And the same pattern of triangular regional exchange helped in the south Asian area, where Europeans, building on older trade flows, used Indian manufactures to pay for island spices. And on newer flows: when the drain of precious metals proved more than Europe wanted to bear, colonial levies and opium, in effect a

Table 5.1 Two estimates of annual average compound percentage rates of growth in the quantum of world trade, 1800–1913 (current prices)

Period	Hanson	Rostow
1800–20	1.8	1.5
1820–40	4.0	2.8
1840–60	5.6	4.8
1860–80	4.3	3.9
1876/80–1896/1900	3.0	3.3
1896/1900–1911/13	4.2	4.4

Note: Over the course of the nineteenth century, prices fell in response to productivity gains associated with the Industrial Revolution – along with the protracted price decline following the Black Death in the mid-fourteenth century, one of the longest deflations of this millennium. As a result, nominal prices tend to underestimate the real increase in trade.
Source: Hanson (1980: 14).

commodity transfer from India to China, eased the burden. In sum, there is more than one way to skin a cat or pay a bill, and what Europe wanted, Europe got.

THE NINETEENTH CENTURY AND NEW TECHNOLOGY

Now for the nineteenth century. The effect of the Industrial Revolution was as follows:

1. To reduce the cost of trade (both transport and transaction costs) and manufacture.
2. To enlarge the geographical scope of trade by making more places accessible at an economic price.
3. To increase effective demand (both movement along the curve and a shift of the curve to the right) on both sides – industrial and raw-materials producers.
4. To promote the search for new materials – in general a substitution of vegetable substances for animal (thus palm oil for tallow) and minerals for vegetable matter (thus mineral fertilisers for animal waste).[2]

The combined effect was a rapid increase in the volume of world trade, with Europe holding pride of place throughout the century (see Tables 5.1 and 5.2).

Table 5.2 Shares in world exports by region, 1840–1900 (per cent)

Region	1840	1860	1880	1900
UK	22	21	17	14
Other Western Europe	33	39	40	41
Other Europe	9	9	8	7
North America	12	11	14	16
Central America	5	2	2	2
South America	5	5	5	5
Northern Africa	<1	<1	1	1
Southern Africa	<1	1	1	1
Asia	12	10	10	9
Oceania	<1	3	2	2

Source: Hanson (1980: 20).

Along with these new technologies went a relatively rapid increase in population, which inevitably reinforced the effects listed above. European death rates fell and birth rates held or in some places even rose in response to better hygiene and medical care and increased earning power for children. (France was a prominent exception.)

The effects of these changes on the commodity composition of trade were as follows:

1. A shift on balance from import to export of manufactures. Britain did not wipe out the Indian hand loom cotton industry; but it effectively stopped importing and re-exporting Indian cottons (except for special prints), and it just about killed cottage spinning. (Hence Gandhi's special attention to revival of the spinning wheel as instrument and symbol of a return to older, more virtuous ways.)

2. Growing reliance on new sources for primary goods: timber from the New World; grain from the United States and Canada; minerals from South America and Malaysia. This was a development that did not really get under way until the middle of the nineteenth century and it was directly related to advances in transportation technology (both railways and marine transport). Before that, Europe made more of its own peripheral areas (thus, south Russia and the Danube basin for grain) and of increased productivity on older soils.

3. Major efforts to change the world botanical and zoological map. Such changes had obvious implications for patterns of exchange. The most spectacular example is no doubt the smuggling of the seeds of *hevea brasiliensis*, source of Para rubber, out of Brazil and the initiation of cultivation, first in India and Ceylon and then (from the 1890s), and much more importantly, in Malaya. The shift, in effect, was from the exploitation of a depletable asset (Brazilian rubber tappers, in their greed, were ready to cut down the trees to augment their immediate gains) to the cultivation of a plantation cash crop. But the transplantation of tea from China to India and Ceylon and of rice around the world was equally momentous, to say nothing of the movement of European and other animal breeds to distant continents (thus camels to the United States and Australia) (Dean 1987; Clark 1988).

Note that such revisions of the inherited botanical and zoological distribution were not to be taken for granted. There were failures as well as successes (thus the camel proved more useful in Australia than in the American southwest); some of the successful transplants resulted in ecological disaster (rabbits in Australia); and it took careful research and nurture to make much of this work (cf. the role of such experimental centres as the Botanical Gardens at Kew).

4. All of this was accompanied and favoured by a rationalisation and an ever closer integration of markets, the result of improved transport and communication technologies, wider networks of information, new organisational arrangements and more effective credit facilities (commodity exchanges, specialised discount houses, integrated commercial–deposit banks). These in turn depended on a continuous movement of Europeans to distant places, whether as settlers or as traders; and where Europeans (or at least northern and central Europeans) were not ready to go, agents and outsiders went and worked for and with them: Greeks and Levantines in Egypt and the Ottoman Empire, Lebanese and Indians in Africa, Chinese and Indians in southeast Asia and Indonesia. Note that some of these outsiders were brought in originally as labourers, but they quickly showed an interest in and talent for trade, sometimes in imitation of more fortunate countrymen.

THE TWENTIETH CENTURY AND ITS PROBLEMS

All of these tendencies continued even more strongly into the twentieth century, with two major amendments. First, the progressive exhaustion of depletable raw materials in Europe. This is true even if one defines Europe in the larger sense of the West, or the North, that is, Europe plus settler colonies (white British dominions, but also the United States). As a result, for the first time Europe (or the advanced industrial world) was obliged to draw heavily for raw materials on what we now call the Third World.

Note that what is destined to become the raw material *par excellence* of a new industrial (motor) civilisation, namely oil, goes through this same cycle beginning in the 1860s. It begins as raw material for illumination (kerosene) but achieves its real importance with the invention of the internal combustion engine and its application in automotive vehicles at the end of the century. Early needs were met largely by United States output, although lesser deposits were tapped in Rumania, Siberia, Burma and the Dutch East Indies. The Middle-East fields were known, or at least suspected, by the early twentieth century, giving rise to territorial dispute (the Mosul area) at the post-war peace conferences; but their exploitation began in the interwar period, and it was not until after the Second World War that the measure of these riches (including the Arabian fields) became known and they began to play the major role in world petroleum supply.

Second, beginning after the Second World War, an end to colonies and the power of compulsory delivery and extraction.

Note that this deliverance from dominion has rarely produced the results hoped for and indeed confidently expected, on either side (Patel 1961). Decolonisation is a complicated process, comprising (like imperialism) formal and informal aspects, economic, political, and cultural, each not necessarily keeping pace with the others. It is a vast subject that I cannot possibly do justice to here. But one element that is relevant to our present discussion is the assumption made by many ideological opponents of imperialism, especially those of the Marxist faith, that the capitalist order rested on the colonial system and that the end of colonies would logically and inexorably signal the end of capitalism – and hence was something devoutly to be wished as part of a larger teleology. Conversely, on the colonial side, the assumption prevailed that it was imperialism that accounted for the technological and economic backwardness of the colonial areas; indeed many believed that capitalism and capitalists, in a kind of betrayal of their own profit credo, had conspired to limit or eschew direct industrial investment in the colonies and had thereby withheld the secrets of modern technology. Hence the faith that once the burden was lifted, unfettered growth and prosperity would follow as the day the night.

These assumptions have been belied by history. The result is a major problem in cognitive dissonance: the world is not what it should be. How to account for this? The most popular explanation has been that colonialism has never died, has never even faded away, but rather persists in the form of neo-colonialism. So there is nothing to explain.

This alleged persistence is linked in turn to the alleged characteristics of international economic relations, some of them especially associated with the patterns and terms of trade. (As the French say, *nous revenons à nos moutons*.) In particular, the argument has been made that trade between rich countries and poor, between industrial and agrarian, advanced and 'backward' (a dirty word now) is intrinsically unequal, as shown first by the high variability of prices for primary products against the relative stability of those for manufactures, and secondly by allegedly persistently deteriorating terms of trade for primary producers. (Note that these were not arguments made in the nineteenth century, when people had a very good conscience about these things. These criticisms – charges – have emerged in our time as a response to new political and ideological challenges, but they have been carried back in time by a number of scholars, especially those of the centre-periphery and dependency schools.)

My reaction to this bill of indictment is that it is both true and not true. It is true above all about intentions: the incorporation of overseas markets into the world economic system did indeed aim at securing cheap and reliable supplies of raw materials and at securing an outlet for domestic products. It is much less true in its assessment of effects and consequently of significance. Here I would make several observations:

1. The deteriorating-terms-of-trade argument is nonsense. Not only is there no such thing in fact or logic as monotonically moving terms of trade between countries, but one could make a good case for the thesis that, thanks to superior gains in productivity in the secondary sector, terms have moved on balance, over the decades, in favour of buyers of manufactures.

2. There is nothing in the exchange of primary products for manufactures that entails or imposes dependency. Everything depends on how one uses the income. This raises the question of the vent-for-surplus argument (staples theory). This model, developed in Canada (by Harold Innes) to explain the course of Canadian growth in terms of an export sequence of primary products (fur, timber, grain) has also been applied with some success to a number of other expanding frontier societies (the United States – tobacco, cotton, wheat; Australia – wool, wheat, meat; Argentina – hides, wool, meat, wheat). It also works pretty well for some older producers of raw materials and semi-finished manufactures: Sweden (timber, pig and wrought iron, iron ore); and should have worked better in India (cottons, tea, raw cotton, and again cotton yarn and fabrics, the second time machine-made). (See pages 35–8 for more information on the theory.)

Why the model seems to have worked so badly in the new countries of the post-Second World War era to the point of making primary-product exports synonymous with dependency and backwardness, is a long story. My own sense is that, other things equal, it is a good thing to be able to export large quantities of primary products where their production accords with comparative advantage. Where such a strategy does not pay off in terms of economic growth, the question one should ask is, what is it that prevents the achievement of comparable efficiencies in the secondary sector? Here trade theory alone will not provide an answer, and one must learn something about such exogenous considerations as the quality of knowledge and human capital, social and cultural institutions and values, and public policy and order.

3. Rational market behaviour becomes especially problematic in the case of depletable assets. There the seller has the special problem of assessing on a continuing basis the future value of a diminishing stock. Some people have argued that it is a mistake, for example, for oil producers to sell oil to today's industrial

nations. Better to sit on it, they say, and use it as needed at home; or to sell it at some later date when it will be worth that much more. They regard such commodity flows as a form of pillage, a drain on the patrimony of the poor.

Yet when one thinks upon it, it is the advanced industrial countries that have given these resources their value, that have in effect created the patrimony. (Oil before kerosene lamps and automobiles was a nasty form of natural pollution.) What's more, it is not always clear what the optimum price and market strategy is. Hold back on a given raw material, raise the price high, and you give a correspondingly strong incentive to the search for a substitute.

And who is to say that a given primary product is irreplaceable? The story of Brazilian rubber could serve as a warning, as Mexico was to learn a century later. The Mexicans built an impressive export pharmaceutical industry after the Second World War on their monopoly of the best natural source of steroid hormones, the roots of the barbasco plant. The major producer was Syntex, a Mexican firm, which was joined by a number of subsidiaries of transnationals which sent quantities of the finished product to their parent companies.

These multinationals were accused of a multitude of sins: tax evasion by transfer pricing (setting the value of shipments too low), exploitation of Mexican peasant barbasco gatherers, failure to pay monopoly rents for this Mexican national resource, export of profits to the home country or, worse yet, to such tax havens as Puerto Rico, Panama and the Bahamas. So in 1975 the Mexican government created a state-owned enterprise named Proquivemex and set about squeezing both the domestic firms and the multinationals with a view to shifting more of the gains to the peasants of the barbasco-growing areas; which made just about everybody in the manufacturing branch unhappy. The locals protested and the foreign-based corporations had the last say, primarily because of technological superiority: what they could not get, they could learn to make, and the Mexican industry needed their products (Gereffi 1983: ch. II).

4. Colonialism brought with it exploitation and neglect, to say nothing of what was probably its most painful and enduring aspect: the spiritual and cultural humiliation of the subject peoples. On the other hand, it gave rise to a two-way process of action and

reaction, and the experience has been for most colonial countries a school in the techniques and values and expectations (in particular, the revolutionary notion that things can be better) of their European masters. Marx understood this very well; his followers have not. While denouncing the abuses of British power in India, he argued that this was the only way to bring this immobile, petrified society into the modern industrial world – better to be ruled by Europe than not to be noticed at all.

5. All exchange relations link stronger and weaker parties. But the relative power and terms of any given transaction are uncertain *ex ante* and vary with circumstances. If they were not, we would have a world in which the rich inevitably got richer and the poor poorer, and where, with experience, no voluntary transactions were possible. But we know that the rank order of rich and poor changes over time, that some become rich and vice versa; also that voluntary exchange continues. Why some of the weak and poor have done better than others remains to be elucidated. If the reasons were obvious, the problem of inequality would have long since been solved.

CONCLUSION

In sum, the logic of anti-trade arguments is their own negation. Things do not get ever worse. Trade may be unequal, but it is not always disadvantageous. Down today may be up tomorrow, and vice versa. Other things being equal, it not only pays to trade; it is more than ever the road to riches. It is also the measure of technological maturity. The commercial pre-eminence of nineteenth-century Europe was not the expression of superior power but of superior performance. The continued success of European producers in world markets, as well as the successful entry of new players, reflects similar considerations: the economic and political map may change, but the pay off to know-how remains.

The implications for practice and policy are clear. The laments of the anti-colonialist are a source of consolation and a way of cultivating guilt as a political instrument. It is always easier to blame someone else for one's misfortunes. But these complaints are no substitute for performance, rather an impediment; so that even if they were true, it would be better to forget them. They just get in the way.

NOTES

1. On the technological creativity of the European Middle Ages, the best sources are the writings of Lynn White, Jr, beginning with a truly seminal article in *Speculum* in 1939, and of Jean Gimpel. See his *The Medieval Machine: The Industrial Revolution of the Middle Ages* (New York: Penguin, 1977). There are numerous historians who in my opinion have best grasped the character and significance of a development that an earlier generation of historians could not have conceived of (they thought of the Middle Ages as a period of intellectual and technological retreat), and that changed the course of world history. The story of the most important of these innovations has now been incorporated into the mainstream of European historiography, but one of the most powerful and yet most ignored because so banal and apparently trivial is the invention of spectacles. White comments on this event and notes that by testimony of a grateful contemporary, we can date it to the beginning of the thirteenth century. But even White does not fully realise the significance of a device that effectively doubled the working lives of those craftsmen and clerks who needed help with reading and close work from about the age of forty, when for purely biological reasons the human eye becomes increasingly presbyopic. Note, moreover, that even in an age of primitive optical technique, corrective lenses for the far-sighted need far less precision than those that correct for myopia. The near-sighted cannot exchange spectacles as the far-sighted can, to the point of being able to buy them from trays in five-and-dime stores. Spectacles remained a European monopoly for 500 years.
2. Guano is a special case of the persistent importance of animal matter, though not for long, since it was essentially a depletable resource. Guano is simply bird droppings, and a conjunction of favourable natural circumstances had over the centuries led to the accumulation of deposits many metres deep on a few small islands off the Pacific coast of South America. Their discovery gave rise in the mid-nineteenth century to a kind of fertiliser rush, sending hundreds of vessels loaded with guano to European and American ports, where it was a major ingredient of the highly commercial farming of that era. The biggest buyer was Britain, which took almost 300,000 tonnes in 1855; the United States was far behind in second place with 65,000 tonnes. See the article 'Engrais' in the *Dictionnaire universel théorique et pratique du commerce et de la navigation* (Paris: Guillaumin, 1859), I, p. 1097.

REFERENCES

Clark, Arthur (1988), 'Camels down under', *Aramco World*, vol. 39, pp. 16–23.
Dean, Warren (1987): *Brazil and the Struggle for Rubber: A Study in*

Environmental History, New York/Cambridge: Cambridge University Press

Dictionnaire universel théorique et pratique du commerce et de la navigation (1859), vol. I, Paris: Guillaumin.

Gereffi, Gary (1983), *The Pharmaceutical Industry and Dependency in the Third World*, Princeton: Princeton University Press.

Gimpel, Jean (1977), *The Medieval Machine: The Industrial Revolution of the Middle Ages*, New York: Penguin.

Hanson, John R., II (1980), *Trade in Transition: Exports from the Third World, 1840–1900*, New York: Academic Press.

Padfield, Peter (1979), *Tide of Empires: Decisive Naval Campaigns in the Rise of the West*, London: Routledge & Kegan Paul.

Patel, S.J. (1961), 'Rates of industrial growth in the last century, 1860–1958', *Economic Development and Cultural Change*, vol. 9, pp. 316–30.

6 · BRITISH COAL ON CONTINENTAL MARKETS, 1850–1913

Rainer Fremdling

INTRODUCTION

The turning from natural sources of power (water and wind) and vegetal fuels (chiefly wood) towards mineral resources (chiefly hard coal) constituted a central element of early industrialisation. Britain's leading role in industrialising her economy largely depended on the early use of hard coal as primary energy in various production processes. Several regions in continental Europe, which industrialised later, also based their development on locally available coal resources, e.g. Wallonie and the Ruhr. But the success of industrialisation during the nineteenth century was not necessarily dependent on the exploitation of local mineral fuel. On the one hand traditional energy sources like water power proved sufficient for early industrialisation (as in Switzerland), and on the other hand hard coal could be transported and stored. Thus, in regions of northern Germany, the Netherlands, or large parts of France a local lack of mineral fuel deposits could be compensated for.[1]

There existed a potentially high and growing demand for mineral fuel in regions far from the coalfields but the major obstacle to meeting this demand was high transportation costs. Coal is a bulky commodity with a low value in relation to its weight. Therefore underdeveloped transportation systems narrowly limited the market areas for coal.[2] After ocean freight rates had declined dramatically in the second half of the nineteenth century, coal was sold

For an extended version of this chapter see Fremdling (1989).

world-wide on a massive scale. This situation continued for a long time so that shortly before the First World War coal had become one of the most important commodities in international trade, surpassed only by raw cotton and grain. During the second half of the nineteenth century freight rates for coal on canals, rivers and especially on railways likewise declined drastically, thereby making the natural distance to the regions far away from the coalfields economically less significant. Thus, coal producers were capable of widening their markets. The spatial expansion led to overlapping markets for different coalfields and hence competition arose among mining areas, which in former times had been pretty isolated. This competition became highly intensive in the Netherlands and northern parts of Germany. Although before the First World War Germany had emerged as the second largest exporter of coal after Britain, she was at the same time one of the foremost importers of coal as well.[3] In northern Germany not only domestic coal-producing regions competed against each other but also foreign suppliers, namely British. Before analysing the competition in specific market areas for coal, I will sketch the importance and direction of British coal exports in general.

BRITISH COAL EXPORTS

During the nineteenth century Britain's coal exports[4] grew at a faster rate than her coal output. According to the recent estimate by Church, British output increased from 63.5 million tons[5] of coal in 1850 to 292.1 million tons in 1913,[6] During the same years exports first comprised little more than 4 million tons and finally nearly 100 million tons. Whereas in 1855 exports (7.5 per cent) had clearly stayed behind the two most important indigenous consumers of coal, namely the iron and steel industry (24.9 per cent) and domestic fuel (20.9 per cent), in 1913 exports outstripped both of them, holding 34.1 per cent as against 11.6 per cent and 12.2 per cent respectively. Coal exports also contributed overproportionally to the growth of the entire British foreign trade. In the total domestic export value, coal had comprised just 1.8 per cent in 1850 but increased to 10.2 per cent in 1913.[7] A major cause for the enormous growth of British coal exports lay in decreasing ocean freight rates.

Table 6.1 Freight rates for coal shipments from Britain[a], 1850–1913 (shillings per ton)

Years	To Hamburg/Le Havre	To Danzig	To Bordeaux	To Genoa	To South America
1850–4	9.7	10.3	11.8	19.4	—
1855–9	10.0	11.7	14.7	26.6	52.0
1860–4	9.2	10.3	14.0	23.6	36.8
1865–9	8.3	9.3	12.6	19.5	32.6
1870–4	8.7	9.2	10.5	17.2	30.0
1875–9	7.3	9.1	9.3	13.9	23.4
1880–4	6.3	8.3	7.8	12.8	23.3
1885–9	4.8	5.9	6.4	10.3	22.4
1890–4	4.7	4.8	4.8	7.5	16.8
1895–9	4.4	4.4	4.6	8.0	13.8
1900–4	4.3	4.8	4.3	7.0	11.8
1905–9	3.8	4.4	4.1	6.5	11.2
1910–13	4.3	5.4	5.3	8.8	17.1

[a] Various ports.
Source: (Harley 1986: 9).

Harley systematically compiled freight rates of coal shipment covering a longer period (see Table 6.1). Starting before the technically far-reaching changes in ocean shipping gained momentum, Harley's data thus include the decisive transition from the wooden sailing vessel to the iron steamer. Harley registers no falling trend in the overall level of freight rates before the 1860s. Thereafter the rates declined dramatically until the early 1890s, in subsequent years they fell rather moderately and shortly before the First World War they increased again. The development of coal freight rates during the nineteenth century differs from North's statement that general ocean freight rates already showed a downward trend in the first half of the nineteenth century.[8]

The steep fall in freight rates from the 1860s was due to innovations which improved the economic performance of steamers.[9] Modern iron steamers had been in use for decades, but less economically than sailing vessels. Steamers lagged behind because for a long time they had to rely on steam engines, which consumed a considerable amount of coal. This had two disadvantages: first, the running costs were high and second, the coal bunkered aboard closely limited the capacity of the shipload. Not before the 1860s did the compound engine (later the triple-expansion engine and further improvements) become standard equipment of steamships. These fuel-saving devices reduced the consumption of coal considerably. Harley shows that in 1855 five pounds of coal were necessary to generate one horsepower for one hour and in 1890 less than two pounds sufficed to generate the same power (Harley 1971: 220). The fuel-saving effect directly lowered the running costs and indirectly increased the freight-earning capacity, which was further enlarged through the smaller dimensions of the improved steam engines.

The steamship itself was decisive in increasing British coal exports. Through forward linkage effects, i.e. decreasing freight rates (caused by the very steamship), the sale of British coal was promoted on foreign markets. To reach these markets powerful backward linkage effects were induced, because this means of transportation itself consumed coal. Nearly one third of the coal leaving Great Britain on the sea was used for running sea shipment.[10]

It is often argued that the coal freight rates could only be so low because they were based on a mixed calculation. And the low rates alone should have guaranteed Britain's merchant fleet the use of its otherwise excessive capacity for return freight. Precisely this argument is examined by Harley with the following conclusion:[11] the great success of the British merchant fleet in non-European trade was not even partly due to coal transportation. The shipment of coal into non-European regions was comparatively very small.[12] Table 6.2 confirms that this trade was concentrated on Europe.

According to Harley, the traffic with foreign North Sea and Channel ports was carried out with special ships, which had to earn their money alone from coal transportation. A different case, however, was the shipment to Scandinavia and to the Baltic Sea: as transportation of timber formed the major source of income, the return freight for coal merely had to defray marginal costs. In the Mediterranean area the coal freights covered the bulk of the receipts, with grain transported as return cargo not having to bear the entire costs of the back and forth journey. In any case it might be stated that the tendency towards downward and finally low freight rates made British coal more and more competitive on foreign markets. In particular so since (disregarding cyclical fluctuations) British coal prices at the pit mouth rather stagnated from the 1850s to the 1880s and increased[13] even thereafter.

How were the British coal exports distributed among the receiv-

Table 6.2 British exports of hard coal, 1853–1913, (five-year averages in per cent)

Country/region	1853–7	1858–62	1863–7	1868–72	1873–7	1878–82	1883–7	1888–92	1893–7	1898–02	1903–7	1908–12/13
Russia	3.1	5.0	5.6	6.5	6.3	7.5	6.1	5.3	5.5	6.4	5.2	6.0
Sweden/Norway	4.2	4.4	4.5	5.2	7.1	7.0	7.4	8.0	9.1	10.0	9.4	9.5
Denmark	7.9	6.5	5.8	5.6	5.0	4.9	5.0	4.8	5.0	5.0	4.8	4.5
Germany	15.5	15.7	14.5	15.2	14.3	12.0	11.6	12.5	13.2	13.3	14.7	14.0
Netherlands	3.9	3.9	2.6	3.3	3.2	2.5	1.5	1.7	1.8	2.8	3.8	3.3
Belgium	0.4	0.7	0.7	1.0	2.0	1.4	1.3	1.5	1.0	1.7	1.9	2.6
France	19.7	19.3	18.3	17.8	19.1	19.6	18.5	16.5	15.8	17.3	15.7	16.3
Portugal/Azores/Madeira	1.8	1.5	1.7	1.6	1.8	1.8	1.8	2.0	1.9	1.9	1.9	1.8
Spain/Canary Islands	3.6	5.2	4.9	4.0	4.0	4.3	4.8	5.6	5.8	5.2	4.8	4.6
Italy	2.4	4.2	5.8	6.0	6.9	8.2	11.1	12.2	13.0	12.7	13.6	14.0
Austria	1.4	1.3	0.7	0.3	0.5	0.3	0.3	0.3	0.6	0.5	1.2	1.5
Rest of Europe	6.3	4.6	4.3	3.3	4.0	5.6	5.9	5.2	4.3	3.5	3.0	3.0
Total Europe	70.2	72.5	69.6	69.7	74.3	75.0	75.3	75.8	76.9	80.4	80.0	81.0
Egypt	1.2	1.4	3.4	3.6	3.9	3.8	4.9	5.4	5.1	4.8	4.7	4.3
Rest of Africa	1.1	0.8	1.5	0.1	0.6	2.1	2.1	2.7	3.2	3.7	3.1	2.7
Turkey	5.1	2.6	2.1	2.3	1.8	1.6	1.5	1.5	1.5	1.0	0.9	0.7
India	3.2	3.0	4.5	3.9	4.8	5.1	5.4	4.3	3.2	1.5	1.1	0.8
Rest of Asia	1.7	2.1	2.6	1.1	1.7	1.7	1.4	1.2	1.1	1.0	1.1	0.5
USA	3.8	4.2	2.1	1.0	0.9	1.2	1.0	0.6	0.5	0.6	0.6	0.0
Canada	1.9	2.0	2.0	1.8	1.2	0.9	0.5	0.3	0.3	0.2	0.2	0.1
Central America	4.4	4.2	5.1	3.6	3.1	2.8	1.9	1.2	1.0	0.4	0.5	0.2
Chile	1.0	0.8	1.1	1.0	1.3	1.0	0.6	0.8	0.9	0.7	0.9	1.0
Brazil	1.8	2.0	2.2	2.5	2.5	2.0	2.0	2.4	2.6	2.1	2.1	2.4
La Plata Region	0.0	0.6	1.2	1.8	1.2	1.3	2.3	3.0	3.4	3.3	4.6	6.0
Rest of South America	0.3	0.2	0.6	0.8	0.8	0.8	0.5	0.3	0.2	0.1	0.1	0.0
Total America	13.2	14.1	14.3	12.5	11.1	10.0	8.9	8.7	8.9	7.4	8.9	9.8
Australia, New Zealand, Pacific Islands	0.9	0.5	0.3	0.0	0.0	0.0	0.0	0.0	0.0	0.0	0.0	0.0
Other countries	3.5	3.0	1.8	6.8	1.7	0.7	0.6	0.4	0.1	0.0	0.2	0.2
Total (tonnes)	5,032,045	7,261,365	9,177,838	11,553,735	14,226,455	17,818,577	22,780,126	28,534,745	32,428,068	41,731,913	52,404,256	66,258,503

Source: Computed from yearly data in the British foreign trade statistics; see Annual Statement.

ing countries or regions? The regional distribution of exports is determined by the receiving port. Table 6.2 shows the already mentioned dominance of European customers. Between 1853 and 1913 this preponderance even increased: initially the European share made up about 70 per cent, during the 1870s and around 1900 it took two further upward batches of 5 percentage points and finally Europe got about 80 per cent of all British coal exports. Outside of Europe large amounts were sent to Egypt, which was due to the opening of the Suez Canal in 1869. This canal helped to diffuse the innovation of steamships to the Far East. It seems likely that coal exports to the rest of Africa mainly served to supply bunker stations. Initially, i.e. in 1853–7, Turkey was an important customer, but the then decreasing export shares seem to indicate an economic stagnation in this area. India took a high level until the 1880s, but, like the rest of Africa, it received rather modest shares in the following decades. The local demand was increasingly met by supplies of newly explored coal mines in the regions themselves. The same applies to South Africa and Australia. Until the 1860s the shares of North America are surprisingly high, but through improved transportation systems there the wealthy indigenous coal resources could soon better be distributed to other North American regions. As in Latin America, rich coal basins had not been explored or exploited before the First World War and British coal could then gain important sales in spite of high transportation costs.

The significance of single countries in Europe and the shifting export ratios over time actually require a differentiated analysis. One might expect countries poorly endowed with coal resources but blessed with a long coast line to have offered an ideal sales market for British coal. Denmark, with her constantly high shares, lends strong support to this. But the shares of Sweden, Norway and above all Italy jumped too high to be fully explained by this hypothesis. The demand for coal depended on the stage of development, i.e. the timing of entering into industrialisation, which mainly was characterised by applying coal-consuming techniques. Hence the shares of British coal exports to the various European countries shifted considerably.[14] France and the Netherlands, serving as contrasting examples of coal imports from Britain, are dealt with separately. The high Russian and the huge German shares point to a further factor of influence. Both Russia and

Germany possessed enormous indigenous coal resources. But for a long time it was cheaper for locations near the coast to import British coal than to rely on domestic supplies. So these British sales were protected against domestic competition by high costs for overland transportation.

Finally a remark on quality differences concerning coal is in order. Quality had a great influence on the market chances of this commodity. Coal is not at all a homogeneous product, but rather a general term. Different coal qualities influenced considerably the spatial dimension of sales markets within certain pricing marges independent of other causes. The British perspective alone is not sufficient to explain the direction and significance of British coal exports. Characteristics of the receiving markets have to be considered as well, which is attempted for France, the Netherlands and northern Germany.

FRANCE

Table 6.2 proves France to have been the major customer of British hard-coal exports from the middle of the nineteenth century until 1913. In the west and southwest of France it was much cheaper to import coal from Britain than to buy it from indigenous coalfields.[15] In the long run, British coal exports to France gained higher market shares than those of Belgium and Germany, rising from 20 to 25 per cent in the middle of the nineteenth century to half of all French coal imports in 1913. Whereas British coal had initially made up roughly 10 per cent of the domestic consumption, it comprised nearly 20 per cent of it shortly before the First World War (see Table 6.3). Crouzet marks off two different stages in the position of British coal on the French market. After rapid gains in the 1830s the market share remained rather stable until 1865 (first stage) followed by large increases (second stage). There are several reasons for the development during the second stage: since the 1870s British coal prices declined as well as the rates of freight across the Channel. Ceding Alsace-Lorraine to Germany, France underwent drastic changes in her foreign trade balance on coal. Belgian coal exports to France stagnated relatively from 1866 onwards and declined after 1883. Coal from Belgium made up the following percentages of total French coal imports: 1834 83 per

Table 6.3 French imports of British coal, 1841–1913 (five-year averages)

Years	Total (1,000 tonnes)	As % share of total imports	of total consumption
1841–5	476	24	9
1846–50	576	24	8
1851–5	702	19	7
1856–60	1,236	22	9
1861–5	1,392	21	8
1866–70	1,854	24	9
1871–5	2,240	30	10
1876–80	3,012	35	12
1881–5	4,032	37	14
1886–90	4,156	40	13
1891–5	4,805	42	13
1896–1900	6,232	48	16
1901–5	7,181	49	15
1906–10	10,235	53	19
1911–13	11,107	49	18

Source: Crouzet (1966: 178).

cent, 1866 60 per cent, 1889 50 per cent, 1901 36 per cent, 1913 20 per cent. The Belgian coal could not fully compete with the coal from the new French mines in the *départements* Nord and Pas-de-Calais. This indigenous coal penetrated mainly into the traditional Belgian market in France leaving the British unmolested. Since the July-Monarchy Britain had gained more and more former Belgian sales areas. Initially she supplied the French Atlantic ports, and under the Second Empire Basse-Seine, Calais and Boulogne supervened.

During the last third of the nineteenth century British and Belgian sales areas barely continued to overlap, with the important exception of the Paris region. But it was not before 1894 that British coal finally exceeded Belgian coal on the French market. Another reason for the partial retreat of Belgian coal from the French market was probably the rapid industrial development in Belgium itself. It even forced Belgium to import German and partly British coal. After 1901 the British market share in France grew less because of the increase of German exports. The German market share in France increased from 12 per cent in 1900 to 27 per cent in 1913. Most of the German coal designed for the metal industry in Lorraine did not compete with British coal in its sales areas directly, but the dynamic price and marketing policy of the Rheinisch–Westfälische Kohlensyndikat produced a successful coal export trade via the Rhine and Rotterdam. In the end German coal even arrived at French ports such as Boulogne, Rouen, Saint-Nazaire, la Rochelle and Bayon. Coal from Germany sometimes held considerable shares in certain coastal *départements*, but by and large Crouzet concludes that the British market position was never seriously undermined by German coal exports to France.

One the one hand, Crouzet states that British coal supported the industrial development in, for instance, Basse-Seine and Basse-Loire because it was cheaper there than French coal. On the other hand, transportation costs made imported British coal significantly dearer than on the other side of the Channel and than French coal in the mining districts themselves. This may partly explain why vast regions, in spite of importing British coal, succeeded less well in industrializing themselves.

THE NETHERLANDS

The timing and nature of the Dutch economic development during the nineteenth century still remains rather obscure. Its periodisation depends on statistical information on the basic economic data, which are not yet sufficient for a generally accepted quantitative framework. The whole discussion has been further confused by the use of different concepts of periodisation: Brugmans places the *Industriële Revolutie* between 1850 and 1870, de Jonge identifies the Dutch *take-off* from 1890 or 1895 to 1910, and van Zanden places the beginning of the process of *moderne economische groei* in the years between 1850 and 1880. In a broader study Maddison includes the Netherlands in the group of countries which were involved in a process of *substantial and sustained growth* (measured in gross domestic product per capita) since 1820 (Brugmans 1983: 201ff.; de Jonge 1976: 236ff., 343ff.; van Zanden 1987: 64ff.; Maddison 1982: 43ff., 166).

Although the evidence is rather inconclusive, most scholars agree on labelling the Netherlands as a late-comer concerning an important part of economic development, namely industrialisation. And this retarded industrialisation has often been explained by the lack of domestic sources of raw materials such as hard coal.[16] It is true that the exploitation of domestic coalfields in Limburg did not take off earlier than the turn of the twentieth century. Before the First World War the rapidly expanding domestic supply of hard coal hardly covered one fifth of domestic consumption (Bos 1978: 111). The high consumption of imported coal, however, severely weakens the argument that Dutch industrialisation should have been hindered by lack of domestic raw material supplies. Even before the railway age the Netherlands had a highly developed system of inland water transportation (rivers and canals) and could thus draw on coal supplies from neighbouring countries. With regard to the transportation costs for coal, major Dutch cities were in a better location than Berlin, for example, which industrialised early and very rapidly during the nineteenth century.[17] Thus an explanation of the retarded industrialisation in the Netherlands should not take the lack of domestically available coal resources into account. Rather, the argument should be reversed to ask why the Netherlands did not make more use of foreign coal supplies than they actually did. But as speculation on this doubtlessly useful question extends beyond the scope of this chapter, I will restrict myself to the facts on coal supplies to the Netherlands.

As shown by the figures in Table 6.2 the Netherlands were a rather moderate importer of *British* coal, though not insignificant for British exporters. However, they could not dominate this nearby market because Ruhr coal had such easy access to the Dutch market (see Table 6.4). It is difficult to explain long-term trends of the Dutch coal market. Production prices at the pit-mouths abroad only had influence on short-term fluctuations of the different market shares (Bos 1978: 123). The crucial points were transportation and related costs. Although one might suppose water transport to be cheaper than railway transport, there were considerable advantages for the railways. From Duisburg or Ruhrort to Rotterdam shipping was always cheaper, but this was not the case with haulage to Amsterdam. Here the costs were forced up by the transportation from the coalmine to the Rhine. As the river Ruhr was hardly navigable for large coalships, railways had to transport the coal from the mines to the Rhine harbours. Furthermore, with differential tariffs set very high for

Table 6.4 Imports (including transit trade) of hard coal into the Netherlands, 1870–1914 (five-year averages)

Years	Total (1,000 tonnes)	From Great Britain (%)	From Belgium (%)	From Germany (%)
1870–4	2,091	21.7	18.5	59.7
1875–9	2,943	15.2	10.5	74.2
1880–4	4,346	10.7	6.7	82.5
1885–9	4,945	7.1	8.0	84.9
1890–4	5,803	9.2	8.2	82.4
1895–9	7,277	12.4	9.7	77.9
1900–4	10,141	11.1	7.3	81.0
1905–9	14,825	17.3	6.1	76.4
1910–4	22,278	9.3	3.0	86.7

Source: Computed from Bos (1978: 362f).

short haulage distances, the railway favoured direct transportation to the Netherlands by rail.[18] Loss of quality through trans-shipping and inadequate facilities for shipment on waterways helped railways maintain an advantage over waterway transportation from the Ruhr to the Netherlands. But this changed after the turn of the century: freight rates on railways did not go down although those on waterways did. Trans-shipping facilities in Rotterdam were much improved and larger vessels lowered transportation costs as well. As a consequence much more coal was brought to the Netherlands by waterway (Nusteling 1974: 288). To sum up, Belgium played a minor role in the Dutch coal market. Since production there could not even meet the internal demand, Belgium herself had to import large quantities (Bos 1978: 119). The dominance of Ruhr coal on the Dutch market was mainly due to lower transportation costs as compared with those of coal from British mines. After losing its initially strong position, British coal by and large served as nothing more than a stopgap for the Dutch market.[19]

NORTHERN GERMANY

In order to explain the development of output and the changing position of foreign coal in Germany a number of influences have to be taken into account. Besides supply side factors, which determined the cost and price levels within the mining districts, there were demand side factors. In the mining regions output was increasing to meet the demands of coal-consuming industries, of which the iron and steel industry was by far the most important (Holtfrerich 1973: 139ff.; Krengel 1983: 131ff.). The close connection between local coal-consuming industries only partly explains the demand-induced growth of output and the changing importance of particular mining districts over time. In addition, sales opportunities outside these areas should be analysed. And these changed fundamentally after the late 1850s when drastically cheapened overland transportation allowed massive coal sales to regions far away from mining areas. Freight rates on rivers and canals fell from the middle of the nineteenth century up to the First World War because of pressure from competing railways and improvements in shipbuilding and the infrastructure in general. This tendency was enhanced by the abolition of river tolls in the 1860s. Until about 1880 railways lowered their freight rates faster than inland waterways, but the position then changed so that by the beginning of the twentieth century freight rates for bulky commodities on water were about half those of the railways (Huber 1978: 161ff.).

By way of example, three important markets are chosen to demonstrate the competition among different German and foreign suppliers of coal. These are Hamburg, Magdeburg and Berlin.

Hamburg

Hamburg was by far the most important port of entry for British coal into the German market. This was not only due to local consumption but also to the fact that British coal was transloaded there and shipped to other German destinations on the river Elbe and her tributaries. Between 1858 and 1870 the British export statistics kept separate figures for Hamburg. Of all British coal exports to German ports Hamburg clearly received more than 40 per cent.[20] Until the 1870s German coal had hardly any chance on the Hamburg market (Heidmann 1897: 5). At that time British coal came mainly from Newcastle or Cardiff. In the beginning it was transported on sailing vessels, which were rapidly replaced by modern steamships from the 1860s.

Various quantitative evidence reveals an overwhelming preponderance of British coal (Königlich Preussisches Ministerium 1860: 29; 1862: 43; 1865: 54; 1871: 41; 1881: 46) and in the years from 1851 to 1865 the proportion of non-British coal in Hamburg was below 1 per cent. However, this preponderance of British coal fell in the middle of the 1870s when special tariffs on the railway allowed increasing quantities of Westphalian coal to reach Hamburg. It became the place for competition between different mining areas and for different transportion systems as well. British coal came as usual by ship, Ruhr coal by railway. By the 1880s the British market share had shrunk considerably, and some British suppliers were nearly driven out of the market entirely. In the middle of the 1890s bituminous coal, for example, which formerly was supplied from South Wales, now came almost exclusively from Westphalia. In 1890 Westphalian colliery owners even established their own marketing organisation for trade in Hamburg (*Entwickelung* 1904: 85ff.). Freight rates for special trains were still dropping or had stabilised on a low level, but also ocean freight rates had declined considerably (see Table 6.1). After the turn of the century freight rates shifted again to the advantage of British suppliers on the Hamburg market (Zentgraf 1913: 495f.). Furthermore, the price policy of the Rheinisch-Westfälische Kohlensyndikat helped British coal sales to stabilise on the rapidly expanding Hamburg market in the early twentieth century (Zentgraf 1913: 500) and Table 6.5 clearly shows that Britain remained the major supplier of coal with market shares fluctuating at around 60 per cent. About one third of Hamburg's coal imports were transloaded to be passed on, mainly to the Berlin region.

Magdeburg

Conveniently situated on the river Elbe, Magdeburg moreover was connected with railway trunk lines to all four points of the compass as early as 1847. By then the high price of wood had forced industry and households to use mainly brown and hard coal as fuel (Voss 1904: 13). In particular the processing of sugar-beet consumed much fuel, so Magdeburg rapidly became one of the major coal-consuming places outside the mining areas (Königlich Preussisches Ministerium 1860: 13ff.). Nearby brown coal collieries competed against distant suppliers of German, British and Bohemian coal but around 1850 this local brown coal was still

Table 6.5 Coal imports into Hamburg, 1894–1911

Year	British (%)	German (%)	Total (1,000 tonnes)
1894	58.2	41.8	2,853
1895	56.5	43.5	2,981
1896	56.0	44.0	3,208
1897	59.8	40.2	3,608
1898	55.4	44.6	3,707
1899	59.5	40.5	4,066
1900	65.3	34.6	4,622
1901	60.8	38.9	4,430
1902	61.0	38.8	4,577
1903	62.1	37.9	4,942
1904	59.0	41.0	4,889
1905	64.3	35.7	5,525
1906	61.8	38.2	6,070
1907	66.9	33.1	7,417
1908	63.1	36.9	7,842
1909	65.9	34.1	7,958
1910	61.9	38.1	8,400
1911	59.4	40.6	7,973

Notes: Between 1900 and 1902 small quantities of American coal reached Hamburg. For the overlapping years (1900–3) Zentgraf gives slightly different figures.
Sources: 1894–1903, *Parliamentary Papers*, vol. 16, 1905: 884; 1904–11, Zentgraf (1913: 502).

solely used by sugar-beet factories located close to the collieries. However, brown coal was regarded as inferior and as it was not processed into compact patent fuel high overland transportation costs further confined its market to the locality. Therefore, hard coal from Britain and Saxony as well as brown coal from Bohemia was transported to Magdeburg on ships. To weaken the dependency on foreign coal, businessmen in Magdeburg were eager to get Prussian coal from Westphalia. In 1849 they complained about the *foreign* Hanoverian state railway not being willing to agree on special low tariffs (Voss 1904: 16). That was grist to the mills of the Westphalian colliery owners and in a pamphlet dated 1858 they recommended increased sales outside the mining area as the only remedy for the expected overproduction of coal. They considered Magdeburg the most important sales market in the east – a place where they had not yet sold any coal (*Absatz* 1858: 10ff.).

Although the *Einpfennigtarif* (a special low railway fare) was

Table 6.6 Coal imports into Magdeburg, 1860–81 (per cent)

Type of coal	1860	1862	1865	1871	1881
British hard coal	25.7	17.4	5.7	18.1	1.0
Westphalian hard coal	6.3	18.2	35.6	20.9	19.9
Bohemian brown coal	24.5	19.9	15.8	26.3	44.8
Local brown coal	34.2	36.5	38.4	27.4	31.1
Saxon hard coal	8.2	6.3	3.7	5.5	1.4
Bohemian hard coal	1.1	1.4	0.3	–	–
Upper Silesian hard coal	–	0.3	0.4	0.6	0.4
Lower Silesian hard coal	–	–	–	–	0.0
Hanoverian hard coal	–	–	–	0.3	1.4
Local hard coal	–	–	–	0.9	–
Total (1,000 tonnes)	395.1	408.7	544.4	622.4	945.1

Source: Königlich Preussisches Ministerium (1860: 25f.; 1862: 38; 1865; 45f.; 1871: 37f.; 1881: 41).

actually not introduced on this connection until 1862, considerable quantities of Ruhr coal were already sold there in 1860 and 1861. The then high price of British coal aided these sales, for which the coal was transported on special trains. But as Westphalian coal possessed some unknown properties, there still was a certain preference for British coal, which held back the substitution of Westphalian for British coal.

In the 1860s and 1870s the share of British hard coal declined rapidly. In 1881 Westphalian coal had driven off nearly all competitors in hard coal (see Table 6.6). During the 1880s British coal disappeared from this market but in 1890, when prices increased and Ruhr collieries could hardly meet the demand, the gap was closed by hard coal from Saxony, Upper Silesia and once again from Britain. Although this was just a short-term cyclical shortage, British coal featured permanently in the 1890s due to the price policy of the Rheinisch-Westfälische Kohlensyndikat. Although the British market share may not have been very large, the buffer function of British coal with its price-depressing effect was highly esteemed by contemporaries: 'This competition has a charitable effect, since undoubtedly the Westphalians would have asked for completely different prices' (Voss 1904: 26). Unfortunately there are no exact statistics available to document the origins of Magdeburg's coal imports until 1913 and even figures for the total amount of coal which arrived on the Elbe are obscure. Shortly before the

First World War it is likely that the British share amounted to 10 per cent of the entire hard coal market. During the period from 1850 to 1913 the British market shares in Magdeburg followed a u-shaped curve, with a capital U in the first half and a small u in the second half.

Berlin

Berlin is situated at the point of intersection of two rivers, which had already been connected by canals before the beginning of the nineteenth century. In the 1840s railways improved the city's convenient location even more. With its developing suburbs, Berlin rapidly became Germany's largest and most densely populated industrial city. Without any local coal resources, Berlin had to rely on imports from mostly very distant mining areas in order to satisfy its needs for primary energy. Towards the end of the nineteenth century this locational disadvantage became less severe because transportation costs had declined. Suppliers from different mining areas competed with each other in Berlin, which thus suffered less than many other regions in Germany from the price policy of cartels.

But in the middle of the nineteenth century the lack of locally available coal resources was still a severe handicap. Transportation costs then were so high that even as late as 1860 wood and peat were the major fuels for domestic use (Königlich Preussisches Ministerium 1860: 13). During the early 1840s Berlin had imported far more wood than hard coal, measured in quantities. Hard coal came exclusively from Great Britain (*Berlin* 1896: 355ff.). Transported via Swinemünde/Stettin (Baltic Sea) and inland waterways, most of it was used to produce coke and town gas as well as smithy coal. Upper Silesian hard coal arrived there for the first time in 1848. This coal probably had a share of barely 10 per cent of hard coal consumed in 1853 (Zentgraf 1913: 450ff.). The available information, although scanty, suggests that the consumption of coal increased very fast from 1840. Apart from hard coal, Berlin also imported much brown coal.

Better data are available from 1860 onwards (see Table 6.7).[21] The tendency in the long run is clearly visible: British coal, which reached Berlin almost exclusively by ship, lost considerable market shares until 1881 and Upper Silesian coal profited heavily from

Table 6.7 Coal imports into Berlin and adjoining factory districts, 1861–81 (per cent)

Type of coal	1860	1862	1865	1871	1881
British hard coal	57.4	41.9	20.6	23.0	4.9
Saxon hard coal	0.6	2.1	1.1	0.3	0.9
Upper Silesian hard coal	18.5	32.1	53.9	52.4	49.8
Lower Silesian hard coal	7.8	6.4	6.6	11.0	9.1
Westphalian hard coal	–	3.2	4.7	1.1	6.2
Hanoverian hard coal	–	–	–	–	0.2
Bohemian brown coal	2.8	2.3	3.6	6.1	16.3
German brown coal	12.8	11.9	9.4	6.1	12.7
Total (1,000 tonnes)	354.2	431.7	652.4	1,073.1	1,545.7

Source: Königlich Preussisches Ministerium (1860: 37; 1862: 37f.; 1865: 42f.; 1871: 33ff.; 1881: 37f).

this loss. Except in 1860, most of the coal was transported by railway. Coal from both Upper and Lower Silesia was able to gain increasing market shares because the railway had reduced its freight rates drastically. Whereas Saxon hard coal hardly achieved much significance, after initial difficulties Westphalian coal even outstripped British coal in 1881, reaching Berlin by railway. In the late 1870s contemporaries believed that British hard coal would disappear completely from the Berlin market (Zentgraf 1913: 452). As shown in Table 6.8, however, British coal increased its market share from just over 5 per cent in 1881 to about one quarter shortly before the First World War. This strong recovery was due both to the unfavourable price policy of the German coal cartels and to the favourable development of water freight rates compared to those of the railway. The market shares of both Silesian mining areas suffered a relative decline in those late years, but in absolute terms Silesia now, as before, delivered most of the hard coal to Berlin. Ruhr coal finally did gain a footing in the Berlin market. Concerning other German mining areas, it was mainly their patent fuel (brown coal) which won notable market shares. Bohemian brown coal, which had done well in the 1870s and 1880s, could not stand up to this competition and was nearly pushed out of the Berlin market before the First World War. In the early twentieth century Berlin was the major consumer of coal outside the coal fields and at least[22] five different mining districts competed there against each other.

	Hard coal, coke, patent fuel					Brown coal, patent fuel		
Year	British	Westphalian	Lower Silesian	Upper Silesian	Saxon	Bohemian	Prussian and Saxon	Total (1,000 tonnes)
1881	5.1	6.4	9.4	50.0	1.6	13.1	13.7	1,029
1882	6.4	6.8	10.1	50.0	0.5	10.9	15.2	1,024
1883	6.4	5.3	9.3	49.6	0.8	10.9	17.7	1,022
1884	7.5	4.9	8.8	48.6	0.6	10.1	19.4	1,065
1885	6.6	4.5	9.0	48.3	0.5	11.2	19.9	1,139
1886	6.7	4.2	9.3	48.5	0.4	9.0	21.9	1,191
1887	5.9	3.9	9.8	47.6	0.2	9.2	22.2	1,203
1888	5.8	4.2	9.0	47.3	0.1	10.2	21.8	1.5	1,292
1889	5.6	4.4	9.0	47.0	0.1	9.8	23.1	1.0	1,320
1890	5.0	4.0	9.2	48.3	0.0	8.4	24.1	1.0	1,407
1891	6.9	3.9	7.1	45.0	0.2	8.9	27.2	0.8	1,332
1892	5.1	3.7	9.1	42.3	0.4	8.7	30.1	0.7	1,270
1893	7.6	3.5	9.0	43.8	0.4	7.3	27.7	0.7	1,420
1894	8.6	3.9	9.5	43.9	0.6	5.7	27.1	0.7	1,458
1895	9.2	4.5	9.1	39.7	0.5	5.0	29.9	1.0	1,427
1896	13.1	5.8	8.7	37.2	0.3	4.1	30.1	0.8	1,635
1897	12.5	7.3	8.0	37.6	0.3	3.7	29.9	0.7	1,689
1898	11.3	7.0	8.2	40.4	0.2	3.0	29.4	0.5	1,693
1899	9.2	8.6	9.6	39.5	0.1	2.5	30.0	0.6	1,707
1900	12.9	6.5	7.8	36.7	0.1	1.7	34.0	0.4	1,793
1901	14.4	5.9	7.8	36.5	0.2	1.4	33.3	0.5	1,948
1902	11.8	6.1	8.3	36.5	0.6	0.8	35.1	0.3	1,762
1903	11.8	6.2	9.3	37.2	0.3	0.6	34.3	0.3	1,875
1904	14.6	5.5	10.1	30.7	0.3	0.8	37.7	0.2	1,819
1905	17.5	6.0	6.5	32.9	0.2	0.8	35.9	0.3	2,045
1906	14.5	7.7	5.5	33.8	0.2	1.0	37.2	0.2	2,037
1907	20.2	7.7	5.6	31.1	0.2	0.8	34.2	0.1	2,332
1908	22.5	7.2	4.9	26.9	0.3	0.3	37.7	0.2	2,228
1909	25.4	7.9	4.2	25.9	0.3	0.2	36.2	0.1	2,372
1910	25.2	8.5	5.0	25.9	0.1	0.1	35.0	0.1	2,159
1911	24.4	7.9	5.3	23.3	0.8	0.1	38.0	0.1	2,062

Note: Since 1888, Prussian and Saxon brown coal have been split up into patent fuel and other coal.
Source: Zentgraf (1913: 453).

Synopsis on Northern Germany

The analysis of regional coal markets in northern Germany revealed clear-cut developments in the long run. In the middle of the nineteenth century hard coal from Great Britain predominated, frequently being the only supply at all. Declining transportation costs of overland haulage by rail allowed suppliers from German mining areas to penetrate these markets and by the 1880s they had succeeded in undermining the British predominance. British suppliers even seemed to have disappeared from some markets for good. But this trend was broken: up to 1913 British coal recovered strongly without ever regaining its former preponderance. There were two main reasons for the British recovery: first, freight rates on sea and inland waterways declined lower than those on railways and second, cartelisation tended to raise the prices of German coal immoderately compared to those for British coal.

CONCLUSION

The industry of the nineteenth century was widely based on coal-consuming techniques, to be sure. Hence, those regions poorly endowed with coal did start with a handicap. They could overcome it through importing coal it is true, but – *ceteris paribus* – the higher price of coal still made industries outside the mining areas less competitive. Nevertheless, the lack of local coal was not altogether prohibitive for successful industrialisation, as several cases show. After all, indigenous coal resources did not guarantee cheap supplies for a successful cartelisation could raise the price well above competitive levels. But lowered transportation costs enabled some regions to draw on the coal resources of competitive mining areas and thus avoid the price-increasing tendencies of cartels. So from the start, neither the lack of local coal resources nor the dependency on powerful indigenous suppliers debarred a region from industrialisation if transportation was cheap enough to overcome these locational disadvantages.

NOTES

1. On the significance of coal and water-power for the European industrialisation see Cameron (1985). He stresses (p. 5.) that water-power

was of major importance even in the mother country of industrialisation, Great Britain, until far into the second half of the nineteenth century. On this see especially von Tunzelmann (1978).
2. Customs duties and similar taxes lost their significance in the second half of the nineteenth century. Therefore I deal with them only occasionally.
3. Lamartine Yates (1959: 150f.) gives figures for 1913. The United Kingdom held a share of 48.6 per cent of world exports, Germany of 22.5 per cent. Of the world-wide import volume, Germany absorbed 7.5 per cent.
4. As far as I know, there is no monography on this subject. Besides short chapters in books on British coal mining in general, see the articles by Palmer (1970), Harley (1986), and the older studies by Thomas (1903), Jevons (1909) and Zimmermann (1911).
5. If not mentioned otherwise, I use metric measures.
6. These and the following figures are taken from Church (1986: 19, 32, 86).
7. Based on the figures in Mitchell and Deane (1962: 283f., 303, 305). Bunker coal for foreign vessels in British ports is not included. After all, in 1913 this comprised 25 per cent of the remaining exports of coal.
8. This is explicitly stated in Harley's paper, see North (1971: 163–74).
9. Only a few aspects of technological improvements are sketched here. For more information see Dyos and Aldcroft (1969: 254ff.; Harley 1971: 216 ff).
10. Thomas even estimated that this share was more than 50 per cent. Thomas (1903: 469); see also Palmer (1970: 337 ff).
11. Harley (1986: *passim*). This argument is set forward, e.g. by Crouzet who points out that 80 per cent of the weight of British exports consisted of coal (Crouzet 1978: 236; see also Zimmermann 1911: 1225, 1261ff).
12. South America alone played a significant role.
13. See the graph in Church (1986: 53). A similar tendency occurred in Ruhr coal mining, see Holtfrerich (1973: 20).
14. Alternative domestic sources of energy also have to be considered, e.g. the richness in wood in the case of Sweden (see Hassel 1905: 122ff).
15. For the following remarks I draw exclusively on Crouzet (1966).
16. Bos (1978: 111) quotes van Dillen and Brugmans as advocates of this view. He also mentions Wieringa who places only secondary importance on the lack of domestic raw materials (see Brugmans 1983: 213; Griffiths 1979: 75ff; Kreeft 1988: 219, 225 ff).
17. In fact, some regions such as Twente, had to wait for railway connections in order to get better access to foreign coal supplies. Indeed, a national railway network emerged rather late in the Netherlands. But from an international perspective de Jonge and Bos are wrong when they see the Netherlands as badly suited for internal communication before the 1880s (see Bos 1978: 112ff). On the

development of the Dutch transportation system, see Brugmans (1983: 226ff).

The careful assessment of the Dutch transportation problem in the first half of the nineteenth century by Griffiths (1979: 66ff.) can be seen as inconsistent with his conclusion. Thus, his and similarly the recent assessment by Kreeft (1988: 226ff.) rather support my argument. It depends on the yardstick for comparison: as compared to Britain or Belgium the Dutch transportation system and hence fuel costs were at a clear disadvantage, but not in the least so as compared to regions in the south, the middle and the north of Germany. And those *handicapped* regions were successfully industrialising, after all.

18. The breakthrough for coal transportation to the Netherlands on railways occurred between 1867 and 1875 (see Nusteling 1974: 176).
19. See also Bos (1978: 116ff.). Going into more detail than Nusteling, Bos discusses the position of British coal on the Dutch market. The stopgap function of British coal becomes very clear since the 1880s (see *ibid.*: 125ff.). According to Bos (*ibid.*: 132ff.), however, Britain had even lost this function by 1909.
20. For source see footnote to Table 6.2. Only in 1865 did Hamburg's share drop below 40 per cent.
21. The source used for Table 6.7 also discriminates between water and rail transportation.
22. One could further differentiate various German brown coal producing areas and British hard coal districts.

REFERENCES

Den Absatz der westphälischen Steinkohlen zur Elbe betreffend, 'Verfasst vom Comité zur Beförderung des Absatzes der westphälischen Steinkohlen nach dem Osten', Essen: 1858.

Annual Statement of the Trade and Navigation of the United Kingdom with Foreign Countries and British Possessions in the Years 1853–1913, *Parliamentary Papers*, 1854/5–1914.

Berlin und seine Eisenbahnen (1846–96), vol. 2, 1896, Berlin: Julius Springer.

Bos, Roeland W.J.M. (1978), *Brits-Nederlandse handel en scheepvaart, 1870–1914, een analyse van machtsafbrokkeling op een markt*, PhD thesis, University of Tilburg: R.W.J.M. Bos.

Brugmans, I.J. (1983), *Paardenkracht en mensenmacht, Sociaaleconomische geschiedenis van Nederland 1795–1940*, reprint, Leiden: Martinus Nijhoff.

Cameron, R. (1985), 'A new view of European industrialization', *Economic History Review*, vol. 38, pp. 1–23.

Church, R. (1986), *The History of the British Coal Industry*, vol. 3, Oxford: Clarendon Press.

Crouzet, F. (1966), 'Le charbon anglais en France au XIXe siècle', in L.

Trénard (ed.) *Charbon et Sciences humaines*, Paris: Mouton, pp. 173-206.
Crouzet, F. (1978), *L'économie de la Grande-Bretagne Victorienne*, Paris: Société d'édition d'enseignement supérieur.
Die Entwickelung des Niederrheinisch-Westfälischen Steinkohlen-Bergbaues in der zweiten Hälfte des 19. Jahrhunderts, (1904), vol. 10, Berlin: Springer.
Dyos, H.J. and D.H. Aldcroft (1969), *British Transport. An Economic Survey from the Seventeenth Century to the Twentieth*, Harmondsworth: Penguin.
Fremdling, R. (1989), 'Britische und deutsche Kohle auf norddeutschen Märkten 1850-1913', in Jürgen Bergmann et al. (eds.) *Regionen im historischen Vergleich*, Opladen: Westdeutscher Verlag.
Griffiths, R.T. (1979), *Industrial Retardation in the Netherlands 1830-1850*, The Hague: Martinus Nijhoff.
Harley, C.K. (1971), 'The shift from sailing ships to steamships, 1850-1890: a study in technological change and its diffusion', in Donald N. McCloskey (ed.) *Essays on a Mature Economy: Britain after 1840*, Princeton: Princeton University Press, pp. 215-34.
Harley, C.K. (1986), *Coal Exports and British Shipping, 1850-1913* (unpublished manuscript), p. 47.
Harley, C.K. (1988), 'Ocean freight rates and productivity, 1740-1913: the primary of mechanical invention reaffirmed', *Journal of Economic History*, vol. 48, pp. 851-76.
Hassel, Theodor (1905), *Der internationale Steinkohlenhandel insbesondere seine wirtschafts-statistische Gestaltung*, Essen: Baedeker.
Heidmann, R. (1897), *Hamburgs Kohlenhandel*, Hamburg: Actiengesellschaft 'Neue Börsen-Halle'.
Holtfrerich, C.-L. (1973), *Quantitative Wirtschaftsgeschichte des Ruhrkohlenbergbaus im 19. Jahrhundert*, Dortmund: Gesellschaft für Westfälische Wirtschaftsgeschichte.
Huber, P. B. (1978), *Die deutsche Eisenbahnentwicklung: Wegweiser für eine zukünftige Fernschnellbahn?*, Köln: Deutsche Forschungs- und Versuchsanstalt für Luft- und Raumfahrt.
Jevons, H. S. (1909), *Foreign Trade in Coal*, London: P.S. King & Son.
de Jonge, J.A. (1976), *De industrialisatie in Nederland tussen 1850 en 1914*, reprint, Nijmegen: Socialistische Uitgeverij.
Königlich Preussisches Ministerium der öffentlichen Arbeiten (ed.), (1860, 1862, 1865, 1871, 1881): *Erläuterungen zu der Karte über die Produktion, Consumtion und Cirkulation der mineralischen Brennstoffe in Preussen während des Jahres 1860, 1862, 1865, 1871, 1881*, Berlin: Landkarten Handlung von J.H. Neumann.
Kreeft, C. (1988), 'Economische groei in Nederland, 1815-1860', *Economisch- en sociaal-historisch jaarboek*, vol. 51, pp. 194-239.
Krengel, J. (1983), *Die deutsche Roheisenindustrie 1871-1913*, Berlin: Duncker & Humblot.
Lamartine Yates, P. (1959), *Forty Years of Foreign Trade*, London: George Allen & Unwin.

Maddison, A. (1982), *Phases of Capitalist Development*, Oxford: Oxford University Press.
Mitchell, B.R. and Deane, P. (1962), *Abstract of British Historical Statistics*, Cambridge: Cambridge University Press.
North, D.C. (1971), 'Sources of productivity change in ocean shipping, in Robert William Fogel and Stanley L. Engerman (eds), *The Reinterpretation of American Economic History*, New York: Harper & Row, pp. 163–74.
Nusteling, H.P.H. (1974), *De rijnvaart in het tijdperk van stoom en steenkool, 1831–1914*, Amsterdam: Holland Universiteits Pers.
Palmer, S. (1970), 'The British coal export trade, 1850–1913, in D. Alexander and R. Ommer (eds), *Voyages and Trade Routes in the North Atlantic*, Newfoundland: Maritime History Group Memorial University, pp. 333–54.
Thomas, D.A. (1903), 'The growth and direction of our foreign trade in coal during the last half century', *Journal of the Royal Statistical Society*, vol. 96, pp. 439–522.
von Tunzelmann, G.N. (1978), *Steam Power and British Industrialization to 1860*, Oxford: Clarendon Press.
Voss, H. (1904), *Magdeburgs Kohlenhandel einst und jetzt*, Magdeburg: Heinrichshofen'sche Buchhandlung.
van Zanden, J.L. (1987), 'Economische groei in Nederland in de negentiende eeuw. Enkele nieuwe resultaten', *Economisch- en sociaalhistorisch jaarboek*, vol. 50, pp. 51–76.
Zentgraf (1913), 'Der Wettbewerb auf dem Berliner Kohlenmarkt', *Glückauf*, vol. 49, pp. 449–503, 533–40, 572–83.
Zimmermann, E. (1911), 'Die britische Kohlenausfuhr, ihre Geschichte, Organisation und Bedeutung', *Glückauf*, vol. 47, pp. 1142–52, 1181–91, 1219–28, 1257–64, 1292–8.

7 · THE GROWTH OF INTERNATIONAL BANKING TO 1914

Rondo Cameron

BANKS: THE FIRST MULTINATIONALS

A strong argument can be made that banks constituted the first multinational business firms.[1] Although it can be argued in rebuttal that the Italian bankers who frequented the fairs of Champagne were only engaged in international trade, and thus were not true multinationals (Bautier 1953), such was clearly not the case for the Italian bankers in England in the thirteenth and fourteenth centuries (Prestwich 1979). The Bardi and Peruzzi were the largest business enterprises in Europe before being forced into bankruptcy by the default of Edward III in 1345; nor were they the only Italian bankers in England. The Medici bank, although somewhat smaller than the Bardi and Peruzzi, was nevertheless the largest business enterprise in the fifteenth century. It pioneered the holding company form of organisation in order to avoid the kind of catastrophe that had overtaken the Bardi and Peruzzi, and had branches in Rome, Venice, Naples, Pisa, Milan, Geneva, Lyons, Basel, Avignon, Bruges and London in addition to its headquarters in Florence (De Roover 1963).

Like international banking, with which it was closely connected, international investment can also be traced to the high middle ages. The Italians initially went to England to engage in the wool trade, but they soon became involved in lending to the sovereign, which ultimately proved to be their undoing. They could also be found in Bruges, Antwerp and several cities of northern Europe as well as in the Levant. As in England, it was probably the opportunity for trade that first lured them to such locations, but in time they engaged in both public and private finance. In the fifteenth century a number of Tuscan merchant bankers financed the silver mining industry of the Balkans (Krekič 1979).

Italian bankers clearly dominated the banking industry throughout the middle ages, with the Aragonese, especially those from Barcelona, as runners up; but at the end of the fifteenth century they began to encounter stiff competition from bankers in south Germany who, in the next century, emerged as leaders of the industry (Bergier 1979). Of these the Fuggers and the Welsers were, of course, the most prominent, but there were many others (Ehrenberg 1928).

The Fuggers owed their prominence in large part to their dealings with the House of Habsburg, in particular with the Emperor Charles V. In the end they suffered the fate of other financiers, such as the Bardi and Peruzzi, who loaned too liberally to sovereigns. In their heyday, however, from the end of the fifteenth to the middle of the sixteenth century, the House of Fugger was pre-eminent in European finance. Under Jacob Fugger II (1459–1525) the family firm, with headquarters in Augsburg, operated branches in several German cities and in Hungary, Poland, Italy, Spain, Lisbon, London and Antwerp. Through their relations with temporal rulers they obtained control of the silver and copper mines of the Tyrol and Hungary from which they supplied the monetary needs of Antwerp before the influx of Spanish silver from the New World (Kellenbenz 1981). From Lisbon and Antwerp they largely controlled the distribution of spices in central Europe, for which they exchanged the silver and copper needed to purchase the spices in India. They also accepted deposits and dealt extensively in bills of exchange. The rise of the Fuggers more or less coincided with the rise of the Antwerp market, but the timing was less than coincidental (Van der Wee 1963).

The decline of Antwerp, after the initial success of the Dutch revolt and the closure of the Scheldt, was even more rapid and dramatic than its rise, but it was paralleled by the equally rapid and spectacular rise of Amsterdam. The ease with which Amsterdam achieved its rank as the principal entrepôt of Europe was due in part to the influx of merchants and financiers from fallen Antwerp, who brought both their capitalist know-how and their liquid capital.

The seventeenth century appears to have witnessed a mild

trough or slowdown in international investment. On the one hand the examples of the Spanish kings in repudiating their debts, followed to some extent by the French and other absolute monarchs, discouraged lenders from trusting their disposable funds with political sovereigns. On the other, the financiers with the most liquid capital – that is, the Dutch – found ample opportunities for investment in shipping, trade and the public securities of their own country. The Dutch did, nevertheless, initiate a pattern of lending to foreign governments which they expanded greatly in the following century (Barbour 1950).

In the first half of the seventeenth century Louis de Geer, a Walloon from Liège who became a naturalised Dutchman and operated from Amsterdam, became the principal financier of Sweden's Gustavus Adolphus. De Geer, along with his in-laws of the Trip family, likewise from Amsterdam, also introduced modern technology into Sweden's iron and copper industry, in which he invested heavily (Edmundson 1891). Dutch investors also participated in financing the reclamation of the fenlands of eastern England, employing Dutch engineers and Dutch technology. Genoa and Geneva continued to function in the seventeenth century on a small scale as markets where funds could be procured for international uses, but it is significant that neither produced great banking dynasties to be compared with those of earlier or later centuries.

The eighteenth century experienced a revival of both international banking and international lending. The Dutch were chiefly responsible for both. The relative decline of Dutch commercial superiority left them with ample reserves of liquid funds but comparatively few profitable outlets for investment. As a result, the Amsterdam capital market attracted borrowers – deficitary governments for the most part – from all of Europe and even, from 1781, the fledgling United States (Riley 1980). The principal debtors included Great Britain, Austria, Denmark, Sweden, Russia, Poland, Spain and France. The process of international lending also produced a new international banking dynasty, Hope & Company, whose founder claimed descent from Scottish nobility (Buist 1974). Geneva likewise took part in the eighteenth-century revival of international lending, largely as a result of the dispersal of French Huguenots after the Revocation of the Edict of Nantes in 1685 (Lüthy 1959–61).

The wars of the French Revolution and the Napoleonic era wrought havoc with international financial relations, bringing with them repudiations, inflation and the disruption of ordinary commercial and financial processes. Indirectly, however, they set the stage for the next episode in the drama of international finance by bringing into prominence those 'five gentlemen of Frankfurt', the brothers Rothschild, and by creating the need for the first large international financial operation of the nineteenth century, the financing of the French indemnity. They also opened the way for the classic era of international merchant banking.

THE ERA OF MERCHANT BANKING

Virtually all of the bankers mentioned above were merchants as well as bankers; most of them, indeed, became bankers by way of their mercantile activities. In the literature of banking history, however, the period from the end of the Napoleonic Wars to the rise of the great international joint stock banks in the latter half of the nineteenth century is generally regarded as the classic era of merchant banking (Chapman 1984). In that period private bankers in international commerce and finance proliferated, and a few of them became so rich and powerful that they numbered among the movers and shakers of the nineteenth century.

What, exactly, were their functions, and what were their characteristics? Since they were, in the first place, merchants, the import and export of commodities were, in the beginning at least, of major concern; and some of them continued active in such business until the second half of the nineteenth century. The international movement of commodities was financed in large part by bills of exchange and acceptances, thus requiring a familiarity with these instruments on the part of the merchants. Some of them, generally the more prominent ones, began to specialise in granting acceptance credits on bills of exchange for others, thereby making the transition from merchanting to banking. According to Chapman (1984), this transition was especially marked in Britain between the crises of 1825 and 1836. In the frequently quoted words of Baron Schroeder, a prominent merchant banker of the later nineteenth century, acceptances were the 'bread and butter' of merchant bankers, but some of them helped themselves to the 'jam' of the issuance of public securities. With time a few – the London House of Rothschild, for example – specialised in the latter almost entirely.

Another common characteristic of the merchant bankers was their international orientation. Many (of the founders, at least) were natives of countries other than the ones in which they made their marks as bankers. A few of the merchant bankers of Paris could trace their origins to the Old Regime, but others were foreigners, mainly Protestants from Switzerland and Jews from the Rhineland who moved to Paris during the Empire or soon after. The foreign-born or foreign-descended also played prominent roles in the English, especially the London, banking community, which helps to account for its cosmopolitan outlook. The Barings, for example, originally came from Germany. Others were of Dutch and German origin, both Jewish and Gentile; French Huguenots; Greeks and others from the eastern Mediterranean; a goodly number of Americans; and of course the Scots from north of the border. Across the Atlantic in America all of the bankers were of course descended from European stock, but many had come directly and recently, from England, Scotland, France, Germany, and elsewhere.

A brief listing of some of the leading figures and families of this international financial community will serve to highlight both the similarities and diversity. At the end of the Napoleonic Wars the Hopes of Amsterdam and the Barings of London were unquestionably the leading international bankers. They had financed a large part of the British war effort and assisted in financing Britain's allies. In 1803 and afterwards they helped finance Jefferson's Louisiana Purchase from France. In 1817 they took the lead in organising France's 'liberation loans', the funds for which were raised mainly through the London market although French bankers and investors also participated.

The Rothschilds did not participate directly in the liberation loans, but they soon began to play a major role in virtually all international financial operations. The family banks originated during the Napoleonic Wars when the Elector of Hesse-Kassel, in flight from Napoleon, engaged Meyer Amschel Rothschild of Frankfurt, the founding father, to look after his fortune.[2] Meyer Amschel had five sons, one of whom, Nathan, had gone to England as early as 1798 and in 1804 established the firm of N.M.

Rothschild & Co. in London. In 1810 Meyer Amschel took his sons into partnership in the Frankfurt firm as M.A. Rothschild & Söhne. Shortly afterwards the youngest son, James, established a branch in Paris where, under the nose of Napoleon, he cooperated with the other branches in financing the Allies. After Napoleon's defeat the firms reorganised. The eldest son, Amschel, had already taken over the management of the Frankfurt house after the death of their father in 1812. The Paris branch became an independent firm, and in 1816 Salomon set up a branch in Vienna to help restore the shattered finances of the Habsburg Monarchy. Karl did likewise in the Kingdom of Naples in 1820.

The principal business of the Rothschild banks, like that of all merchant banks of the period, consisted of the finance of international trade by means of bills of exchange drawn on one another and on other correspondents in the principal centres of commerce. Like the Barings and Hopes before them, however, the Rothschilds quickly began to specialise in government finance, underwriting the issues of government bonds that proliferated in the great restructuring of public finance that occurred after the Napoleonic Wars and in the wake of revolutionary upheavals in the 1820s and 1830s. Baron James soon acquired a virtual monopoly on the issue of French government *rentes* and the securities of other Latin governments.

In the mid-nineteenth century the third most important London merchant bank, after Rothschilds and Barings, was Brown, Shipley & Co., the London branch of the American firm of Brown Brothers, which had originated in Baltimore and had branches in New York, Boston, Philadelphia and Liverpool as well as London (Perkins 1975). In the 1860s and 1870s it was overtaken by another American firm, J.S. Morgan & Co., whose principal had begun as an employee, then partner, of George Peabody, one of the pioneer American bankers in London, and whose son, Pierpont Morgan, Sr, was destined to become one of the most powerful private bankers of all times (Carosso 1987). There were, in addition, numerous other Anglo-American firms based in London.

London also attracted many German Jewish and other German bankers hoping to follow in the footsteps of the Rothschilds. These included the Stern brothers, R. Raphael & Sons, the Seligman brothers, Speyer brothers (Seligman and Speyer also in New York), Alexander Kleinwort (founder of the forerunner of Kleinwort, Benson & Co., eventually the largest acceptance house in London), C.J. Hambro & Son (actually from Copenhagen), Frederick Huth & Co., Ludwig Knoop & Co. and William Brandt (Chapman 1984). Most of these firms, which also maintained branches on the Continent – Hamburg, Frankfurt, St Petersburg and elsewhere – specialised in commercial and financial relations between continental Europe and the rest of the world through London.

Although James de Rothschild was undoubtedly the pre-eminent private banker in Paris during his lifetime (he died in 1868), he both competed and cooperated with numerous old-established Catholic and Protestant firms as well as more recent Jewish arrivals from the Rhineland and central Europe. Among the former were Jacques Laffitte, a governor of the Bank of France (1814–20) and an important financial innovator before his death in 1844, and the Perier family, who produced several regents for the Bank of France as well as some prominent politicians. Notable Protestant banking dynasties included the Mallets, established as bankers in Paris from 1723, and the Delessert, Hottinguer, André, Odier and Vernes families. Among the Jewish financiers, the Foulds came to Paris from the Rhineland soon after James de Rothschild. Adolphe d'Eichthal was the first Jewish regent of the Bank of France (1839–1849) (Cameron 1961: 107–9). Later Jewish arrivals included the Bischoffsheims, the Goldschmidts and the Sterns, all of whom had relatives and correspondents in both London and central Europe. All of the above banking families, along with others, were known collectively as *la haute banque parisienne*.

THE RISE OF JOINT STOCK BANKS

In the second half of the nineteenth century the private merchant bankers encountered the competition of large joint stock banks. The transition from private to joint stock banking in the international economy has been dubbed a 'financial revolution', and its crucial years have been located in the 1850s and 1860s (Landes 1956). Such terminology may be overly dramatic, however, as there was no abrupt shift in either the methods or instruments of international finance. The private banks continued their traditional activities until the First World War and even afterwards, and in many instances the joint stock banks were merely the creations – and creatures – of the private bankers. The transition might more aptly be described as the natural evolution of financial institutions as they responded to changes in the technology of production and communications and to the increase in the capital requirements of both industry and government.

The concept of joint stock investment banking may be traced to the ideas of the utopian theorist Count Henri de Saint-Simon. Saint-Simon argued that the true natural leaders of society were the great bankers and industrialists, and that the means for achieving the reconstruction of society were to be found in the role of credit and the 'spirit of association'. Among Saint-Simon's acquaintances was the banker Jacques Laffitte, who subsidised a number of Saint-Simon's publications and who, less than a year after he was summarily dismissed as governor of the Bank of France, proposed the creation of a company with a capital of 240 million francs to construct all of the canals to be authorised by the French government. The reactionary government of the day, however, fearing the concentration of financial power in the hands of the liberal opposition, of which Laffitte was one of the leaders, rejected the proposal. Four years later Laffitte came up with a new proposal for a Société Commanditaire de l'Industrie to be capitalised at the slightly more modest figure of 100 million francs. The proposed company would function in part as an investment bank, in part as a gigantic holding company for industry. Laffitte enlisted the support of the leading financiers and industrialists including Casimir Perier, Charles Mallet and James de Rothschild, as potential investors and officers, but the government, relying in part on the advice of the Bank of France, again rejected the proposal in October 1825. The financial crisis of the following month temporarily dissipated enthusiasm for the project and the stubborn attitudes of the government and the Bank of France successfully resisted all similar proposals for more than two decades (Cameron 1961: 112).

Meanwhile more practical steps towards the introduction of joint stock investment banking occurred in the southern Netherlands, soon to become independent Belgium. There the foundation in 1822 of the Algemeene Nederlandsche Maatschappji ter Begunstiging van de Volksvlijt, known after 1830 as the Société

Générale de Belgique, laid the foundations of modern investment banking. This is not the place for a detailed account of the activities of the Société Générale and its companion and rival, the Banque de Belgique, in promoting the industrialisation of Belgium (Cameron 1961: 119–25; 1967: ch. 5). What merits emphasis here, in addition to noting the origin of practical joint stock investment banking, is the international aspect: that is, the role of the French capital market and in particular the cooperation of the merchant bankers Rothschild and Hottinguer with the Société Générale and the Banque de Belgique, respectively.

For the next act in the drama of international finance the scene switches back to Paris. (The British joint stock banks, which developed apace from the 1830s, did not engage in international banking until the end of the century, leaving that function to London's merchant banks.) After the *coup d'état* of 1851 and the proclamation of the Second Empire the following year, Napoleon III sought to lessen the dependence of his government on Rothschild and other members of the *haute banque* by creating new financial institutions. He found eager collaborators in the brothers Emile and Isaac Pereire, former employees of Rothschild who struck out on their own. With the blessings of the Emperor they founded in 1852 both the Société Général de Crédit Foncier, a mortgage bank, and the Société Générale de Crédit Mobilier, initially intended as a 'railway bank'.

The Crédit Foncier at first restricted its activities to France, especially in providing mortgage credit for the reconstruction of Paris undertaken by Napoleon's prefect of the Seine, Baron Haussmann; but in 1863 its directors participated in the establishment of the Allgemeine Oesterreichische Boden-Credit-Anstalt, popularly known in France as the Crédit Foncier Autrichien. In subsequent years it assisted in the formation of the Preussische Central Bodencredit A.G. (1870), the United States Mortgage Company (1871), the Banco Hipotecario de España (1873), and played a large role in Egyptian finances (Cameron 1961: 129–31).

Unlike the Crédit Foncier, the Crédit Mobilier launched immediately into international finance. In the spring of 1853, only a few months after its own establishment, it participated in the syndicate promoting the Bank für Handel und Industrie in Darmstadt (Darmstädter), the first of the German 'great banks'.[3] From there it went on to promote banks, railways and industrial enterprises in Switzerland, Austria, Russia, Spain, Italy, the Ottoman Empire, even London! In addition to its own activities, it inspired a host of imitations by both French and other promoters; some, like the Stockholms Enskilda Bank, were soundly conceived and administered and made major contributions to the economic development of their countries; others, like the Crédit Mobilier of America, which had no connection with the original except the pirated name, were fraudulent from the beginning. *The Economist* (12 July 1856) noted with amazement that

> The manner in which the French capitalists are extending their relations is most remarkable. At present they have under their control railways in Switzerland, in Austria, in Italy, in Spain, in Holland, and in Belgium; they have established Crédit Mobiliers in Madrid and Turin, are about to do the same in Lisbon, and are trying to do the same at St Petersburg and Constantinople; they are endeavouring to obtain concessions of railways in Russia; they have established a large bank at Darmstadt, and will not rest until they get one at Constantinople ... they hold important concessions of mines and coal pits in Spain, in the Rhenish provinces, and in Silesia; they hold a large and in some cases a predominating interest in numerous railways, iron works, coal pits and banks in Belgium; they are about to establish lines of gigantic steamers ... ; they are taking the lead in the project for cutting through the Isthmus at Suez; and they have a pretty considerable interest in the omnibuses of London.

James de Rothschild observed the progress of his former employees with growing concern. Although he did not immediately sever relations with them – in April 1852 Emile Pereire presented the annual report for the directors of the French Northern Railway and was re-elected as director for a term of four years – Rothschild withdrew his support from the Pereires' projected Midi Railway, and thus indirectly – and unintentionally – turned them to promote the Crédit Mobilier. When they offered him a token participation in the first block of shares he replied by drafting an indignant letter to none other than the Prince-President in which he charged them with speculation, monopoly and irresponsibility! (Gille 1954). The following year, during the promotion of the Darmstädter Bank, he organised a counter-syndicate to depress the price of the shares, thereby depriving the promoters of most of their expected profits (Cameron 1961: 150).

Of all the Pereires' successes, their purchase of the Austrian State Railway by the Crédit Mobilier in 1854 galled Rothschild the most. The public finances of the Habsburg monarchy had been regarded by the Rothschilds as virtually an exclusive fief, and they resented any transgression on it. Even more ominous, rumours circulated in the spring of 1855 of the impending formation of a large joint stock bank in Vienna by interests affiliated with the Crédit Mobilier. Isaac Pereire, in his annual report to the stockholders of the latter in April 1855, outlined a programme for the creation of affiliated banks in all countries of Europe: 'In creating these establishments it would be necessary, while assuring them of independence of action for the development of their own national industries, to avoid the dangers of isolation. It would be necessary, in fact, to attach them to one another in order to develop their powers of expansion and association' (Cameron 1961: 151). Soon afterwards Isaac himself was in Vienna with a number of proposals for the economic development of the monarchy, including plans for the bank.

The Rothschilds had been handicapped in opposing the purchase of the railway by the absence of any family members in the Austrian capital. Salomon, in charge since 1816, had fled the country with Metternich in 1848, leaving the bank in the care of employees; he died near Paris early in 1855. James, now stung into vigorous action, dispatched Salomon's son Anselm, whom he had trained personally in his Paris counting-house, to prevent further encroachments on the family preserve in Austria. Anselm joined forces with a group of Viennese aristocrats and bankers of the second order who had already petitioned the government to charter a *mobilier*-type bank. Alexander Bach, the interior minister, and Baron von Bruck, the finance minister, at first favoured the Pereires' proposal, but with the return of the Rothschilds suggested an amalgamation of the two groups. The Pereires reluctantly agreed, but Baron James, hastily making amends with the imperial government in Paris, persuaded it to attach conditions that made it impossible for the Crédit Mobilier to participate. Thus, on 6 November 1855 the Austrian government formally chartered the K.K. Privilegirte Österreichischen Creditanstalt für Handel und Gewerbe to a group dominated by the Rothschilds. Baron James, who along with other merchant bankers had frequently denounced the joint stock form of organisation as inconsistent with the banker's function, allowed himself to be persuaded of its utility.

With the Rothschilds' example before them, other merchant bankers flocked to create joint stock banks. In 1856 the Rothschilds themselves, with the assistance of Gerson Bleichroeder, took part in establishing the Berliner Handels-Gesellschaft on the model of the Crédit Mobilier except that, unable to secure a charter as an *Aktiengesellschaft* from the Prussian administration, the founders organised it as a *Kommanditgesellschaft*. In the same year David Hansemann reorganised the Disconto-Gesellschaft, also a *Kommanditgesellschaft* founded in 1851 as a simple discount bank on the model of the French Comptoir d'Escompte, as a *mobilier*-type operation. Although the Prussian administration was adamant in refusing charters for true joint stock banks, other German principalities were more liberal; in the single year 1856 no fewer than a dozen joint stock banks, mostly modelled on the Crédit Mobilier, were established in German cities including Breslau, Coburg, Dessau, Hamburg (two), Leipzig and Oldenburg (Riesser 1911). 1856 was also a banner year for the creation of banks in other countries, with three in Switzerland, three in Spain (all with French capital, including affiliates of Rothschild and the Crédit Mobilier), and others in Sweden, the Kingdom of Sardinia (Piedmont) and Constantinople. Attempts to establish *mobilier*-type banks were also made in Belgium, the Netherlands, Rumania and Serbia, but in all cases the proposals were refused by the governments.

Why were there no new banks in France in 1856? In fact, Rothschild and several other prominent merchant bankers, a group known informally as the *Syndicat des banquiers* and the *Réunion financière*, had planned to establish one but the government, fearing a financial crisis (a year prematurely, as it turned out) announced on 6 March that it would approve no further *sociétés anonymes* for the remainder of the year. The next French joint stock bank, the Crédit Industriel et Commercial, came in 1859. Its founders, who included David Hansemann and William Gladstone of London (*not* the politician) as well as several French bankers, announced that they intended to create a large deposit bank on the English model and 'naturalise' in France the English practice of payment by cheque; in fact, its operations in its early years resembled that of the Crédit Mobilier. (Meanwhile the

Comptoir d'Escompte de Paris, created as a temporary emergency measure in 1848, received a new charter as an independent *société anonyme* in 1854, doubled its capital in 1856, and by 1870, with a capital of 100 million francs, had branches in London, Alexandria, Bombay, Calcutta, Hongkong, Saigon, Shanghai and Yokohama.)

The next great wave of financial promotions reached a peak in 1863, with dozens of new banks and credit companies setting up throughout Europe: in France, Switzerland, Italy, Belgium, the Netherlands, Sweden, the Czech Crownlands and Hungary as well as Austria proper, Russia, and even in well-banked England. Two of these new institutions deserve special note: the International Financial Society of London, an English affiliate of the Crédit Mobilier (Cottrell 1985); and the Banque de Paris et des Pays-Bas (Paribas).

The latter began as a nominally Dutch institution, the Nederlandsche Credit- en Deposito-Bank of Amsterdam. Although it had a Dutch charter, the majority of shareholders owning more than three fourths of its shares resided in France, and it immediately opened a branch in Paris which quickly outran the main office in Amsterdam in its volume of business. Its energising spirit was Louis Bischoffsheim, a Jewish financier who moved from Amsterdam to Paris in 1850 and set up a private bank, which he subsequently merged with the new institution. From the beginning it operated internationally; by 1870 it had branches in Geneva, Antwerp and Brussels, and participated in banks and industrial enterprises in France, Belgium, and overseas. In 1871 it amalgamated with the recently established Banque de Paris, changed its name, and moved its headquarters to Paris (Cameron 1961: 177–8).

In 1863 the Crédit Industriel established a *filial*, the Société de Dépôts et de Comptes Courants, also in Paris. More auspicious for the future, Henri Germain, using the new law permitting free incorporation with limited liability for companies capitalised at not more than 20 million francs, founded the Crédit Lyonnais with exactly 20 million as a purely local bank. It did not long remain such. In 1864 it established a branch in Paris, which became its head office in 1878 (Bouvier 1961).

Rothschild and his friends in the *Réunion financière* had intended to launch their long-delayed rival of the Crédit Mobilier, the Société Générale pour favoriser le développement du Commerce et de l'Industrie en France ('Société Générale') in 1863, but bureaucratic foot-dragging in the *Conseil d'Etat* held up approval of their request for a full year. Meanwhile the English friends of the *Réunion financière* had succeeded in bringing out the Société Générale's 'twin', the General Credit and Finance Company (Cottrell 1990). Within a few years the latter transformed itself into an acceptance house, but the Société Générale, engaging in both ordinary commercial and investment banking, was probably the closest exemplar in France of Germany's universal banks.

Germany did not participate significantly in the financial promotions of the 1860s. In part, perhaps, the creations of the 1850s sufficed; but more important was Prussia's continued refusal to permit joint stock banks. When the law was modified in 1870 to permit free incorporation – together with the euphoria generated by the victory over France later the same year – the *Gründerjahre* of 1870–2 made the experience of 1856 pale by comparison. In little more than three years more than one hundred new banks were founded in Germany alone. The crisis and depression of 1873 wiped out almost three-quarters of those, but of those that survived the Deutsche Bank and the Dresdner Bank were destined to play a large role (Born 1983). A new chapter in the history of international banking had begun.

INTERNATIONAL BANKING IN ITS PRIME, 1870–1914

In the generation or so before the First World War international investment reached dimensions previously unknown, and the banking systems of the world achieved a degree of internationalisation also without precedent. The juxtaposition was not coincidental. Although the resources for investment were generated by the advances in technology and the enormous increase in international trade that characterised the nineteenth century, the allocation of those resources, both domestically and internationally, increasingly depended on the banking systems. The following brief summary will focus on international banking and investment between 1870 and 1914.[4]

As is well known, Great Britain – or, more accurately, the private investors of Great Britain – was far and away the largest foreign investor before 1914. At the latter date British investments abroad amounted to about £4 billion (approximately $20 billion in 1914 values), or 43 per cent of the world total. Before about 1850 British investors purchased government bonds of several European countries and invested in private enterprises there, especially the early French railways. They also bought the securities of American state governments, and of Latin American countries as well. From the 1850s they turned their attention increasingly to American railways, mines and ranches, to similar investments in Latin America and Asia and, above all, to the British Empire. In 1914 the self-governing dominions accounted for 37 per cent of British foreign investments and India another 9 per cent, the United States for 21 per cent, and Latin America, 18 per cent. Only 5 per cent of Britain's total foreign investments were to be found in Europe.

France (or the French) was the second largest foreign investor, with total investments in 1914 of more than fifty billion francs (about $10 billion). In the first half of the century Frenchmen invested chiefly in their near neighbours: the securities of both revolutionary and reactionary governments in Spain, Portugal, and the several Italian states; bonds of the new government of Belgium after the successful revolution of 1830; mines and other industrial enterprises in Belgium both before and after 1830; and similar but smaller investments in Switzerland, Austria and the German states, especially western Germany. Between 1851 and about 1880 French investors and engineers, under the guidance of banks like the Crédit Mobilier, took it upon themselves to build the railway networks of much of southern and eastern Europe. They also invested in industrial enterprises in the same areas, and financed the perennial government deficits of the countries located there, as well as the Ottoman Empire and Egypt. After the Franco-Russian *rapprochement* of 1891 French investors, with the active encouragement of their government, invested huge sums in both public and private Russian securities. In 1914, at the outbreak of the First World War, fully one quarter of all French foreign investment was in Russia. About 12 per cent each was in Mediterranean Europe (Iberia, Italy, Greece), the Near East (Ottoman Empire, Egypt, Suez), and Latin America, with smaller amounts in the United States, the Scandinavian countries, Austria-Hungary, the Balkans and elsewhere. Unlike the case of Britain, less than 10 per cent of French investments went to French colonies.

Germany presents the interesting case of a nation that made the transition from net debtor to net creditor in the course of the century. In the middle decades of the century the western provinces benefited from an inflow of French, Belgian and British capital which helped develop powerful industries and a booming export surplus that provided the funds with which, first, to repatriate the foreign captial and then to accumulate investments abroad. Most of the latter were in Germany's poorer neighbours to the east and southeast, including its ally, the Habsburg monarchy, and its eventual enemy, Imperial Russia, although Germans also had important investments in the United States, Latin America and elsewhere (including miniscule amounts in the African and Pacific colonies). The German government, like the French, sometimes tried to use private foreign investment as a weapon of foreign policy; in 1887 it closed the Berlin stock exchange to Russian securities, and later it urged the Deutsche Bank to undertake the Anatolian (the so-called Berlin-to-Baghdad) railway.

The smaller developed nations of Western Europe – Belgium, the Netherlands and Switzerland – all of which had benefited from foreign investment in their economies during the century, had likewise become net creditors by the end of the century. In 1914 their combined foreign investments amounted to about six billion dollars, almost as much as Germany. Austria, the western half of the Habsburg monarchy, had investments in Hungary and also in the Balkans, although on balance the empire was a net debtor.

Among the recipients of foreign investment the United States was, in total, by far the largest. As indicated, foreign, especially British capital helped build railways, open up mineral resources, finance cattle ranches and numerous other endeavours. After the Civil War, however, and especially from the late 1890s, American investors began to purchase foreign securities and, even more importantly, American corporations began to invest directly abroad in a variety of industrial, commercial and agricultural operations. Most of these were in the western hemisphere (Latin America and Canada), but some were in Europe, the Near and Middle East and the Far East. In 1914, when total foreign investments in the United States amounted to slightly more than seven billion dollars, American investors had invested almost half as much abroad. In the next four years of the First World War, as a result of American loans to the Allies, the United States became the world's largest creditor nation.

Within Europe the largest single recipient of foreign investment was Russia. The Russian railway network, like the American, was built largely with foreign capital, which was channelled into both private securities (stocks and bonds) and government and government-guaranteed bonds. Foreigners, especially foreign banks, also invested heavily in Russian joint stock banks and in the great metallurgical enterprises of the Donbas, Krivoi Rog and elsewhere. The largest borrower of all, however, was the Russian government, which used the money not only to build railways but also to finance its army and navy. The largest investors were the French, but Germans, British, Belgians, Dutch and others also took part.

Most of the nations of Europe borrowed at one time or another during the nineteenth century. Germany and some of the smaller developed nations made the transition from net debtor to net creditor. Of those that did not, the record for both productive uses of the funds and repayment was poorest in the Mediterranean countries, southeast Europe, and the Near and Middle East. Frequently, the proceeds of both private investments and government loans were used wastefully and at times corruptly. In brilliant contrast to the poor record of those areas, most investments in the Scandinavian countries not only paid for themselves but made positive contributions to the development of the economies in which they were made. Indeed, although the absolute amounts were relatively small, on a per capita basis foreign investments in Sweden, Denmark and Norway were the largest in Europe. The amounts borrowed were invested wisely and, along with the high educational attainments of the populations of those countries, should be credited with the rapid development of their economies in the late nineteenth century.

Australia, New Zealand and Canada also had large foreign investments in relation to the size of their populations, which, as in the cases of the Scandinavian countries, helps to account for their high growth rates and high standards of living at the beginning of the twentieth century. By 1914 Canada had received the equivalent of $3.85 billion (1914 values), mostly from Great Britain, although US citizens and firms had invested about $900 million there. Australia had $1.8 billion and New Zealand about $300 million, over 95 per cent in both cases from Great Britain. The greater part of the funds in all three cases was invested in public (government) securities, and went to finance social overhead capital (railways, port facilities, public utilities, etc.), although substantial sums also went into mining in Australia and Canada.

Investments in Latin America and Asia, although substantial in total, were much smaller in relation to the populations of the recipient nations than the countries just considered. In them, and in Africa to an even greater degree, the principal result of foreign investment was to develop sources of raw materials for European industries without transforming the internal structures of the economy. In 1914 foreign investments in Latin America amounted to approximately $8.9 billion; in Asia, to $7.1 billion; and in Africa to slightly more than $4 billion. In every case Great Britain was the largest single source of funds, accounting for 42 per cent in Latin America, 50 per cent in Asia and more than 60 per cent in Africa.

Britain's leading role as foreign investor helps to explain the predominance of London as the world's financial and banking centre, but other factors also contributed. Britain was still the world's largest commercial nation, and most of that commerce was financed by bills on London. Indeed, much of the commerce of other nations with one another was also financed through London. Britain's adherence to the gold standard, and the role of the Bank of England in maintaining that standard, also contributed to London's predominance.

The British financial structure continued to evolve even after 1870. At the latter date the commercial banking system still consisted predominantly of unit banks, both private (the survivors of the 'country banks' of the eighteenth century) and joint stock, numbering approximately 365 altogether. Thereafter a process of concentration set in, involving both the growth of the larger joint stock banks by amalgamation and the expansion of branch networks. By 1913 the system consisted of about seventy banks nationwide, of which roughly a dozen were headquartered in London and maintained over 2,500 branches throughout the country. Most of the commercial banks still concerned themselves primarily with local and regional finance, but by the 1890s the largest London banks had begun to deal in international bills and even in issues of foreign securities. The pattern for the latter had been set as early as 1857 when the London and Westminster Bank, in collaboration with Baring Brothers, issued a loan for the Australian state of Victoria; by the 1880s it acted on behalf of other Australian states as well.

Another novelty of the 1850s and 1860s which became commonplace after 1870 was the rise of the so-called Anglo-International and Anglo-Imperial banks, joint stock banks with headquarters in London and branches overseas. In 1870 seventeen of these maintained branches in East Asia, South America and Europe. By 1910 their number had grown to twenty-five, with fewer branches in Europe but more in the Near and Middle East. Their main business was the finance of trade with the areas where they maintained branches, but they also got into the business of issuing foreign securities. These banks generally maintained close relations with private merchant bankers, who frequently sat on their boards of directors.

Other new entrants on the London financial scene from the 1870s onward were branches or offices of foreign banks, such as the Comptoir d'Escompte, the Crédit Lyonnais, the Deutsche Bank, the Dresdner, and the Russian Bank for Foreign Trade (St Petersburg). Their main business was the finance of trade with their respective countries, but they also occasionally cooperated with London's private merchant bankers in the issuance of securities.

In spite of this new competition, the private merchant bankers continued their leadership in the City. Stanley Chapman (1984: 105–6) has estimated that just seven of them – Rothschild, Baring, Kleinwort, Schroeder, Hambro, Brandt and Gibbs – accounted for 45 per cent of the acceptance credit on the London market on the eve of the First World War. Between 1870 and 1914 the merchant banks were primarily responsible (in some cases in cooperation with joint stock banks or other agencies) for about 40 per cent of the new issues of foreign securities. Increasingly the merchant banks acted as members of international syndicates. The 'Rothschild consortium', for example, generally included the three family banks (London, Paris and Vienna; the original bank in Frankfurt had been phased out), four German Jewish private banks, three Austro-Hungarian joint stock banks in which the family had interests, the Disconto-Gesellschaft, and occasionally the Darmstädter. Other combinations were also possible, depending upon the circumstances and purposes of the project at hand.

In France a number of new joint stock banks came into existence in the 1870s. A number of them were designed specifically to develop economic relations with foreign countries – for example the Banque Franco-Egyptienne, the Banque Française et Italienne, the Banque Franco-Hollandaise, the Banque Russe et Française and the Banque Transatlantique – and to that end established *filials* in the countries of their interest. Another joint stock investment bank, the Union Générale, had a less happy history. Patterned on the Crédit Mobilier, it was however touted as a 'Catholic bank' intended to wrest control of French finances from the 'monopoly' of Jewish and Protestant financiers. (Its manager had acquired his on-the-job training as an employee of the Austrian railway enterprises of both the Pereires and the Rothschilds.) It undertook numerous industrial and financial enterprises in both Austria and France, but overextended itself and came toppling down at the beginning of 1882, touching off a general financial crisis and inaugurating a depression that lasted almost fifteen years (Bouvier 1960).

That crisis, together with other disappointments, led some of the larger French joint stock banks to change their tactics, to develop their deposit business along the lines of the English joint stock banks. The Crédit Lyonnais under Henri Germain led the way as early as the 1870s. Even so, it continued to lend its *guichets* on a commission basis to underwriting syndicates in which it occasionally participated on its own account. It was especially active in placing Russian securities in France.

The Comptoir d'Escompte continued its mixed banking functions through the 1880s, even to the extent of becoming involved in a scheme to corner the world market in copper. That adventure led to its failure and the suicide of its principal officer in 1889. To prevent another major crisis the Ministry of Finance and the Bank of France guaranteed its depositors against losses and reorganised it as the Comptoir Nationale d'Escompte, an ordinary deposit and discount bank, but even that did not prevent it from taking part in further foreign financial affairs. It was especially strong in the Orient before 1889, somewhat less so thereafter.

The Société Générale gave up its investment banking functions more slowly. As late as 1890, 22 per cent of its total assets were in the form of securities and participations in other enterprises. This figure dropped to 13 per cent in 1900 and by 1912, with assets of more than two billion francs, only 5 per cent were in the form of participations and securities. It was, nevertheless, extremely active in eastern Europe, especially Russia and the Ottoman Empire. The Société Générale frequently cooperated with German and Austrian as well as other French banks.

As the majority of French banks gradually shifted their operations to short-term commercial credit, investment banking in France came to be concentrated in institutions created especially for the purpose and operating largely with their own capitals. Foremost among these was the Banque de Paris et des Pays-Bas. Although active in French railways and public utilities (especially the electrical industry after 1880), Paribas devoted by far the greater part of its resources to foreign operations. It participated in railways from Portugal to Russia, from Argentina to China; mining and metallurgical enterprises in Russia, Sweden, Spain and North Africa; electricity in Norway, Germany and Russia; gold mines in Russia, Australia and South Africa. Very few of the millions of foreign securities which came on the French market did so without the assistance of Paribas. In most of its operations it had the cooperation of other French and foreign banks, especially Hambro, Baring, Hope, Bleichroeder, the Disconto-Gesellschaft and the Deutsche Bank.

Several other, smaller banks were formed on the model of Paribas. These included the Crédit Mobilier Français, a reorganised version of the original Crédit Mobilier (1871); the Banque Française pour le Commerce et l'Industrie (1901); and the Banque de l'Union Parisienne, founded in 1874 but reorganised in 1904 by several Protestant members of the *haute banque* (Mallet, Mirabaud, Hottinguer, etc.) to assist them in their foreign undertakings. All of these banks had *filials* or participated in the ownership and control of other banks throughout eastern and southern Europe, the Near and Middle East and Latin America.

In 1875 the Comptoir d'Escompte, the Crédit Industriel et Commercial, and Paribas, together with the French government created the Banque de l'Indo-Chine as a bank of issue for French possessions in Asia. In addition to its issue function, however, it also served as a commercial and investment bank, with participations in tea and rubber plantations, mines, distilleries and a variety of other industries. It also established branches outside French territory: Hong Kong (1895), Bangkok (1897) and Singapore (1905) (Bonin 1987).

The Imperial Ottoman Bank was a most unusual financial institution. Founded in 1856 in Constantinople as an ordinary joint stock bank by a group of British financiers, it was greatly enlarged and obtained a new charter in 1863 by a French group including the Crédit Mobilier and several members of the *haute banque*. According to its new charter it had a monopoly of note issue for the whole of the Ottoman Empire, served as fiscal agent for the government, could buy and sell securities, specie, and commodities, and 'finally, [could] undertake any operation relating to the functions of a banking institution' (BIO 1863). In later years the bank became an almost exclusively French institution and dominated the economic and financial life of the Empire. In the early years of the twentieth century the list of French directors might easily have been mistaken for the names of the regents of the Bank of France or a register of the *haute banque*.

In Germany private merchant bankers dominated both domestic and international banking well into the 1870s. Several of them founded joint stock banks both to secure command over greater amounts of capital and to reduce risks. By 1880, however, unlike the situation in Britain and France, the joint stock banks under professional managers like Gustav Mevissen (Schaaffhausen'scher, Darmstädter), the Hansemanns (Disconto-Gesellschaft) and Georg Siemens and Herman Wallich (Deutsche Bank) dealt with the private bankers as equals or even subordinates. Thereafter they quickly established their dominance.

German foreign investments, like those of Britain and France, were largely guided by the banks, both private and joint stock; but the precise relations differed according to the area of the world in which the investments were made. In the United States, for example, where several of the important private banks (Kuhn, Loeb & Co., Speyer & Co., W.G. Hallgarten & Co., Warburgs, Seligman) had been founded by immigrant German Jews, personal and family relationships greatly influenced the flow of investment. In South America and Asia trading relationships led to the establishment of overseas banks: the Deutsch-Belgische La Plata Bank (founded in 1872 by Oppenheim and the Disconto-Gesellschaft, sold to the Deutsche Bank in 1874, liquidated in 1885); the

Deutsche Übersee-Bank (founded in 1886 by the Deutsche Bank, and far more successful than the former); Brasilianische Bank für Deutschland (1887) and the Bank für Chile und Deutschland (1895), both founded by the Disconto-Gesellschaft; and the Deutsche-Asiatische Bank, founded in 1889 by a consortium of all the leading German banks, both joint stock and private. Finally, the sizeable foreign investments in Austria-Hungary, the Balkans, the Ottoman Empire and Russia undertaken by virtually all of the German banks were motivated primarily by the expectation of a high rate of return, but political factors and the pressure of the government – both positive and negative – were not negligible.

Belgium, the country that pioneered joint stock investment banking, was also a pioneer in another important financial institution, the international holding company. In both cases the Société Générale de Belgique was the pioneering instrument. The Société Générale took the lead in expanding abroad after 1870 and especially after 1890. Its motives at first were to find foreign markets for the Belgian industries that it patronised, especially heavy industries, and to this end it founded or participated in foreign railways and tramways. Subsequently, after those markets were saturated or nearly so, it branched out into heavy industry and financial institutions. Between 1891 and 1913 it participated in at least nineteen foreign banks and financial institutions. In heavy industry it was especially active in developing the iron and steel industry of southern Russia, but had many other participations as well. As in the earlier period (before 1870), other Belgian banks eagerly imitated the Société Générale, not always with such success.

The financial structure in the United States was quite different from that in Europe. Under the National Banking System, introduced by the federal government during the Civil War as a measure of war finance, joint stock banks generally were prohibited from establishing branches, including overseas branches. This meant that the banking system was characterised by many – literally thousands – of small unit banks mainly concerned with local business. Moreover, joint stock banks were also prevented from accepting drafts or bills of exchange, the principal instruments of international finance. Another feature of the American banking system, offsetting to some extent the rigidity of the joint stock banks, was the existence of many – again thousands – private (unincorporated) banks, entirely free of the regulations that encumbered the joint stock banks except that they were prohibited from issuing their own notes. Most of these were also relatively small and concerned with local business, but a few – a score or so – located in New York, Philadelphia and Boston, specialised in international finance. They not only accepted bills of exchange but also, usually in partnership with European firms, undertook the placement of American securities abroad. Many of these firms had offices in London and/or Paris: Brown Brothers & Co., J. & W. Seligman & Co., Morton, Bliss & Co., Drexel & Co., Lazard Frères (actually an American firm before establishing itself in Paris), and so on. Some acted as American agents for European merchant banks: for example, August Belmont & Co. for the Rothschilds, Kidder, Peabody & Co. for Barings. The most famous, of course was J.P. Morgan & Co.; Pierpont Morgan in New York served as the American agent for his father's firm, J.S. Morgan & Co. of London, until he succeeded his father on the latter's death in 1890. Thereafter he was senior partner in both New York and London until his own death in 1913.

The financial structures of the debtor countries of Europe were profoundly affected by their international connections. Most of the banks of southern and southeastern Europe had either been founded directly by banks or financiers from the creditor countries or else depended upon them for both financial and technical assistance. For example the Credito Mobiliare Italiano and the Banca di Credito Italiano, founded on the same day in 1863, were *filials* of, respectively, the Crédit Mobilier and the Crédit Industriel and for some years maintained committees of directors in Paris. When the Credito Mobiliare (which took over the Credito Italiano in 1892) failed in the financial crisis of 1893, it was replaced the following year by the Banca Commerciale Italiana, which depended in large part on German capital and expertise. The Germans shortly withdrew, however, to be replaced in turn by the Banque de Paris et des Pays-Bas.

Banking in the Scandinavian countries differed from that in the Mediterranean lands in that already in 1870 they had relatively sophisticated banking structures that did not depend significantly on either foreign capital or technical expertise. In the next four decades, however, during which their economies developed and modernised very rapidly, they borrowed abroad extensively and their banks played a crucial role in both borrowing and allocating the borrowed funds. In both Sweden and Denmark three large joint stock banks dominated international financial relations: Stockholms Enskilda Bank (1856), Skandinaviska Banken (1864) and Stockholms Handelsbank (1871, subsequently the Svenska Handelsbank) for Sweden; the Privatbank (1857), Landsmanbanken (1871) and Handelsbanken (1873) for Denmark. Although domestically owned and controlled, all of them – especially Stockholms Enskilda Bank – had been influenced by the Crédit Mobilier and subsequently by the German banks. Sweden also had the Sveriges Allmänna Hypoteksbank, a state-owned mortgage bank established in 1861 on the model of the Crédit Foncier, which issued large quantities of mortgage bonds abroad; in 1914 the French owned 99.5 per cent of them.

The banking system of Russia, one of the last in Europe to develop, owed much – financially and otherwise – to Western models. The wholly state-owned State Bank, established in 1860 to replace a number of pre-reform state banking institutions, played a larger role in international financial relations than central banks in other nations owing to Russia's large foreign-held government debt and its efforts to adopt the gold standard in 1897. But the most important foreign influence occurred through the joint stock banks. The first of these, the St Petersburg Private Commercial Bank (half government-owned in spite of its name), came into existence in 1864. By 1914 fifty such banks existed, mostly headquartered in St Petersburg and Moscow, with more than 800 branches nation-wide. The twelve largest banks, eight of them based in St Petersburg, controlled 80 per cent of total assets. Many of them had been founded or were managed by French, German, British and other bankers. In 1916 foreign banks owned 45 per cent of the capital of the ten largest banks; of that, more than 50 per cent was French, 37 per cent German, and 9 per cent British. Many foreign banks had initially invested directly in Russian industrial enterprises, but later shifted their investments to the banks, both because the Russian banks could monitor the industrial investments more closely and could also benefit from government favours.

Japan, another late-comer to modern industrialisation, also adopted Western models for its financial institutions. Space does not permit a detailed account, but it is worth noting that after the Meiji Restoration the new Japanese government first took the relatively new National Banking System of the United States as its model. When that failed to produce satisfactory results the government withdrew the right of note issue from the banks, converted them to ordinary deposit banks *à l'anglaise*, and created a new central bank, the Bank of Japan, on the model of the Banque Nationale de Belgique.

CONCLUSIONS

What conclusions can be drawn from this all-too-hasty survey of the development of international banking from the Middle Ages to the First World War? In the first place it is clear that, with a few exceptions, the international banks, bankers and the banking system (in so far as it *was* a system) were instruments of material progress. The international investments which they made or facilitated provided capital for economic growth. Moreover, and perhaps more importantly, the international movements of capital also usually involved the international diffusion of technology, a crucial determinant of economic development. The exceptions occurred when foreign investments were used for the purchase or production of armaments and other means of warfare. But the banks and bankers can scarcely be held responsible for the uses made of their capital by sovereign governments. Many examples could be cited in which bankers opposed, not always successfully, the military use of their funds.

Secondly, international banking was an instrument not only of material progress, but of moral progress as well. Not only was technology diffused, but ideas more generally: ideas in the realms of literature, the arts, politics and philosophy. International banking and the international commerce which it made possible were certainly not the only means of diffusion, nor was it the intention or purpose of the bankers to serve as diffusers of knowledge; as Adam Smith said of merchants in general – and bankers were, after all, merchants – they were 'led by an invisible hand' to promote an end which was no part of their intention.

The tragedy of the First World War for which the bankers cannot be held responsible, put an end to that benign system, for a time at least. Attempts were made to revive it in the interwar years, and in recent years we have witnessed the proliferation of 'global banking' which makes the pre-war system look simple by comparison. But without that simple system the global world economy of today could never have come into existence.

NOTES

1. By multinational business firms I mean enterprises that carried on productive activities beyond mere trade across political boundaries in two or more countries. See Wilkins (1970: ix) and Hertner and Jones (1986: 1).
2. There is an enormous literature on the Rothschilds. Among the better and more recent books are Gille (1965–7) and Bouvier (1983). Among the older works E.C. Corti's two volumes (1928 a and b) are still worth reading.
3. Cameron (1961: 148–50). Actually the first one was the A. Schaaffhausen'scher Bankverein, created in the crisis year 1848 on the ruins of the bankrupt private bank, Abraham Schaaffhausen & Co. In the panic of the revolution the Prussian administration departed temporarily from its firm rule against joint stock banks, to which it soon returned, which is why the promotors of the Darmstädter could not locate their bank in Cologne, as they desired.
4. The following pages present a drastic condensation of the studies contained in Bovykin and Cameron (1990, forthcoming). Citations of individual chapters have not been made.

REFERENCES

[BIO] Banque Impériale Ottomane (1863), *Acte de concession et statutes*, Paris: BIO.
Barbour, Violet (1950), *Capitalism in Amsterdam in the Seventeenth Century*, Baltimore: Johns Hopkins University Press.
Bautier, Robert-Henri (1953), 'Les foires de Champagne: recherches sur une évolution historique', *Bulletin de la Société Jean Bodin*, V, *La Foire*, pp. 97–145. Trans. as 'The fairs of Champagne' in R. Cameron (ed.), *Essays in French Economic History* (1970), Homewood, IL: Richard D. Irwin, pp. 42–63.
Bergier, Jean-François (1979), 'From the fifteenth century in Italy to the sixteenth century in Germany: a new banking concept?' in Center for Medieval and Renaissance Studies (ed.), *The Dawn of Modern Banking*, New Haven/London: Yale University Press, pp. 105–29.
Bonin, Hubert (1987), *Indosuez: l'autre grande banque d'affaires*, Paris: Economica.

Born, Karl Erich (1983), *International Banking in the 19th and 20th Centuries*, New York: St. Martin's Press.
Bouvier, Jean (1960), *Le Krach de l'Union Générale*, Paris: Presses Universitaires de France.
Bouvier, Jean (1961), *Le Crédit Lyonnais de 1863 à 1882*, 2 vols, Paris: SEVPEN.
Bouvier, Jean (1983), *Les Rothschild*, 2nd edn, Paris: Fayard.
Bovykin, Valerii, and Rondo Cameron (eds) (1990, forthcoming) *International Banking, Investment, and Industrial Finance, 1870–1914*, New York/Oxford: Oxford University Press.
Buist, Marten G. (1974), *At Spes Non Fracta: Hope & Co. 1770–1815*, The Hague: Martinus Nijhoff.
Cameron, Rondo (1961), *France and the Economic Development of Europe, 1800–1915*, Princeton: Princeton University Press.
Cameron, Rondo, with the collaboration of Olga Crisp, Hugh T. Patrick and Richard Tilly (1967), *Banking in the Early Stages of Industrialization*, New York/Oxford: Oxford University Press.
Carosso, Vincent (1987), *The Morgans, Private International Bankers, 1854–1913*, Cambridge, MA: Harvard University Press.
Center for Medieval and Renaissance Studies, University of California, Los Angeles (1979), *The Dawn of Modern Banking*. New Haven/London: Yale University Press.
Chapman, Stanley (1984), *The Rise of Merchant Banking*, London/Boston: Allen & Unwin.
Corti, Egon C. (1928a), *The Rise of the House of Rothschild*. London: Gollancz.
Corti, Egon C. (1928b), *The Reign of the House of Rothschild*, London: Gollancz.
Cottrell, Philip L. (1985), *Investment Banking in England, 1856–81: A Case Study of the International Financial Society*, 2 vols, New York: Garland.
Cottrell, Philip L. (1990, forthcoming), 'Britain, 1870–1913' in V. Bovykin and R. Cameron (eds), *International Banking, Investment, and Industrial Finance, 1870–1914*, New York/Oxford: Oxford University Press.
De Roover, Raymond (1963), *The Rise and Fall of the Medici Bank, 1397–1484*, Cambridge, MA: Harvard University Press.
Economist, The (1856), 12 July.
Edmundson, George (1891), 'Louis de Geer', *English Historical Review*, vol. 6, pp. 685–712.
Ehrenberg, Richard (1928),: *Capital and Finance in the Age of the Renaissance: A Study of the Fuggers and their Connections*, trans. from the German by H.M. Lucas (1963), New York: Augustus M. Kelley.
Gille, Bertrand (1954), 'La fondation du Crédit Mobilier et les idées financières des frères Pereire', *Bulletin du Centre de Recherches sur l'histoire des Entreprises*, vol. 3, pp. 1–22.
Gille, Bertrand (1965–7), *Histoire de la Maison Rothschild*, 2 vols, Geneva: Librairie Droz.

Hertner, Peter and Geoffrey Jones (eds) (1986), *Multinationals: Theory and History*, Aldershot: Gower.
Kellenbenz, Hermann (ed.) (1981), *Precious Metals in the Age of Expansion: Papers of the XIVth International Congress of the Historical Sciences*, Stuttgart: Klett-Cotta.
Krekić, Bariša (1979), 'Italian creditors in Dubrovnik (Ragusa) and the Balkan trade, thirteenth through fifteenth Centuries', in Center for Medieval and Renaissance Studies (ed.), *The Dawn of Modern Banking*, New Haven/London: Yale University Press, pp. 77–104.
Landes, David S. (1956), 'Vieille banque et banque nouvelle: la révolution financière du dix-neuvième siècle', *Revue d'histoire moderne et contemporaine*, vol. 3, pp. 204–22.
Lüthy, Herbert (1959–61), *La Banque Protestante en France de la Révocation de l'Edit de Nantes à la Revolution*, 2 vols, Paris: SEVPEN.
Perkins, Edwin J. (1975), *Financing Anglo-American Trade: The House of Brown, 1800–1880*, Cambridge, MA: Harvard University Press.
Prestwich, Michael (1979), 'Italian merchants in late thirteenth and early fourteenth century England', in Center for Medieval and Renaissance Studies (ed.), *The Dawn of Modern Banking*, New Haven/London: Yale University Press, pp. 77–104.
Riesser, Jakob (1911), *The German Great Banks and their Concentration in Connection with the Economic Development of Germany*, Washington: Publications of the National Monetary Commission (vol. 14).
Riley, James C. (1980), *International Government Finance and the Amsterdam Capital Market, 1740–1815*, Cambridge, MA: Harvard University Press.
Van der Wee, Herman (1963), *The Growth of the Antwerp Market and the European Economy (fourteenth-sixteenth centuries)*, 3 vols, The Hague: Martinus Nijhoff.
Wilkins, Mira (1970), *The Emergence of Multinational Enterprise: American Business Abroad from the Colonial Era to 1914*, Cambridge, MA: Harvard University Press.

PART IV

ASPECTS OF GROWTH AND STAGNATION IN THE WORLD ECONOMY DURING THE TWENTIETH CENTURY

8 · WORLD ECONOMIC PERFORMANCE SINCE 1870

Angus Maddison

As there are now about 200 separate 'countries' and GDP estimates back to 1870 are available for only twenty-five of them, one cannot hope for comprehensive retrospective monitoring of the 'world economy'. If we exploited the available estimates to the full, the sample would be heavily biassed towards the advanced countries. I have therefore confined the sample to ten big countries – the five biggest OECD and the five biggest non-OECD economies. The sample completely ignores Africa and the Middle East, but it covers 74 per cent of the GDP of OECD countries, 68 per cent of the Soviet bloc, 52 per cent of developing Asia and 60 per cent of Latin America. It covers 68 per cent of world product, 60 per cent of world population and half of world exports.

THE LONG-TERM RECORD

Table 8.1 summarises performance over the 117 years since 1870. It shows both coefficients of multiplication and compound growth rates. For analytical purposes, growth rates are preferable. The coefficients show inter-country variations in performance more dramatically, but they exaggerate differences in inter-country performance.

Table 8.1 shows both weighted and unweighted averages. For the purpose of assessing inter-country performance the arithmetic average is preferable, but when we use the ten countries as a proxy measure for the world aggregate, weighted averages are needed. The latter showed an average GDP growth of 2.7 per cent a year and an average growth of per capita income of 1.5 per cent over

Table 8.1 Summary indicators of long-term performance, 1870–1987

	Coefficients of multiplication			Annual average compound growth rates		
	GDP	Population	GDP per capita	GDP	Population	GDP per capita
France	13	1.4	9	2.2	0.3	1.9
Germany	26	2.4	10	2.8	0.8	2.0
Japan	84	3.6	24	3.9	1.1	2.7
UK	9	1.9	5	1.9	0.6	1.3
USA	53	6.1	9	3.4	1.6	1.9
Arithmetic average (5 countries)	37	3.1	11	2.8	0.9	1.9
Weighted average (5 countries)	31	3.2	10	3.0	1.0	2.0
Brazil	157	14.4	11	4.4	2.3	2.1
China	17	3.1	6	2.5	1.0	1.5
India	7	3.8	2	1.7	1.1	0.5
Mexico	44	8.9	5	3.2	1.9	1.4
USSR	27	3.6	8	2.9	1.1	1.8
Arithmetic average (5 countries)	50	6.8	6	2.9	1.5	1.5
Weighted average (5 countries)	18	3.6	4	2.5	1.1	1.3
Arithmetic average (10 countries)	44	4.9	9	2.6	1.2	1.7
Weighted average (10 countries)	24	3.5	6	2.7	1.1	1.5

Source: See Appendix.

Table 8.2 Per capita GDP growth rates, 1820–1987

	1820–70	1870–1913	1913–50	1950–73	1973–87
France	1.3	1.4	1.1	3.8	1.7
Germany	1.1	1.6	0.7	4.9	2.0
Japan	0.1[a]	1.5	0.9	8.1	2.8
UK	1.2	1.0	0.8	2.5	1.5
USA	1.5	2.0	1.6	2.2	1.5
Arithmetic average	1.0	1.5	1.0	4.3	1.9
Brazil	–	0.2	2.7	4.5	2.4
China	–	0.5	−0.5	4.0	5.7
India	–	0.1	−0.4	1.6	2.3
Mexico	–	0.9	1.0	3.3	0.8
USSR	–	0.6	2.5	3.6	0.4
Arithmetic average	0.1[a]	0.5	1.1	3.4	2.3

[a] Author's guesstimate.
Source: See Appendix.

the 117 years. In the first group of 'advanced' countries, per capita income grew at an (arithmetic) average rate of 1.9 per cent per annum, and 2.0 per cent per annum on a weighted basis. In the second group it grew more slowly: 1.5 per cent a year using the arithmetic average and 1.3 on a weighted basis. Thus there was no convergence in income levels between the two groups over the long run, the percentage gap being slightly wider in 1987 than in 1870.

One can see in Table 8.2 that modern economic growth (defined in Kuznets' sense of reasonably sustained per capita growth) did not start in 1870 in our first group. Most of these countries already had significant per capita growth from 1820 onwards, but the little evidence there is for the second group suggests that 1870 was more or less the starting point of their per capita growth. The fastest GDP growth for 1870–1987 was recorded in Brazil, the slowest in India. The fastest per capita growth took place in Japan, the slowest in India.

Table 8.3 shows per capita real income levels in comparable units, i.e. US dollars of 1965. These estimates were derived by using the time series for GDP and population described in the appendix and merging them with 1965 benchmark estimates of GDP level contained for the most part in Maddison (1970). In comparison across countries with very wide differences in per

Table 8.3 GDP per capita at 1965 factor cost (US dollars at 1965 US prices)

	1870	1913	1950	1973	1987
France	416	768	1,168	2,963	3,762
Germany	346	694	913	2,764	3,626
Japan	175	332	466	2,815	4,120
UK	689	1,057	1,438	2,557	3,165
USA	566	1,344	2,386	3,971	4,893
Arithmetic average	438	839	1,274	3,014	3,913
Weighted average	440	925	1,505	3,293	4,276
Brazil	109	118	311	853	1,187
China	118	149	126	308	673
India	155	164	146	209	286
Mexico	167	241	349	737	825
USSR	286	373	914	2,083	2,209
Arithmetic average	167	209	369	838	1,036
Weighted average	170	195	267	556	764

capita output and income, I prefer this benchmark to the more recent International Comparison Project (ICP) estimates for 1980 (see Table 8.14 and 8.15, on page 236) available in UN (1986), because I think the ICP exaggerates the income of developing countries as explained in Maddison (1983a). The table shows that the USA became the lead country in terms of real income per head somewhere between 1870 and 1913 (elsewhere I have argued for a date around 1890). It has kept this lead ever since. The second place is now occupied by Japan, but the relatively high Japanese real income depends, in part, on unusually high labour input per head of population (long working weeks, short holidays and high activity rates). Unfortunately we do not have adequate data for measuring labour productivity levels for these ten countries, but for the top five see Maddison (1987).

Table 8.4 compares the ranking of countries in terms of total product. In 1870 China was the biggest economy, India the second, Russia third and the United States fourth. In 1987 the United States was first, China second, USSR third and Japan fourth. This table (unlike most of the others) is not adjusted for territorial change, but see Table 8.12, page 235, for figures which are so adjusted.

In 1870 our top group had only three-quarters of the total product of our second group; by 1987 the situation had been

Table 8.4 Total GDP in 1870 and 1987 (boundaries of epoch) (million US dollars at 1965 US prices)

	1870	1987
France	15,978	209,507
Germany	13,949	220,735
Japan	6,035	505,971
UK	20,851	179,394
USA	22,645	1,194,551
Total 5 countries	79,458	2,310,158
Brazil	1,063	166,372
China	41,491	724,096
India	39,239	225,466
Mexico	1,540	67,821
USSR	23,161	623,613
Total 5 countries	106,494	1,807,368

Table 8.5 Total exports in 1870 and 1985 (million US dollars in current prices)

	1870	1985
France	541	97,726
Germany	424	183,406
Japan	15	175,683
UK	971	101,332
USA	403	213,146
Total 5 countries	2,354	771,293
Brazil	76	25,639
China	104	27,343
India	255	8,397
Mexico	25	21,822
USSR	216	87,041
Total 5 countries	676	170,242
Total 10 countries	3,030	941,535
World	5,132	1,930,104

Sources: Lewis (1981), Maddison (1962) and national sources for 1870. UN, *Monthly Bulletin of Statistics* for 1985.

reversed. The relative size of the different economies in terms of GDP is not a good indicator of their influence on world economic developments. This is better approximated by the size of their trade, shown in Table 8.5. In 1870, the United Kingdom held first place, followed by France, Germany and the United States. In

Table 8.6 Phases of development, 1870–1987 (annual average rate of GDP growth at constant prices)

	1870–1913	1913–50	1950–73	1973–87
France	1.6	1.1	5.1	2.2
Germany	2.8	1.3	5.9	1.8
Japan	2.5	2.2	9.4	3.7
UK	1.9	1.3	3.0	1.6
USA	4.2	2.8	3.7	2.5
Arithmetic average	2.6	1.7	5.4	2.4
Weighted average	2.9	2.2	4.6	2.6
Brazil	2.3	4.9	7.5	4.9
China	1.0	0.2	6.2	7.1
India	0.6	0.7	3.7	4.5
Mexico	2.0	2.7	6.6	3.5
USSR	2.5	2.5	5.1	1.7
Arithmetic average	1.7	2.2	5.8	4.3
Weighted average	1.2	1.6	5.4	4.0
Grand total				
(arithmetic average)	2.4	2.1	5.6	3.4
(weighted average)	2.1	2.0	4.9	3.2

Source: See Appendix. Figures are adjusted to offset effect of changed boundaries.

1987, the United States held first place, followed by Germany, Japan and the United Kingdom.

PHASES OF GROWTH

Table 8.6 shows four phases of growth of GDP within the period 1870–1987. I developed this periodicity while analysing long-term growth in sixteen advanced countries (Maddison 1982) and it has some validity for the world economy as well.

The first phase, 1870–1913, shows performance in a situation of minimalist government intervention in economic life, with a stable international monetary order, freedom of international capital movements and migration, and with trade impediments confined to tariffs. The latter were very low in the United Kingdom and its colonies, and also in countries like China, Egypt, Turkey, and Thailand which were subject to treaties limiting their sovereignty in this respect. The United States, Russia and Brazil were high-tariff countries, so the world order of that time was not one of pure liberalism.

Domestic policy rules in the advanced countries were generally those of sound finance, with balanced budgets, sound money, and only the very beginnings of social security. Brazil went furthest in degree of unorthodoxy with *de facto* floating exchange rates and tolerance of inflation, but it was a mild transgression by later standards. Gerschenkron distinguished between latecomers where government intervened in the growth process by fostering railways and banks, and the *laissez-faire* of the United Kingdom which had the pioneer experience of early modern growth. By retrospective standards the dichotomy seems perhaps exaggerated, but it has some validity for Meiji Japan, Tsarist Russia and Mexico under Porfirio Diaz, and it is true that British growth performance was relatively poor in this period, during which it lost its status as lead country to the United States.

In 1870–1913, growth performance was highest in the United States and worst in the Asian countries subject to colonial rule or foreign hegemony. US dynamism in this period was strongly associated with its natural resource advantages and its capacity to attract migrants and foreign capital. The available evidence suggests much higher rates of investment in the United States than elsewhere (Maddison 1982: 40).

Our second phase, 1913–50, was a time of troubles with two world wars and a major world depression, which had a particularly adverse effect on Europe and Asia. However, in Latin America the collapse of the liberal world order in 1929–32 sparked off a new kind of government activism in the development process, of an import substitution kind. Several Latin American countries did rather well in this period, particularly Brazil. The United States had rapid growth of GDP in the 1940s, due to the stimulus of war.

In this period the USSR embarked on a very radical and ambitious experiment with confiscation of capitalist property, establishment of state owned enterprise in agriculture and industry, and forced accumulation with the idea of getting accelerated growth through higher rates of investment. Within the capitalist group, older precepts of economic policy were largely abandoned in Germany and Japan. In the 1930s and 1940s both countries had a high degree of government intervention.

With the breakdown in the liberal world order after 1929, world

Table 8.7 World export volume (billion US dollars)

World exports at 1973 prices	
1720	1.02
1820	2.44
1870	18.87
1913	75.48
1929	106.81
1950	114.35
1973	578.10
1985	855.70
Annual compound growth rate of world exports	
1720–1820	0.9
1820–70	4.2
1870–1913	3.3
1913–50	1.1
1950–73	7.3
1973–85	3.3

Source: 1720–1970 Maddison (1982): 254; 1973–85 from IMF, *International Financial Statistics Yearbook*, 1986 edition.

trade collapsed and so did the international capital market (see Tables 8.7 and 8.8). Growth processes were much more autarkic and less diffused than in the old liberal order, with a general fall in the ratio of trade to GDP.

The third phase 1950–73 was a golden age in which growth processes seem to have entered a virtuous circle. In all countries, except the lead country (the United States), growth was much higher than in any earlier period. To some extent this reflected an element of recovery from the destruction and wasted opportunities of the 1913–50 period. There was also an efficiency bonus from restoration of a liberal world-trading order and the rehabilitation of the international monetary system at Bretton Woods facilitated the prospects for expansionist policy. But on top of this there were other elements, notably a commitment to fuller use of economic potential on the part of governments in the advanced capitalist countries and in the newly independent Third World. The old establishment view of the role of government had undergone major change.

A remarkable feature of the period was the universal rise in rates of investment throughout the world. This undoubtedly was a

Table 8.8 Gross value of foreign capital liabilities of developing countries (billion US dollars at year-end)

	1870	1914	1938	1950	1973	1985
Total in current prices	5.3	22.7	23.1	13.6	172.0	1,118.0
Total in 1973 prices	17.9	96.6	72.3	25.1	172.0	508.8

Sources: UK, French and German investment 1870–1914 from H. Feis, *Europe: The World's Banker 1870–1914* (New York: Kelley 1961); USA from C. Lewis, *America's Stake in International Investments*, (Washington, DC: Brookings Institution, 1938), and other from *International Capital Movements in the Interwar Period* (Lake Success: UN, 1949). 1939 from C. Lewis, *The United States and Foreign Investment Problems*, (Washington DC: Brookings Institution, 1948) and Bank of England, *United Kingdom Overseas Investments 1938–1948* (London, 1950). 1950 estimated mainly from UK and USA official sources. 1973 estimated from OECD, *Development Cooperation*, various issues (includes $119 billion debt plus an estimated $53 billion of direct investment). 1985 figure represents $948 billion of debt, see OECD, *External Debt Statistics* (Paris: OECD, 1987), plus an estimated $170 billion of direct investment. Deflator is US consumer price index.

major reason why such growth was possible. Ease of communication, efforts to promote technical interchange, the big surge in international private investment all made it easier for follower countries to mimic the lead country's technology, and made this investment effort profitworthy.

Since 1973 world economic growth has slowed down markedly though aggregate growth for the ten countries has been fairly respectable by historical standards (see Table 8.6). The slowdown has affected all the advanced OECD countries, Latin America and the USSR. The exceptions are China and India.

For the advanced capitalist countries, I have argued (Maddison 1983b) that three major influences were operative: (a) some 'normal' slowdown in European countries and Japan as they exhausted the special opportunities for growth they had in the post-war age (catching up with the lead country, improvements in efficiency through expansion of intra-trade and elimination of low productivity employment in agriculture); (b) some unavoidable loss in order to respond to shocks coming from the collapse of the fixed rate international monetary system of Bretton Woods, from the two OPEC shocks and from the acceleration of inflation; (c) substantial changes in the 'establishment' view of policy objectives and weaponry.

In my view the advanced countries are growing below their

Table 8.9 Growth of total reproducible capital stock

	1913–50	1950–73	1973–84
France	0.9	3.6	4.0
Germany	0.7	5.4	3.4
Japan	1.6	8.0	7.2
UK	1.2	3.3	2.5
USA	1.8	3.4	2.8
Arithmetic average	1.2	4.7	4.0
Brazil	2.5	6.2	9.4[a]
China	n.a.	n.a.	n.a.
India	n.a.	5.8	4.9[b]
Mexico	n.a.	6.8	5.5
USSR	4.7[c]	8.6	n.a.

[a] 1973–80; [b] 1973–81; [c] 1929–51.
Sources: Maddison (1987: 690) for first 5 countries. Brazil net fixed capital stock from R.G. Goldsmith, *Brasil 1850–1984: Desenvolvimento Financeiro sob um secolo de Inflacao*, (Sao Paulo: Harper & Row, 1986, p. 154). India from J. Kumar, R.P. Katyal and S.P. Sharma, 'Estimates of fixed capital stock in India', Delhi, (mimeo., 1986, p. 54), which refers to the net fixed capital stock in the public and private corporate sector. Mexico net fixed capital stock 1950–60 from *Cuentas nacionales y Acervos de Capital 1950–67* (Banco de Mexico, 1969); 1960–85 from L.H. Villalpando Hernández and J. Fernández Moran, *La Encuesta de Acervos, Depreciación y Formación de Capital del Banco de Mexico 1975–1985* (Bank of Mexico, 1986). USSR gross capital stock without deduction of depreciation, 1929–51 from R. Moorsteen and R.P. Powell, *The Soviet Capital Stock 1928–1962*, (Homewood, Illinois: R. D. Irwin, 1966, p. 615); 1950–73 from A. Bergson and H.S. Levine, *The Soviet Economy Towards the Year 2000* (London: Allen and Unwin, 1983, p. 37).

potential, as evidenced by their high levels of unemployment, and the fact that their capital stock is still growing much faster than historical norms (see Table 8.9). I do not attach much value to 'structural' explanations of Western slowdown, or to Eurosclerosis.

Latin American countries appeared to be bucking the world economic trend in phase 4 until 1982, financing expansionary policies by heavy foreign borrowing. This was ended by the debt crisis, which has brought very disappointing or negative growth. Here too it seems clear that post-1982 growth has been below long-run potential, and previous debt experience suggests that the problem will be resolved by delinquency (Maddison 1985). However, it is clear that Latin America also has very major problems of inflation and that the attack on inflationary expectations via heterodox policy has not been successful.

In the USSR (and incidentally in Eastern Europe as well), the slowdown has been remarkably similar in timing to that in Western countries, but the causality seems different. Here there do seem to be more genuine structural problems, some of the Latin American debt syndrome, with some threat of inflation and unemployment implicit in the *perestroika* policy menu.

India and China are economies with low productivity and a good deal more catch-up potential than the others, which they are exploiting by major efforts to raise the level of physical (and human) capital. In China's case, the high level of resource mobilisation for growth (ratio of gross investment to GDP up from 10 per cent in 1952 to 38 per cent in 1985) has been supplemented by considerable liberalisation of the economy in the past decade. Neither of these countries has had debt or inflation problems on anything like the scale of Latin America.

CONCLUSIONS

It is obvious that there have been some forces in the 'world economy', that have affected growth momentum of the various countries in similar ways (the phase phenomenon). There have also been changes in the relative wealth and power of individual countries without much long-run evidence of convergence in income levels between our two major groups.

This chapter is cursory and rather descriptive with no overt model of the forces making for growth. However, it is clear that these forces are very complex and that proximate growth accounts (such as Maddison 1987) are only part of the story. Figure 8.1 summarises my view of the underlying causality.

APPENDIX

Sources for population
For OECD countries from Maddison (1987). Brazil 1870–1940 from *O Brasil — Numeros*, Rio: IBGE, 1960, p. 5; thereafter supplied by Brazilian statistical office. China 1870–1933 from

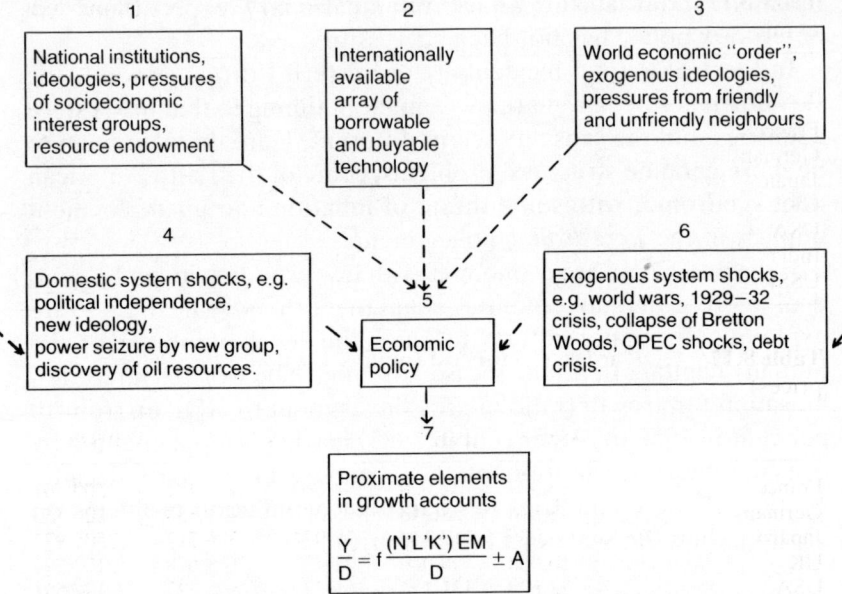

$$\frac{Y}{D} = f \frac{(N'L'K')\,EM}{D} \pm A$$

Y = GDP; D = population; N' = natural resources developed and augmented; L' = human capital, i.e. labour force augmented by investment in health, education and training; K' = stock of all kinds of physical capital augmented by technical progress; E = microeconomic efficiency of resource allocation; M = macroeconomic efficiency; A = foreign funds.

Figure 8.1 Ultimate and proximate elements in economic performance: a box diagram.

Table 8.10 Population 1870–1987 adjusted to present-day boundaries (thousands at mid-year)

	1870	1913	1950	1973	1987
France	38,440	41,690	41,836	52,119	55,685
Germany	24,870	40,825	49,983	61,976	60,858
Japan	34,437	51,672	83,662	108,660	122,897
UK	29,185	42,622	50,363	56,210	56,687
USA	40,061	97,606	152,271	211,909	244,171
Total	166,993	274,415	378,115	490,874	540,298
Brazil	9,797	23,660	51,942	99,836	140,694
China	350,000	430,000	551,960	892,110	1,072,076
India	208,312	250,057	359,943	579,000	787,930
Mexico	9,219	14,930	27,376	56,481	82,234
USSR	79,354	158,371	180,050	249,800	282,296
Total	656,682	877,018	1,171,271	1,877,227	2,365,230
Grand total	823,675	1,151,433	1,549,386	2,368,101	2,905,528

Table 8.11 Population 1870–1987 with frontiers of year cited (thousands at mid-year)

	1870	1913	1950	1973	1987
France	38,440	39,770	41,836	52,119	55,685
Germany	39,231	66,978	49,983	61,976	60,858
Japan	34,437	51,672	82,900	108,660	122,897
UK	31,393	45,649	50,363	56,210	56,687
USA	39,905	97,227	151,683	211,909	244,171
India	253,000	303,700	359,943	579,000	787,930
USSR	(81,000)	165,700	180,050	249,800	282,296

Table 8.12 GDP at 1965 factor cost (million US dollars at 1965 US prices)

	1870	1913	1950	1973	1987
France	15,978	32,020	48,863	154,432	209,507
Germany	8,616	28,343	45,632	171,333	220,735
Japan	6,035	17,144	38,934	305,712	505,971
UK	20,088	45,040	72,424	143,678	179,394
USA	22,690	131,154	363,297	841,222	1,194,551
Total 5 countries	73,407	253,701	569,150	1,616,377	2,310,158
Brazil	1,063	2,782	16,080	84,859	166,372
China	41,491	64,267	69,717	275,834	724,096
India	32,308	40,964	52,598	121,049	225,466
Mexico	1,540	3,598	9,542	41,620	67,821
USSR	22,690	59,088	164,560	520,268	623,613
Total 5 countries	99,092	170,699	312,497	1,044,415	1,807,368
Grand total	172,499	424,400	881,647	2,660,792	4,117,526

Table 8.13 Exports per head of population[a] (US dollars at current prices and exchange rates)

	1870	1913	1950	1973	1985
France	14.1	33.4	73.7	702.9	1,843.2
Germany	10.8	35.9	39.9	1,090.1	3,014.2
Japan	0.4	6.9	10.0	340.7	1,467.1
UK	30.9	56.0	125.6	527.3	1,788.3
USA	12.8	24.5	67.5	337.0	890.8
Brazil	7.8	13.3	26.2	62.1	191.4
China	0.3	0.7	1.0	6.6	26.2
India	1.0	2.6	3.2	5.0	10.6
Mexico	3.2[b]	9.9	19.4	40.0	283.7
USSR	2.7	4.7	10.0	85.9	313.8

[a] Population within boundaries of years specified.
[b] 1877–8 exports.

Table 8.14 Alternative estimate of real GDP at 1980 market prices (multilateral ICP weights) (million US dollars)

	1870	1913	1950	1973	1980	1987
France	44,856	89,892	137,175	433,548	526,946	588,162
Germany	27,156	89,328	143,817	539,985	627,973	695,683
Japan	15,025	42,684	96,935	761,140	982,755	1,259,731
UK	69,822	136,373	219,288	435,030	464,759	543,173
USA	60,852	351,745	974,334	2,256,092	2,607,134	3,203,694
Total	208,711	710,022	1,571,549	4,425,795	5,209,567	6,290,443
Brazil	3,075	8,060	46,592	245,866	396,917	482,041
China	120,094	186,024	201,805	798,342	1,142,017	2,095,951
India	79,330	100,579	129,096	297,179	387,030	553,564
Mexico	4,911	11,468[a]	30,410	132,650	205,179	216,157
USSR	56,110	146,113	406,888	1,286,579	1,473,747	1,542,104
Total	263,520	452,244	814,791	2,760,616	3,604,890	4,889,817

[a] 1910.
Source: UN/Eurostat (1986, 1987), Marer (1985).

Table 8.15 Alternative estimate of real GDP per capita at 1980 market prices

	1870	1913	1950	1973	1980	1987
France	1,167	2,156	3,279	8,318	9,780	10,562
Germany	1,092	2,188	2,877	8,713	10,200	11,431
Japan	436	826	1,159	7,005	8,414	10,250
UK	2,084	3,200	4,354	7,739	8,253	9,582
USA	1,519	3,611	6,399	10,647	11,447	13,121
Brazil	314	341	897	2,463	3,349	3,426
China	343	433	366	895	1,157	1,955
India	381	402	359	513	570	703
Mexico	532	768	1,111	2,349	2,946	2,663
USSR	707	923	2,260	5,150	5,550	5,463

Source: UN/Eurostat (1986, 1987), and Marer (1985).

D.H. Perkins, *Agricultural Development in China 1368–1968* (Chicago: Aldine, 1969, p.16); thereafter from World Bank, *World Tables*. India from A. Maddison, *Class Structure and Economic Growth* (New York: Norton, 1971, pp. 164–5) and World Bank, *World Tables*. Mexico from A. Maddison, *The Political Economy of Poverty Equity and Growth in Brazil and Mexico* (forthcoming). USSR from B.R. Mitchell, *European Historical*

Statistics 1750–1970 (London: Macmillan, 1975; p. 65); *Narodnoe Khoziastvo* (Moscow) and UN *Monthly Bulletin of Statistics*.

Sources for GDP time series
France from J-C. Toutain, *Le Produit Interieur Brut de la France de 1789 à 1982* (Grenoble: Presses Universitaires de Grenoble, 1987). Germany, Japan, UK and USA from Maddison (1987). Brazil and Mexico from Maddison (*op. cit.*, forthcoming). China from Maddison (March 1983). India 1870–1900 from A. Heston, 'National income', in D. Kumar and M. Desai, *Cambridge Economic History of India* (Cambridge: Cambridge University Press, 1983); 1900–46 from A. Maddison, 'Alternative estimates of the real product of India, 1900–46', *Indian Economic and Social History Review*, vol. 22, no. 2, 1985; 1946–50 from Maddison (1971); 1950 onwards from *National Accounts Statistics 1970–71 – 1984–5* (Delhi: CSO, 1987). USSR 1870–1950 from A. Maddison, *Economic Growth in Japan and the USSR* (London: Allen & Unwin, 1969), thereafter from US Joint Economic Committee, *Gorbachev's Modernization Programme: A Status Report* (US Congress, 1987).

REFERENCES

Lewis, Arthur (1981), 'The rate of growth of world trade, 1830–1973, in Sven Grassman and Erik Lundberg (eds), *The World Economic Order: Past and Prospects*, London: Macmillan.

Maddison, Angus (1962) 'Growth and fluctuation in the world economy, 1870–1960', *Banca Nazionale del Lavoro Quarterly Review*, no. 61, pp. 127–95.

Maddison, Angus (1970), *Economic Progress and Policy in Developing Countries*, London: Allen & Unwin.

Maddison, Angus (1982), *Phases of Capitalist Development*, Oxford: Oxford University Press.

Maddison, Angus (1983a), 'A comparison of levels of GDP per capita in developed and developing countries, 1700–1980', *Journal of Economic History*, vol. 43, no. 1, pp. 27–41.

Maddison, Angus (1983b), 'Economic stagnation since 1973, its nature and causes: a six country survey', *De Economist*, vol. 131, no. 4, pp. 585–608.

Maddison, Angus (1985), *Two Crises: Latin America and Asia, 1929–38 and 1973–83*. Paris: OECD

Maddison, Angus (1987), 'Growth and slowdown in advanced capitalist economies: techniques of quantitative assessment, *Journal of Economic Literature*, vol. 25, pp. 649–98.

Marer, Paul (1985), *Dollar GNPs of the USSR and Eastern Europe*, Baltimore: Johns Hopkins University Press.

Summers, Robert, and Alan Heston (1984), 'Improved international comparisons of real product and its composition, 1950–1980', *Review of Income and Wealth*, vol. 30, pp. 207–62.

United Nations/Eurostat (1986 and 1987), *World Comparisons of Purchasing Power and Real Product for 1980: Phase IV of the International Comparison Project*, parts I and II, New York.

9 · EUROPE AND THE WORLD ECONOMY DURING THE INTER-WAR PERIOD

Herman Van der Wee and Erik Buyst

INTRODUCTION

Despite some interest from historians and economists in the 1950s and 1960s, the interwar economy has only become a major topic of research since the late 1970s. The first and especially the second oil shock led to problems in the world economy that resembled in some respects those of the 1930s. The debt crisis of the developing countries, the large imbalances in international trade, monetary instability and high unemployment all suggest parallels with the inter-war period. The stock market crash of October 1987 could only heighten interest in comparing current economic difficulties with those of the 1930s. Whether the aftermath of the 1987 crash will be like that of 1929, only time will tell. What the stock market crash of 1987 did highlight was the economic interdependence among countries. This was also true, to a somewhat lesser extent, in the inter-war period. Here we will show how the lack of international cooperation drove the European and world economies to complete collapse in the 1930s and thwarted subsequent recovery.

THE AFTERMATH OF THE FIRST WORLD WAR (1918–25)

The First World War had far-reaching consequences for the European economy. More than 60 million men were involved in

The authors wish to thank Peter Solar for help with preparation of this chapter.

the armed conflict, and governments came to intervene significantly in the organisation of economic activity. When the Armistice was finally signed in November 1918, Europe had to deal with severe population losses, extensive devastation, financial and political disorganisation and a serious reduction in civilian output. Reconstruction took several years. It proved far more difficult to restore the economic institutions than to rebuild the physical capacity to produce goods and services.

The post-war recovery

After four years of savage warfare Europe could start to count its losses. The number of soldiers killed in active service was estimated at 8.5 million. If we include the permanently disabled, the estimates rise to 15.5 million casualties, or about 14 per cent of Europe's adult male working population, not counting civilian casualties. The impact of these losses was greater than the figures indicate since they were concentrated among men in the most productive years of their lives. Moreover, it took considerable time to replace the skilled workers killed in action.

Capital losses are more difficult to measure, but the value of the European capital stock undoubtedly fell during the war as the result of destruction, the collapse of private investment, and the neglect of maintenance. Massive losses of houses, factories and infrastructure occurred where the war was actually fought. In areas occupied by the Central Powers, such as Belgium and northern France, equipment containing metal useful for the war effort was dismantled and sent to Germany. At the end of the war machinery and equipment were deliberately destroyed. Large tracts of agricultural land in many parts of Europe were laid waste and the cattle stock was severely depleted. The destruction and deterioration of railway equipment and roadbeds caused serious transport problems in much of continental Europe.

Where damage was extensive the recovery proved long. Most nations hit by the war had drawn down their gold and exchange reserves and thus faced difficulties in financing imports of necessary raw materials, capital goods and even food. They could have been helped by the organisation of a large-scale relief programme. Unfortunately, effective action fell far short of this. Food relief, for example, was inadequate and undertaken with very little international cooperation. Victorious countries were generally able to obtain provisions on credit, but Germany and its allies had to pay in cash. Less than 10 per cent of food relief took the form of outright gifts. Famine, therefore, remained a threat in central and eastern Europe for several years.

Recovery was further delayed by the disruption of traditional trading links during the war. Some markets were lost for ever; others had to be painfully rewon. The extensive territorial changes in central and eastern Europe made things even more complicated. Economic relationships established during the last half of the nineteenth century were smashed by the creation of new nations and the redrawing of almost all borders. One striking instance is the fate of the textile industry of Austria-Hungary. Its spinning mills were located primarily in Bohemia and Moravia and became part of Czechoslovakia, while much of its weaving capacity was in and around Vienna. New patterns of communication had to be created in a climate of old rivalries and resentments.

The central and eastern European countries faced the task of becoming coherent political and economic entities. In a context of political instability and shortages of food, raw materials and capital goods this was not easy to achieve. Moreover, in a number of these countries industrialisation had not proceeded very far, leaving much of the population dependent on agriculture. In a time when the traditional safety-valve of emigration was closing up, population pressure became more acute. Governments responded by extensive land reforms, which in practice led only to the fragmentation of holdings and a significant increase in small-scale subsistence farming. Labour productivity in agriculture remained low, and savings that could be used for investment in and out of agriculture were limited. A shift towards industry, the only long-term solution, was thus impeded by structural problems.

It is not surprising, then, that it took considerable time before most belligerent countries regained their pre-war levels of output. At the same time, the neutral countries in Europe, the United States, Japan, and other countries outside Europe whose economies had already been greatly stimulated by wartime demand, continued to grow. Over-capacity in certain sectors, notably heavy manufacturing and agriculture, became apparent in the 1920s. As France, Belgium and other participants rebuilt their iron and steel industries with the latest technology, they added to the already inflated capacity outside Europe. The belligerent nations also faced new competition in traditional export markets. Some outlets in Latin America and Asia had been taken over by the United States and Japan. Other markets were increasingly supplied by local import substitution. As a result, international competition in semi-finished goods and in agricultural products became severe in the course of the 1920s and exerted a long-term downward pressure on prices.

Despite these problems, Europe as a whole had regained its pre-war level of output by about 1925. But the war left a more persistent legacy in continued impediments to international trade and imbalances in the monetary system (Lewis 1949: 35).

Internal war debts, inflation and currency stabilisation

Government expenditures rose dramatically during the war, financed not so much by taxation as by large-scale borrowing. Central banks were encouraged or compelled to extend advances to the state which created an abundance of liquidity. This policy made it easy for the government to issue liquid assets, like Treasury bills, in the home market. Both elements induced an dramatic increase in the money supply which fuelled inflation (Eichengreen 1986: 37–8; Holtfrerich 1986a: 58). At the end of the war the inflationary problem was not for the most part unmanageable, but continued lax monetary and fiscal policies made things worse in several countries.

During the war governments took extraordinary measures to keep exchange rates from deviating too far from their pre-war levels. They included unprecedented controls on merchandise trade and capital movements. These were so successful that in November 1918 only small deviations from pre-war exchange rates existed (Brown 1940: Table 1). This strengthened popular belief that a quick return to 'normalcy', as embodied in the pre-war gold standard, was possible.

But once the artificial pegging of exchange rates was suspended, inflationary pressures led to the depreciation of most European currencies. Although it was considered a matter of some urgency that each nation should return to a fixed gold parity, the stabilisation process proved far more difficult than was anticipated.

Many countries faced a vicious circle of large budget deficits, money creation, inflation and currency depreciation. High reconstruction costs, continued military spending, and expensive social programmes boosted government spending at a time when savings were low and tax systems inefficient. As a result, Belgium, France and Italy, among other countries, were forced to stabilise their currencies at rates well below pre-war values. Austria, Germany, Hungary and Poland failed to bring inflation under control and their currencies became valueless. New monetary units had to be introduced in these countries before hyperinflation could be brought under control and new parities established. Britain and most neutral countries were thus exceptional inasmuch as they regained their pre-war rate against gold.

The way in which stabilisation was carried out had implications for economic recovery. Britain, for instance, imposed severe retrenchment policies designed to lower domestic prices, with the effect of slowing domestic growth. Where inflation was not excessive, as in Belgium, France and Italy, depreciation stimulated economic recovery. Since the public believed that the authorities would ultimately reverse the course of price inflation, workers in these countries were less militant in demanding wage increases to compensate for the rise in the cost of living. Creditors loaned money at rates that did not anticipate future inflation. So production costs declined, thereby promoting exports. Government also benefited from 'moderate' inflation as its debt burden was lightened (Eichengreen 1986: 48–51; Van der Wee and Tavernier 1975: 79–207).

Where price increases accelerated into hyperinflation the consequences for the real economy were dramatic. Savings dried up as money lost its value. Some dissaving probably even took place as people liquidated their assets. Massive capital flight occurred. Where government, firms and households all tried to run deficits at the same time, the monetary system collapsed. People stopped using the domestic currency as a unit of account, and reform was only successful after a new monetary unit had been introduced (Kindleberger 1984: 314–19). Moreover, to restore confidence government followed a tight financial policy which restrained economic growth. The banking system was not well placed to finance growth, having lost much of its capital during hyperinflation.

External war debts, international financial flows and reparations

The belligerent countries not only financed their war effort by borrowing at home, but also by issuing loans abroad. Many went on borrowing after the Armistice to pay for reconstruction and to finance balance of payments shortages, confident that the losers would be forced to settle the bill. In 1921 inter-allied war debt amounted to some $26.5 billion. The United States and Britain were the major creditors; France the major debtor. Britain, which was owed more by the other Allies than it had borrowed from the United States, was willing to cancel all payments, but the Americans would not agree. The United States remained deaf to the European argument that they had paid in terms of human life. Furthermore, the United States wanted to be paid in gold or dollars (Aldcroft 1987: 92–6). Since the American trade balance showed a large surplus, it was not easy to achieve this transfer. Repayment was made even more difficult by the higher import duties in the Fordney-McCumber tariff of 1922 (Poulson 1981: 508; Holtfrerich 1986a: 186). Debtor countries found it harder and harder to export to the United States and thus to earn the dollars and gold necessary to repay their debts.

The problem of German reparations further complicated the matter. When the Armistice was signed Germany knew that it would have to pay reparations to the victorious Allies, but the amount remained an open question. In January 1921 the Reparations Commission presented a bill for $33 billion, the greater part of which was to be paid to Britain, France and Belgium. The Germans regarded this as excessive, especially given their current financial and economic conditions. During the course of 1922 German inflation accelerated, but requests for a moratorium on reparations were repeatedly refused. By the end of 1922 Germany could no longer meet its obligations. French and Belgian troops invaded the Ruhr, but workers there went on strike and blocked this attempt to extract reparations in kind. To finance resistance the German government turned to the printing press, which was the death-blow for an already shaky monetary system. The mark depreciated faster and faster. It soon became clear to the French and the Belgians that the occupation of the Ruhr was a failure and they returned to negotiations. After long and difficult talks, the Dawes Plan emerged, which scaled down reparations payments and made provision for a loan of 800 million Reichsmarks to Germany. The loan was a phenomenal success, its New York tranch being oversubscribed by more than ten times (Kindleberger 1984: 303).

The success of the Dawes loan and the high interest rates in Germany – the result of its tight financial policy after the hyperinflation – attracted through the London money market a flow of foreign capital during the following years. This helped finance German industrial recovery but created a dangerous chain of transactions involving loans and reparations. The United States, and to a lesser extent other countries, loaned money to Germany, which then transferred it in part as 'reparations' to the Allies. The latter used these to pay their own debts with the United States. Such a spiral of credits could not continue indefinitely. In the long run it posed a serious threat to the stability of the international financial system.

MISLEADING STABILITY (1925-9)

By the middle of the 1920s reconstruction and recovery in Europe were virtually complete. International confidence grew and offered the prospect of sustained prosperity.

Economic activity in the second half of the 1920s

The 1920s were hardly roaring. In most countries the growth of real gross domestic product was only modest (3 per cent per annum in the United States, 2 per cent in Britain) (Kendrick 1961: 293; Feinstein 1972: Table 14). Thus it is not surprising that there was no pressure on real resources at the peak of the cycle. Prices were even trending downward slowly. Most countries still had a margin of underutilised capacity. Unemployment rates remained high and real wages showed only marginal gains. An exception to this picture was, perhaps, the upsurge of business profits.

The misperception of economic activity by contemporaries probably stems from the intense stock market speculation which occurred in the United States, and to a lesser extent in some European countries, in 1928 and 1929. Continuously rising share prices created a euphoric atmosphere. Another important psychological element was the Locarno Pact of 1925. International confidence seemed to have returned and reduced considerably the sometimes severe political tensions of the early 1920s. Most of the great inflations were under control, and Britain's return to the gold standard in 1925 was seen as a sign that the return to 'normalcy' was just around the corner (Aldcroft 1982: 53).

Although economic growth in general was far from impressive, some countries, such as France, Belgium and Germany, experienced a rapid growth of industrial production in the late 1920s. France and Belgium had stabilised their currencies in 1926 at somewhat undervalued exchange rates which boosted exports. At the same time France was in the process of modernising its industry by investments in promising sectors such as chemicals, electricity, engineering, automobiles and rayon (Caron 1981: 194, 231). Germany's situation was quite different in the mid-1920s. Hyperinflation had shaken its economy and a tight monetary policy exerted deflationary pressure. Expansion thus started from a relatively low level, which in part accounts for its high growth rate. With the help of a flood of foreign capital, Germany achieved a remarkable modernisation with striking progress in heavy capital goods, chemicals and electrical goods. But this prosperity was misleading. It was only in the last years of the 1920s that German real income surpassed its pre-war level (James 1986: 114–16), and it would soon appear that its growth was built on shifting sand.

The gold standard under pressure

The attainment of monetary stability proved far more difficult than anticipated in many countries. Moreover, the stabilisation in individual countries was accomplished without much international coordination. Little attention was paid to the question of correct parity values. The dollar, which had returned to gold in 1919, served as a rough benchmark, but it was often speculative and political considerations that determined the level at which countries stabilised their exchange rates.

The problems of currency misalignment can be seen in the case of the pound sterling, the traditional lynchpin of the international monetary system. In early 1925 speculative capital inflows, based on expectations that the pre-war parity would be re-established, pushed up the sterling exchange rate. When the pound approached its pre-war parity, Chancellor of the Exchequer Winston Churchill tied it once more to gold. But British prices and wages had not declined as fast as the exchange rate had risen, so the pound became overvalued with respect to the domestic price level. Other overvalued currencies included those of Denmark, Italy, Norway and Sweden, while the currencies of the United States, Belgium , France, Germany and Poland were undervalued (Redmond 1984: 520-1).

Once the pattern was set in the mid-1920s, the chosen rates came to be regarded as sacrosanct. Authorities were reluctant to adjust them even when misalignment was apparent. Thus the system started off from a point of disequilibrium, which gave the gold standard less of a chance to function as smoothly as before the war. The misaligned currencies magnified balance of payments problems, but few countries were prepared to sacrifice domestic growth for external equilibrium. Countries with overvalued currencies were reluctant to put pressure on domestic prices and increase unemployment. Gold and exchange reserves thus flowed from them to the countries with undervalued currencies, which continued to accumulate reserves rather than let their exchange rates rise.

These flows worsened the maldistribution of the world's monetary reserves that had resulted from the war. Gold was accumulated by countries that did not really need it, either because their currencies were not used as reserves (France, Belgium, European neutrals) or because they already had more than enough gold in relation to their international liabilities (United States). Britain, which was losing gold, had a much greater need of it. Given its status as a reserve currency and its large international liabilities, Britain would be the weak link in the system in a period of crisis (Drummond 1987: 33-9).

Another structural element increased the vulnerability of the monetary system during the late 1920s. Full convertibility into gold had largely been abandoned. Most countries, for lack of adequate gold reserves or for other motives, opted for a gold exchange standard as recommended by the Genoa Conference of 1922. In this system the monetary authorities held international reserves consisting largely of dollars and sterling balances backed by gold. Since London was no longer so dominant in financial markets, these funds could easily be shifted from one financial centre to another as interest rates and confidence changed. As a result, the key centres, London and New York, needed larger gold stocks than those required for normal trading purposes. There was always the possibility of speculation against a key currency or a sudden demand to convert foreign claims into gold. Because of its low gold reserves, London was again the weak link in the system (Aldcroft 1987: 168-70).

International lending: another source of instability

The First World War changed the pattern of international lending and left many countries with a considerable burden of foreign debt. From 1924 foreign lending on a large scale resumed as economic prospects improved. Currency stabilisation was well under way and the political climate had improved.

Most foreign capital went to central and southeastern Europe. Unfortunately, these loans were often used to finance balance of payments deficits and contributed little to rectifying underlying imbalances through economic development. Some loans were used for investment, but the returns were often disappointing. Agricultural investments boosted production and exports, but in a world market already facing overproduction in primary products this only put further downward pressure on prices. The extension of manufacturing capacity was often directed towards import substitution. The result was inefficient, technically backward industries producing inferior goods and dependent for survival on protection and government support (Pollard 1981: 289). Moreover, some long-term projects were financed with short-term credit, which posed potential liquidity problems.

By the end of the 1920s the debt burden of several central and southeastern European countries had reached alarming proportions. Debt service payments constituted a quarter or more of the value of current exports (Drabek 1985: 425). Since the servicing of foreign loans called for strong currencies obtainable from a limited range of exports, this made the situation even worse. As a result, some countries were forced to raise new loans to pay the interest on old debts, a practice that had its limits.

Not only the borrowing nations made mistakes. Creditors often financed risky projects and allowed central and south eastern

European countries to pile up foreign debts to an extent which could never be justified by their potential export earnings.

The German situation was somewhat different. Reparations complicated matters, with a curious debt triangle among Germany, the European Allies and the United States. But Germany managed to use some foreign capital in the modernisation of its industrial structure. This led to significant growth in industrial output, although it did little to boost export earnings, which complicated debt service in the long run. Another weakness of the German position stemmed from the fact that a large part of capital inflow consisted of short-term loans to German banks, which they then invested in long-term projects in industry. In the case of a sudden withdrawal of funds the German banking system would face great difficulty in meeting its obligations.

THE GREAT DEPRESSION (1929–39)

In the late 1920s structural imbalances became more and more acute. Overproduction in certain sectors, growing tension in the monetary system and the huge problems related to debt management posed serious threats to sustained economic growth in Europe and in the world as a whole. Painful adjustments were inevitable, but the question remained whether they could be executed in a controlled manner before the economic system collapsed.

The onset of the Depression (1928–30)

In the second quarter of 1928 prices on the New York stock market started to rise rapidly. This diverted funds from foreign lending to the domestic financial market. American capital exports were further hindered by the failure of the Federal Reserve to accommodate the rising demand for credit, which led to a rise in interest rates. US new capital issues for foreign account fell by over 50 per cent between the first and second halves of 1928 (Kindleberger 1987: 70–1; Holtfrerich 1986b: 1–32). This dramatic curtailment of lending exerted a powerful deflationary pressure on the debtor countries which was first felt through the balance of payments, since most borrowing nations used the loans to finance current account deficits. For a limited time they could depend on their small reserves of gold and foreign exchange, but soon more drastic measures, including domestic deflation and trade restrictions, became necessary.

The process of adjustment became even more difficult as US economic activity started to decline in the summer of 1929 and as the stock market crash of October 1929 weakened business confidence. American foreign lending declined further and US import demand contracted (Kindleberger 1987: 126). Since the United States accounted for more than 40 per cent of the primary product consumption of the fifteen leading industrial nations, the impact on the export prospects of many debtor countries was severe. Agricultural prices, which had already been falling in the late 1920s, started a more precipitate fall. Primary product producers were caught in a squeeze between severely declining export receipts and continued high interest payments fixed in terms of gold (Nötel 1986: 217–25). Deflation and import restrictions alone turned out to be insufficient remedies.

Debtor countries were soon faced with the need either to devalue their currencies or to default on their debts. In general they chose first to sacrifice the exchange rate, since default would preclude further foreign borrowing. In late 1929 and early 1930 several Latin American countries, Australia and New Zealand abandoned the gold standard (Eichengreen and Portes 1987: 20). Inasmuch as this step helped to restrain these countries' imports of manufactures and stimulate their exports, it put pressure on those nations that remained on gold. The demand for their manufactures fell, with the perverse effect of further reducing their imports of raw materials. Desperate attempts by the debtor countries to increase the volume of agricultural exports only put more pressure on prices.

Among the borrowing countries Germany was in a somewhat different situation, and not only because of the burden of reparations. In contrast to most central and southeastern European countries it was not dependent on primary product exports. Its economic activity had slackened even before the decline in the inflow of foreign capital, which, of course, made the situation worse (Falkus 1975: 465). In spring 1929 a foreign exchange run caused a temporary monetary crisis. Foreign banks feared that negotiators would not be able to reach agreement on a new reparations schedule (what became the Young Plan) and called in their short-term loans (James 1984: 69).

During the first half of 1930 the European economy was in bad shape, but events were still under control. The American economy showed some signs of recovery and lending to Europe revived. The writing-off of reparations and a more liberal commercial policy on the part of the United States could possibly have alleviated the difficulties of the European debtors. Unfortunately, the United States took neither of these steps.

The collapse of the European economy (1930–2)

The Hawley–Smoot Tariff Act

Under pressure from the farm lobby, the US Congress tightened, rather than loosened, its commercial policy. It passed the Hawley-Smoot Tariff Act, which brought in one of the largest duty increases in international trade history. The rates on agricultural products, including cotton, dairy products, meat and sugar, underwent particularly large increases. In spite of protests from thirty-three foreign governments, many US industries with foreign markets and hundreds of American economists, President Hoover signed the bill into law in June 1930. It was a mistake with far-reaching consequences. The United States already had a large trade surplus, so there were no balance-of-payments problems that required restrictions on imports. Moreover, the restraints on imports made it extremely difficult for debtor countries to pay their American loans. In any case the Hawley-Smoot Tariff provoked widespread retaliation. This wave of protectionism produced a massive contraction of international trade (Saint-Etienne 1984: 11–15). US lending virtually ceased and American banks started to demand repayment of outstanding loans. The worst hit were, of course, the primary product producers of central and southeastern Europe and Latin America, with economic collapse only a matter of time. Industrialised countries in Europe were also seriously affected. Falling export demand led to large-scale unemployment.

The situation of the financial sector was dire. The repatriation of commercial bank balances by the United States, France and other countries put further strain on the already weak finances of central

European nations. In September 1930 the overwhelming victory of the Nazi Party in the German elections led to a run on German banks, though the German government managed to keep things under control.

The financial crisis in Latin America and Central Europe
The crash of the financial and monetary system did not, however, start in Europe. In Latin America declining economic activity undermined tax receipts and boosted government expenditures, while a rapid fall in export revenues eroded foreign exchange reserves. These countries had neither the money to service foreign debts nor the foreign exchange necessary to transfer revenues abroad. In January 1931 Bolivia defaulted on its foreign debt and its example was quickly followed by several other Latin American countries (Eichengreen and Portes 1986: 621). This seriously undermined international confidence and led to an increased demand for liquidity.

In Europe the demands of creditors put severe pressure on the banking system, which had its funds tied up in loans to depressed industries. In May 1931 the Austrian Creditanstalt, which accounted for over two-thirds of the total deposits of the Austrian banking system, failed. Lack of international cooperation made it impossible for the Austrian government to rescue the bank, with the result that depositors panicked and there were runs on banks not only in Austria but in Czechoslovakia, Hungary, Poland and Rumania (Kindleberger 1984: 372).

The financial crisis in central and southeastern Europe could not leave Germany unaffected. There was a flight of capital that put pressure on the banking system. In June 1931 Prime Minister H. Brüning announced that Germany was unable to continue its reparation payments, which led to a run on the German banks. Both domestic and foreign lenders tried to call in their loans. The government had to impose a two-day bank holiday in July and a standstill on foreign credits. As the German banks put pressure on firms to repay their loans rapidly, undermining their finances, industrial production fell spectacularly and unemployment rose (James 1984: 78–80). This decline in economic activity increased political tensions and weakened the already vulnerable Weimar Republic.

Devaluation of the pound sterling

The financial crisis in central and southeastern Europe and in Germany soon affected the London money market, which had served as the conduit for the flow of capital to these areas. Large short-term credits became frozen. Given the already low gold reserves of the Bank of England, confidence in the stability of the pound faded away. Capital fled the country and political difficulties further weakened the position of sterling. Finally, excessive publicity over a naval pay dispute precipitated a run against the pound in mid-September 1931 and on 21 September Parliament approved legislation suspending the Bank of England's obligation to sell gold. Within a few months sterling fell by more than 30 per cent against the dollar (Kindleberger 1984: 378–80).

The pound was not well defended against speculation. Foreign credits were available, but the Bank of England did not use its principal instrument, the discount rate, until after the devaluation. It appears that Britain was unwilling to defend its currency until the bitter end. One reason was the widespread belief that sterling was overvalued. It had certainly been pegged too high when Britain went back on gold in 1925 (Matthews 1986: 572), but whether it was still overvalued in the late 1920s is far less certain (Redmond, 1984: 582). Contemporaries pointed to persistently high unemployment and balance-of-payments deficits as evidence that it was.

Modern research suggests that contemporaries overdramatised the British economic situation. National product was growing more rapidly in the late 1920s than it had before the First World War. Unemployment had an important structural component, as some major export industries, such as cotton, coal and shipbuilding, declined while other sectors more oriented to the domestic market expanded. The large merchandise trade deficits in the balance of payments were more than offset by huge surpluses on services. In the late 1920s the current account was always positive, with the exception of 1926, the year of the General Strike (Saint-Etienne 1984: 21–3).

If the British economy was stronger than contemporaries believed, then the deep devaluation of the pound was probably unnecessary. Strong action by the Bank of England, coupled with full international cooperation, could have tackled the British problem and contained the financial crisis in central and southeastern Europe. Instead the depression was given new impetus.

Further deepening of the Depression (1931–2)
The devaluation of sterling was a serious shock to the world economy. Countries with strong economic ties to Britain, including much of the Empire and the Scandinavian countries, soon abandoned gold and devalued their currencies. At the same time a whole battery of restrictions on trade were installed to shield domestic economies from external influences. A wave of tariffs, imports quotas, prohibitions, licensing systems, and clearing agreements spelled the end of multilateral trade and payments. Trade wars raged as never before.

By the third quarter of 1932 the trade of European countries had fallen below 40 per cent of its 1929 level. Countries that remained on the gold standard, such as Belgium, France, the Netherlands, Italy, Poland and Switzerland, found themselves in increasing difficulties. Their export prices were no longer competitive. Severe deflation designed to reduce domestic costs seemed the only option.

Primary product producers fared the worst since agricultural prices continued to fall more sharply than industrial prices. Currency depreciation increased the burden of their foreign debts. In the absence of further financing from abroad, several central and southeastern European countries defaulted on their debts in the course of 1932.

By the summer of 1932 the economic situation in Europe was grim. The international financial and monetary systems were badly shattered and international trade was much reduced. Economic activity stood at a very low level almost everywhere, with both capital and labour severely underutilised. Some feared a total breakdown of the economic system. The situation was thoroughly unstable, as exchange rates were subject to speculative capital movements, the prospect of competitive devaluations and the threat of retaliatory tariffs (Aldcroft 1982: 92–6).

Incomplete recovery (1933–7)

In late 1932 faint signs of recovery could be detected in some countries. In some cases the revival was only a brief pause before a further fall, but in others recovery did indeed take root.

Recovery in the United States was only temporary, ended by a final wave of bank failures in 1932–3. In April 1933 President F. Roosevelt prohibited gold exports, a *de facto* suspension of the gold standard. This was a classic case of competitive currency depreciation, for there were no pressures on the American current account and gold reserves were immense (Foreman-Peck 1983: 251). A new cascade of devaluations followed the American action. For the 'Gold Bloc', those countries which persisted in maintaining parity with gold, this put increasing pressure on their economies. Recovery was thus cut short in France, Belgium, the Netherlands, Italy, Poland and Switzerland (Eichengreen and Sachs 1985: 930).

The economic revival was more lasting in Britain and Sweden. In Britain expansionary monetary policy, in conjunction with balanced government budgets, helped the economy to finance a reorientation of production from exports to the domestic market. From 1934 vigorous growth was apparent in housing, consumer durables and chemicals. In Sweden the recovery was powered by a large programme of public works from 1933. The resulting budgetary deficit was met by extensive borrowing. In addition, cheap money boosted the housing construction and industrial investment, and currency devaluation stimulated exports.

By the middle of the 1930s nearly all countries had registered at least slight increases in economic activity from the troughs of the Depression. Such recovery as did occur owed virtually nothing to international cooperation. The World Economic Conference in London in June–July 1933 was not only a failure, but was the last major international effort to cope with economic problems before the Second World War. Instead restrictions on trade and capital movements tended to increase. International lending never revived to any extent and, not surprisingly, exports played very little role in growth (an exception here was Sweden). Trade became bilateral or was increasingly confined to economic blocs. A good example is the system of Imperial Preference introduced at the Commonwealth Conference of August 1932 in Ottawa. Since exports offered little stimulus to economic activity, it was home demand that had to provide the basis for recovery.

As private initiatives for growth were wanting, states began to intervene more extensively in economic activity. Besides the restrictions on trade and capital movements, they supported monopolistic arrangements in sectors such as coal, iron and steel, railways, agriculture and shipbuilding. Some governments tried to stimulate activity through a policy of cheap money. Expansionary fiscal policy, by contrast, was rare, thwarted by an unreasonable fear of inflation and adherence to balanced budgets.

The impact of government policy on recovery was, in general, not impressive (Aldcroft 1982: 97–104). The basis for sustained growth was structural change from old staple industries to newer lines of development in motor cars, electrical and chemical goods, and services. Governments did little to promote or assist this change in productive orientation. In a few cases it was counterproductive. French economic policy, for example, was little short of disastrous. In the late 1920s the French economy was strong, and its downturn came later and was less severe than that of most other countries. France's large gold stock enabled it to follow an independent monetary policy. But French adherence to the gold standard meant that an increasingly large burden of adjustment was being imposed on the domestic economy. Deflationary policy reduced investment, with the effect that production and employment continued to decline even during the period of world-wide recovery between 1934 and 1936. The expansionary policy implemented by the left-wing coalition that came to power in 1936 meant that the link to gold would have to be broken. When the franc was at last devalued a short recovery followed, though France never exceeded its 1929 level of output before the Second World War (Saint-Etienne 1984: 37).

The German recovery from the Depression was a notable success. In 1933 the disastrous deflationary policy of the last Weimar governments was abandoned. The Nazis, on assuming power, launched a massive programme of public works, taking up many projects conceived during the Weimar Republic but never realised. The 'motorisation' of the German economy, with mass production of automobiles and extensive road building, played an essential role in sustaining the initial upswing by absorbing many unemployed resources (Overy 1975: 482). At the same time comprehensive economic planning was instituted. Extensive regulations on trade, payments and exchange restricted inessential imports and, where possible, boosted exports. The drawback of this economic success was, of course, the introduction of a totalitarian political regime. Moreover, from 1936 onward public control of the economy was used to shift resources away from private consumption to military expenditure.

Preparations for war

Economic conditions in the late 1930s were, in general, not propitious. In 1937 American economic growth started to slacken again. International trade received another setback as a hesitant liberalising movement proved abortive and tariffs were raised widely in 1938. One country after another tightened up exchange controls. The European recession of 1937 was not particularly severe, but this was probably due to the stimulus to demand provided by rearmament. Nazi Germany initiated the military build-up, soon followed by Britain and France after the remilitarisation of the Rhineland in 1936 (Kindleberger 1987: 278–84).

During this period Germany strengthened its regional political and economic position by concluding a number of bilateral trade agreements with countries in central and southeastern Europe. These countries, whose economies had been devastated by the Depression, had foregone help from abroad by defaulting on their debts and were seemingly condemned to development along autarchic lines. Bilateral trading arrangements with Germany helped them to find outlets for their goods and to obtain capital goods without the need for scarce foreign exchange.

CONCLUSION

The inter-war years leave a bitter taste. The Armistice of November 1918 did not bring the better world for which the soldiers in the trenches had hoped. It might even be suggested that the war seems to have been continued on the economic front. Lack of international cooperation delayed and complicated the post-war recovery. International debts, reparations and misaligned currencies created an unstable economic structure and hindered the economic development of Europe. By the late 1920s some imbalances had reached alarming proportions and painful adjustments were inevitable. Shortsighted economic policies, such as protectionism, wrecked international trade and led to the breakdown of the international financial and monetary systems. Sharp declines in economic activity and mass unemployment complete the picture. The subsequent recovery proceeded slowly in an unfriendly environment of competitive devaluations and extreme protectionism. Even in 1937–8 international trade remained well below its 1929 level and many countries were still plagued by high unemployment and unused productive capacity. The economic plight of Europe was made all the more dismal by the increasing political tensions and the threat of war.

REFERENCES

Aldcroft, Derek H. (1982), *The European Economy, 1914–1980*, London: Croom Helm.
Aldcroft, Derek H. (1987), *From Versailles to Wall Street 1919–1929*, Harmondsworth: Penguin Books.
Brown, William A. (1940), *The International Gold Standard Reinterpreted, 1914–1934*, Princeton: Princeton University Press.
Caron, François (1981), *Histoire économique de la France: XIXe-XXe siècles*, Paris: Colin.
Drabek, Z. (1985), 'Foreign trade performance and policy', in Michael C. Kaser and Edward A. Radice (eds), *The Economic History of Eastern Europe 1919–1975*, I, Oxford: Oxford University Press, pp. 379–531.
Drummond, Ian M. (1987), *The Gold Standard and the International Monetary System 1900–1939*, Basingstoke: Macmillan.
Eichengreen, Barry (1986), 'Understanding 1921–1927: Inflation and economic recovery in the 1920s', *Revista di storia economica*, vol. 3, pp. 34–66.
Eichengreen, Barry and Jeffrey Sachs (1985), 'Exchange rates and economy recovery in the 1930s', *Journal of Economic History*, vol. 45, pp. 925–46.
Eichengreen, Barry and Richard Portes (1986), 'Debt and default in the 1930s. Causes and consequences', *European Economic Review*, vol. 30, pp. 599–640.
Eichengreen, Barry and Richard Portes (1987), 'The anatomy of financial crises', in Richard Portes and Alexander K. Swoboda (eds), *Threats to International Financial Stability*, Cambridge: Cambridge University Press, 10–66.
Falkus, Malcom (1975), 'The German business cycle in the 1920s', *Economic History Review*, vol. 38, pp. 451–65.
Feinstein, Charles H. (1972), *National Income, Expenditure and Output of the United Kingdom 1855–1965*, Cambridge: Cambridge University Press.
Foreman-Peck, James (1983), *A History of the World Economy. Interna-*

tional Relations since 1850, Hemel Hempstead: Harvester Wheatsheaf.
Holtfrerich, Carl-Ludwig (1986a), *The German Inflation, 1914–1923: Causes and Effects in International Perspective*, Berlin: Walter de Gruyter.
Holtfrerich, Carl-Ludwig (1986b), 'US capital exports to Germany, 1919–1923, compared to 1924–1929', *Explorations in Economic History*, vol. 23, pp. 1–32.
James, Harold (1984), 'The causes of the German banking crisis of 1931', *Economic History Review*, vol. 37, pp. 68–87.
James, Harold (1986), *The German Slump: Politics and Economics 1924–1936*, Oxford: Clarendon Press.
Kendrick, John (1961), *Productivity Trends in the United States*, Princeton: Princeton University Press.
Kindleberger, Charles P. (1984), *A Financial History of Western Europe*, London: Allen & Unwin.
Kindleberger, Charles P. (1987), *The World in Depression 1929–1939*, Harmondsworth: Penguin Books.
Lewis, William A. (1949), *Economic Survey, 1919–1939*, London: Unwin University Books.
Matthews, Kent G.P. (1986), 'Was sterling overvalued in 1925?', *Economic History Review*, vol. 39, pp. 572–87.
Nötel, R. (1986), 'International credit and finance', in Michael C. Kaser and Edward A. Radice (eds), *The Economic History of Eastern Europe 1919–1975*, II, Oxford: Oxford University Press, pp. 170–295.
Overy, R.J. (1975), 'Cars, roads and economic recovery in Germany, 1932–1938', *Economic History Review*, vol. 38, pp. 466–83.
Pollard, Sidney (1981), *Peaceful Conquest. The Industrialization of Europe 1760–1970*, Oxford: Oxford University Press.
Poulson, Barry W. (1981), *Economic History of the United States*, New York: Macmillan.
Redmond, John (1984), 'The sterling overevaluation in 1925: a multilateral approach', *Economic History Review*, vol. 37, pp. 520–32.
Saint-Etienne, Christian (1984), *The Great Depression 1929–1938. Lessons for the 1980s*, Stanford: Hoover Institution Press.
Van der Wee, Herman and Karel Tavernier (1975), *La Banque Nationale de Belgique et la politique monetaire entre les deux guerres mondiales*, Brussels: Weissenbruch.

10 · MOTIVES FOR CURRENCY CONVERTIBILITY: THE POUND AND THE DEUTSCHMARK, 1950–5

Alan S. Milward

In accepting the terms of the Anglo-American Financial Agreements in 1944 the British government had accepted that all sterling earned internationally on current account would be declared freely convertible into dollars from July 1947. This was at the insistence of the United States which wanted to use the dollar loan to Britain to create a post-war international economy based on multilateral trade without discrimination and with a minimum of trade and payments restrictions. Automatic currency convertibility between the two currencies in which two-thirds of post-war foreign trade would be carried on was seen as the guarantee that the protectionist exchange controls of the 1930s would be removed. Although there was much disagreement about the date, on the whole most political opinion in Britain agreed with the idea, also regarding the convertibility of the pound as a guarantee of a more liberal international economy and judging this to be in the long-run interests of the United Kingdom as well (Gardner 1956). After the ignominious collapse of the first attempt at sterling-dollar convertibility in August 1947 there does not seem to have been any change of heart. The Labour government made no attempt to erect the reimposed currency and trade controls into any permanent system for controlling the economy. Policy was pragmatic, apparently waiting for such time as currency convertibility could be restored once more without danger to the reserves. In the eyes of the Treasury the situation seems to have been similar to that after 1918, when there was a minimum level of reserves at which it was thought safe to establish convertibility and that first this had to be reached.

'OPERATION ROBOT' AND THE 'COLLECTIVE APPROACH'

The discontent of the Bank of England and some of the Treasury officials with this waiting game came to a head in the 1951 balance-of-payments crisis. After the experiences of 1947 and 1949 this third crisis in six years seemed to show that reserves might never reach the required level unless there was a change of policy. It was in these circumstances that some of the Treasury officials and the Bank governor mainly responsible for overseas finance, Sir George Bolton, persuaded the Chancellor of the Exchequer of the newly formed Conservative government, R.A. Butler, to try to replace the existing policy by a secret plan, 'Operation Robot'.[1] In its initial version, the only version that stood a chance of being accepted, Operation Robot was designed to declare convertibility into the dollar for a new special category of sterling, 'external sterling'. This was sterling held by non-residents and by foreign central banks and earned on current account. The proposals as they appear in the records of the Treasury and the Bank of England were to establish convertibility for external sterling at a freely floating exchange rate, but there are indications that in the event the pound would not have been allowed to fall below a rate of $2.40 from its actual par rate of $2.80 – what we would now call a 'dirty float'. The existing sterling balances, which were still as large as they had been at the time of the Bretton Woods agreements, although their composition had become much less volatile, were to be either frozen or funded into long-term debt, the policy which had been so sternly rejected at the time of the Anglo-American financial agreements. These actions would be taken unilaterally; there would be no consultation with the United States or the IMF.[2] If necessary, and it would surely have proved to be so, trade controls would have been reimposed against exporters to Britain whose currencies remained inconvertible. Leaving aside its deflationary aspects, Operation Robot clearly broke with the line of thinking about convertibility which Bretton Woods and the dollar loan had established. Firstly, it was an unilateral action and secondly, it would result in an increase in trade controls.

Opposition to this scheme in the Cabinet had various motives. Some members, including the future prime minister Harold Macmillan and Churchill's private adviser Lord Cherwell, saw it as a threat to the consensus politics which they considered to be the wisest way forward for the Conservative party in the post-war world. Others, particularly the Foreign Secretary Anthony Eden, saw it as running counter to the main lines of foreign policy. Yet others feared it might end all chance of the hoped-for 'special relationship' with the United States. The Secretary of State for Commonwealth Affairs saw the plan to freeze the sterling balances as inimical to future Commonwealth relationships. No one, though, appears to have opposed the proposals in cabinet on commercial grounds.

Robot, after being rejected by ministers as a feasible course of action for the second time in summer 1952, by which time the balance-of-payments crisis had been safely negotiated, was succeeded by a variety of other plans to make sterling convertible, all of which went under the name 'Collective Approach' but were in fact substantially different. What they had in common with each other and with Robot was their willingness to see an increase in trade restrictions, albeit, it was hoped, only a temporary one, in return for establishing sterling–dollar convertibility safely. Convertibility itself, rather than the advantages which it appeared to offer for an increase in commodity trade, had become the objective of a small but influential group. Why?

Their motives were mixed. Sir George Bolton and the two Treasury officials Sir Richard Clarke and Sir Leslie Rowan who had backed his proposals all agreed, as did the Chancellor, that the 1951–2 balance-of-payments crisis was a sign that the similar difficulties of 1947 and 1949 had not been just reconstruction phenomena. It was at this point that their views diverged. Clarke thought that, although this was not the prime motive for convertibility, it would divert the flow of British foreign trade towards dollar markets and so help both to restore an overall payments equilibrium and to produce an industrial and commercial restructuring. Bolton and Rowan were concerned solely with the balance-of-payments advantages it would bring. These, though, remained unspecified, seldom going further than the statement that currency convertibility had always brought gains of this kind because of the extent of Britain's financial involvement in the international economy through merchanting, brokerage, shipping, insurance and foreign investment. All three, and presumably Butler, felt that if convertibility were not restored there would ultimately be large losses and that since it remained the intention of Washington and the capitalist world to restore it, it was important that Britain should do so first among European countries so as not to incur these potential losses. Underlying this haste was also the fear that the longer the pound remained inconvertible, the more business would be lost to the United States. Butler appears to have thought that convertibility was the only sure external regulator of the economy. All of them were deeply concerned by the higher levels of public expenditure to which post-war politics appeared to have irrevocably committed government. This alone was a serious threat to confidence in the pound, Butler thought, and it would be better, given these new commitments, for the exchange rate and not the reserves to take the strain. He was therefore from the beginning of his period of office, as were the other advocates of Robot and the Collective Approach, opposed to the Bretton Woods conception of fixed exchange rates.[3]

One of the difficulties was that Robot was clearly incompatible with the EPU agreement of 1950. In spite of a series of ingenious proposals for combining convertible and inconvertible currencies in one payments system, no one could find a way round the basic problem that everyone in the EPU would try to earn the currency that was convertible into dollars. The United Kingdom would have become the target for West European exports. So it was always accepted that if Robot went ahead Britain would, if necessary, protect itself against too great an increase in imports from western Europe by restoring the non-tariff barriers to trade which the OEEC (Organization for European Economic Cooperation) programme of trade liberalisation – a programme actually initiated by Britain itself in 1949 – was in the course of removing. This would constitute a flagrant breach of the trade rules of EPU, which forbade discrimination within the Union. But it seems even more likely that western European markets would have protected themselves against British exports, which for them would have become the equivalent of dollar imports. It was impossible to suppose without excessive optimism that in an international trading system where discrimination against dollar imports was temporarily accepted by all, there would not also have been discrimination against imports priced in convertible sterling. Clarke rationalised this difficulty for world trade out of existence by imagining an increase of sterling exports to the dollar zone so rapid as to cancel out the effect of the loss of a proportion of sterling exports to western Europe, a solution only for Britain. For the Bank of England the EPU appears to have been seen as a dangerous thing in itself, irrespective of its diversionary effects on trade, because it still enshrined, albeit remotely, the original Marshall Aid concept of a single European currency in its unit of account, the écu, in which the settlements were reckoned, and also because it took away from the power of central banks. The banks had to report all their working balances on foreign transactions monthly to the BIS (Bank of International Settlements) and make them available in their entirety for the multilateral compensations which the BIS effectuated.

Although Robot was twice rejected by the cabinet in 1952 this mixture of motives continued to prevail so that commercial considerations were no longer thought of as the primary reason for re-establishing convertibility. From June 1952, the date of the definitive rejection of Robot, until March 1953 the Collective Approach was concerned with the attempt to reach an accord with the United States to rewrite the Bretton Woods agreements. The United States was to be offered a fresh start. The clock would be put back to 1945, the mistakes made at that time acknowledged, and a wholly new basis for a return to world-wide currency convertibility against the dollar established as in 1947 through the prior establishment of pound-dollar convertibility. A new US line of credit would be provided to fund the sterling balances. The preferred solution in London was that this would be done through an increase in the funding of the IMF, needed in any case, it was argued, because of the growth in value of world trade since 1945. Commonwealth officials were told at the end of 1952 that it was assumed the increase would be of the order of $5,000 million, of which $2,500 million would be set aside to back sterling convertibility together with the convertibility of other European currencies which would be made convertible at the same time, the last point being of course something on which the Americans were particularly insistent for it would be neither desirable nor possible on their part to go to Congress for another loan purely for sterling.[4] At the end of 1953 the total working capital of IMF was still only about $3,000 million.

The proposals were really designed to replace the EPU as the focus of multilateral settlements by a more world-wide focus as envisaged at Bretton Woods. One question which never received any clear answer in these British proposals however, was which European currencies would go convertible at the same time as sterling. The Deutschmark, the guilder, the Belgian and French francs, and the three main Scandinavian currencies were all mentioned in 1952 as possibilities. After the start of 1953, as French foreign deficits increased, the French franc was mentioned no more.

Whatever the possibilities, the central difficulty in EPU remained the same as it had been when Robot had been the plan: either other important West European currencies would remain inconvertible with the same consequences for trade liberalisation as under Robot, or the pound would have to wait for other central banks, especially the Bank of France, to be in a position to establish convertibility. To counter this objection the United States was to be invited to replace the trade rules of EPU, which guaranteed members against discrimination, by a world-wide set of trade rules formulated jointly by IMF and GATT. No one could believe that these could have the same force as the rules enforced by the Management Board of EPU, which was effectively a committee of OEEC, because a more world-wide body could simply not be a club of the same kind. In return for American backing for these proposals the United Kingdom was still only prepared to declare convertibility for non-resident sterling (more or less as it would have been defined under Robot) and to end all discrimination against dollar imports. Given the extent of dollar discrimination still prevailing even at the end of 1957, this was, though, an important commercial offer.[5]

A REPLACEMENT FOR BRETTON WOODS?

The proposals still differed from the original conceptions of Bretton Woods through their insistence on a greater margin of fluctuation for exchange rates. The idea of a floating exchange rate had been dropped, mainly because of the political opposition in Cabinet to anything that looked like deflation, but it had been substituted by a proposal for flexible rates. The currencies would be allowed to fluctuate in a flexible band up to 5 per cent on each side of the registered par rate. The hope of the Bank of England was that once the flexible rates were introduced, some European currencies would peg on sterling, as they had done after 1931, while others would fluctuate against sterling within their own flexible bands, rather like the rules used to operate some of the more recent versions of the EMS where the Deutschmark has been the marker currency. This was a rewriting of Bretton Woods with a vengeance, a straightforward reassertion of the 'key currency' idea, which the United States had rejected at the end of the war in spite of the support it had found in Wall Street and from certain economists. Commonwealth prime ministers were told that in future there would be a 'nuclear group' of currencies which would set the rules, the US dollar, sterling, the Canadian dollar, the Deutschmark, the French franc and the Belgian franc, an earlier and smaller version of the Club of Seven.

These proposals were rejected in Washington on several weighty grounds. One was that they implied a return to trade discrimination in western Europe, perhaps even to bilateralism between countries whose currencies were left inconvertible, and so ran counter to the whole thrust of American policy in Europe since the war. Another was that extra backing for the IMF to allow it to support progress to convertibility looked to the State Department uncommonly like the stabilisation loans of the 1920s all over again, instead of the progress towards the integration of western Europe which it wanted to generate and which it saw in part arising from an increase in the volume of intra-West European trade. The first test for the State Department was whether British plans would advance or retard political unity in western Europe. The answer was only too obvious.[6] Since Bretton Woods, American priorities had also changed. Although the Marshall Plan had kept alive the rhetoric of Bretton Woods, it had displaced general currency convertibility to a lower policy priority, something which, too, must advance the cause of western European unity. Dulles mentioned 1959 as a probable date for the return to general convertibility, the year in which it did in fact arrive.[7] On these grounds, also, flexible rates were rejected. They would, it was argued, only make the implementation of the European Defence Community Treaty and the European Political Community more difficult. The Presidents' Commission on Foreign Economic Policy, established in August 1953 under the chairmanship of Clarence Randall (the Randall Commission) was eventually given the task of reporting on convertibility as well as other issues in American international policy, but as far as the Bank of England was concerned this was tantamount to a burial of the proposals.

The second stage of the Collective Approach lasted from March 1953, when the British proposals met such a flat response in Washington, to March 1954. It aimed at achieving what the Bank was fond of calling *de facto* convertibility, progressing towards effective convertibility without any comprehensive international agreement. Part of this programme aimed at increasing the ease with which sterling could be transferred by reducing the variety of sterling accounts, the 'unification of sterling' as the Bank called it. This was accompanied by the reduction of trade and exchange controls and the reopening of commodity markets in London. The Bank had a coherent order of procession for these piecemeal policies but it was substantially altered by the Chancellor's frequent reluctance and hesitation, as well as by outside events. Official policy towards the EPU was schizophrenic in thought and deed. The Bank continued to insist on the maximum possible liberty of action, which meant insisting on renewals of the Union for six months, when the government had little choice but to renew membership for another year, and then insisting on a right to withdraw at any time – equally difficult for the government to negotiate. A further difficulty with withdrawal was that the United Kingdom was the biggest debtor because of the sterling area deficits on trade with western Europe and so would have had to diminish its reserves to make substantial gold payments. *De facto* convertibility therefore had to be fitted in to continued EPU membership and to common action with the OEEC members. This achieved the reopening of arbitrage markets on 18 May 1953 for the Belgian, Swiss and French francs, the Danish and Swedish kroner, the guilder and the Deutschmark. This was soon followed by the introduction of certain kinds of forward dealing in these currencies by central banks. In the twelve months after the agreement the value of automatic compensations through BIS (Bank for International Settlements) in Basel fell by 57 per cent and it must be assumed that much of this reduction, plus the increase in the value of intra-West European trade was moved out into settlements in the London money markets (Triffin 1957: 213).

Although this was viewed by all parties as a further step in freeing trade from controls, the general trend of British policy, together with the numerous official conversations which the Collective Approach demanded, could only increase distrust about Britain's commitment to the EPU. After the rejection of the first Collective Approach proposals by Washington, however, the Bank turned towards western Europe. Bolton decided that the only viable policy was that London should become one of two centres of a two-world system of convertibility, a place for all non-dollar settlements, and consoled himself with the thought that eventually the Soviet Union and its satellites would enter the London non-dollar world. This required joint progress to convertibility of the main western European currencies, the nuclear group, and thus it required, in particular, some measure of agreement with the Deutschmark, the currency of the second-biggest trader.

APPROACH TO THE FEDERAL REPUBLIC

The Bank was well aware of the German Minister for the Economy, Ludwig Erhard's dislike of the EPU and his desire for a convertible mark. If, the Bank argued, Britain and the Federal Republic could change the settlement terms within EPU to the point where all settlements were made, even in the first tranche of debt, in gold or hard currency, effective convertibility with the dollar would have been established even though discrimination against dollar imports into western Europe remained. This was precisely Erhard's own policy. His support for a convertible mark had grown from the start of 1952 with the growth of the Federal Republic's reserves. As far as he was concerned, the EPU confined German exports unnecessarily to western Europe, so preventing the German 'return to world markets' which his book so stridently proclaimed (Erhard 1953). Worse, it allowed France to acquire German imports against EPU balances and to do so by overtly inflationary means which weakened the force of German monetary policy. His officials argued that the German commodity trade surplus within western Europe was structural, so that if the existing payments system persisted German exports would remain unrequited. By contrast, world-wide exports and a convertible mark would further reduce prices, increase output and improve productivity.[8] It seemed a reasonable assumption that when the British payments position in EPU improved, Erhard could be brought in behind a proposal to harden EPU settlements until they had attained *de facto* convertibility.

What the Bank of England failed to take into account was the constraints which both foreign policy and commercial realities imposed on the Minister for the Economy. Policy on future convertibility was referred to an inter-ministerial committee. Here the *Auswärtiges Amt* took the view that European integration now meant that no action which was inimical to France could be taken in EPU.[9] The Council of Economic Advisers held that the purpose of making the Deutschmark convertible should be primarily a commercial one, an increase in commodity exports.[10] The *Deutscher Industrie- und Handelstag* commissioned a study which emphasised the danger to German exports of any rift in the EPU between convertible and inconvertible currencies. In particular they were concerned about German exports to France, Italy, Austria, Turkey and Greece, the five EPU members whom they judged to have no chance of convertibility in 1953 and who were opposed to hardening the settlements.[11] These markets had been responsible for 21.5 per cent of all German exports in 1952. The outcome of the discussions in Bonn was that in spite of Erhard's discontent and the even greater displeasure of some of his officials, no step towards convertibility along the lines proposed by the British was to be taken unless at the same time the trade rules of the EPU were confirmed, which meant further steps towards trade liberalisation by the United Kingdom and proscribed any steps away from it in order to defend convertibility. This in turn meant retaining the supervisory powers over trade rules of the OEEC through the Managing Board of the EPU. Policy thus came down on the same side as manufacturers and exporters.

In retrospect this appears also as the wisest economic course. The extraordinarily rapid growth of German exports in the first four years of the Federal Republic had been overwhelmingly to the Benelux, to Austria and Switzerland, and to the three Scandinavian countries. For them the Federal Republic was playing the role which Britain had played in a larger context to other rapidly industrialising countries in the nineteenth century; it was exporting capital goods and at the same time because of its low tariffs offering a niche on its own market to their specialised manufactured exports. It was in this narrow geographical symbiosis that the Federal Republic's trade and income (and its reserves) were growing. The 'return to world markets' was a chimera whereas a return to trade liberalisation in the OEEC was an immediate vital interest, as was retaining an EPU settlements mechanism acceptable to the weaker members. No matter how restive Erhard subsequently was with these conclusions, the outcome of the policy debate in the Federal Republic by 1953 was conclusive. There was to be no progressive hardening of the settlements mechanism without retaining a firm set of rules of the game. It followed from the ambivalent British motives for seeking a joint agreement on convertibility that they did not value its commercial advantages so highly as to want to retain the commercial rules of the EPU, which might be a handicap to them if convertibility proved troublesome and which kept them fixed in a western European trade system with which they had little sympathy.

The British hoped to turn the European trade and payments system into a world-wide system by securing German support for a European Fund, to be created out of the working capital of a dissolved EPU and which could provide loans on strictly commercial terms to help the weaker members of EPU attain dollar convertibility. Agreement on the European Fund would go hand in hand with a mutual agreement to harden the settlements in EPU until *de facto* convertibility was reached. Negotiations between Britain and the Federal Republic over the scope of this European Fund occupied much of the third stage of the Collective Approach, because the British proposals fell far short of the policy which it had been determined in Bonn was the only acceptable compromise. The British wanted the Fund to last for only one year and to have no executive power other than the supervision of the transition to fully convertible settlements. Maintaining the rules of the game could then be left to the major central banks. This was in line with the concept of the 'nuclear group' and would bring the OEEC's supervision of trade to an end. It was in line with the Bank of England's idea that the best model was the pre-war

Tripartite Agreement based on frequent central bank consultations but with no firm permanent commitments on commercial policy or even on rates of exchange.[12] The Bank deutscher Länder simply did not believe in the goodwill of the British proposals, regarding them as a trick to buy time until the Conservatives could call another election, win it with a large majority, and unilaterally declare the convertibility of the pound the day afterwards.[13] This would have been the worst of all situations for the Federal Republic. Erhard took the view that the only satisfactory German response to such a move would be to establish Deutschmark convertibility immediately afterwards. Whether this would have happened was never put to the test because of the failure of the United Kingdom to find one single ally in western Europe and because of the fall in the sterling reserves in 1955.

THE SMALLER EUROPEAN COUNTRIES

The growing symbiosis with the Federal Republic had entirely altered the stance of two potential British allies, Belgium and the Netherlands. From the start of the EPU agreement in 1950 Belgium had given every appearance of being the least willing participant. With large surpluses on western European transactions, which in a system of world-wide convertibility could comfortably have offset its dollar deficits, Belgium had originally seen little to gain from the EPU and the Bank of Belgium had preferred an arrangement not only world-wide but more akin to the gold standard and less favourable to debtors. Between 1950 and 1952 it had energetically sought repayment in some convertible form of the debts owed to it in EPU, and even in spring 1952 was still threatening to leave the Union if special arrangements of this kind were not made.[14] After the agreement in March 1952 with France and Britain to offset some of these repayments by military aid and contracts, the Belgians were still expected by the British representatives to oppose the renewal of EPU in the summer for any period longer than one year, which was also British policy. At the meeting in June to determine the conditions for renewal, however, the Belgian delegation arrived with last-minute instructions to support a renewal for two years because of the commercial advantages of the Union.[15] The period between March and June had seen a decisive change in policy, the main grounds for which are readily comprehended; the EPU countries were responsible for about 80 per cent of Belgian exports by value in that year. By November Belgium was arguing strongly in the OEEC against any joint steps towards convertibility by the 'nuclear group' because it would increase discrimination against exports priced in Belgian francs. By May 1953 it was scarcely prepared to take part in official discussions with the United Kingdom on the British proposals under the Collective Approach.

As for the Netherlands, it seems clear that from 1950 onwards a set of irreversible rules of the game for intra-West European trade had become a priority for Dutch foreign policy in Europe.[16] This had been the objective of the Dutch Foreign Minister Dirk Stikker's proposals to the OEEC in summer 1950 called the 'Plan of Action'. It was the objective of Foreign Minister Jan Willem Beyen's demand that the other foreign ministers of the six ECSC countries accept a customs union with common rules and a common tariff as a concomitant of the Defence Community and the Political Community, a demand which they reluctantly conceded in 1953. And it was to be the objective of Beyen's revised proposals for a common market made to the Spaak Committee in 1955. All these proposals envisaged a set of mutually enforced trade regulations, and in the Beyen proposals these were to be enforced by an authority whose collective powers would be greater than the cooperative will of the OEEC and the managing board of EPU and which would have the power also to enforce some rules of the game on tariffs. It was made clear by Beyen to Erhard that the minimum acceptable position for the Netherlands was a resumption of trade liberalisation by the OEEC.[17] There was support for the Dutch proposals that tariffs should also be regulated in Europe and the European Fund proposals as they stood in March 1954 were subject to heavy criticism in the OEEC. Two of the members in the weakest international position, Denmark and Greece, wanted to replace the British proposals by a collective OEEC agreement with the IMF under which the EPU and its trade rules would be a regional unit of the IMF. Nobody except the British was prepared to revert to Bretton Woods without maintaining the special regime for the management of European trade which had been developed since 1950. The Swiss delegation to the OEEC even said the British proposals ought to produce a good luck telegram from the dead Stalin.[18]

US POLICY

There were still lingering hopes in London that the Randall Report would back the British proposals. It was known that H.J. Williams, a firm supporter of the key currency argument at the time of the Bretton Woods negotiations, was trying to write the small section on convertibility in as favourable a way as possible to the British point of view. There was considerable pressure within the IMF itself to break free from the American shackles imposed in 1948 which had confined the Fund to so insignificant a role in the world. Some of its officers, Edward Bernstein for example, were strongly in favour of using the Fund to support sterling–dollar convertibility as a way of re-establishing its importance. The Federal Reserve Board also rated sterling–dollar convertibility as a higher priority than European 'integration' (in which of course it was not particularly interested) and contemplated supporting it by a direct loan to the Bank of England, like the stabilisation loans of the 1920s. The US Treasury had always regarded European integration as an irritating interference with financial priorities, and it even displayed considerable enthusiasm for the British idea that in any return to world-wide convertibility the Bretton Woods concept of fixed rates should be jettisoned in favour of the 'flexible bands' which London had proposed.[19]

In the event the Randall Report said very little about convertibility and there really were few grounds for optimism that American policy would change. In July 1954 the National Advisory Council agreed that the OEEC must be kept intact in the impending transition to currency convertibility, adding as a sop to Britain that there should be liaison with the IMF and GATT. After convertibility the OEEC must be able to enforce trade rules so that convertibility did not lead to an increase in discrimination. Even after this decision and the cautious exegesis in Washington of the Randall Report to the effect that it supported a move towards convertibility but within the existing framework (although not sufficiently to satisfy the State Department), British policy did not

Table 10.1 Value of sterling-area reserves at end of year (million US dollars) (revised figures)

Year	Reserves
1945	2476
1946	2696
1947	2079
1948	1856
1949	1688
1950	3300
1951	2335
1952	1846
1953	2518
1954	2762
1955	2120
1956	2133
1957	2273
1958	3069
1959	2736

Source: UK Central Statistical Office, *Economic Trends, Annual Supplement*, 1984.

change and the European Fund proposals remained unacceptable to everyone in the OEEC. It was only the weakening of the British balance of payments in 1955 and the fall in the reserves which changed British policy.

BRITAIN'S FALLING RESERVES

Over the previous two years it had been possible to believe that the removal of trade and exchange controls was producing a gradual growth of reserves. By 1955 it was becoming evident that reserves were falling and would still be lower at the end of the year than in 1950 (see Table 10.1) There was no basis for the unilateral declaration of sterling–dollar convertibility that the *Bank deutscher Länder* feared and which the only half-secret negotiations for the Collective Approach had always suggested might be a possibility. Perhaps the shift in policy was also helped by the demise of the Defence Community treaty. But underlying this change of direction can also be detected a mounting unease that British exports were not growing as quickly as those of other West European countries, and that one reason for this might be that too small a proportion of them was directed towards the rapidly-growing western European markets. A Board of Trade enquiry into this hypothesis gave it only lukewarm support, but it was symptomatic of the mounting anxiety that one of the reasons why the British reserve position remained too weak to support convertibility might be a commercial one, that in spite of the much more rapid growth of British exports than in the inter-war period, their performance was too weak, partly because of their geographical distribution.

In the final terms of agreement on the European Fund the stipulation was that countries with a total of 50 per cent of the total EPU quotas could agree to replace the EPU with the European Fund. This meant that the United Kingdom and the Federal Republic between them could take the decision, a conclusion which prevented unilateral action by Britain while sheltering the Federal Republic from the more extreme pressures within EPU for giving the European Fund power to supervise tariff reductions or lend large sums for development to the Italian national development agency for the south, the *Cassa per il Mezzogiorno*. On its part the United Kingdom conceded that the European Fund should also serve as guarantor of the existing EPU trade rules. At the start of the EPU renewal meetings in June the Federal Vice-Chancellor Blücher was taken aside by Butler before the discussions began and personally assured that the United Kingdom had now abandoned all thought of unilateral action.[20] Both parties then agreed to support at the EPU renewal meetings in June a proposal that the settlements mechanism should be hardened so that debt settlements be made up to 75 per cent in gold in the first tranche.

BRITISH AND GERMAN EXPORTS

There was no earlier period at which the United Kingdom would have been prepared to make such concessions and in that sense the European Monetary Agreement marks a return to the conception, to which of course only lip-service had been paid in 1945–7 and which may never have been taken too seriously in London, that the first purpose of currency convertibility was to facilitate commodity trade. In 1947 it had been acceptable to establish convertibility while still maintaining an armoury of trade controls; the European Monetary Agreement accepted that trade liberalisation and convertibility must be combined. This did not mean that the prime motives for convertibility were not still the maintenance, perhaps even the extension, of the sterling area and the nostalgia for the past role of sterling. But a new element, anxiety over trade competition with the Federal Republic and the fear that this might have to be in Europe, had entered the scene. An increase in the use of sterling in intra-European trade and payments and an increase in the volume and proportion of British exports to western Europe were obviously not incompatible. It was not, however, so obvious, that given the universal political prejudice in favour of the sterling area and empire, and given the tendency of the main financial institutions to seek profits from overseas investment and other sources of invisible earnings, that they would always prove compatible.

If the performance of British exports in the 1950s is compared to their performance in earlier periods, it can certainly be argued, as Cairncross does, that the balance on commodity trade was much stronger in that decade than could ever have been expected from the historical record (Cairncross 1985). In so far as the weakness of the balance of payments originated from purely British causes, it would be more reasonable to attribute it to the failure of invisible earnings to grow after 1951 sufficiently to compensate for the increasing volume of capital imports. But it seems wholly misleading to compare British foreign trade success in the 1950s only to its performance in other decades. It should be compared to the foreign trade performance of other West European countries, of which the Federal Republic is much the most apposite because its foreign trade both in volume and structure by the early 1950s was the most like that of Britain, although not of course in its geographical distribution. It is this comparison which shows how poorly British exports performed relatively, because after 1955 the Federal Republic's export gains from Britain were at the expense of British *pre-war* markets.

The growth of the Federal Republic's exports was overwhelmingly due to the strength of western European demand; in 1959 60 per cent of its exports by value still went to EPU markets. The *Bundesverband der deutschen Industrie*, commenting on the Anglo-German proposals to the OEEC for the European Monetary Agreement, insisted on the value of maintaining under any regime of general convertibility the same international payments facilities and the formalised committee structure of the OEEC, and entered a cautionary note about any tendency to move to flexible exchange rates to make convertibility easier. The high proportion of capital goods in the Federal Republic's exports to western Europe demanded, they argued, a system of fixed exchange rates to facilitate the financing of these exports, often financed on five or ten-year loans.[21] The opinion of British manufacturers does not appear to have been sought at any higher level than the Board of Trade, if it was sought there. The accord reached with the Federal Republic indicated the acceptance of the idea that restrictions on British trade in western Europe would not be an acceptable price for reducing trade restrictions elsewhere and so presaged the proposals for the Free Trade Area. This still remained a very generalised standpoint compared to the specific trades which the German government, to Erhard's annoyance, was being called on to defend.

This is not the place to enter into the complex and unresolved debate over the reasons for the relative weakness of British exports in the 1950s.[22] The most rapidly growing markets for manufactured exports throughout the decade were all, however, in western Europe, and it must be asked whether the willingness to risk a drop in trade with western Europe in return for a limited form of convertibility was not one example of the neglect of the manufacturing and exporting sectors of the economy in favour of its financial sector which has been so emphasised by certain economists and historians as the root cause of the United Kingdom's post-war economic weakness.[23] In their view, the Bank and the Treasury represented the international financial interests of the City more than those of the manufacturing sector and retained a dominance over policy formulation, particularly under Conservative governments, which has impeded industrial investment and the growth of the manufacturing sector.

German manufacturers protested against the risk which the British proposals carried to the 21.5 per cent of total German exports going in 1952 to the five EPU countries, which in their view would certainly have been unable to establish convertibility and consequently if EPU had been dissolved would have had to resort to discrimination against Deutschmark imports and perhaps to bilateral trade. The fear that a premature declaration of sterling–dollar convertibility might set in motion a general return to bilateral trade in western Europe was widespread. It was a factor in America's discouraging attitude, as well as in the opposition to general convertibility of all those debtors in intra-EPU trade whose deficits the EPU was financing. In this light the possible outcome of the British proposals was even more threatening. In so far as the dynamic expansion of intra-West European trade depended not only on an adequate payments mechanism but on the credit which it provided, the collapse of the EPU might have reversed the tendency to trade expansion. Both by its own generous terms for debtors and by the pressures which the OEEC brought on the Federal Republic to finance its own exports in the EPU even beyond the limit of its original quotas the EPU was indirectly responsible for the growth of the exports of all the Federal Republic's smaller trading partners who remained in trade deficit with Germany. And where the Federal Republic was not the dominant trade partner, as in the case of Denmark or Norway, the increase in the exports of these two countries to other EPU markets such as the United Kingdom depended on the generous funding of trade deficits which EPU provided. Erhard's counter-argument was that because the Federal Republic was piling up large trade surpluses in western Europe – part of which were settled only in cumulative EPU debts – whereas it had a trade deficit with the dollar zone, convertibility in a world-wide framework would be a contribution to settling the dollar deficit, like the Belgian argument before summer 1952. Maintaining EPU, he argued, only increased the tendency of German exports to flow in the 'wrong' direction. German manufacturers were a vested interest clinging to a secure position to the detriment of the economy as a whole.

THE ADVANTAGES AND DISADVANTAGES OF CONVERTIBILITY

In calculating the commercial risk to the Federal Republic or the United Kingdom in establishing dollar convertibility without the general concurrence of the other EPU members, we must assume that some proportion of exports to the five countries singled out by

German manufacturers would have continued. These countries, Austria, France, Greece, Italy and Turkey, are a minimum list. It is probable that Denmark, for example, would have found the transition to convertibility equally difficult. But if we assume that these five countries would have returned to the bilateral trading arrangements of the period 1945–50, the most appropriate measure of their capacity to take German or British exports is probably the value of their exports to both countries. In reality, the bilateral arrangements of 1945–50 allowed for a larger 'swing' on each side of equilibrium in the balance than those of the 1930s, but it is difficult to believe that such provisions could have continued in one direction only over the whole period 1952–8 until general convertibility was established, whereas under the EPU regime of multilateral settlements the Federal Republic was able, for example, to run persistently large surpluses with Austria. Over the period 1952–8, until the coming of general convertibility, the Federal Republic's imports from these five countries amounted to only 74 per cent of its exports to them. This suggests that under bilateral trading conditions German exports to these countries would have amounted to $6,671 million instead of the $9,053 million which they actually totalled. They amounted over the whole period to 20 per cent of all German exports, the share of these markets dropping only slightly and still being 19.6 per cent in 1958.

Is it possible that the Federal Republic could have made up this export loss of $2,372 million by increasing its exports to the dollar zone? The total value of the Federal Republic's exports to North America over the same period was $3,406.5 million. Had the Federal Republic's exports to Austria, France, Greece, Italy and Turkey to be requited by being paid for in goods, hard currency or gold, this would have meant an increase of almost 70 per cent in exports to North America, which seems wholly improbable. And if this had been the outcome of British policy, what would then have occurred to British exports to North America? Especially, it might be asked, when they were failing to compete successfully with German exports even in sheltered sterling-area markets. The United States, it should be added, remained a heavily protected market in the 1950s.

If these were the risks entailed in British policy, and in Erhard's version of it, what were the compensatory gains? We could simplify the issues by assuming that there was a clear economic rationale behind the pressure for convertibility, to increase the value of invisible earnings. Motives were by no means so rational, though, and it is impossible to find any unambiguous statement that the motivation was to strengthen invisibles. British exports to the five countries in question were only 6.5 per cent of total exports in 1952. Over the period as a whole they amounted to 6.1 per cent of total exports. This was equivalent to a sum of $3.477 million. Making the same assumption as for the Federal Republic, that their value under a bilateral trading system would have been the equivalent of the value of their recipients' exports to Britain, leads to the hypothetical conclusion that had the EPU not existed the United Kingdom would have still achieved the same value of exports because the value of its imports from the five countries was $3,651 million. In the narrowest sense, therefore, there was no commercial risk to the United Kingdom in return for the hypothetical gain in invisibles.

Estimating the hypothetical gain, however, involves counterfactual assumptions which probably put a greater strain on historical reality than it should be asked to bear. One method would be to compare them to the increase in invisible earnings over the equivalent period after the establishment of general convertibility from the start of 1959, but this increase occurred in entirely different historical conditions. Cohen and Shonfield have both tried to estimate the proportion of British invisible earnings in the 1950s which was dependent on the international use of sterling (Cohen 1971; Shonfield 1958). This of course is not the same as being dependent on the convertibility of sterling, but we may assume that convertibility would in fact have increased the use of the pound in international transactions. This was certainly one of the main motives. Both estimated that about one-third of the income from merchanting, brokerage and trade financing depended on the international use of sterling. It is not easy to sort out these items from the United Kingdom balance-of-payments data, and Cohen and Shonfield are by no means in agreement on what proportion of earnings under each item depended on the use of sterling as an international currency. One-third of the increase in earnings in these particular items between 1958 and 1964 was roughly, however, $244 million current (Clarke 1967: 12). The value of invisible earnings from particular sources in the 1950s is harder to determine, but using the Treasury estimates for 1956 the total income dependent on the use of sterling as an international currency could be put at $350 million annually. The one thing that can be said is that even if British trade with the five countries was in deficit and thus the immediate commercial risk to it through the disruption of EPU was absent, the potential gains from invisibles in return was very small compared to the value of commodity trade involved.

The issue needs to be decided by a more dynamic analysis. It tended to be seen at the time as a dispute over the geographical sphere of influence of the British economy, not as a choice between commodity trade and services. Both for the expansion of foreign trade and international services, Sir George Bolton and his allies would have argued that a world-wide system of trade resting on currency convertibility, in turn resting on the pillar of sterling–dollar convertibility, was essential. But the more rapid expansion of the foreign trade of all Britain's West European competitors, in part because their trade was with each other through the transferable currency arrangements of the EPU, called this analysis into question because the growth of commodity trade might actually have suffered from the priority given to the objective of the attainment of convertibility. It depends on what the outcome for the EPU would have been. Could it have survived a British withdrawal and had it done so could it still have been, without the sterling area, as dynamic a force for trade expansion? The likelihood is that intra-West European trade would have reverted to a regime like that of 1949 which, although it was still supervised by the OEEC, rested essentially on a network of bilateral trade and payments agreements, within which shortages of specific currencies inevitably invoked quotas and other non-tariff restrictions. Even though only a quarter of the United Kingdom's exports went to western Europe, the general effects of a slower growth, perhaps even a period of decline, in intra-West European trade would surely have had their impact on the British economy too. The indifference to the prospects for other western European economies which British policy preferences revealed between 1951 and 1955 was probably not even in the United Kingdom's own interests. Had western Europe's markets not continued to absorb western Europe's exports during the American recession of 1953, might not the long-sustained post-war boom have come to an end?

The surplus on invisible earnings, in any case, ceased to grow after 1951, whereas it had grown rapidly for the previous six years. The failure of shipping earnings to continue to grow, the increase in capital imports both into Britain and into the sterling area, and the higher interest rates and service charges paid on these and on the sterling balances, were the main causes of the failure of invisibles to continue to contribute to the growth of the reserves. This seems to indicate that export expansion might have offered a surer way to increase the size of the reserves, as the example of the Federal Republic so resoundingly demonstrated, and might therefore have been the surer road to currency convertibility. The international influences operating on the rest of the sterling area were so powerful, though, that the movement of the sterling area reserves was not dominated by the United Kingdom's own choices of economic policy. In that sense the estimated gains of giving trade expansion the first priority, rather than the establishment of convertibility itself, could have been relatively small in comparison to the effects of the exogenous influences on the sterling area reserves, for example the great annual fluctuations in the United States' annual demand for raw material imports. Exactly the same point could be made about the impact on the reserves of an increase in invisible earnings due to the establishment of a form of limited, or even of *de facto*, convertibility.

CONCLUSION

The Bank of England still dreamt of asserting the hegemony of sterling in western Europe, from time to time nostalgically considering the possiblity of bringing Scandinavian countries into the sterling area. It is obvious that German policy could only be a set of reactions to more or less well-informed guesses about the British government's intentions. Hegemony, however, requires leadership and this the Bank notably failed to provide. No single country in western Europe supported its policy between 1951 and 1955, because for all of them the commercial priorities came first and progress towards convertibility depended on that first priority being satisfied. Fortunately the real power lay in Washington, because once Robot had been rejected all the subsequent proposals under the Collective Approach depended on American financial backing for sterling. In this case the British may perhaps count themselves lucky that this was so. The Germans certainly can.

NOTES

1. Cairncross (1985: 234 ff.) and Newton (1986) give substantial accounts of the scheme.
2. Public Record Office (PRO), T 236/3240, 'External action', draft of a note by the Chancellor, n.d.
3. 'There is nothing sacrosanct about a fixed rate (except the decree of the IMF Founding Fathers)', PRO, T 236/3240, Clarke to Rowan, 25 January 1952.
4. Bank of England (BOE), OV 44/52, 'Borrowing from the IMF etc.', 11 November 1952.
5. The calculations by Hemming, Miles and Ray (1958/9) show that there was very little reduction between 1953 and the start of 1958 in the extent of British discrimination against dollar imports.
6. Eisenhower Library, White House Central Files. Confidential File, Box 67, Van Hollen to Hauge, 'US position for conversation', 4 March 1953.
7. PRO, T 232/408, Owen to Copleston, 30 March 1954.
8. Bundesarchiv (BA), B 102/12655/2, Bundeswirtschaftsministerium (BWM), 'Herstellung der Konvertierbarkeit', 22 July 1953; 'Besprechungen über das deutsche Programm zur Erreichung der Konvertierbarkeit . . .', 23 July 1953.
9. BA, B 102/12655/1, 'Londoner Besprechungen über Währungsfragen', 30 April 1953.
10. BA, B 102/12650/2, 'Aufzeichnung über den Stand der Diskussionen zur Frage der Reform der EZU', 17 January 1953.
11. BA, B 102/12651/2, IFO, 'Zur Frage der Konvertierbarkeit der D-Mark', May 1953.
12. BA, B 102/12651-2, 'OEEC ministerial examination group on convertibility', note by the United Kingdom, 4 June 1954; BOE, OV 44/61, Thompson-McCausland to France, 19 January 1953.
13. BA, B 102/12652/2, Bank deutscher Länder to Erhard, 25 January 1955.
14. The fullest discussion is in Rees (1963). For Belgium's original opposition to the EPU, see Milward (1984).
15. PRO, T 230/210, UK Delegation to OEEC to Foreign Office, 27 June 1952.
16. R.T. Griffiths and A.S. Milward, 'The Beyen Plan and the European political community', in Maihofer (1986).
17. BA, B 102/12653/1, 'Deutsch-niederländische Gespräche über Konvertibilitätsfragen', 10 June 1954.
18. BA, B 102/12652/1, 'Bericht über die Expertensitzung der OEEC am 15/17 Juni 1954'.
19. BOE, OV 44/61, Makins to Butler, 7 December 1953.
20. BA, B 102/12653/2, Blücher to Adenauer, 20 June 1955.
21. BA, B 102/12653/3, Bundesverband der deutschen Industrie, 'Die Handelspolitik in der Übergangsphase zur Konvertibilität', 7 June 1955.

22. There has not been much advance on the best contemporary study, Wells (1964).
23. See, for example, in chronological order, Shonfield (1958) Hirsch (1965) Pollard (1982), Newton and Porter (1988).

REFERENCES

Cairncross, Alec (1985), *Years of Recovery. British Economic Policy, 1945–1951*, London: Methuen.
Clarke, William M. (ed.) (1967), *Britain's Invisible Earnings. The Report of the Committee on Invisible Exports*, London: British Export Council.
Cohen, Benjamin J. (1971), *The Future of Sterling as an International Currency*, London: Macmillan.
Erhard, Ludwig (ed.) (1953) *Deutschlands Rückkehr zum Weltmarkt*, Düsseldorf: Econ-Verlag.
Gardner, Richard N. (1956), *Sterling–Dollar Diplomacy. Anglo-American Collaboration in the Reconstruction of Multilateral Trade*, Oxford: Clarendon Press.
Hemming, M.F.W., C.M. Miles and G.F. Ray (1958/59), 'A statistical summary of the extent of import control', *Review of Economic Studies*, vol. 26, pp. 75–109.
Hirsch, Fred (1965), *The Pound Sterling: A Polemic*, London: Gollancz.
Maihofer, Werner (ed.) (1986), *Noi si mura*, Florence: European University Institute.
Milward, Alan S. (1984), *The Reconstruction of Western Europe, 1945–1951*, London: Methuen.
Newton, C.C.S. (1986), 'Operation Robot and the political economy of sterling convertibility, 1951/1952', *European University Institute Working Paper*, no. 86/256, Florence.
Newton, S. and D. Porter (1988), *Modernization Frustrated. The Politics of Industrial Decline in Britain since 1900*, London: Unwin Hyman.
Pollard, Sidney (1982), *The Wasting of the British Economy*, London/Canberra: Croom Helm.
Rees, Graham L. (1963), *Britain and the Postwar European Payments System*, Cardiff: University of Wales Press.
Shonfield, Andrew (1958), *British Economic Policy Since the War*, London: Wyman & Sons.
Triffin, Robert (1957), *Europe and the Money Muddle: From Bilateralism to Near-convertibility, 1947–1956*, New Haven: Yale University Press.
Wells, Sidney John (1964), *British Export Performance: A Comparative Study*, Cambridge: Cambridge University Press.

PART V

THE CENTRE AND THE PERIPHERY OF THE TWENTIETH-CENTURY WORLD ECONOMY

11 · THE UNITED STATES AND THE WORLD ECONOMY IN THE TWENTIETH CENTURY

Charles P. Kindleberger

The twentieth was said by Henry Luce, the founder of *Time* Magazine, to be the American century. If so, like Adolph Hitler's 1,000-year Reich, it did not last as long as advertised. When it started and when it ended are questions that will be addressed, or at least posed, in what follows. But it is perhaps fair to say that the country was an economic youth as the century dawned, and now may be in some sort of economic decline.

I choose not to try to fit the country into the Rostovian stages of pre-conditions, take-off, drive to maturity and age of high mass consumption (Rostow 1960). I have some objection to any and all stage theories, but that particular paradigm lacks a stage of decline. Decline may be implied by high mass consumption, however, if one gives credence to the Cipolla view of the decline of empires – that improvements in the standards of living brought about by a rising economy lead to more and more people demanding to share the benefits, and that incomes increase and extravagances develop as new needs replace those which have begun to be satisfied (Cipolla 1970, from the back cover of the paperback).

One could perhaps fit the country into another paradigm related to the balance of indebtedness: young debtor, mature debtor, young creditor and mature creditor, although the symmetry of the scheme hides the fact that the United States went from the first to the third in the three or four years of the First World War, stayed there for sixty years, and reached the fourth stage only in the middle 1970s. This pattern, too, lacks much attention to the stage of capital consumption, as the mature creditor is presumed to live off foreign income rather than to borrow for consumption and/or consume the capital invested abroad.

There are other patterns one could experiment with, the Gompertz or S-curve of material transformation as the metallurgist, Cyril Stanley Smith (1975) calls it, or the Kondratieff model of recurring fifty-year cycles, at least prices, and possibly – though I have no faith in them – in such other economic variables as production, income, technical change, or wars that serve as hothouses of economic growth, speeding up capital formation and growth in young countries, decline through capital consumption in ageing countries.

One can of course compare the United States in the world economy with the United Kingdom: when Britain was the world's economic leader it had sterling and the British Navy; the United States in its turn had the dollar and the atom bomb (Hogan 1987: 213). Hawtrey (1952) stated that power is the capacity to produce goods and to move them over distances – a view that focuses on the British navy more than on the battleship: the US analogue presumably lies in the civil air fleet and the air force. Or one could approach the ninety-year (present century) history of the United States in the terms of Paul Kennedy (1987) or of Mancur Olson (1982). Kennedy claims that leading powers take on commitments that grow until they mount beyond the capacity of the country, or its willingness, to discharge them. Olson makes a distinction between countries that remain at peace or undefeated for years on end, in which distributional coalitions form and fight for a growing share, or at least against a declining one, of the national income, blocking the agenda of solutions to problems of production and trade. Thurow (1980) calls it a zero-sum society; Krueger (1974) puts it that a shift occurs from output and marketing to rent-seeking. A scheme that focuses more on the world economy and less on the United States is that of Wallerstein (1980) in which the world is organised about a centre and consists for the most part of a periphery. On this showing the United States could be said to have started in the periphery, or possibly the semi-periphery as the later versions of the pattern provide (Senghaas 1985), and moved unevenly to take over the position of the centre, and in recent years to drift out again.

I hope I may be permitted to pursue my own rather different line which focuses on external economic relations, and in particular on five functions that a world economic leader should perform: the maintenance of open markets in terms of glut, and the sharing of scarce commodities in acute shortage; maintenance of the international monetary system, which could mean an open market for precious metals (the Netherlands in the seventeenth century), running the gold standard (Britain from the Congress of Vienna to the outbreak of the First World War), the United States' management of the dollar and the Bretton Woods system from 1946 to some such date as 1971 or 1973; maintaining a flow of capital from the rich countries of the world to the poor; fostering the coordination of macro-economic policy; and provision of a lender of last resort in financial crisis (Kindleberger 1986: ch. 14). The first and fifth functions involve crisis management; the intermediate three have to do with the steady state or trend. It is perhaps overstating the matter to suggest that if the trend is not managed in some fashion, crises are likely to develop. Some crises are exogenous. The distinction between trend and crisis is none the less useful. An outline of the schema by functions and time periods is furnished in Table 11.1 as a guide to the overall discussion.

I propose to demonstrate that the United States was a free rider from 1901 to 1914, and gave no thought to any of these tasks until after the First World War; that in the inter-war period it became aware of the need for some country to discharge the functions but chose to leave them to others, participating, when at all, too little and too late; towards the end of the inter-war period, under Roosevelt, the isolationist stand of the country was abandoned after peaking in 1933, and bit by bit for one function and another the country began to assert some leadership. The beginnings were slow: the Reciprocal Trade Agreements Act in 1934 could be taken as a start, but it was limited. In foreign exchange the Tripartite Monetary Agreement of September 1936 was again a feeble start, but none the less a foot in the door. Strong leadership did not appear until perhaps Lend-Lease in 1942, or the international institutions of UNRRA (United Nations Relief and Rehabilitation Agency), FAO (Food and Agriculture Organization of the United Nations), Bretton Woods, etc. at the end of the war and immediately afterwards. With the Marshall Plan and Point IV, the country reached the apogee of its leadership role.

Table 11.1 The United States and the world economy – twentieth century

Function	1901–14	1919–29	1930–9	1945–70	1971 to present	Notes
Goods markets	Strong protection moderated 1913	Anti-dumping tariff, ignored 1927 tariff truce, resist Stevenson rubber plan	Hawley–Smoot irresponsible Begin reversal RTAA, 1934	ITO, GATT, Dillon, Kennedy etc. rounds sale out of strategic reserve Combined Boards NTBs	Bilateral XR, MFA, soya bean 'shocku', AOPEC embargo left to oil countries	Gephardt threat of bilateral retaliation, ambivalence commodity agreements, GSP
Foreign Exchange	'Automatic' under gold standard	FRBNY interest in European cooperation	Thomas amendment, change gold price, torpedo WEC Tripartite Monetary Agreement silver price	Bretton Woods, British loan, Marshall Plan, gold pool swaps, G-10 SDR	10% devaluation floating, benign neglect, Baker Plan, Louvre to correct 1982–5, appreciation	Gold bugs: Mundell, etc., free fall? Liquidity a non-problem
Capital flows	Mature debtor repays FDI	Dawes loan, spurt X 1924–8, halted 1928 when NYSE boom	Widespread default, lending stopped to all but Canada	X–M Bank, World Bank, regional DBs, IET, VCRP, MCP	Bank Lending sovereign states after 'crime of 1971', big inflow, Treasury bonds real estate, equities	Baker insistence on banks continued lending, Black Monday

Coordination monetary, fiscal policy	Gold standard, Aldrich Comm., Fed. Res. Act	Sterilise war gold, 1927 Ogden Mills, CB meeting	Feeble attempt to coordinate B of E	IMF, OECD, WP #3, Chequers	Carter programme, locomotives, summit meetings ineffective	Inability of US to persuade Japan to limit export-led growth, FRG to relax about inflation
Lender of last resort	Not needed	Isolationism, insist on war debts	Too little too late, sabotage World Economic Conference	Marshall Plan etc., swaps, Paris Club	Mexico 1982, Basel protocol 1975	Unclear where responsibility lies today

Abbreviations:

AOPEC – Arab Organization of Petroleum Exporting Countries; B of E – Bank of England; CB – central banks; DB – development banks; FDI – foreign direct investment; FRBNY – Federal Reserve Bank of New York; FRG – Federal Republic of Germany; GATT – General Agreement on Tariffs and Trade; GSP – Generalized System of Preferences; IET – Interest Equalization Tax; IMF – International Monetary Fund; ITO – International Trade Organization; MCP – Mandatory Control Program; MFA – Multi-Fiber Agreement; NTB – Non-Tariff Barrier; NYSE – New York Stock Exchange; OECD – Organisation for Economic Co-operation and Development; SDR – Specialized Drawing Rights; VCRP – Voluntary Credit Restraint Program; WEC – World Economic Conference; WP – Working Party; X – export of capital; X – M – exports minus imports, or trade balance; XR – export restraints.

The dating of decline again presents a problem: one could take the breakup of the London gold pool in 1968, the closing of the gold window in August 1971, floating the dollar in 1973 (at the insistance of the Bundesbank). Benign neglect applied to the dollar exchange rate under President Nixon and later President Reagan while Donald Regan was Secretary of the Treasury, produced a reaction of reasserted US concern under James Baker, Mr Regan's successor, in the Plaza (1985) and Louvre (1987) agreements and the Seoul declaration on Third World debt. As I write the country seems to be slipping – in the heat of a forthcoming election campaign – into a catatonic state in so far as it tries to cope with the deficit in the balance of payments, trade and exchange policy, and preparing for upcoming incidents in the continuing Third World debt crisis and a possible free fall in the dollar. A number of proposals of more or less insight are put forward, ranging from a return to the gold standard advocated by Congressman Kemp and a former candidate for governor of New York, Lewis Lehrman, to large-scale negotiations about Third World debt (Senator Bill Bradley, Felix Rohatyn, Peter Kenen, *et al.*), balanced-budget constitutional amendments, rigorous abstention of government from interfering with markets, regulation of markets, reregulation of banking, etc., but no one seems to be listening.

GOODS MARKETS

The task of a leading country in the world in relation to commodity markets has been interpreted as leaving them alone in ordinary times, but intervening in crisis. Leaving them alone means free trade, that is, imposing no tariffs. The United States is constitutionally unable to tax exports so that this means keeping down tariffs and other restrictions for imports. There are various possible sorts of crises. In periods of glut, the task of a leader is to keep its market open for imports, as Britain did from 1846 to 1860 on to 1915. In periods of acute shortage, it means continuing to supply the good or goods in question to buyers. Crises which affect the resources engaged in an import-competing good, sometimes called market disrupting, pose difficult questions. If the resources involved, especially labour, have opportunities for other employment, even at lower wages, there is a case for doing nothing. If they are isolated and the only alternative is unemployment, some economists would want to impose tariffs on second-best grounds that call for interfering with markets when they don't work. Others would intervene to improve or assist the functions of the labour market. Where the industry is capable of recovery there may be a case for a temporary and disappearing tariff, and so on. Much depends upon whether the authorities are concerned with the welfare of a limited group, of consumers within the nation as a group, or of optimal allocation of world resources. Presumably less-developed countries have limited responsibility for the allocation of resources in the world as a whole, while a leading country looks beyond its borders. As a country declines in the world relative to others its horizons shrink again.

The United States entered the twentieth century with high tariffs enacted in 1890 (McKinley), 1894 (Wilson) and 1897 (Dingley). The British Board of Trade estimated at the turn of the century that its most important export goods paid duties in the United States averaging 70 per cent *ad valorem*. The Payne–Aldrich tariff of 1909, a Republican enactment, changed the details but left the general level more or less the same. A Democratic tariff adjustment in 1913 (Underwood) lowered duties on about half the more important items, left others unchanged, established an official Tariff Commission.

The immediate post-war period was one of considerable chaos in trade. Exchange rates pegged during the war were let go, and many countries adopted new tariffs to counteract 'exchange dumping'. In the United States this took the form of the Fordney–McCumber tariff of 1922. The United States protested vigorously but vainly against the 1923–4 Stevenson rubber plan to raise prices in the Malay States and Ceylon; ultimately the scheme was undermined by rapidly expanding native production in Indonesia. Along with other countries, the United States participated in the World Economic Conference of 1927 that negotiated a truce in tariff increases, but like other countries, paid little attention to it.

Maintaining high tariffs during the 1920s after it had paid off a lot of its overseas debt during the war, accumulated claims on the rest of the world, and engaging in substantial new lending especially in the period from 1924 to 1928, the United States was attacked as failing to act as a creditor nation should. The reference, of course, was to British free trade from 1860 to 1913 and substantial foreign lending. Modern economic theorists, however, are in general agreement that the criticism was misplaced: tariffs are a micro-economic distortion with but little macro-economic effect as impact on the balance of payments. A particular tariff may make it hard for a debtor to export to the United States a particular good in which it has a comparative advantage, but the expansionary effect of the restriction in the importing creditor, and contractive effect in the exporting debtor, however objectionable in themselves, will correct most of the effect of the tariff on the balance of payments.

The 1929 depression is usually credited with having given rise to the Hawley-Smoot tariff of 1930. In fact, the origin of the Hawley-Smoot goes back to the presidential campaign of 1928 when President Hoover promised to do something for agriculture, and the Congress reached for what Schumpeter called 'the Republican sovereign remedy', the tariff. Log-rolling let the matter get quickly out of hand. Increases in duties spread from agricultural products to other raw materials and to manufactured products. Democrats joined Republicans in the exercise, and both were pushed aside by the lobbyists for particular interests. The decline in business may have induced President Hoover to sign the monstrous bill into law in June 1930, over the protests of 1,028 economists inside the country and of forty-five foreign countries. It was a beggar-my-neighbour action of the most parochial sort.

In the first years of the Roosevelt administration that began in March 1933, the US government was even more acutely isolationist in economic terms than it had been under Hoover. The World Economic Conference of June–July 1933 was torpedoed, as will be shown, on unwillingness to stabilise the foreign value of the dollar. The farm programme required limiting imports from Canada of products the prices of which had been raised domestically. Strong demands for agricultural protection were voiced within the government by one George Peek in the Department of Agriculture. The Secretary of State, however, was Cordell Hull, a former Congressman and former chairman of the Ways and Means Committee under Democratic regimes, who came from a district in Eastern Tennessee that exported tobacco, and was adamantly, almost fanatically, a free trader, and especially an opponent of British Empire and Commonwealth preference that discriminated against United States farm products. He kept pushing in the

Cabinet for a liberalisation of trade, partly also as a political gesture against the autarkic Fascist countries.

In 1934 the President acceded to his programme, against that of Peek, and went forward with the Reciprocal Trade Agreement Act. Under this legislation Congress turned the tariff-making function over to the Administration for limited periods of time, and within restrictions, as a means of eliminating log-rolling. The first Act provided that tariffs could be reduced by 50 per cent (or half the Hawley–Smoot level) against reciprocal concessions made by a bilateral agreement partner. Concessions made to one country were extended to all others with whom the United States had a treaty of Friendship, Commerce and Navigation containing the most-favoured-nation clause. The first agreements were relatively innocuous, with Latin American countries, and then, just before the war, new ones with Canada and the United Kingdom, but highly restricted in the commodities and products for which concessions were granted (or obtained). Subsequent renewals, especially after the war, provided for 50 per cent reductions not from Hawley–Smoot but from the existing lowered level, for reductions to zero under certain circumstances, few of which were realised in practice, and for multilateral negotiations (actually simultaneous bilateral negotiations in which concessions exchange between countries where one was the principal supplier of the other in a given good were generalised to all other countries in the negotiation).

All this time the Congress and the lobbyists representing the interests of particular commodities and products were yielding ground grudgingly. Each renewal of the legislation imposed new limitations: 'peril points' beyond which tariffs in specified commodities could not be reduced, an 'escape clause', which provided that a given concession could be withdrawn if it led to a very damaging increase in imports, and the like. In due course the Administration gave further ground by negotiating special agreements with foreign exporting countries to restrict exports to the United States, originally one country-supplier at a time, but when this raised US prices and attracted imports from other foreign countries, at first in successive bilateral agreements and then multilaterally.

The movement of the United States from a protectionist to a relatively free-trade country is explained by economists as the consequence of the rising importance of large-scale industry which exported, as against small-scale industry which was import-competing. Business in the former was organised into such a group as the Committee for Economic Development which was liberal, in the latter in the National Association of Manufacturers, which was protectionist. The position in labour was more complex, as the American Federation of Labor on a craft basis and originally protectionist, merged with the Congress of Industrial Organizations, an industrial union, the biggest constituents of which came from large-scale production and were for low tariffs to stimulate exports. In the early post-war period the AFL–CIO supported the trade agreement acts; as world recovery and growth outside the United States began to lead to imports of such products as automobiles, radio and television sets, and the like, the liberality of the unions weakened. Large-scale industry also lost cohesion on the issue. Some companies undertook foreign direct investment to produce whole products or components abroad and remained in favour of free trade, while others such as steel resisted. Labour's opposition to liberal trade arrangements was expressed in the push for passage of a Burke–Hartke bill, which failed, but would have both restricted imports and put penalties on foreign direct investment.

At the time of writing, one presidential candidate, Representative Richard Gephardt from Missouri, proposed to mingle the trade issue with balance-of-payments again, calling for negotiations with separate countries that have bilateral surpluses in payments with the United States. This appears to be a disguised version of geriatric tariffs, such as have been called for in Britain by the late Lord Kaldor. Whether these will come to pass cannot be foretold, but the discussion indicates that the United States has receded a long distance from its role as a leader in promoting freer world trade.

It must be admitted that there was a strong element of national interest in promoting free trade so long as the United States was a leading producer of the latest manufactured goods. The British equivalent was called 'free-trade imperialism' (Gallagher and Robinson 1953; Semmel 1970). When the competition from Japan and Germany became intense, enthusiasm for free trade diminished. The Reagan administration professed an ideological predilection for free markets, but like that of Roosevelt, Truman and others, made concessions to protectionist forces when it judged it expedient. One defence against the protectionist forces in the country was to pressure Japan to reduce its infant industry restrictions faster, a process that became known as 'Japan-bashing'.

Attention to particular trade items was intense in the First and Second World Wars, when scarce shipping space was allocated in transatlantic carriage, and when the United States organised allied Combined Boards to allocate the supplies of food, raw materials and capital equipment. Pressure was exerted to bring such neutral countries as Argentina within the allocation schemes, and to keep them there during the period of acute scarcity after the war. In due course government allocations were relaxed in favour of free markets. When raw materials became abundant after 1951, some residual anxiety over the availability of supplies built up, and the United States acquired substantial stockpiles of commodities, such as non-ferrous metals, that might run short. When scarcities returned with the Korean War, some of these US stockpiles were released to the market, to dampen the rise in prices.

In the 1950s and 1960s as Japanese production rose with a strong export drive, the United States kept its market open for Japanese goods when those in Europe were for the most part closed. In 1973, however, two episodes suggested that the United States was no longer willing to take a leadership role in commodities. An Arab Organization of Petroleum Exporting Countries embargo, a reduction by 25 per cent for most countries, but 100 per cent for those it deemed hostile – the Netherlands and the United States – hurt the Netherlands with far more reliance on imports than the United States, which has substantial domestic production. Neither the EEC (European Economic Community) nor the US government took action to assist the Netherlands – although they locked the door in November 1974, after the horse had been stolen, by organising an International Energy Agency. The Netherlands was assisted, however, by the international oil companies which rearranged the distribution of Iranian supplies that lay outside the embargo to spread the hurt more equitably.

In the summer of 1973, moreover, President Nixon cut off the export of soybeans from the United States to hold down the price which had gone sky-high. Since Japan's diet depended upon imports of soybeans, and US production and consumption were on a far bigger scale, this was an unconscionable act for a world stabiliser to take in the commodity field, and indicated a shift away from attention to world stability to the narrow interest of the United States.

A complete account of US leadership in goods markets would require attention to commodity agreements in which US policy has varied from opposition to tolerance, the latter qualified by the condition that some attention be paid to consumer interests, and to acceptance of some financing of balance-of-payments deficits by the IMF when an exporting country's prices fall. The issue is complicated, and lies outside the present interest in leadership functions.

FOREIGN EXCHANGE

In my taxonomy of leadership functions in the world economy I duck the question of what the appropriate policy for a foreign-exchange regime should be – though I have views on that subject – to say merely that the regime should be managed. In the nineteenth century to 1914 the regime is characterised as the gold standard, though it is sometimes regarded as a sterling standard, disguised as an objective, immutable, and autonomous institution to which Britain conformed rather than which it directed. In any event, the United States played an entirely subordinate and passive role until the establishment of the Federal Reserve System in 1913 and its operation in the world economy in 1919 and thereafter. Even then it is appropriate to observe that interest in the subject was restricted for the most part to New York, and that the rest of the country, including Washington, was uninterested or antagonistic to involvement in the exchange problems of post-war Europe.

In the 1920s Benjamin Strong, the governor of the Federal Reserve Bank of New York, was an advocate of rapid reconstruction of the system of exchange rates in Europe. He continuously urged the Bank of England to restore the pound to par, consulted with the Bank of France and the Bank of Italy as to what the rates for the franc and lira should be, tried to smooth the ruffled relations between Montagu Norman of the Bank of England and Emile Moreau of the Bank of France. As noted below, he was prepared to accommodate US monetary policy to some degree to the interests of Europe but not, however, to the extent of expanding the money supply by the full range made possible by the gold received by the United States from Europe during and after the war.

The exchange regime laboriously reconstructed after 1925 broke down in 1931 as capital withdrawals, first from Austria and then successively from Germany and Britain, led to restrictions on the one hand, especially the German Standstill Agreement, and then British exchange depreciation on the other. In due course the Japanese yen, which had been restored to gold only late in 1929, was depreciated to relieve the strong deflationary pressure of declining export prices, especially silk. This occurred in December 1931. Continued price declines after sterling depreciation drove the United States off gold in April 1933, and the gold bloc ultimately followed in 1935 and 1936.

There is an open historical debate as to whether the United States and France could have forestalled the spreading collapse in foreign exchanges by a substantial lender-of-last-resort operation for Austria in May 1931. The weakened Britain, a victim of overvaluation from the restoration of the pound to par in 1925, lacked the resources to bolster the Austrian schilling. The United States was reluctant to take strong action. France restricted its modest assistance on Austrian acceptance of political conditions. The United States attempted to assist Germany with a moratorium on war debts and reparations, but France raised legal questions and while they were being discussed, capital withdrawals picked up and drove Germany to inconvertibility. Rescues for Britain were too little, too late, and regarded by the British Labour Party as too political. The appreciation of the dollar and gold currencies (depreciation of sterling and its many linked currencies) in September 1931, accelerated the decline of world gold and dollar prices.

In all this, the United States acted as one among the other states, solicitous of its own interest and disregarding the repair or reconstruction of the system. In April 1933 President Roosevelt accepted the so-called Thomas amendment put forward by inflationists in Congress which would allow him to cut the link of the dollar to gold. There followed abandonment of convertibility. When the delegates to the World Economic Conference of June–July 1933 agreed on an exchange of concessions in which the United Kingdom would stabilise the pound, Germany would relax foreign-exchange control, France give up its trade quotas, and the United States settle war debts, lower tariffs, and stabilise the dollar. Roosevelt backed off as the hint of dollar stability knocked down US commodity and stock-market prices.

Some observers have maintained that the United States was altogether wrong to devalue the dollar because the current account of the balance of payments was in surplus, which meant that international transactions were giving a lift to the US economy (Nurkse 1949). This analysis has a narrow base in a foreign-trade-multiplier model, and neglects the effects of exchange rates on prices. In actuality the appreciation of the dollar after the pound sterling, yen, etc., went off gold was so deflationary for US prices and incomes that it produced an export surplus as a residual. The surplus was not an independent autonomous force.

In the autumn of 1933 the United States experimented in raising prices through changes in the gold price. At first higher prices for gold were applied to domestic production. Gradually it was recognised that the lift to prices – in the Greenback period from 1863 to 1879 which supplied the data on which the experiment was based – had come from the exchange rate not the gold price; the gold price was an effect, not a cause. A change was then made to buying gold at higher prices abroad, with the dollars used to buy, say, sterling, driving down the dollar rate. But the connection between gold prices and commodity prices was generally loose and the United States quickly became disenchanted with the experiment. A year later the government approached the Bank of England to ask whether it would be interested in stabilisation, and received a negative reply.

During this period the US Treasury also raised the price it paid for silver at the behest of senators from silver-mining states, dismissing the initial negative impact the action had on the currencies of the two main countries on the silver standard, Mexico and China.

Slowly the US view on exchange-rate management changed. Roosevelt and his Secretary of the Treasury, Henry Morgenthau, became bored with manipulating the gold price and finally stabilised it without British cooperation in February 1934 at $35 an ounce, up from $20.67. Morgenthau developed fairly romantic notions about the excitement of international finance and participated with the British in providing a cover for French devaluation in September 1936, the so-called Tripartite Monetary Agreement which was limited in its actual effect. The participants agreed to hold each others' currencies only for twenty-four hours before turning them into gold, as contrasted with the six months or more under the swap arrangements that sprang into being in March 1961. The Administration, however, held steady, rather than reducing the price of gold again when the so-called 'Golden Avalanche' poured gold into the United States, as private citizens and even central banks sold gold for dollars in a Gresham's Law episode (Graham and Whittlesey 1939).

By the time of the Second World War, the United States took a leading role in preparing the way for a new foreign-exchange regime. The White plan from the US Treasury dominated the Keynes plan from Britain to constitute the core of the Articles of Agreement of the International Monetary Fund worked out at Bretton Woods in 1944. The British loan and the Marshall Plan were put into place to prepare the ground before the IMF could be put into action. When it became impossible to separate trade from capital movements and prohibit the latter without undertaking the impossible task of regulating the credit terms of current transactions, the United States led the way in enlarging the quotas of the IMF. It agreed at Basel in March 1961 on a swap arrangement, under which, in crisis, a country under attack could obtain temporary assistance by swapping its currency for foreign exchange, and in the autumn of that year to extend the Fund's Articles by incorporating the General Arrangements to Borrow, the provision of foreign exchange to this Fund from Group of Ten countries with extensive financial markets.

In the late 1950s foreigners began to accumulate dollar balances in New York and it was thought that the United States balance of payments had changed from positive to negative. The gold-exchange standard was attacked by leading economists, Robert Triffin (1960) and Jacques Rueff (1965) on the ground that the United States was able to extract goods and assets abroad from the rest of the world by persuading it to hold dollars. Triffin, in particular, asserted that when the US corrected its balance the world would be short of liquidity because there was insufficient gold coming into central bank reserves to support the demand for more money. He advocated the creation of a new international (paper) asset and its substitution for dollars and gold in international bank reserves. It was argued, in opposition, that there was an abundance of liquidity in the system, as any country wanting more could borrow dollars long and hold them short, with the United States acting as a bank to the world and supplying liquidity to countries of good credit standing on demand. Just as banks were not in deficit when they lent long and borrowed short, so the United States was not in deficit either (Despres, Kindleberger and Salant 1965).

There was, however, a significant difference in that the United States as bank was expanding its deposits and long-term assets, but its reserves were static or declining, as newly-mined gold went into hoarding or industrial use, and the rest of the world borrowed long and bought gold. President de Gaulle of France declared war on the dollar standard in February 1965, and after taking incremental surpluses in gold rather than dollars in 1964, began systematically to convert dollars into gold, $1 billion in 1965 and another $500 million in 1966 before the French balance of payments turned adverse. To buttress the dollar, the United States in 1965 put forward a proposal for the creation of Special Drawing Rights (called SDRs), primarily, I judge, to permit its own reserves to grow, even though any scheme would have to provide reserves for all. The proposal was adopted as part of the IMF, but not pursued after the advent of floating exchanges.

The Vietnam War in the second half of the 1960s produced a real deficit in the current account of the US balance of payments and the run accelerated. In 1968 the United States broke up the gold pool under which it had furnished at least half of the gold bid for at the $35 an ounce price in the London fixing. In August 1971 it closed the gold window, refusing to convert dollars into gold, and additionally imposed a 10 per cent tax on all imports in an effort to get the other countries of the world to agree to a depreciation of the dollar. If it had raised the gold price other countries might have followed to achieve the same set of exchange rates at a higher gold price. The 10 per cent depreciation was achieved in December 1971 at the Smithsonian agreement, named after a museum in Washington, DC where the conference was held, that raised the gold price to $42. The dollar remained under pressure in the next years until finally the notion of a dollar tied to the price of gold or of any other currency was abandoned altogether.

There followed a period of what has been called 'benign neglect' of the exchange rate by the United States. Other countries might intervene in their own currencies by buying or selling dollars already owned or acquired through swaps, but the United States took no steps to control the rate of the dollar until tight money under the Federal Reserve's attempt to raise interest rates to bring down the rate of inflation led to five years of appreciation ending in February 1985, followed by two years of depreciation. In September 1985 Secretary of the Treasury James Baker negotiated the Plaza Agreement with Britain, France, Japan and West Germany to stabilise foreign-exchange rates. When this wobbled a further negotiation produced the Louvre agreement in 1987. The emphasis was clearly on correcting the fluctuating dollar that was embarrassing the United States rather than providing a stable world system.

CAPITAL FLOWS

To achieve economic stability the world needs a steady flow of capital from rich countries with excess savings to those embarked on the development process with capital needs in excess of national saving. Some economists recommend counter-cyclical lending, to provide exchange to developing countries when depression or recession in industrialised areas cuts down on purchases of less developed countries' exports. It is awkward, however, to have a spurt of foreign lending suddenly cut off by the diversion of savings to home use. As it happens the rhythm of capital flows is not readily subject to policy control. There tends to be a regular pattern in the course of development, borrowing while rapidly developing, paying back as a country achieves new industries and expands exports, then accumulating foreign investments. Ultimately a country lives off the income of accumulated investment and may even consume its foreign capital.

At the start of the twentieth century the United States was in the process of moving from the stage of young debtor to mature debtor. The country was also beginning to undertake direct foreign investment abroad in those industries in which it had innovated – agricultural machinery, office machinery and the like – typically labour-saving devices, and in oil, an industry in which it had pioneered. The outbreak of the First World War speeded the process of change inordinately, allowing the United States to pass rapidly to the stage of young creditor in a few years. Much of the accumulation of claims on the rest of the world took the form of intergovernmental debts, provided to European allies during the war and in its immediate aftermath. J.P. Morgan & Co. took the lead after the war in private lending for stabilisation purposes, but after the successful oversubscription of the New York tranche of the Dawes loan in 1924, the rush to lend abroad became general – especially to Germany, Latin America, Australia, New Zealand and Canada.

When the New York stock market started an ascent in the spring of 1928, however, sale of foreign bonds in New York became difficult. Foreign borrowers shifted from long-term issues to short-run bank loans, based not on trade credits but on accommodation. Some US houses such as Lee, Higginson of Boston kept trying to float funds for preferred clients, for instance Germany and Ivar Krueger, and went bankrupt in the process. With the spread of depression world-wide, default on outstanding debt became general in Latin America and Germany. New lending continued during the 1930s only for Canada and Israel, the latter selling bonds to supporters in the United States on drives in which the economic motive was diluted by political and religious ties.

It seemed clear after the Second World War that private lending would take a long time to recover from the defaults of the 1930s. Accordingly the United States made generous settlements on Lend–Lease and various relief loans – in place of the business attitude towards war debts after the First World War. At Bretton Woods US proposals provided for an International Bank of Reconstruction and Development (the World Bank) to lend government monies to borrowers in need of capital, and also to mobilise private savings for the purpose by selling to the public its bonds bearing government guarantees. The first issues were sold in the United States for dollars, the currency then most in demand. Gradually, as national capital markets recovered the Euro-bond market grew to strength and goods became available from other sources, monies were raised outside the United States in the Euro-currency market, Germany, Switzerland and Japan, and after 1973 in the oil-producing Arab states. While the World Bank was getting organised in 1945 the United States enlarged the capital of the Export–Import Bank from $1 billion to $4 billion, took the lion's share of the assistance furnished by UNRRA and in 1946 undertook a $3.75 billion loan to the United Kingdom to assist sterling's postwar recovery as a key currency. When these measures proved inadequate to the task of reconstruction the United States in 1948 enacted a European Recovery Program – the so-called Marshall Plan – with assistance made available partly on a loan basis, but for the most part in grants.

The recovery generated by this governmental assistance finally began to attract private capital abroad from the United States, initially as direct foreign investment and ultimately in debt form, both as new bond issues and as bank loans. In the 1960s the capital outflow began to exceed the US current account surplus in the balance of payments by a substantial margin. First President Eisenhower, then Kennedy and Johnson, became concerned about the balance of payments and tried to inhibit the outflow. A tax levied on interest received from bonds, the so-called IET (Interest Equalization Tax), was set at a prohibitive level. Subsequent legislation, known as the Gore amendment, applied the tax to bank loans to which the lending had shifted. When the wedge between returns available in the United States and those in Europe widened, the flow shifted once again to direct investment. In 1964 President Johnson called for a Voluntary Credit Restraint Program that permitted direct investment but tried to limit the amount of capital brought from the United States. In 1968 the programme was made mandatory.

None of these measures proved effective. The IET applied to bonds had a major loophole in that it did not apply to foreign bonds bought from other residents in the United States, and the procedures for establishing the residence of the sellers were poorly enforced. In direct investment, allowing new investments made with foreign profits which would otherwise have been repatriated had the same impact on the balance of payments as allowing a capital outflow. Moreover, loans raised abroad by Americans had to be repaid, so that direct investment undertaken with foreign loans was equivalent, with a time lag, to the export of capital or direct investment.

In the early 1970s the monetary authorities in the United States made a mistake with substantial consequences for the world economy. Largely to assist in the re-election of President Nixon in the autumn of 1972, the Federal Reserve System loosened credit in 1970 and 1971 to stimulate business (Greider 1987). The action was taken at a time when the Bundesbank in Germany was trying to control inflationary tendencies by tightening interest rates. The result was that an enormous outflow of short-term capital went abroad to the Euro-currency market that had been gradually building up since about 1960. There it was borrowed by German residents, including multinational corporations, to pay off internal debt, and when sold to the Bundesbank for Deutschmarks was redeposited by the Bank in the Euro-currency market. The 'deficit' on the balance of payments of the United States under the (unacceptable) liquidity definition, rose from an average of $2–$4 billions a year to $20 billions in 1971 and $30 billions in 1972. Interest rates fell in the Euro-dollar markets, and Euro-banks started to look for loan outlets. Well before the Yom Kippur war of November 1973, the large price increase in oil, and the accumulation by OPEC (Organization of Petroleum Exporting Countries) of massive dollar balances which were deposited in New York and the Euro-currency market and recycled by major banks to Third World oil importing countries, the burst of sovereign lending by syndicates of banks had begun. The sudden and unanticipated fall in interest rates stimulated foreign lending much as had happened in the 1820s and 1880s in Britain when government debt conversion to lower levels had taken place.

The burst of lending to Third World debtors, notably Mexico, Brazil and Argentina, continued with a spurt for oil-producing countries like Mexico in 1979 when the second OPEC price increase occurred. This increase was short-lived, however, as new production came into play in the North Sea, the North Slope in Alaska and elsewhere. When Mexico found it impossible to maintain debt service at lower oil prices without help, the Third World debt crisis ensued in August 1982. Various stop-gap measures to adjust the position were worked out. The United States made a bridging loan to Mexico, and an emergency purchase of $1 billion worth of petroleum to be delivered to the US Strategic Reserve while the commercial banks and the International Monetary Fund negotiated a debt rescheduling. This and subsequent reschedulings undertook to provide for new loans so as to avoid the disastrous pattern for world stability of 1873, 1890 and 1928 when rapidly rising lending was suddenly stopped. The commercial banks in general, and especially the regional banks in the United States which had been drawn into the lending syndicates belatedly, were reluctant to lend more. Handling of the debt problem proceeded country by country, year by year, on a thoroughly *ad hoc* basis.

Not only did the United States stop lending to Third World countries after 1982, but it began to attract the savings of the rest of the world, not for investment so much as for consumption. Private consumption as personal savings continued to decline in the country, and public consumption as the US government deficit mounted in the 1980s, along with the deficit on the balance of payments on current account. Much of the effect can be traced to tight monetary policy after 1979 when an attempt was made to reduce the rate of inflation which had risen over 10 per cent a year, while loose fiscal policy with substantial tax reductions in 1981 and a rising rate of military spending continued. The tax reductions failed to raise personal savings: the government and household spending attracted imports and crowded out exports. Countries like Japan, Germany and Taiwan piled up savings and dollar balances that they invested in government bonds, takeovers of US companies, real estate and ordinary equities. While figures of balances of indebtedness are notoriously uncertain because of problems of valuation, it is generally believed that the United States went from a creditor position *vis-à-vis* the rest of the world of some several hundred billions in 1980 to a net debtor position of half a trillion dollars by 1987.

COORDINATION OF MACRO-ECONOMIC POLICY

Under the gold standard, in effect at the opening of this century, monetary policy was understood to be coordinated automatically: countries receiving gold expanded their money supplies; those losing it (apart from newly-minted specie) contracted. In addition, in the pre-Keynesian era, governmental budgets were expected to be balanced in peacetime, if not overbalanced to pay down government debt.

US interest in monetary policy in the years before the First World War arose primarily from financial crises experienced in 1893 and 1907. A National Monetary Commission was appointed in 1910, under the chairmanship of Nelson Aldrich, and produced a series of studies of central and commercial banking in the United States and in other countries. The concern was primarily with the inelasticity of the money supply in crisis and, despite the fact that the 1907 panic had been communicated through London and Paris to Italy, its focus was local.

Following the First World War the country got drawn in to questions of policy at the international level. The United States had accumulated a large stock of gold during the war through exports to the Allied powers, and it was anticipated that this would lead to increased money supplies and higher prices. Sterilisation of much of the gold frustrated this hope. In Britain, which was struggling to restore the pound to par in the first half of the 1920s, it was sometimes proposed that she should send $100 millions in gold as a payment on war-debt account to cause inflation in the United States. The suggestion was vetoed by Montagu Norman of the Bank of England on the ground that the Federal Reserve System would probably sterilise that too.

The imbalance between the pound, restored to par and overvalued in 1925, and the French franc, stabilised *de facto* in 1926 and undervalued, led in 1927 to an *ad hoc* attempt to coordinate monetary policy internationally. Benjamin Strong, Montagu Norman, Hjalmar Schacht of the Reichsbank and Charles Rist, the deputy governor of the Bank of France, met on Long Island in July 1927 at the estate of the secretary of the US Treasury, Ogden Mills, to discuss what steps might be taken to ease the British difficulties. It was agreed that the Federal Reserve Bank of New York would lower its discount rate to discourage the inflow of capital from London, and adjust its gold price so that the Bank of France would purchase gold to match its balance-of-payments surplus from New York rather than from London. The exercise in international cooperation is regarded by some as a mistake in so far as it contributed to the rise of the stock market in New York, and a detour from an appropriate policy based on US requirements (Friedman and Schwartz 1963: 289 ff).

Coordination of macroeconomic policy became a non-issue during the depression, the war, and the immediate years after the Second World War when each country was fully preoccupied with its own problems. With the establishment of the Bank for International Settlements in Basle in 1930 as part of the Young plan dealing with German reparation, there were monthly meetings of central bankers that permitted an exchange of views, but the

United States was not represented formally as the Federal Reserve System was not a stockholder of the Bank in spite of its having an American president from time to time and an observer attending the meeting, usually in the person of the US Treasury attaché in Paris. It was not until after the war, of course, that transatlantic air travel developed to the point where it was feasible to bring members of the Washington establishment to Europe for meetings on a regular basis.

In the course of the Marshall Plan, economic policies came under discussion in the OEEC, at which the United States had a representative of the US Economic Cooperation Agency in the person of its Special Representative. When the OEEC was converted, after the termination of aid under the Marshall Plan, to the OECD, with the United States as a regular member along with Canada and later Australia and New Zealand, a series of working parties was established of which No. 3 dealt with macroeconomic questions. This functioned for a number of years with regular meetings attended by representatives of the US Treasury, the Council of Economic Advisors and the Federal Reserve system. Its work was gradually allowed to lapse, as it was recognised that various countries had different objectives as in achieving low unemployment, low inflation, balance-of-payments equilibrium and the like. In 1966 Secretary of the Treasury Henry Fowler urged at a meeting of finance ministers at Chequers in England that the Europeans lower their interest rates. This was largely an *ad hoc* appeal to assist the US balance of payments. Under the Carter administration from 1976 to 1980 the United States appealed for the major powers, especially Germany and Japan, to join it in expansionary fiscal policy as 'locomotives' to pull the rest of the world and each other into greater prosperity. The response was at most half-hearted, and US efforts to expand income and employment largely alone worsened the country's balance of payments. Under Presidents Carter and Reagan there began a series of Summit Meetings among seven leading countries – the United States, Germany, Japan, France, Italy, Canada and the United Kingdom – that met for a few days a year, with elaborate agendas prepared by staff, covering a wide variety of political and economic subjects but reaching few agreements, and constituting, for the most part, ceremonial meetings for photographic opportunities.

On this showing, coordination of macroeconomic policies –

monetary and fiscal – has been both sporadic and ineffectual. There is, moreover, the disastrous experience of 1970 and 1971 when the Federal Reserve System and the Bundesbank pulled strongly in different directions, the United States to lower and the Bundesbank to tighten interest rates. Such lapses into cross purposes have happily been rare.

THE LENDER OF LAST RESORT

I have written so profusely and redundantly on this issue at various earlier times (Kindleberger 1978) that I can afford to be brief here. In the pre-war period the United States was preoccupied with its own affairs and took little if any interest in how it might assist the troubles of others, if only to prevent their spread. The war loans of 1918 and 1919 can be interpreted as rescue or salvage operations, though not in the narrow sense of relieving finance markets in acute distress. Insistence on collecting war debts and denying any connection between reparation and war debts can be interpreted as the opposite of last-resort lending; refusing to relieve economic trauma because of the potential cost in giving up a good asset for a poor one. (The analogy that comes to mind is that of the Intra-European Payments Scheme of 1949 under the Marshall Plan, where possibilities of a given country cancelling its claims against its liabilities were divided into two classes: those on the same country, which proceeded automatically, and those where a claim on A was cancelled against a liability to B which was turned over to A. In this latter case the cancellation was undertaken only if the creditor agreed to accept the claim on the debtor. Few cancellations of this order took place.)

It is generally recognised that the United States (and France) were niggardly and dilatory in serving as lenders of last resort to Austria, Germany and Britain in 1931, permitting international disintermediation to ramify. In addition, the French attached political conditions to their limited assistance, not to Britain but to Austria and Germany, and followed up the depreciation of sterling by accelerating the liquidity crisis, converting dollars into gold, as did Belgium, the Netherlands and Switzerland. As indicated earlier, the Tripartite Monetary Agreement provided little assistance among the several partners – holding foreign exchange by agreement only twenty-four hours. It did, however, turn the direction of pressure from liquidation to support.

During and after the Second World War Lend-Lease, the Bretton Woods institutions, the Export–Import Bank capital infusion, British loan and Marshall Plan transferred resources for more or less long periods rather than serving as last-resort lending. That came into being spontaneously at Basle in March 1961 with swaps, the provision of instant foreign exchange to help in this case Britain, later Canada, Italy, Britain again, the United States. The swaps were expected to be reversed at the end of a fixed time period, usually six months, and if this could not be done with the besieged country's resources because the reversal of capital flow had not been complete, it was expected that any unreconstituted portion would be otherwise funded, usually by a drawing on the International Monetary Fund. The Fund was of little avail as a lender of last resort on its own because of the time-consuming nature of its decision-making when rescue operations were often needed in hours and days rather than weeks and months.

A residual ambiguity as to which country could undertake responsibility for meeting the liabilities of its banks arose in 1974 when the German authorities delayed meeting obligations of the bankrupt Herstatt Bank of Cologne to foreign banks with which it had exchange contracts. The so-called Basle protocol of 1975 provided that each national authority should be responsible for the obligations of its national institutions worldwide. In 1982, however, the Bank of Italy declined to meet the liabilities of the Banco Ambrosiano's Luxembourg subsidiary (as contrasted with branch) when that bank failed. The 1984 failure of the Continental Illinois Bank found the US Federal Deposit Insurance Corporation making good Japanese-held certificates of deposit in excess of the prescribed $100,000 limit in order to restore confidence in the international money market.

In 1988 there is some uncertainty as to where matters stand with respect to the lender-of-last resort function. The Plaza and Louvre accords negotiated by Baker call on the leading five financial powers to stabilise each other's currencies but make no provision, as under the swap arrangements, for any country whose currency is supported by the others to compensate a foreign central bank that experiences losses on its foreign-exchange holdings from depreciation or devaluation of the currency in question. The central banks of West Germany and Japan, in particular, hold large amounts of dollars bought at rates well above present levels. Swaps would doubtless be set in motion if other currencies than the yen, Deutschmark or dollar were to be dumped on the market by speculators. The Bank of Japan and the Bundesbank have large holdings of dollars with which they can support their currencies. But if the dollar were to come under attack and threaten to go into a free fall it is not clear at what point, in terms of exchange rate or amounts of support, other countries would rally around. As the US role as world stabiliser is undermined, there is no clear country interested to take its place. We approach again the position in the early 1930s when the former stabiliser has weakened in relative strength and zeal to uphold the role and other possible candidates for the post hold back.

Some economists and political scientists put faith in bilateral or trilateral arrangements to stabilise the world economy in the foregoing respects. A distinguished German banker and legislator, Ludwig Bamberger, commenting on the need for a central bank, made a remark that bears on the point: 'shared responsibility is no responsibility' (Zucker 1975: 78).

REFERENCES

Cipolla, Carlo M. (ed.) (1970), *The Economic Decline of Empires*, London: Methuen.
Despres, Emile, Charles P. Kindleberger and Walter S. Salant (1965), 'The dollar and world liquidity: a minority view', *The Economist*, vol. 218, no. 6389, London (5 February).
Friedman, Milton and Anna Jacobson Schwartz (1963), *A Monetary History of the United States*, Princeton: Princeton University Press.
Gallagher, John and Roland Robinson (1953), 'The imperialism of free trade, 1815–1914', *Economic History Review*, 2nd ser., vol. 6, pp. 1–15.
Graham, Frank D. and Charles P. Whittlesey (1939), *Golden Avalanche*, Princeton: Princeton University Press.
Greider, William (1987), *The Secrets of the Temple: How the Federal Reserve Runs the Country*, New York: Simon & Schuster.
Hawtrey, Ralph G. (1952), *Economic Aspects of Sovereignty*, London: Longmans, Green.
Hogan, Michael L. (1987), *The Marshall Plan: America, Britain and the Reconstruction of Western Europe, 1947–1952*, New York: Cambridge University Press.

Kennedy, Paul (1987), *The Rise and Fall of Great Powers: Economic Change and Military Conflict from 1500 to 2000*, New York: Random House.
Kindleberger, Charles P. (1978), *Manias, Panics and Crashes: A History of Financial Crises*, New York: Basic Books.
Kindleberger, Charles P. (1986), *The World in Depression, 1929–1939*, 2nd edition, Berkeley: University of California Press.
Krueger, Anne O. (1974), 'The political economy of the rent-seeking society', *American Economic Review*, vol. 64, no. 3 (June), pp. 291–303.
Nurske, Ragnar (1949), 'Conditions of international monetary equilibrium', in American Economic Association, *Reading in the International Trade*, Philadelphia: Blakiston.
Olson, Mancur (1982), *The Rise and Decline of Nations: Economic Growth, Stagnation and Social Rigidities*, New Haven: Yale University Press.
Rostow, Walt W. (1960), *The Stages of Growth: A Non-Communist Manifesto*, Cambridge: Cambridge University Press.
Rueff, Jacques (1965) in J. Rueff and Fred Hirsch, 'The rule and role of gold, an argument', *Essays in International Finance*, no. 47, Princeton: Princeton University Press.
Semmel, Bernard (1970), *The Rise of Free Trade Imperialism: Classical Political Economy, the Empire of Free Trade, and Imperialism, 1750–1850*, Cambridge: Cambridge University Press.
Senghaas, Dieter (1985), *The European Experience: A Historical Critique of Development Theory*, Dover, NH: Berg Publishers.
Smith, Cyril Stanley (1975), 'Metallurgy as human experience. The 1974 distinguished lectureship in materials and society', *Metallurgical Transactions*, vol. 6Aa, no. 4, pp. 604–14.
Thorow, Lester (1980), *The Zero-Sum Society*, New York: Basic Books.
Triffin, Robert (1960), *Gold and the Dollar Crisis*, New Haven: Yale University Press.
Wallerstein, Immanuel (1980), *The Modern World System II: Mercantilism and the Consolidation of the European-World Economy, 1600–1750*, New York: Academic Press.
Zucker, Stanley (1975), *Ludwig Bamberger: German Liberal Politician and Social Critic, 1823–1899*, Pittsburgh: University of Pittsburgh Press.

12 · HARD TIMES: LATIN AMERICA IN THE 1930s AND 1980s

Albert Fishlow

INTRODUCTION

The experience of the Great Depression was central to the formulation of Latin American economic policy in the post-Second World War period. The vigorous import substitution policies implemented in the region in the 1940s and 1950s reflected as much a continuity of a successful defensive strategy implemented in the 1930s as a conversion to a new theoretical approach. The 1930s were a decade that saw declining reliance on world trade as an engine of growth and emergence of a larger role for internal demand under the auspices of a more active state.

Now in the 1980s, for the first time since 1945 Latin American countries have again been subject to a reversal of economic activity. Regional per capita gross domestic product in 1988 was more than 6 per cent below its 1980 level. The pervasiveness of the decline is even more impressive. Of the twenty-three countries for which data are presented in the *Preliminary Overview of the Latin American Economy* (Economic Commission for Latin America and the Caribbean 1980–7), all but four – Barbados, Chile, Colombia and the Dominican Republic – show reduced per capita output. A decade of development, and for some countries more, has been lost.

This result, standing in sharp contrast to the adaptation to even more serious deterioration of the external economic environment in the 1930s, has now led some to speculate on another apparent lesson from the Great Depression. Did the widespread and continuing Latin American default on outstanding external debt at that time contribute to a more positive outcome? This subject has been recently explicitly addressed in two very useful papers.[1] Here I seek to integrate some of those results into a broader comparative view of the two downturns that extends earlier contributions.[2]

In this chapter I emphasise three points. First is the different origin of Latin American economic collapse in the two periods. In the 1930s decline was caused by deterioration of export earnings, to which both quantities and prices contributed; in the 1980s increases in interest rates and a reduction in capital inflows were much more prominent factors in inducing a balance-of-payments crisis. Second is the different role of adjustment of the merchandise account to restoring income growth. In the 1930s, owing to higher export prices and volume recovery after 1932, trade played a positive role despite protectionist forces and income contraction in industrial countries. In the 1980s exports have not been as buoyant, as terms of trade deterioration has persisted and volume growth has been erratic. Joined together with continuing debt service, the recent pattern has required continuing import compression. Third is the differential susceptibility to the debt overhang. In the 1930s claims on export proceeds for debt service were smaller compared to the 1980s. Moreover, the external and internal climate permitted partial default which allowed rapid growth of imports needed to underwrite economic recovery. That ability to help sustain needed import expansion and new investment through relaxing external claims has so far eluded policy-makers in the 1980s.

These differences add up to circumstances in the 1930s that were more favourable to an internal dynamic of industrial expansion and a more prominent public sector role. Once the very sharp initial contraction in trade occurred, and was buffered against full domestic impact by increased domestic production, recovery in trade reinforced demand. In the 1980s the external constraint has been more binding and far-reaching in its impact through the nexus with debt. In particular, there has been a new combination of inflation, public sector deficits and slow growth that has so far defied effective solution.

The importance of debt service in the 1980s as a determinant of performance has led to vigorous efforts by Latin American countries to reduce the adverse resource transfer. In a final section, I therefore briefly consider current proposals for debt relief against

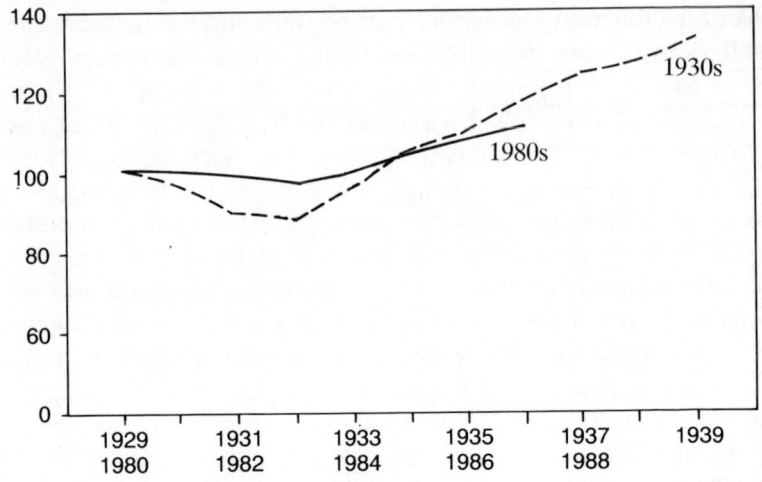

Figure 12.1 Gross domestic product of Latin American countries (1929 = 100; 1980 = 100). *Source*: Table 12.1.

the backdrop of the discussions and the actual procedures followed in the 1930s.

ORIGINS OF THE DECLINE

Figure 12.1 graphs the output performance of the region in the two periods. It is immediately apparent that the decline after 1929 and subsequent recovery were much more pronounced than in the 1980s. The recent pattern is much shallower and more persistent than the V-shaped trajectory of the Great Depression. Note, however, that the conventional wisdom of a better Latin American response to the crisis of the 1930s partially derives from comparison with the industrialised countries. Between 1929 and 1932 income falls by 11 per cent in Latin America, 28 per cent in the United States. In the 1980s Latin American performance seems even worse when compared to the East Asian success.

Table 12.1 adds evidence on export quantum and terms of trade to the output series portrayed in Figure 12.1. The collapse of exports after 1929 is evident. Export quantum for the region as a whole fell by an average of more than 10 per cent a year for three years. Declining relative prices for Latin American exports almost

Table 12.1 Regional product and trade performance of Latin American countries

	Gross domestic product[a]	Export quantum[b]	Terms of trade	Import capacity
1929=100				
1929	100	100	100	100
1930	96	83	82	69
1931	90	88	66	59
1932	89	71	72	52
1933	97	76	66	51
1934	105	88	75	66
1935	109	91	72	66
1936	117	92	77	71
1937	124	103	80	84
1938	127	84	75	64
1939	132	88	75	67
1980=100				
1980	100	100	100	100
1981	100	109	94	102
1982	99	112	85	95
1983	97	120	86	105
1984	100	131	92	119
1985	104	131	88	114
1986	108	131	78	100
1987	111	142	78	107

[a] For 1930s, average of five countries representing about 75 per cent of regional exports (see Table 12.2).
[b] Export quantum, pieced together from annual growth rates in 1980s, is not exactly equal to import capacity divided by terms of trade.
Sources: Thorp (1984); Economic Commission for Latin America and the Caribbean 1980–7.

match the decline in quantity. The joint effect is captured in the series on import capacity.

The shock to Latin American countries in 1929, although they were also recipients of capital flows during the 1920s, came primarily from the trade side. Exports were of an order of 20 per cent of output and sometimes greater. Thus they might have been expected to influence economic activity more generally through at least three channels. Reductions in external income affected domestic aggregate demand. Second, because half and more of government revenues derived from trade, there was an immediate fiscal effect. Third, under gold standard rules, deterioration in the balance of payments also implied contraction of the money supply.

But the large potential effect was offset by several factors. Because declining terms of trade were such a large part of the reduction in export earnings, and domestic prices were flexible, employment, and internal demand, were buffered. Such attenuation was aided by the resource intensity of many exports and the importance of foreign investment: the impact was felt on foreign profits rather than domestic employment. Although revenues fell, and governments sought to curtail expenditures, many could not do so fully, thereby sustaining aggregate demand. In similar fashion, while initially monetary contraction was experienced in most countries, that link to international reserves was soon broken as governments moved to devalue exchange rates.

On the supply side, there was a high elasticity of response as imports were sharply curtailed, reflecting their non-essential character and the substitutability of domestic production in foodstuffs, textiles and other consumer goods. The lack of complexity of Latin American economies was an asset. In the end, product fell by about 10 per cent while import capacity was reduced by 50 per cent. Fixed import coefficients would have yielded much larger declines in income to restore balance-of-payments equilibrium in the absence of external finance.

In the early 1980s, by contrast, export volume grew at quite respectable rates. Indeed, Latin American performance improves upon the earlier record of the region in the 1970s and also outstrips that of developing countries as a whole. Despite the world recession, Latin American countries gained market share over this period. Terms of trade are unfavourable, reducing purchasing power over imports, but not comparably with the fall of primary commodity prices after 1929. Import capacity falls by only 6 per cent between 1980 and 1982 and exceeds its 1980 level in 1983.

A measure of the difference in origins and subsequent evolution of the two crises is provided by the simple relationship between output and import capacity. For Latin America in the 1930s, there is a strong positive influence between the two rates of growth, after adjusting for autocorrelation. The elasticity is 0.2 for the decade as a whole, and 0.3 until 1937. Including 1938 and 1939 reduces the role of import capacity and weakens the fit because the larger countries in Latin America sustained expansion despite the recession of 1937; expanded domestic productive capacity and greater policy experience yielded dividends. In the 1980s the elasticity is very small, negative and not statistically significant.

This distinction can be put another way. Angus Maddison has calculated the direct consequences on Latin American income of export volume and terms-of-trade changes in 1929–32 and 1979–83. For the former, he finds that more than 11 percentage points of growth out of 20 can be ascribed to declining export receipts. In the recent period there is a *positive* contribution of export volume, reduced but not fully offset by worsened terms of trade, while the real income change is negative (Maddison 1985: 20, 55).

The missing ingredient in the 1980s is the important role of rising real interest rates and the abrupt change in capital availability upon the balance of payments. Although conventional decompositions of the oil shocks now recognise the former, the latter is usually treated as response rather than cause. The distinction is critical. In the early 1980s conditions of capital supply underwent significant change as commercial banks re-evaluated their exposures in the aftermath of rising interest rates and slowing industrial-country growth.

High debt/product ratios made Latin American countries especially susceptible to shocks from the side of the capital account, while the higher export/product ratios of the Asian countries made them more vulnerable to adverse effects on trade. Leaving out the former makes the poorer Latin American recent performance more of a puzzle than it need be. In addition, when the total negative impact of changing international conditions is related to exports rather than product, the Latin American countries emerge as the most seriously affected. That is the right measure. Adjustment had to occur in the balance of payments. When it did, because capital inflows were unavailable as a buffer, imports had to be reduced. The smaller the import ratio, and the more industrial the economies, the less the flexibility that had been shown in the 1930s and the larger the size of the income reduction required for the given shock (Fishlow 1987).

Thus far the discussion has been in aggregate terms. Table 12.2 provides some additional country detail. The degree of product decline in the 1930s is closely ordered by the fall in import capacity. Chile does worst and Colombia best on both measures. Argentina does more poorly than it should. This corresponds both

Table 12.2 Country product and import capacity annual growth rates (per cent)

	1929–32		1932–7		1980–3		1983–7	
	Product	Import capacity	Product	Import capacity	Product	Import capacity	Product	Import capacity
Latin America[a]	−4.0	−19.8	6.9	12.9	−1.0	1.6	3.4	0.5
Argentina	−4.9	−13.0	5.9	15.3	−3.2	2.0	1.2	−7.2
Brazil	−0.3	−18.3	7.5	8.2	−1.1	1.4	6.3	6.9
Chile	−12.5	−46.0	9.0	46.7	−2.8	−1.5	4.8	7.2
Colombia	1.3	−10.7	4.2	4.3	1.7	−6.4	4.7	18.8
Mexico	−5.6	−29.7	8.8	19.0	1.1	17.3	0.8	−3.6

[a] For the 1930s, product is 1929 weighted average of the five countries.
Source: See Table 12.1.

to its more complex economy and policies that tended to be conservative. The use of exchange controls rather than real devaluation to reduce imports meant that there was less of an inducement through relative prices for import substituting domestic production. Taxes were also increased after an initial deficit opened in 1930, and monetary policy remained restrictive until 1935.[3]

In the early 1980s the correspondence is much less clear because it is filtered through the effect of outstanding debt. Colombia's performance is the best, notwithstanding declining import capacity; it is also the only country not yet required to reschedule. Argentina, Brazil and especially Mexico all do poorly despite increasing import capacity. Their debts dominate movements in the balance of payments.

Latin American growth was reversed in the 1980s, as in the 1930s, as a result of flawed integration into the world economy. In the earlier period it was concentration upon exports of primary products whose supply had begun to outstrip demand in the 1920s, thereby provoking a sharp and immediate reaction in world markets after 1929. More recently it was an asymmetric opening to reversible financial inflows without a corresponding increase in export penetration. Because the Latin American countries were the principal developing-country debtors, the consequences of disinflation in the industrial countries upon interest rates had a disproportionate effect upon them.[4]

ADJUSTMENT OF THE BALANCE-OF-PAYMENTS DISEQUILIBRIUM

If the origins of the crisis were different, so was the structure of adjustment in the two downturns, as has already been suggested. Both do share a large initial reduction in imports as the balance of payments deteriorated for different reasons. In the Great Depression the magnitude of the export decline dictated immediate and severe curbs on imports, both through direct intervention and devaluation. Import volume fell by some 60 per cent between 1929 and 1932, matching import capacity. Similarly, between 1980 and 1983 import volume dropped by almost 40 per cent. It is a measure of the difference in the origins of the two crises that such a large compression in imports was necessary in the 1980s even as import capacity was increasing. In the recent experience, adjustment of the trade account was the only option to compensate for sudden deterioration of the capital account and interest payments.

In the recovery phases after 1932 and 1983, two important distinctions should be drawn. One relates to exports, the other to imports. During the 1930s there was a stronger and more continuous rebound of exports, both in volume as well as the terms of trade. In Table 12.1 one notes an increase in export quantum between 1932 and 1937 of 9.7 per cent a year, and the terms of trade improve by 2.1 per cent. The corresponding results between 1983 and 1987 are 4.3 per cent for volume, while terms of trade worsen by 2.4 per cent.

Better export performance in the 1930s was not due to stronger international recovery. That was mixed, and protectionism was a serious barrier. Policy in the Latin American countries also contributed to the favourable results. Almost all the larger countries in the region opted for significant real exchange rate devaluation by 1932 as a result of large changes in nominal rates unaccompanied by offsetting inflation. The extent of the change was upwards of 50 per cent. That realignment of export prices was sufficient, without much further devaluation during the decade, to permit Latin American export quantum to increase by 45 per cent between 1932 and 1937 while the increase in world primary trade was 16 per cent. That still left the region, as for world trade generally, barely back at 1929 levels.[5]

In the 1980s deliberate efforts to encourage exports also met with some success as countries sought to follow the counsel of trade expansion to solve their balance-of-payments problems. Real exchange rate devaluation was again an important factor, amounting for the region to a change of some 50 per cent between 1980 and 1987.[6] In addition there were a variety of subsidy programmes to encourage the sale of non-traditional products. But the results were far from spectacular as volume increases faltered after the gains in 1984, and larger sales encountered price weakness. Note also that real devaluation was more costly in the indexed economies of the 1980s than those of the 1930s. It implied accelerating inflation that came to rival the original balance-of-payments problem it was designed to help; I return to this point subsequently.

After substantially outperforming the developing country aggregate increase between 1980 and 1984, Latin America has fallen behind since 1985. Asian NICs, with a much greater specialisation in manufactures, have done considerably better in a world where trade volume has itself slowed compared to the 1970s. To some extent the Latin American performance has reflected the greater attraction of the internal market for producers. As efforts to stimulate recovery occurred in many countries after 1985, rising demand was met at the expense of external sales. With investment limited, new capital was not allocated to produce specifically for world markets.

The essential contribution of the rapid export recovery in the 1930s was less its direct stimulus upon demand than its provision of foreign exchange to purchase imports. The calculated primary impact of expanded export volume and improved terms of trade explains less than a fifth of the realised growth in real income in 1932–7.[7] Acceleration of export revenues translated into a significant relaxation of the foreign exchange constraint after 1932 and did not frustrate the positive effects of significantly increased internal demand.

That is the second important difference between the 1930s and the 1980s. During the first episode, imports much more than accompany exports in the recovery of the 1930s while in the 1980s they less exceed the rise in exports: a very strong gain of 18.4 per cent a year in the Great Depression, 6.8 per cent a year in the 1980s. Note as well that the import response in the 1930s is widely shared; in the 1980s there is a significant country dispersion, with Mexico and Chile being substantially above average and Argentina, Brazil and Colombia much below. Indeed, for the non-oil countries as a group, real imports increase by only 3.8 per cent between 1983 and 1987, less than the corresponding 5.2 per cent rise in import capacity; Mexico's drastic reduction in imports by 1983 and subsequent recovery distorts the regional aggregate.

In the 1980s, paradoxically, it has thus proved much harder to export one's way out of the balance-of-payments crisis than from the depths of the Great Depression. Ocampo's conclusion for Colombia that 'the growing manufacturing capital-intensive sectors had sufficient foreign exchange to finance the expansion of production capacity and the imports of intermediate goods' applies to the region more generally (Ocampo 1984: 141). Restrictive import policies further insured that required inputs would be favoured relative to non-essential consumer goods. The composition, and not only the relative importance, of imports changed during the 1930s. In the 1980s there was much more limited scope for substitution, and expansion more quickly posed the threat of limited imports.[8]

Additionally, in the 1980s there was continuing allocation of considerable foreign exchange for mandated debt service, whereas in the 1930s at least partial default quickly became the regional pattern. I therefore turn now to a direct examination of the differences in the extent and form of foreign obligations and their implications for economic performance.

FOREIGN CAPITAL

Table 12.3 sets out estimates of the public debt and total foreign capital both for 1929 and 1980, and relates them to the respective levels of exports. Use of a 1938 estimate for total foreign capital should not much overstate the 1929 levels since capital flows were subsequently small. The stock of direct foreign investment in 1980 is possibly understated, but not seriously; some 80 per cent of total debits for factor payments were accounted for by interest.

In 1929 total foreign capital was larger relative to export earnings than in 1980 by a substantial margin, while the reverse was true of the relative size of public or publicly guaranteed debt in the two periods.[9] In 1929, as in the nineteenth century, foreign private investment both through equity and debentures much exceeded public borrowing in Latin America. Return payments on such capital were the responsibility of private debtors, not governments. Thus the 1929 balance of payments was more subject to adjustment in the event of economic downturn. In the later period, as a result of repeated entry into the new Euro-dollar capital market of the 1970s and the ready availability of credit attendant upon petro-dollar recycling, Latin America's situation was far different. Servicing obligations were now overwhelmingly in the form of interest and the responsibility of the public sector.

The ratio of foreign capital could be as large as it was in 1929 because interest (and profit) rates were low and maturities long. For Latin American dollar securities issued at the end of the 1920s

Latin America in the 1930s and 1980s

Table 12.3 Debt levels (billion US dollars)

	1929				1980		
	Public debt	Total foreign capital[a]	Debt/exports of goods ratio	Capital/exports of goods ratio	Public debt	Total foreign capital[b]	Debt/exports of goods ratio	Capital/exports of goods ratio
Latin America	4.1	11.3	1.5	4.1	222.5	270.3	2.5	3.0
Argentina	1.2	3.2	1.3	3.6	27.2	31.3	3.4	3.9
Brazil	1.1	2.0	2.4	4.4	68.4	84.7	3.4	4.2
Chile	0.5	1.3	1.8	4.6	11.1	12.9	2.4	2.7
Colombia	0.1	0.3	0.7	2.5	6.3	7.9	1.5	1.9
Mexico	0.8	1.8	2.9	6.4	50.7	60.1	3.1	3.7

[a] 1938.
[b] 1977 Stock of foreign investment according to OECD, *Development Co-Operation, 1979 Review* (1980), supplemented by direct investment flows reported in Inter-American Development Bank, *Social and Economic Progress in Latin America* (1988).
Sources: Economic Commission for Latin America and the Caribbean (1980–7); Economic Commission for Latin America (1965); Woodruff (1966).

the median interest rate was a little above 6 per cent and the term was thirty-five years. Older issues carried somewhat lower interest rates as the average rate of 4.8 per cent on outstanding sterling bonds confirms.[10] Taking a rate of 5.5 per cent implies annual interest and profit payments of less than 23 per cent of exports, with amortisation on the fixed debt bringing total service to about 30 per cent. An average ratio of 1.5 for the public debt/exports ratio translated into a claim of only a little more than 12 per cent of exports for government service. Only for Brazil and Mexico are the proportions much larger. (One of the reasons for the high Mexican value is the arrears accumulated during years of previous non-payment.)

In 1980 actual interest and profit payments were comparable to the 1929 relative claims despite a much lower foreign capital/exports ratio, while amortisation added fully another 15 percentage points.[11] That was because bank borrowing in the 1970s typically ranged from only six to eight years. And payments in the 1980s were largely a public sector obligation. This added considerably to the vulnerability inherent in the recent period. On top of that, interest rates on bank loans varied with only a six-month lag behind market rates so that debt service was immediately sensitive to changes in current interest rates.

After both 1929 and 1980 the weight of debt service claims sharply increased. With the sharp decline in the value of export earnings after 1929, the relative requirements of public debt service rapidly escalated. At the nadir of the Great Depression in 1932, public obligations would have absorbed 30 per cent of export earnings and further crowded out already reduced imports. Such a hypothetical level was never reached. Country after country adjusted their actual payments by entering into partial defaults on interest and sinking-fund payments. Bolivia began on 1 January 1931 and by the end of 1933 virtually all the others had joined; Argentina was the prominent exception. In 1935 more than 70 per cent of outstanding Latin American dollar bonds were in at least partial default. Only Haiti and the Dominican Republic remained current. Sterling bonds, excepting continuing full Argentine service under the Roca-Runciman agreements, fared only slightly better.

The percentage of dollar bonds in arrears subsequently rose to 85 per cent in 1937. Note that even as conditions were improving in Latin America as a result of economic recovery, debt service payments were not fully reinstated. They remained substantially within the control of the debtor countries, and were adjusted to conform to domestic needs. Brazil, for example, fully stopped payments in 1938 and 1939 and resumed partial payment in 1940 at lower than previously prevailing rates.

Similar large increases in obligations occurred in the 1980s. But this time the deterioration of the ratios had its origin in the numerator rather than export performance. The debt/exports ratio of 2.5 in 1980 gave way to one of 4.6 in 1987 despite export growth. Interest payments reached 48 per cent of goods exports in 1982 before receding to 36 per cent in 1987. For Argentina in 1987 the percentage was 65; Brazil 36; Chile 32; Colombia 25; and Mexico 40.

Yet, excepting Peru's 1985 decision to limit payments as a percentage of exports and Brazil's temporary moratorium in 1987–8, Latin American countries have been more compliant than in the Great Depression. There has been much rhetoric about the need to meet the social debt before the foreign debt, and formation of the Cartagena group of debtors, but at the end of the day debt service has been full by the largest debtors. They have managed to do so by a substantial and immediate realignment of their external accounts. Overall, Latin American countries began to achieve large export surpluses to cover their interest obligations and thus to transfer real resources abroad. The total transfer by reason of debt service from 1982 to 1987 exceeded $125 billion.

The ubiquity of default in the Great Depression compared to the recent experience owes itself to several related factors. For one there is the origin of the crisis in declining export receipts. Not only was the rise in obligations relative to foreign exchange earnings greater after 1929 than after 1980, but inability to pay was more credible in the context of a global depression that also had strong impact on the industrial countries. In the second instance the decline in foreign trade directly eroded the revenue bases of governments at a time when half and more of receipts came from export taxes and import tariffs. The public sector could not be expected to meet external obligations in the midst of general retrenchment and austerity. The larger role of government in recent years, and its more extensive tax base, have given rise to greater expectations in debt service.

Third, the structure of debt service in the 1930s, being dominantly interest payments, lent itself to an early unilateral adjustment of obligations. In the 1980s, by contrast, there was initially a large repayment of principal as noted above. Bank creditors could in the first instance extend maturity dates as a concession to encourage countries to remain current on interest. Additional credits, moreover, were organised under the auspices of the IMF from private as well as public sources. This concerted involuntary lending, especially since exports were growing – unlike the early 1930s – elicited continuing country negotiation and serial reschedulings.

A fourth factor was the ubiquity not only of export decline but partial default. Latin America may have led the parade, but they were far from being the only marchers. By the beginning of 1932 defaults had spread to southern and eastern Europe. And even before the final German default in 1933, Hoover had called for a one-year moratorium on inter-governmental debts in 1931. Reparations were ended at the Lausanne Conference in July 1932. Latin American debts were caught up in the deterioration of the whole international economic fabric. Creditor countries, especially the United States, were more preoccupied with export markets than debt repayment. In those circumstances, the Latin American countries were able to enjoy much greater freedom of action.

Finally, default in the Great Depression did not trigger any substantial internal opposition. Argentina was a possible exception, even resisting British suggestions of dollar bond default to provide larger scope for Anglo-Argentine trade. Three special characteristics differentiate that situation from other countries. First is the 'substantial amount of the Argentine sterling- and dollar-denominated debt that was held by Argentines.' Default might directly cause losses to groups within the country. Second is the continuing 'conviction that prosperity would be regained ... under an open economic environment' as a result of the favourable economic growth earlier experienced. This view was certainly strongly enough held by the cattle interests that default would not be universally popular. Third is the much higher level of public debt issued internally in Argentina: a comparative international table places that country far in advance of other Latin American countries and comparable with Japan and Canada. Domestic creditors had much potentially to fear from policies abrogating contractual commitments. These considerations were very much weaker elsewhere in the region and default correspondingly more prevalent. Currently, with larger internal debts, more commitment to market-oriented policies and a rising fear of populism in elite circles, the Argentine circumstances of the Great Depression may be more widely descriptive of the region as a whole.[12]

Countries, then as now, were careful not to repudiate, however. Debt service was most typically partial rather than totally absent. Initially, before the full extent of the export decline was anticipated, payment was sometimes made in funding bonds or scrip. As the decade wore on, and despite rising exports after 1932, service did not increase. On the contrary, the percentage of bonds in default tended to increase; countries took advantage of declining commodity prices after 1937 still further to reduce their payments. Domestic expansion was infectious. New nationalist political leaders gave priority to import requirements for domestic recovery and took advantage of emerging European conflict to rebuff private creditor pressure. The lack of cost to default, and support of the United States for settlement rather than resumption, validated other uses of foreign exchange.

Among those uses was repurchase of debt at the much lower market prices prevailing as a result of default. By the mid-1930s the average value was 25 cents on the dollar. One estimate suggests as much as 40 per cent of dollar bonds issued by debtor countries were held outside of the United States at the end of 1935; another suggests that a dozen countries had repurchased between 15 and 50 per cent of their outstanding debt since the beginning of the 1930s. For Latin America the leader was Peru, which failed to service at all, and repurchased an estimated 31 per cent at an average price of 21 (Royal Institute 1937: 318; Eichengreen and Portes 1988: 33).

Recent proposals for debt repurchase at current discounted prices to reduce the overhang, either by countries or through an international facility, have met with theoretical scepticism (Dooley 1988; Bulow and Rogoff 1988). The basic argument is that bondholders largely benefit from the rise in market price pursuant on repurchase while debtors have better alternative use of the resources used. The 1930s experience was not enthusiastically endorsed by creditors, however, nor regarded unfavourably by debtors. The Council of the Corporation of Foreign Bondholders wrote: 'The Council has always upheld the principle that a Government which declares itself temporarily unable to meet interest upon its External Bonds should not profit by the occasion to effect amortization at prices which are depressed by its own default.' Creditors might acquiesce, but only when there was partial and agreed interest payment in addition to such repurchase. The Economic Commission on Latin America opined: 'The Latin American Governments obviously could not fail to take advantage of so suitable an opportunity to meet some of their financial commitments abroad on favorable terms.'[13]

Eichengreen and Portes fail to discern systematic reaction of prices to country participation in the market (Eichengreen and Portes 1988: 34). Neither the deliberate depression of prices associated with 'moral hazard' nor a rise as a result of equilibrium pricing are apparent. Debt repurchase came after the large exogeneous decline in exports made continuing service improbable; creditors recognised inability rather than unwillingness to pay. On the other side, debtors could have correctly and differentially anticipated a significant economic recovery that would have left them subject to higher future payments in the absence of amortisation at bargain rates. Had they not used the foreign exchange in this way, as Chile did explicitly, moreover, it might simply have gone towards larger interest payments. There was neither a constant and shared probability distribution of outcomes nor the full freedom to use resources that are implicit in the theoretical formulation.

EFFECTS OF REDUCED DEBT SERVICE

How much did default condition the recovery in the 1930s? For a broad set of countries economic performance seems to vary directly with the extent of default (Eichengreen and Portes 1988: 12–19). On the other side, the 1937 Report of the Royal Institute of International Affairs asserts that 'figures of the total outstanding volume of defaulted bonds give an exaggerated impression of the losses which creditors experienced ... In other words, defaults reduced the incomes of the two principal creditor countries ... by not more than one-quarter.' Defaults were, however, concentrated in Latin America and Central Europe. For the former, average payments on sterling investments of all kinds were down

Table 12.4 Export surplus (as percentage of goods exports)

	1929	1932	1937	1980	1983	1987
Latin America[a]	11.2	42.8	27.3	−13.7	32.0	25.6
Argentina	9.6	35.1	36.4	−17.5	47.4	15.7
Brazil	8.6	39.9	4.3	−13.9	29.7	42.6
Chile	30.5	24.1	54.4	−16.2	26.3	23.5
Colombia	−3.5	47.7	−11.6	−4.9	−50.5	32.0
Mexico	36.5	29.7	22.4	−16.6	61.9	40.8
Latin America (full public debt service)[b]	11.2	61.5	35.5	−	−	−

[a] Excludes Venezuela, 1980 to 1987.
[b] Calculated on the assumption that debt service of 8.2 per cent was paid throughout the period versus estimates of actual payments of 3.3 per cent in 1932 and 1937. The latter presume partial payments of 40 per cent in both years based on the information on sterling bonds in 1932 (Royal Institute of International Affairs (1937: 303); Brazil at both dates, Maddison (1985: 27).
Sources: CEPAL, Relación; Economic Commission for Latin America and the Caribbean 1980–7.

two-thirds, from 4.5 per cent in 1929 to little over 1.5 per cent in 1934 (Royal Institute 1937: 303, 311).

Table 12.4 presents direct information on the relative size of the Latin American trade surplus in the 1930s and the 1980s. This provides a reasonably accurate measure of actual resource transfers in the two periods as a result of the lack of offsetting capital inflows; when both sets of data are available, relative resource transfers are 18 per cent in 1980, 35 per cent in 1983 and 19 per cent in 1987.

In 1929 the region and all countries except Colombia were in surplus, reflecting deficits on invisibles as well as the reduced inflows already experienced in that year. Predictably, the surplus increases in 1932 as a result of the sharp reduction in exports and continuing debt service at partial levels. But with the exception of Chile and Argentina, and clearly for Latin America as a whole, there is considerable lessening of the relative surplus by 1937. Note in particular the actual declines for Brazil, Colombia and Mexico from 1929 levels.

In 1980, all five countries, and the region as a whole, were in deficit as a result of capital inflows. By 1983, excepting the erratic movement for Colombia, all countries had moved to a substantial surplus. Because of falling interest rates and rescheduling, the

1987 regional transfer was reduced. Argentina and Mexico stand out in this regard. Despite the Brazilian moratorium, the surplus relatively increased, measuring not only accumulation of reserves but continuing actual payments of interest on much of the debt. In 1987, despite some greater scope for imports than in 1983, the situation remained dramatically different than in 1980.

It is thus clear that the two experiences are quite distinct. But default is not the whole story. Suppose that public debt had been integrally serviced in the Great Depression. Then the evolution of the regional surplus, as indicated in Table 12.4, would not have looked all that different in the 1930s. Different assumptions as to the degree of partial service would not alter this conclusion. A greater reduction in imports would have been necessary in 1932, of an order of one-third. But the 1937 difference would have been only about 10 per cent, and compatible with rapid growth and a high import elasticity.

The two determinants of this result are the dominance of the export cycle and the limited place of public debt in total foreign capital in the 1930s. By contrast, a partial default of the same magnitude in the 1980s would have allowed for expanded imports of close to a third in each of 1982 and 1987, and permitted a significant expansion in demand without confronting a foreign exchange constraint.

Moreover, it has been harder to adjust to such a constraint in the 1980s than in the 1930s for three reasons. One is the internal counterpart of the large external transfer, the greater problem of the public sector in securing the needed debt service in domestic currency. The second is the prevalence of indexation that translates exchange rate changes into accelerating inflation. The third is the impact of debt service in reducing investment rates and inhibiting productivity growth.

Public sector management in much of the region is precarious. Not only do interest payments have to be met, but important and productive public sector expenditures have had to be curtailed. Still, deficits exceed those of the Great Depression. They have largely been financed by issue of internal debt to attract the surpluses of the private sector. This has contributed to high interest rates, which only add to the financial problems of governments in later years. As long as the rate of interest exceeds the rate of growth of the economy, there is a tendency for the internal debt/product ratio to rise until the point where dynamic instability can threaten.[14] Much higher taxes could obviate the need to resort to debt, or to money issues that sustain high inflation, but such policies are not only difficult to impose in the midst of lagging economic activity but also create disincentives to private investment.

Many Latin American economies today are indexed, formally or informally. Such rules are responses to high rates of inflation that in turn perpetuate and accelerate price increases. In particular, the use of the exchange rate to stimulate export surpluses through real devaluation has been a significant inflationary force. Real wages only decline when current rates of inflation are greater than last period's price increases to which nominal wage increases have been geared. This sets in motion demands for greater frequency of adjustments that only accelerates the inflationary spiral. It is no accident that the record export surpluses of the Latin American countries in the 1980s have also coincided with record increases in inflation that have verged on hyperinflation in some. Soaring prices only aggravate the interest rate problem. A priority external objective has been achieved, but at the expense of internal equilibrium.

Finally, an important effect of debt service in the 1980s has been to crowd out real investment. On average, debt service has absorbed 5 to 6 percentage points of gross product in the Latin American countries in recent years while investment has fallen to a corresponding degree. External transfers have not been accomplished by reducing consumption. Real interest rates of 15 to 20 per cent instead have helped to funnel the domestic resources needed to service debt from private capital formation. The consequence has been costly. Trade expansion has not been a vehicle for new technology and productivity increase. Instead exports have come from existing capacity and have been competitive by reason of falling real wages.

In the Great Depression investment apparently also declined substantially but with lesser consequence. Industrial expansion was for the domestic market and labour, rather than capital, intensive. Exports were agricultural and did not require large investment inputs to be competitive. One was able to attract capital formation to new sectors even though aggregate levels had fallen. Those mitigating circumstances in the Great Depression do not now apply.

DEBT RELIEF IN HISTORICAL PERSPECTIVE

In view of these negative effects of debt service upon economic activity, even as Latin American countries have individually continued to reschedule and negotiate with their private creditors they have advocated more far-reaching solutions. Three response phases can be identified. In 1985 came the Baker Plan whose centrepiece was larger capital inflows in return for internal adjustment. When these failed to materialise, Baker emphasised in early 1987 mechanisms for reducing debt through debt/equity swaps and other options. In May of the same year, with aggressive commercial bank provisions against potential losses, a new impulse was given to ways of reducing debt through private market solutions. The Mexican bond issue and Bolivian buy-back of the debt were direct results.

In the Great Depression a similar sequence can be identified. Various efforts at global debt relief were offered early on, but never succeeded (Eichengreen 1988). The first schemes were directed, as in the Baker Plan, to restoring capital flows as a means of reviving trade and world economic activity. There was also a recognition of the possibility of servicing debt in domestic currency as a means of freeing resources for needed imports. The surplus countries, the United States and France, were counted on for support but failed to see the merits of their special obligation to underwrite global financial recovery. Although debtor countries supported the proposal at the World Economic Conference in 1933, the creditors were not as eager. The United States excluded discussion of the inter-war debts, as it had earlier in the context of reparations in the 1920s, dissipating the interest of the Europeans. In the end it was impossible to orchestrate the needed degree of political commitment and cooperation.

In the Great Depression it was left to repeated bilateral negotiations between creditor representatives and Latin American debtor countries to find solutions of partial default that lasted through the crisis. Definitive settlements awaited a more active political interest by the United States in improving hemispheric relations, an improved Latin American balance of payments and the assistance of Second-World-War inflation in reducing the real value of claims. The latter was of importance, as it had been after the First World War, in allowing debtors to adjust to their greater exposure and questions the meaning of calculations showing positive nominal returns to creditors (Skiles 1988: 34ff.).

There has also been muddling through in the 1980s as generalised schemes of debt rescheduling have met the same inability to reach agreement as in the Great Depression. It has differed, however, by virtue of active creditor-government pressure to assure timely payment and the presence of the multilateral international institutions to enforce such preferences. Private creditors have been better organised as well. In conjunction with slowly growing world trade, these factors have added up to a much larger repayment than in the Great Depression.

The current debt crisis has moved to the chronic problem rather than solution stage. Resolution will require, as it did historically, political incentive on the part of the creditor governments. In 1989, as new administrations are installed throughout the Western Hemisphere, eyes are turned to Washington to say whether there will be a repetition of Franklin Delano Roosevelt's 1939 speech terming defaulted Latin American bonds 'ancient frauds' and blaming bondholders for the failure to settle.[15]

NOTES

1. Eichengreen and Portes (1988) build on previous research including Eichengreen and Portes (1986) and Skiles (1988).
2. An early comparative treatment of the Great Depression is Diaz Alejandro (1983). A comprehensive discussion of the Great Depression experience in Latin America is Thorp (1984; see also Maddison 1985).
3. O'Connell (1984). Other case studies in the volume provide detail on other countries.
4. Eichengreen and Portes (1988) correctly point to other factors than trade variability in provoking default in the 1930s, including fiscal deficit and political commitment. But the balance of payments crisis, which is the point here, clearly has its cause on the merchandise account in the 1930s versus the capital account in the 1980s.
5. Trade data are from Lewis (1952: 107). Real exchange rates are calculated by Diaz Alejandro (1983: 14).

6. Real exchange rates are presented in Inter-American Development Bank (1988: 15).
7. Maddison (1985: 21). Note that the direct role of external trade in stimulating recovery was much greater in Argentina and Chile than in Brazil, Colombia and Mexico, where domestic demand was more important.
8. Eichengreen and Portes's test of the efficiency of import substitution during the Depression is less that than a confirmation of the importance of import growth to output growth as I have argued. They take imports relative to their average value in the 1930s. Import substitution occurred because even with rapid import growth, the import/output ratio at the end of the 1930s was much lower than it had been in the 1920s. See Eichengreen and Portes (1988: 18).
9. Three-quarters of the long-term debt in 1980 was public or publicly guaranteed, and a smaller ratio of the short-term debt. Overall the percentage is close to two-thirds. See Inter-American Development Bank (1988: 580ff.).
10. Skiles (1988: 30); Royal Institute of International Affairs (1937: 303). With adjustment for defaulted bonds paying no interest.
11. International Monetary Fund (1988: 182–3). Adjusted to exports of goods rather than goods and services.
12. Diaz Alejandro (1983: 27); O'Connell (1984: 204). For ratios of external public debt to total debt see Royal Institute of International Affairs (1937: 225).
13. Economic Commission for Latin America (1965: 29); Royal Institute of International Affairs (1937: 320). See also the distinction between public and private creditor views in Eichengreen and Portes (1988: 34–6).
14. For discussion of the instability question, see Fishlow and Morley (1987).
15. Quoted in Skiles (1988: 28).

REFERENCES

Bulow, Jeremy and Kenneth Rogoff (1988), 'The buyback boondoggle', *Brookings Papers on Economic Activity*, December 1988, pp. 675–98.
CEPAL (1977), *Relación de Precios de Intercambio, 1928–1876*, E/CEPAL/1040.
Diaz, Alejandro Carlos (1983), 'Stories of the 1930s for the 1980s', in Pedro Aspe Armella, Rudiger Dornbusch and Maurice Obstfeld (eds), *Financial Policies and the World Capital Market*. Chicago: University of Chicago Press, pp. 5–40.
Dooley, Michael P. (1988), 'Buy-backs and market valuation of external debt', *IMF Staff Papers*, vol. 35, no. 2, pp. 215–29.
Economic Commission for Latin America (1965), *External Financing in Latin America*, New York: United Nations.

Economic Commission for Latin America and the Caribbean (1980–7), *Preliminary Overview of the Latin American Economy*, New York: United Nations.

Eichengreen, Barry (1988), *Resolving Debt Crises: An Historical Perspective*, mimeo, January 1988.

Eichengreen, Barry and Richard Portes (1986), 'Debt and default in the 1930s: causes and consequences', *European Economic Review*, vol. 30, pp. 599–640.

Eichengreen, Barry and Richard Portes (1988), *Dealing with Debt: The 1930s and 1980s*, mimeo, December 1988.

Fishlow, Albert (1987), *Some Reflections on Comparative Latin American Economic Performance and Policy*, University of California, Berkeley Economics Working Paper 8754, September 1987.

Fishlow, Albert and Samuel A. Morley (1987), 'Deficits, debt and destabilization', *Journal of Development Economics*, vol. 27, pp. 227–44.

Inter-American Development Bank (1988), *Economic and Social Progress in Latin America, 1988*, Washington DC: IADB.

International Monetary Fund (1988), *World Economic Outlook, 1988*, Washington DC: IMF.

Lewis, W. Arthur (1952), 'World production, prices and trade, 1870–1960', *Manchester School*, vol. 20, no. 2, pp. 105–38.

Maddison, Angus (1985), *Two Crises: Latin America and Asia 1929–38 and 1973–83*, Paris: OECD.

Ocampo, Jose Antonio (1984), 'The Columbian economy in the 1930s', in Rosemary Thorp (ed.), *Latin America in the 1930s*, London: Macmillan, pp. 117–43.

O'Connell, Arturo (1984), 'Argentina into the depression: problems of an open economy', in Rosemary Thorp (ed.) *Latin America in the 1930s*, London: Macmillan, pp. 188–221.

OECD (1980), *Development Co-Operation, 1979 Review*, Paris: OECD.

Royal Institute of International Affairs (1937), *The Problem of International Investment*, London/New York: Oxford University Press.

Skiles, Marilyn (1988), *Latin American International Loan Defaults in the 1930s: Lessons for the 1980s?*, Research Paper No. 8812, New York: Federal Reserve Bank of New York.

Thorp, Rosemary (ed.) (1984), *Latin America in the 1930s*, London: Macmillan.

Woodruff, William (1966), *The Impact of Western Man*. London: Macmillan.

13 · NEWLY INDUSTRIALISING COUNTRIES IN THE WORLD ECONOMY: NICs, SICs, NECs, EPZs OR TEs?

Detlef Lorenz

INTRODUCTION

Though until today the so-called NICs quantatively represent only a relatively small sector of the world economy, their challenge as well as their policy influence is far greater. The fields of interest involved are many and are indeed quite relevant: the new international division of labour as a chance for the NICs but also entailing reversals of comparative advantages for the old industrialised countries – the NDCs (newly declining countries); new protectionism as a barrier to market penetration as well as graduation as a problem for the NICs; 'positive' adjustment policies for NDCs and successful NICs alike; competition between NICs and next-tier countries; amplification of regional imbalances raised by the world economic dynamics of the NICs, etc.

Against this background it appears inadvisable to dare to make a *tour d'horizon* and produce something like a survey chapter. Approaching the subject more selectively and critically, then, in the face of the vast literature and the attention the NICs have attracted, three following astonishing statements should not be overlooked:

1. Although mainstream economics, in particular the 'new orthodoxy', will strongly oppose Krugman's dictum (1986: 443) that 'conventional trade models' are unable to explain 'one of

the key riddles of economic development' it should be taken seriously.
2. Since 1970, when the seminal study by Little, Scitovsky and Scott was published, economists have been hard at work eliminating a state of affairs Wolf (1983: 14) ascribed to the NDCs – namely confronting the 'largely unanticipated comparative advantages' of the NICs 'in what may be described as a fit of absence of mind'. Nevertheless, it has to be noted that the OECD did not start things moving much before 1979 and the GATT practically postponed the opportunity to take developing countries as 'bargaining partners' seriously until the Uruguay Round!
3. Last but not least and not at all isolated from the two points just referred to, we are still facing the unsettled priority problem of identifying the NICs. Otherwise Bradford and Branson (1987: 6) would not have been entitled to say quite recently: 'Development of a clear theory that would predict which countries will be the next NICs rather than establish criteria for the designation of NICs *ex post*, is one of the central problems of the field of economic development.'

This chapter proceeds by examining at first very briefly the issue of identification and a more extensive interpretation of the 'Gang of Four' (see pages 339–43). We then pursue different approaches broadening the NICs-dimension (see pages 343–9). In the next section implications of 'geographically'-based peculiarities are taken into consideration before we return to evaluating at some length socio-economic foundations regarding the identification issue (see pages 349–59). Finally, in the last section some conclusions are drawn.

JUST SUCCESSFUL DEVELOPING COUNTRIES?

Without a doubt NICs have played an increasingly important role in the modern world economy since the Second World War, particularly since the mid-1960s. They most certainly became a very successful group of the so-called Third World and a hallmark of the North–South world economy. Furthermore, as it turned out, the NICs accomplished the process of integration into the world economy while conforming considerably both to the 'old' world economic order (Bretton Woods) and to the traditional concept of the international division of labour. Industrialisation was the main goal as well as the basis for exporting manufactured goods and pursuing an ES (export-led growth strategy). In both respects they definitely differ from the second successful group, OPEC, which pursued above all a power strategy by means of an old commodity together with a new world economic order aiming at putting a stop to 'exploitation' and deteriorating terms of trade. As we all know today, this spectacular success of the OPEC countries' strategy hardly lasted a decade. The success of the NICs, on the contrary, appears to be far more constant. Nevertheless, doubts regarding the extent of their on-going success, based on conclusions drawn from the outcome of the 1980s and from prognoses as to the development of the world economy in the near future, could prove to be well founded.[1]

In order to form a more precise opinion regarding the position the NICs have gained in the world economy, we have to know more about them other than that they have become a successful group in a process of differentiation of the Third World. That is for the most part a problem of identification. Just as it is not easy to determine what exactly is a typical developing country, so, too, difficult problems arise when attempting to define newly industrialising countries. The group has no legal or established definition and international organisations like OECD, the World Bank or UNCTAD (United Nations Conference on Trade and Development). Its members prefer to 'go it alone'. Certainly, 'there are about as many lists of which countries are NICs as there are authors on the topic of their emergence and growth. So we have an initial problem of identification of countries' (Branson 1987: 30). In the end, for both pragmatic and political reasons there might even be an argument for letting the developing countries do the job for themselves, a procedure already applied by the GSP (General System of Preferences) and suggested in GATT for the problem of graduation. That, however, does not bring us very far. Knowing just when the threshold has been crossed and the developing country no longer considers itself a *newly* developing country is one thing but it is far more relevant to determine which qualifications are pre-conditional for entering the stage of a 'transitional economy' (Bradford 1987).

G-4 AND THE ASIAN NICs RESPECTIVELY

Nevertheless, not only international organisations and economic experts but also every average person knows quite well what has become the core of the NICs, i.e. the famous G-4 ('Gang of Four'), the four little dragons or tigers in East Asia (Hongkong, Singapore, Taiwan and South Korea). Because of evident peculiarities as far as the two *city* states are concerned, Taiwan and Korea are the only *countries* of the 'Gang'. Moreover, they are quite often considered as 'mini-Japans', an aspect to which not only historical significance can be attributed (Turner and McMullen 1982: 1).

Officially *Japan* did not join the ranks of the developed industrialised countries (of the north!) until 1964 when it became a member of the OECD. Though from the perspective of economic history NICs 'have always existed' (Michaely 1984: 123), Japan appears to enjoy a different or unique status. It was dubbed 'the first NIC' and at least two distinguishing characteristics should be mentioned: first, Japan does not belong to the European or Atlantic family of countries (it is a *foreign* country in the *Far East*!); second, Japan has the reputation of having been the leading *imitator* of the world economy demonstrating as the first NIC the innovation of an amazingly successful selective strategy, i.e. 'the catching-up product cycle of development' (Yamazawa 1986: 1). In so far as the new international division of labour in the South–North context could be widely characterised as a dynamic process of innovation and imitation, the newcomers following the leading countries, the NICs might perhaps be even better dubbed *SICs = successfully imitating countries*! With regard to the second generation of NICs (see Figure 13.1), economic history has a very important additional point to make. Each of the 'mini-Japans' passed through decisive pre-take-off periods. Certainly, without the many-sided paradoxical influence of the Japanese colonial regime both countries would not be the VIPs of the NICs (Cumings 1984; Pack and Westphal 1986: 92, 102–3; Lau 1986)!

Apart from the Japanese ingredient of the East Asian NICs the *Chinese* input has equally to be recognised. In the case of Taiwan both influences overlap considerably. Furthermore, it is not by chance that three of the members of the G-4 are Chinese 'regions'. To a certain extent Hongkong, Singapore, Taiwan and the EPZs

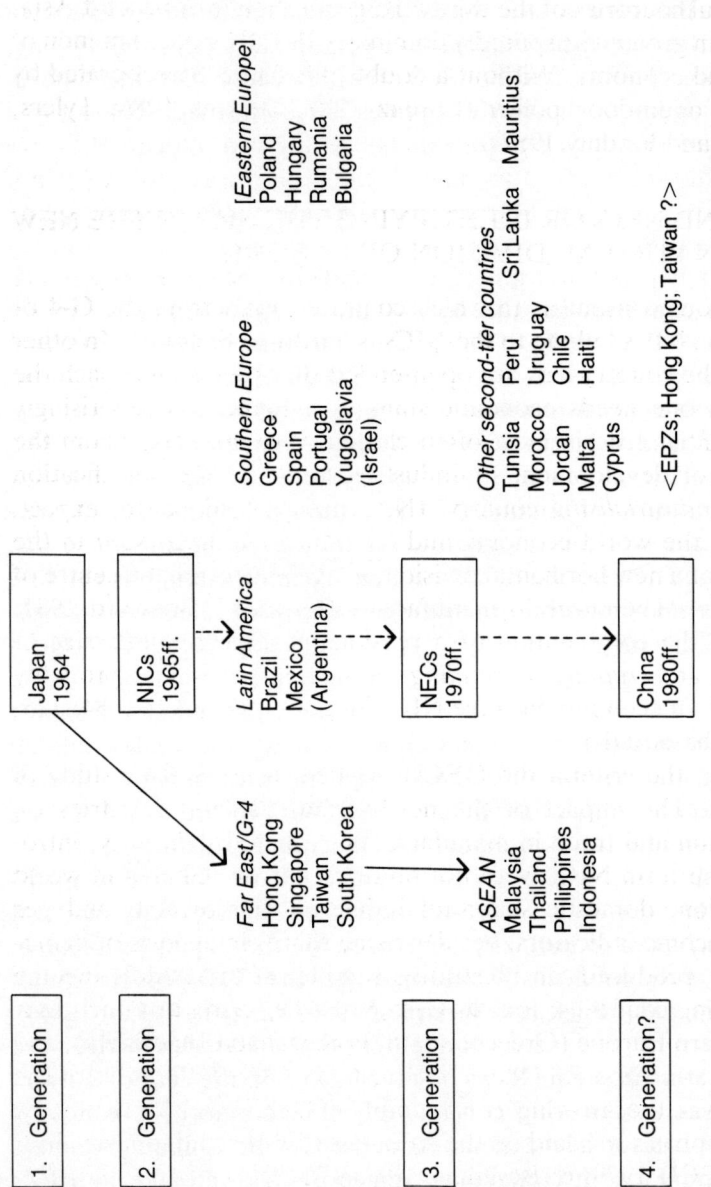

Figure 13.1 Generations of newly industrialising countries

(export processing zones) of mainland China could also be regarded as a collective Chinese 'unit'. At all events the core of the NICs is definitely characterised by the Japanese–Chinese element. Together with Malaysia and Thailand, the two most important and successful countries of the third NIC generation in Southeast Asia, the Asian group undisputedly dominates the NICs phenomenon of the world economy. Without a doubt, this fact is corroborated by China's open-door policy (Lorenz 1987; Perkins 1986; Tylers, Phillips and Findlay 1987).

NICs AND NECs OR IDENTIFYING THE NICs IN THE NEW INTERNATIONAL DIVISION OF LABOUR

Unanimous consent as to which countries apart from the G-4 or the Asian NICs belong to the NICs is hardly to be found. In other words: the country lists are open-ended. In order to approach the problem one needs economic standards. Somewhat surprisingly the essential criteria most often chosen were not taken from the process of development or industrialisation as the specification 'newly *industrialising* country' (N*I*C) would lead one to expect. Instead, the world economy and *international competition* in the context of a new horizontal division of labour became the centre of analysis – 'The *surge* in manufactured *exports*' (Bradford 1987: 302) or 'the combination of a reasonably large *absolute size* of exports and *rapidly expanding* industrial *exports* ... probably classifies an economy into the NIC category' (Michaely 1984: 125; my emphasis, DL).

Surely, the criteria the OECD applied in its pioneer study of 1979 on 'The impact of the newly industrializing countries on production and trade in manufactures', which, by the way, introduced the term NIC, were not quite so narrow. Shares in world production, domestic shares of industrial employment and per capita income indicators, besides rising shares in exports of manufactures, produced 'an illustrative sample' of ten middle-income developing countries: four in East Asia, the 'Gang of Four', four in southern Europe (Greece, Spain, Portugal and Jugoslavia), and two in Latin America (Mexico, Brazil). However, the basis of the report was the growing *competition* in OECD markets and the main emphasis was laid on the *consequences* of rapid industrialisation (OECD 1979: 6; Bergmann 1983: 72–3).

Of course, what the OECD countries were concerned about was a very important development in the world economy since the middle of the 1960s, when more and more developing countries changed from the policy of import substitution to the strategy of outward-looking or export orientation which pursued trade as the famous 'engine' of domestic growth (export-led growth). As a consequence of the rapidly developing *substitutive* trade flows of manufactures from the South, severe displacement competition came into existence in the domestic markets of the North. Adjustment processes and problems of structural change in the international division of labour, as well as the *presumed* dangers of de-industrialisation and rising unemployment because of 'a flood' of low-wage imports, explain the focus of the OECD report.[2]

The ongoing fast expansion of manufactured exports during the 1970s equally explains why two well-known studies, published only three years later than the first OECD study, again chose export indicators to find out whether a second generation of NICs or 'next tier' countries could be established. Twelve or sixteen countries respectively were isolated and dubbed NECs ('newly *exporting* countries') (Havrylyshyn and Alikhani 1982; OECD/DAC 1982; and see Table 13.1). They were identified mainly by the indicator export growth rate for the period 1970–9 which had to exceed even those of the NICs!

But what really distinguishes the NECs from the NICs? As we have argued, the essential criterion characterising a NIC apparently has equally been rapid development of manufactured exports. That they were a bit less new, having started earlier, and being of a higher income level does not count for much. Whereas the two World Bank authors explicitly wanted to demonstrate the ability of the NECs 'to repeat the experience of the newly industrialised countries in the face of slower world growth in trade' (Havrylyshyn and Alikhani 1982: 656), the OECD/DAC study (1982: 125) was far more cautious with respect to their capacity to become NICs.

Two points, moreover, appear quite remarkable. One underlines similarity, namely the preponderance of the Asian group members: only three ASEAN countries hold a share of roughly 50 per cent of the total export volume in both of the mentioned NEC samples comparable to the share of the Asian NICs in the original sample of the OECD (Athukorala 1986: 35; and see Tables 13.1 and 13.2). The other point underlines the eminent difference in

Table 13.1 Manufactured exports of NECs (1979): value of exports (million US dollars)

Second tier (OECD/DAC)		NECs (Havrylyshyn/Alikhani)	
Sri Lanka	132	Sri Lanka	121.4
Haiti	203	Cyprus	226.8
Indonesia	448	*Thailand*	1,195.8
Thailand	1,213	Indonesia	448.2
Philippines	991	Peru	495.5
Peru	400	Jordan	97.5
Morocco	460	Uruguay	373.3
Tunisia	604	*Malaysia*	1,935.5
Mauritius	101	Tunisia	604.5
Jordan	157	*Philippines*	988.1
Malaysia	1,947	Colombia	648.8
Macau	370	Morocco	460.0
Chile	650		
Uruguay	374		
Malta	368		
Cyprus	227		
Total second tier	8.645	NECs Total	7.595.3
NICs (non-OECD)[a]	61.761	NICs Total[b]	73.830.4

[a] The term 'non-OECD' excludes Greece, Spain and Portugal.
[b] The term 'NICs Total' adds three countries: Argentina, Israel and India (!) to the 1979 OECD NICs.

Table 13.2 Exports of manufactures from developing countries (at constant 1980 prices)

	Total exports (billion US$) (1)	Shares in total exports (%)		Total NICs (2+3) (4)	NECs (DAC) (5)	Other DCs (6)
		Four NICs East Asia (G-4) (2)	Other NICs (OECD) (3)			
1970	27.8	35.1	49.6	84.7	4.9	10.4
1975	58.4	38.4	48.3	86.7	6.2	7.1
1980	118.0	52.9	34.6	87.5	8.7	3.8
1983	125.6	53.5	31.5	85.0	9.1	5.9
Annual Averages						
1970–83		45.1	41.8	86.9	7.0	6.1
1980–3		53.5	32.8	86.3	8.7	5.0

Source: Adapted from Athukorala (1986: 32).

absolute size of exports, an especially important point regarding the world economy, particularly South–North competition in the field of manufactures. The two NEC samples only reached a share of 10 per cent or 14 per cent respectively in 1979 (see Table 13.1); in 1983 according to figures presented by Athukorala the shares were as follows: NECs 9.1 per cent, Asian NICs 53.5 per cent and total NICs of the OECD sample 85 per cent (Table 13.2).

To the general conclusion one can draw from adding NECs to NICs – namely that the expansion of the sheer number of NECs only demonstrates the spread of the ES policy while increasing the supply potential clearly underproportionately – a recent UNCTAD study (1986: 11–12) on trade in manufactures also gives evidence. On the basis of a minimum value of $100 million manufactured exports to twenty-one developed market economies, the study presents forty-five developing countries or NECs in our context holding 98 per cent of the total the Third World has to offer. However, only a dozen countries export more than $1 billion but reach a share of 85 per cent, which happens to be the same percentage stated above for the NICs of the 1979 OECD study.

Though both samples are not quite adequately comparable, the following argument might be defensible. Whereas the 'UNCTAD dozen' does not include the three Southern European NICs, Greece, Spain and Portugal of the 'OECD dozen' – meanwhile 'graduated' into the enlarged EC – it does, however, include four ASEAN countries (Malaysia, Philippines, Thailand, Indonesia) which were also part of the two NEC samples quoted above. So, in the end – and not without some manipulation – we might dare to say: in the course of about twenty years within a small group of relevant exporters, only three rather old NICs have been substituted by four new ones. The 'next tier' not only have the advantage of being located adjacent to the G-4 but three of them (Malaysia, Philippines and Thailand) are also the only ones that have successfully diversified into sophisticated and dynamic areas of export (Athukorala 1986: 16–18). Whether that is a sufficient criterion to qualify as NICs is a matter of opinion and will be discussed later (see pages 354–9). The majority of the newly exporting countries selected in the UNCTAD and the two NEC samples, however, still stick to the 'traditional trio' of exports (textiles, clothing and miscellaneous manufactures).

Thus, more basically, we could argue as follows. The ES policies may be internationally transferred alternatively as an *endogenous* or as an *exogenous* strategy. Not surprisingly, most of the NECs seem to have participated only in the second approach. This emerges quite clearly in so far as the expansion of exports has been greatly influenced by establishing EPZs, 'quota propelled growth' or 'quota hopping' (Athukorala 1986: 16–18; Hughes and Newberry 1986).[3] This appears to be predominantly the case in one important field. 'The emergence of NECs in recent years reflects, to a significant extent, the worldwide spread of the textile and clothing industry as an outcome of restrictions imposed by the industrialised countries' (Athukorala 1986: 16). Apparently, neo-protectionism, especially the *management* of the Multi-Fibre Arrangement but also offshore production on the basis of direct foreign investments played a role, assisted by multinational companies interestingly stemming more and more from the Third World or East Asian NICs respectively (Hughes and Newberry 1986: 418–23). Well-known examples of this transfer of superficial and sometimes also discontinuous *elements* of the export-oriented strategy are a few small island economies, for instance Malta, Cyprus, Mauritius, Haiti, Sri Lanka and Macao (see Athukorala 1986: 14–15; OECD/DAC 1982: 128), but we also find similar evidence in ASEAN countries. Last but not least, the resource-rich Latin American countries generally put less emphasis on a steady endogenous ES, Brazil being somewhat of an exception (cf. pages 354–9).

EMULATING A MODEL OF A SEQUENCE OF STAGES?

Very often NICs are rather rashly identified with the outward-looking policy or ES, the more so when the number of NICs is enlarged by further generations of NECs. Or, to put it the other way round, NICs/NECs are supposed to be created by efficiently advertising the stylised (!) experience of the 'Gang of Four'. The so-called 'new orthodoxy' within and outside influential international organisations quite successfully contributed to the propagation of the emulation tests. Apart from problems on the supply side of particular countries, just touched upon at the end of the previous section, the emulation strategy, however, faces the limits set by aggregation head-on. So long as, principally, each country is held eligible to be a NIC, provided the appropriate policy has been applied ('getting relative prices right'), it seems legitimate to follow the simulation experiment by Cline (1982) asking the question:'Can the East Asian model of development be generalised?'.

The study was published in the same year as the two NEC papers mentioned above; it aimed at something like 'built in' limitations of the NIC phenomenon. Naturally, if a *generalised* recommendation is derived on the basis of the microeconomics of price competition and market shares, as well as on the basis of the premiss of the *small* country in the neo-classical international trade theory, then the dangers of the 'fallacy of composition' are overdue. While the model may work well if pursued by a limited number of countries, it may break down if a large majority of developing countries seeks to pursue it at the same time, because the resulting outpouring of manufactured exports might be more than western markets could absorb. Consequently, protectionist response might be the result of attempts to generalise the East Asian export model of growth also (Lorenz 1988: 439–43).

Of course, this method does not identify individual countries nor does it tell us how many NICs have to get a licence, so to speak. Moreover, the apparent impossibility (illogic) of providing every developing country with G-4 dimensions or of finding the penetration threshold for the import markets in developed countries is *not* the decisive problem. What does matter, however, is that there are limits facing international competition which the new orthodoxy likes to deny. The fact that the industrialised countries' capacity to absorb or to transform could be overstrained and that overcapacities arise, is neither a product of the imagination nor is it always necessarily the consequence of wrong policies. Clearly, prices, if allowed to be flexible, can overcome some 'myths of external constraints' (Riedel 1987) but the results of displacement competition are not success and profits for *all* who even pursue the right or sound policies recommended. Furthermore, they are not at all independent of the realities of demand is a thorny dilemma with regard to *ex ante* and *ex post*. Who will know *ex ante* how much supply is appropriate, but equally, who can tell the story about the consequences if *ex post* it wasn't?!

One possibility to circumvent the principal difficulties in a seemingly elegant manner appears to be the widely acknowledged 'stages approach to comparative advantage' (Balassa 1977), although the approach implicitly recognises that demand constraints, too, are part of the process! Otherwise stages would not be conceived of as an element of 'adjustment' breeding less protection, *ceteris paribus*. In fact, historical development processes are characterised by sequences of events resembling generations; the same applies to developing countries climbing up the ladder of comparative advantage, one after the other. Not all of them offer the same range of products in the same period of time because development endows them with different and changing advantages. Then we get what has become known as country or product substitution among the developing country suppliers. The underlying idea is that replacement instead of competition takes place and consequently adjustment processes in the importing industrialised countries are divided over a couple of periods.

Empirical investigations do not generally support the theory of stages (Cline 1984: 26–32; Athukorala 1986: 21–2). Yet that is not the real problem, which should rather be understood as one of 'adding-up' (Lorenz 1988: 422, 442). Even when the leading countries (NICs) climb up the ladder and shift production – which has become disadvantageous – to newcomers at a lower level (NECs), only export competition among the different generations of *developing* countries is reduced. Import competition in *developed* countries, however, will rise, the reason being a broadening of the imitation process between North and South. If by country substitution Japan, the NICs or the NECs give way to next tier countries, the leading countries do not go out of business at all or shift supply to *domestic* markets. Rather, they add a more or less broad range of new sectors and extend competition to different lines of import penetration in developed countries. An OECD report on protection (1985: 186) illustrated the point cogently by an 'innocent' graph without, however, elaborating on the problem (cf. Figure 13.2 and Table 13.3).

A CLOSER LOOK AT NICs SPLITTING UP IN 'HINTERLAND' RELATIONSHIPS

International competition in manufactures spans a very broad spectrum indeed. New sources and a variety of dynamic exporters

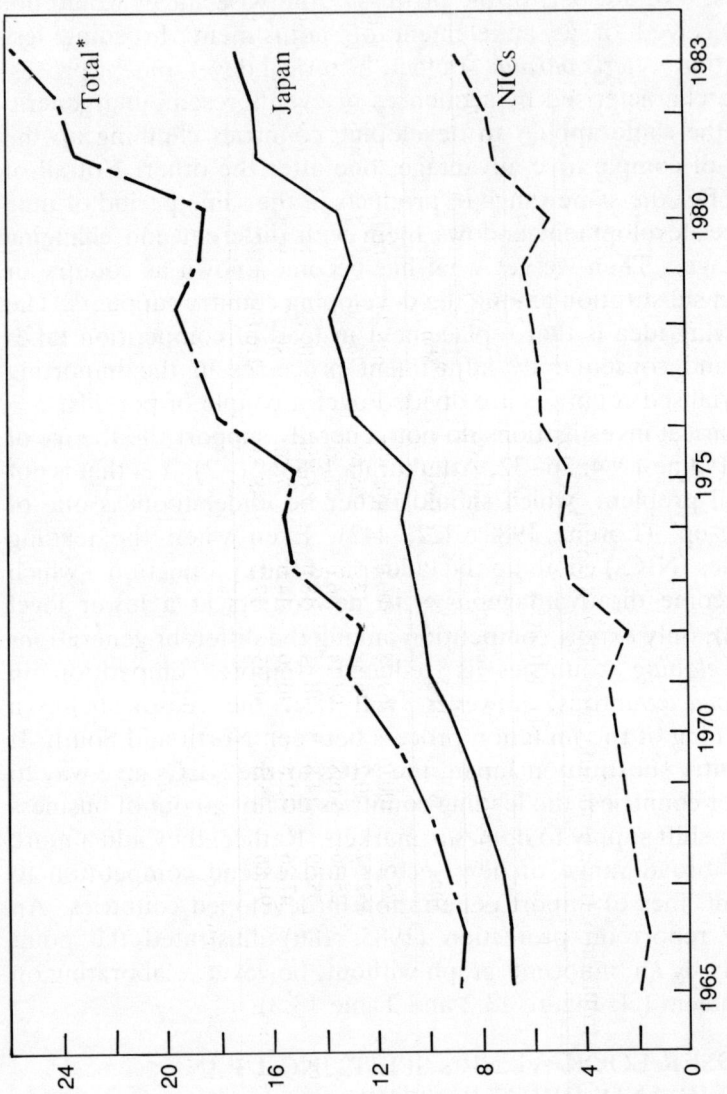

Figure 13.2 OECD imports of manufactures from Japan and the NICs as a percentage of total OECD manufactured imports. (*Japan, Singapore, Hong Kong, Korea, Taiwan, Mexico, Brazil.)
Source: OECD 1985: 1, 186.

Table 13.3 Distribution of trade in manufactures 1983–6 (total)

	Asian NICs/G-4						Japan					
	Exports		Imports		Balance		Exports		Imports		Balance	
	$bn	%	$bn	%	$bn		$bn	%	$bn	%	$bn	
World	375.25	100.0	269.78	100.0	105.47		675.44	100.0	132.98	100.0	542.45	
USA	152.57	40.7	46.88	17.4	105.69		244.50	36.2	51.80	39.0	192.70	
Japan	25.36	6.8	97.14	36.0	−71.78		–	–	–	–	–	
Western Europe	55.39	14.8	48.64	18.0	6.75		107.68	15.9	36.50	27.4	71.81	
EC	47.26	12.6	40.10	14.9	7.16		89.15	13.2	29.80	22.4	59.35	
Developing countries	94.86	25.3	46.53	17.2	48.33		216.64	32.1	32.37	24.3	184.27	

Source: GATT (1987 Appendix: 163, 169).

– especially from the Far East but also including eastern Europe – have to be taken into consideration if we care for the new international division of labour with substitutive exports supplied by the NICs and NECs. One important positive aspect of the aforementioned rather heterogenous OECD sample (1979) is the geographical extension of the NICs group: besides the four Asian NICs, four (five) European NICs and two (three) Latin American countries.[5] Although meanwhile the three EC (European Community) members and Israel no longer are categorised as developing countries, Mexico has developed a heavy oil bias, and Argentina still holds a very weak NIC position, nevertheless the OECD group of the NICs commands attention because of remarkable 'hinterland relations' the NICs display opposite to 'their' gravity centres. The point is seldom recognised but it is of great significance for Europe and the United States, as well as having further consequences for the world economy in general (Lorenz 1989b).

A rough quantitative survey is given in Table 13.4.[6] The data provide two interesting aspects for western Europe or the EC respectively. Western Europe is the only region in which all groups of NICs including a few semi-industrialised *socialist* countries of eastern Europe have pronounced supplier interest.[7] As the European NICs in southern and eastern Europe do far less business in other parts of the world economy, clearly in contrast to the international ('footloose') Asian NICs, western Europe or the EC have become the areas where NICs compete among themselves most intensively. Though competition between the various NICs groups is partly not very close because of product- or specialisation-differentiation, in the end the many-folded supply adds up to an important potential of import penetration competition. If we include Japanese exports, which, as argued above, would make sense, the point could be adequately underlined. This particular constellation in Europe is unique and should be regarded, too, as a special ingredient with respect to the patterns and attitudes of European protectionism. In addition the effect of protection is increased, if we add a further European event. Three NICs – Spain, Portugal and Greece – have joined the EC. Officially they disappeared as NICs but they also changed sides, which probably had the effect of strengthening protection towards third countries (Lorenz 1988: 432–3).

The 'hinterland relations' *vis-à-vis* the respective industrialised

Table 13.4 Trade in manufactures of the EC, the United States and Japan (1980) (billion US dollars)

	EC[a]			USA			Japan		
	Exports	Imports	Balance	Exports	Imports	Balance	Exports	Imports	Balance
Total world	295.9	221.1	+74.8	167.5	162.0	+5.5	127.4	48.6	+78.8
Southern Europe	*30.8*	*19.5*	*+11.3*	4.8	3.0	+1.8	2.1	0.5	+1.6
Socialist countries	*20.9*	*16.8*	*+4.1*	1.3	1.3	−0.1	3.4	1.0	+2.4
East Asian NICs	7.3	11.6	−4.3	10.9	18.2	−7.3	*18.6*	6.1	*+12.5*
Latin America	17.8	14.1	+3.7	32.2	22.8	+9.4	8.3	2.4	+5.9

[a] Excluding intra-EC trade
Source: Adapted from Bradford and Branson (1987: 63).

[M] p.461, Table-13.4

countries, moreover, conceal a second remarkable problem. Each 'developed region' realises comfortable trade balances in manufactures with regard to 'their' NICs. However, that goes hand in hand with significant inter-regional asymmetries as Branson (1987) rightly emphasised. The inter-regional imbalances developed not only for the US but also for the EC (see Table 13.4): both regions are facing high surpluses *vis-à-vis* the NICs in Latin America and southern or eastern Europe respectively, while at the same time realising mounting deficits opposite the East Asian NICs. Furthermore, these inter-regional imbalances could be seen as a counterpart to the int*ra*-regional imbalances Japan has with regard to 'its' Asian NICs and which could hardly be compensated because Japan developed surpluses with every other NIC group including eastern Europe. On the other hand, the risks of such a triangular trade remained with the NICs of Latin America or Europe, which faced problems exporting more primary commodities (terms of trade; agricultural protection) and at the same time, the United States was facing a mix-up of debt problems and structural imbalances with regard to Latin America. 'Overall the United States had a deficit in manufactures trade of 10.3 billion dollars with the Asian NICs and a surplus of 2.6 billion dollars with the Latin Americans in 1981 ... this highlights the exposure of US trade to the debt situation in Latin America' (Branson 1987: 55). In constrast, Japan and the Asian NICs in this way settled their *intra*-regional problems by accommodating *extra*-regional difficulties (Lorenz 1989a)![8]

THE CONSTRAINT OF BEING A TRANSITIONAL ECONOMY (TE)

As we have seen in different ways, the NICs and their model-function are heavily characterised by their surprising and eminently successful development of exports, the famous export surges and export-led growth policies. They are widely understood as the outcome of an outward-looking policy. This strategy has been centred on *external* influence and a liberal *foreign trade* policy under the auspices of a competitive order avoiding or eliminating distortions: 'getting prices right' as a popular slogan demands. This policy stance did not mean a policy of *laissez-faire* (Little 1987:

46). Rather, what was aimed at was a limitation or guidance of government policies in order to secure an undistorted export development via efficient markets, not a discriminating (neutral!) allocation of resources (Balassa 1980). Apart from avoiding or abolishing distortions in industrialised countries, i.e. neo-protectionism, clearly the emphasis on price competition in open markets is essential for promoting *substitutive* trade flows and 'workable' displacement competitition (import penetration). This strategy has become known as the hallmark of an efficient international supply policy denying export pessimism and justifying export optimism (Meier 1985; Riedel 1987).

However, is this stylised trade and price model of the NICs sufficient and convincing for identifying NICs? Don't we have to transcend the trade surface whatever international trade as an indicator otherwise means from the viewpoint of world economics? And, indeed, the so-called 'new orthodoxy' has come under severe attack recently, along the lines of the decisive *internal* inputs the development experience of NICs suggests. But before evaluating some arguments critics have more recently raised, two remarks might be in order.

Even the OECD's original study (1979) did not solely rely on trade indicators, but also used indicators for industrial production and employment as well as per capita income (NICs as middle-income countries in World Bank terminology). However, they were more of a secondary nature and, moreover, they appear to have played a doubtful role, for countries with a remarkable potential for industrial production like India, Pakistan, Egypt or Chile were disregarded because of a wrong trade strategy (OECD 1979: 22). Presumably, NICs above all have to be NECs! Nevertheless, the OECD report also contains an illuminating statement which is particularly important in relation to the many small, resource-poor countries where off-shore production (EPZs) has been mainly concentrated on export surges. Furthermore, as regards the section of this chapter on identifying NICs, and the relevant number of NECs or NICs, the following quotation is still topical: 'None of these countries appears to have as yet the entrepreneurial skills and other conditions needed to embark on industrial development along the Hongkong or Singapore models.'[9] Additionally, East Asian premisses (clichés?) for a trade-oriented *growth* policy were explicitly underscored: a disciplined population, well-educated, efficient and active entrepreneurs, and political stability in general (OECD/DAC 1982: 124).

Interestingly, too, investigations with far more diversified catalogues of indicators, including socio-economic and geopolitical criteria, in the end hardly differed from the result of the OECD study with respect to the countries that should qualify as NICs (compare the representative report by Bergmann 1983: 57). Even a quite differently motivated, sophisticated approach by Menzela and Senghaas (1984) comes out with top marks for the two 'arch-NICs', Taiwan and Korea! Possibly, rather than following the often too mechanically designed clusters of indicators, a few avenues of recently elaborated positive criticism are far more rewarding, not the least in the provision of some solid and stimulating arguments for identifying 'true NICs'.

More often, and meanwhile quite frequently, many attempts of different methodological origin have been undertaken to present extensively the significance of 'intelligent' and cooperative policies of intervention, guiding and exploiting the allocation *via markets*.[10] By far transcending the trade sector, sectoral and macroeconomic policy in general proved decisive for what was dubbed 'getting policies right' (Bradford 1987: 315–16). Most remarkably, together with attempts to find the causal demands explaining *endogenous or autonomous growth* typical for TEs, international trade, too, has been differently evaluated. Completely in the tradition of the seminal approach by Kravis (1970), who transformed trade from an 'engine' to a 'handmaiden' (see also Riedel 1987), two authors from the Pacific region, Lee and Naya (1986), reinterpreted trade in an East Asian (NICs) context. Without denying trade the position as a leading sector, they think the impetus for export expansion did not come from abroad:

> What has made trade a leading sector is expansion in the supply capacity for exports and not in demand for them. What has expanded the supply capacity is a question still to be answered satisfactorily and is in fact a far more interesting and challenging question than what proximate effects trade has had on economic growth. (p. 35)

More is revealed about the strategic importance of supply capacity if economic growth and development is analysed as accelerating structrual change, heavily influenced by what Kindleberger and others called the 'capacity to transform'. Of particular interest appears to be the influence of policies guiding capital formation. The promotion of structural flexibility via macropolicies aiming at the costs of capital goods and the availability of financial funds is an old cornerstone of development economics in market and socialist economies alike. Marxist theorising and the Russian experience with regard to 'division I and II', as well as many examples from the European history of industrialisation demonstrate fairly well the central position of that significant factor. No wonder Bradford (1987) found relatively convincing empirical evidence in that respect explaining the high performance of the NICs. Just in comparison with World Bank arguments regarding the link between price distortions and development or trade strategies, Bradford's dictum warrants particular attention: 'Underpricing investment goods for a time through deliberate policies may be an important means of accelerating structural change and a key instrument in the strategy *for becoming a NIC*' (Bradford 1987: 307, 314; my emphasis, DL).

Closely related to economic growth and structural change is the ability to compete, which could be made a forceful indicator of export success. If export promotion is not only targeted superficially to rising market shares but is part of a true growth strategy, 'changes in the economic policy framework and in the structure of the economy will have to occur first' (Paus 1985: 39). In particular, they have to make sure that competitiveness is based on rising productivity and real wages. In an instructive investigation of four Latin American countries (Argentina, Colombia, Peru and Brazil) empirical evidence for a solid degree of competitiveness was only found in the case of Brazil!

Interestingly, the studies undertaken by Bradford and Paus also give evidence for a plausible thesis: the more comprehensive and pretentious the approaches for the analysis of 'transitional economies' are, the smaller the number of NICs becomes. Analysing sixteen TEs, Bradford reaches the tentative conclusion:

> There is a question of whether Columbia, Thailand, India and the Philippines are in fact in the process of becoming NICs. The evidence here is not conclusive, but it suggests they are not. From the figures in this section Malaysia appears to be the only next tier NIC to be on the NIC path rather than on the general development path. (Bradford 1987: 310)

The remark about Malaysia seems of equal importance as the mentioned exception of Brazil in the paper by Paus (cp. Ranis 1981: 219; Williamson 1985: 509).

In the same vein, the exclusion of countries regarding the status of a TE appears to be a consequence of two other factors that are rather heterogeneous but apparently converge: the transferability of the East Asian model and the different endowment of countries with respect to natural resources. Regarding the first factor, transferability, especially Latin America is a case in point. Many more or less convincing arguments have been put forward to explain why the East Asian model was not, and could not really be, applied in Latin America – if we again put aside Brazil as a possible exception! However, closer inspection of Latin American development performance brought into the open a very remarkable point that is directly related to the 'intelligent management' of markets already briefly touched upon above. While there seems to be much more overlapping in economic policies in general between East Asia and Latin America than is commonly held – in particular the problem 'is not a question of state intervention versus free market' – the real difference should be looked for on the instrumental level: 'it is a much more subtle issue of the goals to which state intervention is directed and *how that intervention is managed*' (Macomber 1987: 472; my emphasis, DL).[11]

The second factor, rich endowment with natural resources as a fundamental constraint or disincentive for an aggressive development policy/strategy on the lines of the G-4, at first was impressively made clear by the work of Ranis (1981), for instance. His detailed comparative analysis of import substitution versus export promotion phases and policies explained why the skipping of the 'primary export substitution sub-phase' in Latin America was important and for which reasons, namely not the least because of a natural resource bias (Ranis 1981: 215–20).[12] The disincentive regarding the full exploitation of simple labour-intensive exports is equally emphasised by Bradford when comparing Latin American countries with Asian ones (Bradford 1987: 302–5).

Most instructive, and surprising at the same time, is the extension and generalising of the argument by Lee and Naya (1986). They argue in the closer context of comparing Asian NICs and Asian NECs. Furthermore, besides the natural resource-bias of ASEAN countries they rightly emphasise the different 'character' of trade flows:

Although the governments profess to be committed to economic growth, there seems to be less urgency in the commitment. As the exports of the countries in Southeast Asia are as yet largely in resources and resource-based products, they do not often *compete* with commodities produced in importing countries ... there is thus *less urgency to be efficient and competitive* in the Southeast Asian countries than in the resource-poor East Asian countries. Moreover, rents constitute a large portion of the export revenues. As a result, in comparison with their counterparts in East Asia the governments in Southeast Asia are engaged more in the role of distributing rents and less in the role of promoting exports and economic growth. (Lee and Naya 1986: 7, 34; my emphasis, DL)

This is an interesting comparison indeed, but also a harsh judgement!

Hence, the status as TE is doubted for countries of the second/third generation of NICs/NECs, which commonly are regarded as very successful candidates. Parallel to the exception of Brazil in Latin America, one country in Southeast Asia, namely Malaysia, remarkably plays an outsider's role. 'There is a clear difference in the average outcomes between the NICs and Malaysia, on the one hand, and India and the next tier NICs on the other' (Bradford 1987: 309; cp. Ariff and Hill 1985: 60). If, moreover, the difference between Malaysia and the Philippines is considered more thoroughly (Ranis 1981: 219–20), then we might even *speculate* on a distinction between Chinese and Latin American 'style' in resource-rich Southeast Asian countries.[13] Possibly, it is not just by chance that until today also two large, relatively resource-poor countries like India and China showed apparently different NICs/TEs qualities. Some typical evidence presumably could be found in the different success EPZs displayed respectively.

DANGEROUS GENERALISATIONS VERSUS NICs REVISITED

Until today the NICs have remained a small but *demanding* group of developing 'transitional' countries. Learned discussions and topical publications of international organisations (OECD 1988; UN 1987; GATT 1987) alike document that statement reasonably well. By choosing the qualification 'demanding' the identification problem of the NICs is focused. Only if the *development* of developing countries is not seen from the initial stage of a *'newly'* industrialising or exporting country but rather is oriented at the ability and propensity to graduate into the stage of a developed country, the significance for the world economy likewise becomes better understood. The extension and lasting enforcement of the first 'Japan-shock' by the second East Asian NICs-shock has really been the core of the most effective dynamisation of development and competition in the South–North world economy.

This important and *particular* historical experience should not be generalised too easily, however. A follower group of equally successful worldwide countries is hardly to be expected as well as 'a simple linear process of continuously rising generations of national economies' (OECD 1988: 87), although apparently this was of concern when looking for NICs, recommending Asian models or developing a theory of stages. Perhaps even more inadequate appears to be the methodology of the 'new orthodoxy' founding political recommendation simply on prices, markets or foreign trade regimes – something like 'world markets without hinterlands' – instead of analysing developing countries as socioeconomic macro-units endowed with *domestic* markets and developmental states.

If we enlarge the approach as '*supply* economics' in the latter and general meaning then most NIC problems seem to alter to realistic dimensions and qualities although, of course, difficult problems of adjustment for the world economy and the countries in North and South still have to be solved. Equally, as the identification problem is eased, we could be less concerned than in the past about the rightly deplored 'artificiality' of group building. But then there is no need still to *underline* 'the very fluid and changing borders between groups of countries' (OECD 1988: 82). For the same reason one should not refer to 'a broad continuum from which new "NICs" can emerge' (OECD 1988: 87). As a matter of fact and of more differentiated considerations, the NICs/NECs continuum in Southeast Asia and Latin America appears to be rather narrow.

OPEN RESEARCH QUESTIONS

Three important fields remain for further research:

1. What about the procedures by which NICs/TEs will be assimilated in developed countries? Is that really a *country* pro-

blem or is it 'a phenomenon of successive upgrading in certain activities' (OECD 1988: 87)? Is the enlargement of integration areas – compare Europe/EC – a solution to graduate NICs? Will the United States follow a similar approach, and did it already start that way by looking at the Caribbean Basin Initiative or the Mexico policy? Furthermore, is the Pacific challenge of the twenty-first century possibly to be understood as a Pacific community of the Asian NICs with or without Japan and China respectively? (Lorenz 1989b).

2. Regional problems or problems of international regionalism – burdened with the particular problems of such second-best regimes – interestingly would also come into existence if the generally neglected *large* countries/NICs got closer attention. Hitherto they played no particular role (China, India) or they were classified simply as NICs (Brazil, Mexico, India, Indonesia) which was rather unsatisfying.[14] Do they prefer or avoid some kind of economic South–South dominance? To what extent might *extra*-regional trade be transformed into *intra*-regional or even into 'domestic' trade (Lorenz 1989a)? Are the constellations different for East Asia and for Latin America?

3. Finally, what can we say about the more or less large number of the residual of the 'less-developed countries'? Do they have no chance of becoming NICs, even with outward-looking policies or – to say it the other way around – will they have success without the mainstream medicine?

NOTES

1. Compare, for instance, OECD (1988), UN (1987, ch. 8), Balassa and Williamson (1987, chs 1 and 7), Athukorala (1986), Oshima (1986).
2. Compare for more details Lorenz (1988: 435–49) and Lorenz (1985).
3. Regarding EPZs and discussion in the section on a development model, it has to be emphasised that they 'cannot create comparative advantage' and that 'governments which adopt export processing zones as a policy instrument are acknowledging that their domestic policy frames have a substantial anti-export bias. They are also acknowledging that there is little hope, or even desire, to remove that bias in the short to medium run' (Wall 1987: 5). Spinanger (1984) speaks of the 'danger of EPZs being used by politicians as their "alibi" trade liberalisation policy' (p. 86); but he also underscores the

importance of country-specific linkages which are remarkably different (see Malaysia v. the Philippines, pp. 74–7).
4. This seems all the more true if we disregard the *untypical* import *surge* of the US economy in the 1980s (OECD 1985: 171–5; cp. also Table 13.3). The ability to penetrate import markets through relative competitiveness could be outweighted by the slowing down of demand in developed countries (see Athukorala 1986: 22–3)!
5. For a while, Israel and Argentina were added to the OECD sample. The 1988 report refers to only the G-4 and Mexico/Brazil.
6. In 1981, for instance, there is further information about the import shares of manufactures for the EC: Japan 5.8 per cent, eastern and southern Europe 5.0 per cent, the G-4 plus 3 ASEAN countries 4.0 per cent (Lorenz 1988: 431). Brazil and Mexico are not documented separately.
7. The recent statement of the OECD (1988: 82) that 'the European countries, on the whole, are much less exposed to the NICs than the non-European Members' (of the OECD) thus does not appear fully justified because the OECD–NIC group of six (!) is at least too small for Europe. Compare also Hughes and Newberry (1986: 436) and Poznanski (1986) as well as the literature quoted in Lorenz (1988: 427, footnote 3).
8. Cp. also Table 13.3. With regard to the United States and Japan the NICs are 'an intermediary participant in trade flows which intensify the trade imbalances of the two major OECD countries' (OECD 1988: 82).
9. Quite apart from the world economic dimensions these two city-states have developed!
10. For the eminent role the so-called 'developmental state' has played in the Asian NICs, compare, for instance, the two conference volumes edited by R.A. Scalapino *et al.* (1985) and by F.C. Deyo (1987) as well as Pack and Westphal (1986), Bradford and Branson (1987: 16–23) and Sachs (1985: 548–60).
11. Williamson (1985: 568) adds a very important and plausible point: 'My basic explanation of differential performance would run in terms of farsightedness of policy formation'!
12. The resource bias includes what is now called 'Dutch disease' and what Ranis dubbed 'Kuwait effect'. Interestingly, Teitel and Thoumi (1985/1986: 486) argue slightly differently because of a divergent evaluation of the determinants of the growth process in the case of Brazil and Argentina. The new manufactured exports of the 1970s were not really the exclusive results of export incentives, but rather the 'natural' consequences with regard to the 'wisdom . . . to follow, as in Southeast Asia, an export-oriented strategy largely based on unskilled labour-intensive industries'.
13. See also the comment by H.W. Singer (1986: 302–3) on the comparative study of South Korea and the Philippines by Datta Chaudhuri.
14. Compare the group of 'natural resource NICs' (Brazil, Mexico, Argentina, Indonesia) on the one hand (Bradford and Branson 1987:

8), and the 'case India' on the other hand – considered as a NIC by Bradford and Branson as well as by Havrylyshyn and Alikhani (1982: 652) – in either case without adequate or convincing reasons!

REFERENCES

Ariff, Mohamed and Hall Hill (1985), *Export-oriented Industrialization: The ASEAN Experience*, Sydney: Macmillan.
Athukorala, Premachandra (1986), *Export Performance of 'New Exporting Countries': How valid is the optimism?*, mimeo, Victoria, Australia: La Trabe University.
Balassa, Bela (1977), 'A 'stages' approach to comparative advantage', *World Bank Staff Working Paper*, no. 256.
Balassa, Bela (1980), 'The process of industrial development and alternative development strategies', *Essays in International Finance*, no. 141, Princeton.
Balassa, Bela and John Williamson (1987), *Ajusting to Success: Balance of Payments Policy in the East Asian NICs*, Washington: Institute for International Economics.
Bergmann, Christel (1983), *Schwellenländer. Kriterien und Konzepte*, Münich: Weltforum Verlag.
Bradford, Colin I. (1987), 'Trade and structural change: NICs and next tier NICs as transitional economies', *World Development*, vol. 15, pp. 299–316.
Bradford, Colin I., Jr and William H. Branson (1987), *Trade and Structural Change in Pacific Asia*, Chicago/London: University of Chicago Press.
Branson, William H. (1987), 'Trade and structural interdependence between the United States and the newly industrializing countries', in Colin I. Bradford Jr and William H. Branson (eds) *Trade and Structural Change in Pacific Asia*, Chicago: University of Chicago Press, pp. 27–60.
Cline, William R. (1982), 'Can the East Asian model of development be generalized?', *World Development*, vol. 10, pp. 81–90.
Cline, William R. (1984), *Exports of Manufactures from Developing Countries. Performance and Prospects for Market Access*, Washington: Brookings Institution.
Cumings, Bruce (1984), 'The origins of the Northeast Asian political economy: industrial sectors and political consequences 1900–1980', *International Organisation*, vol. 38, pp. 1–40.
Deyo, Frederic C. (ed.) (1987), *The Political Economy of the New Asian Industrialism*, Ithaca, NY: Cornell University Press.
GATT (1987), *International Trade 86–87*, Geneva.
Havrylyshyn, Oli and Iradj Alikhani (1982), 'Is there cause for export optimism? An inquiry into the existence of a second generation of successful exporters', *Weltwirtschaftliches Archiv*, vol. 118, pp. 651–63.

Hughes, Gordon A. and David M.G. Newberry (1986), 'Protection and developing countries' exports of manufactures', *European Policy*, vol. 1, pp. 410–41.
Kravis, Irving B. (1970), 'Trade as a handmaiden of growth: similarities between the nineteenth and twentieth centuries', *The Economic Journal*, vol. 80, pp. 850–72.
Krugman, Paul R. (1986), 'Comment on the paper by Hughes and Newberry', *European Policy*, vol. 1, pp. 443–5.
Lau, Lawrence J. (ed.) (1986), *Models of Development. A Comparative Study of Economic Growth in South Korea and Taiwan*, San Francisco: ICS Press.
Lee, Chung H., and Seigi Naya (1986), *Trade in East Asian Development with Comparative Reference to Southeast Asian Experiences*, paper presented at the conference on 'Why does overcrowded resource-poor East Asia succeed – Lessons for the LDCs?', mimeo, Nashville: Vanderbilt University.
Little, Ian M.D. (1987), 'A comment on Professor Toye's paper' in Louis Emmerij (ed.), *Development Policies and the Crisis of the 1980s*, Paris: Development Center of the OECD, pp. 42–8.
Little, Ian, Tibor Scitovsky and Maurice Scott (1970), *Industry and Trade in Some Developing Countries: A Comparative Study*, London: Oxford University Press.
Lorenz, Detlef (1985), 'Deficiencies of orthodox foreign trade theory with regard to employment', *Intereconomics*, vol. 20, pp. 122–9.
Lorenz, Detlef (1986), 'New situations facing the NICs in East Asia', *Intereconomics*, vol. 21, pp. 263–8.
Lorenz, Detlef (1987), 'NICs, China and Pacific cooperation', *Sino-Soviet Affairs*, vol. 11, pp. 51–64.
Lorenz, Detlef (1988), 'Industrial imports from the Asian NICs, principal adjustment problems and European strategies of protectionism', paper presented at the East-West Center Conference, Honolulu (April 1983), in Hans W. Singer, Neclamber Hatti and Rameswar Tandon (eds), *New World Order Series, Vol, IV: New Protectionism and Restructuring*. New Delhi: Ashish Publishing House, pp. 421–58.
Lorenz, Detlef (1989a), 'Intra-regional trade and Pacific cooperation: problems and prospects', in Wolfgang Klenner (ed.), *Trends of Economic Development in East Asia*, Berlin: Springer, pp. 65–74.
Lorenz, Detlef (1989b), 'Trade in manufactures, newly industrialising countries (NICs) and regional development in the world economy – a European view' in *The Developing Economies*, vol. 27, no. 3.
Macomber, John D. (1987), 'East Asia's lessons for Latin American resurgence', *The World Economy*, vol. 10, pp.469–82.
Meier, Gerald M. (1985), 'The new export pessimism', in Toshio Shishido and Ryvzo Sato (eds), *Economic Policy and Development*, Dover, Mass.: Auburn House Publishing, pp. 19–32.
Menzel, Ulrich and Dieter Senghaas (1984), *Indikatoren zur Bestimmung von Schwellenländern. Ein Vorschlag zur Operationalisierung*, Bre-

men: Berichte aus dem Weltwirtschaftlichen Colloquium der Universität Bremen.
Michaely, Michael (1984), 'The demand for protection against exports of newly-industrializing countries', *Journal of Policy Modelling*, vol. 7, pp. 123–132.
Naja, Seiji (1986), *Role of Trade Policies: Competition and Cooperation*, Honolulu/Hawaii: mimeo, Resource Systems Institute, East–West Center.
OECD (1979), *The Impact of the Newly-Industrialising Countries on Production and Trade in Manufactures*, Paris.
OECD/DAC (1982), *Development Co-operation*, review, Paris (ch. 12).
OECD (1985), *Costs and Benefits of Protection*, Paris.
OECD (1988), *The Newly-Industrialising Countries: Challenge and Opportunity for OECD Industries*, Paris.
Oshima, Harry T. (1986), 'The construction boom of the 1970s: the end of high growth in the NICs and Asean?', *The Developing Economics*, vol. 24, pp. 207–28.
Pack, Howard and Larry E. Westphal (1986), 'Industrial strategy and technological change: theory versus reality', *Journal of Development Economics*, vol. 22, pp. 87–128.
Paus, Eva (1985), *Manufactured Export Growth in Latin America in the 1970s: Reflection of Improved Competitiveness?*, mimeo, Diskussionsbeiträge des Ibero-Amerika Instituts für Wirtschaftsforschung, no. 37, Göttingen. Extended version forthcoming in *Journal of Developing Areas* (1989).
Perkins, Dwight H. (1986), *China: Asia's Next Economic Giant?*, Seattle; University of Washington Press.
Poznanski, Kasimierz (1986), *Competition Between Eastern Europe and Developing Countries in the Western Market for Manufactured Goods*. Eastern European volume, Washington: The Joint Economic Committee of US Congress.
Ranis, Gustav (1981), 'Challenges and opportunities by Asia's superexporters: implications for manufactured exports from Latin America', in Werner Baer and Malcolm Gillis (eds), *Export Diversification and the New Protectionism*, Champaign: University of Illinois Press, pp. 204–21.
Riedel, James (1987), *Myths and Realities of External Constraints on Development*, London: Gower, for the Trade Policy Research Centre.
Sachs, Jeffrey D. (1985), 'External debt and macroeconomic performance in Latin American and East Asia', *Brookings Papers on Economic Activity*, pp. 523–64.
Scalapino, Robert A., Seizaburo Sato and Jusuf Wanandi (eds) (1985), *Asian Economic Development. Present and Future*, Berkeley: University of California, Institute of East Asian Studies.
Singer, Hans W. and Parrin Alizadeh (1986), 'Import substitution revisited in a darkening external environment', *Razvoy/Development – International*, vol. I/2, pp. 295–321.

Spinanger, Dean (1984), 'Objectives and impact of economic activity zones – some evidence from Asia', *Weltwirtschaftliches Archiv*, vol. 120, pp. 64–89.

Teitel, Simon and Francesco Thoumi (1985/86), 'From import substitution to exports: the manufacturing exports experience of Argentina and Brazil', *Economic Development and Cultural Exchange*, vol. 34, pp. 455–90.

Turner, Louis and Neil McMullen (eds) (1982), *The Newly Industrializing Countries: Trade and Adjustment*, London: Publication for the Royal Institute for International Affairs.

Tylers, Rodney, Prue Phillips and Christopher Findlay (1987), 'ASEAN and China exports of labour-intensive manufactures: performance and prospects', *ASEAN Economic Bulletin*, vol. 3, pp. 339–67.

UNCTAD (1986), *Salient Features of Trends and Policies in Trade of Manufactures*, Geneva (TD/B/C. 2/223, Parts I and II).

United Nations (1987), *World Economic Survey 1987*, New York (ch. VIII).

Wall, David (1987), *The Nature, Rationale and Role of Export Processing Zones with Special Reference to China*, mimeo, University of Sussex.

Williamson, John (1985), 'Comment on the paper by J.D. Sachs', *Brookings Papers on Economic Activity*, pp. 565–70.

Wolf, Martin (1983), *'Fortress Europe' and 'Collective Self-Reliance'*, Hamburg: Deutsches Übersee Institut.

Yamazawa, Ippei (1986), *Industrialization through the Full Utilization of Foreign Trade: The case of some East Asian countries*, paper presented at the 8th World Congress of the International Economic Association, mimeo, New Delhi.

INDEX

acceptances in merchant banking, 194–5
Africa, foreign investment in, 208
Allarde, Pierre Le Roy d', Atlantic trade, 92–3, 97–100
America
 Latin *see* Latin America
 United States *see* United States of America
Amsterdam, financial centre, 192, 193, 203
animals, transplantation to other continents, 160
Antwerp, financial centre, 191–2
Argentina
 debt, 326, 327, 328–9, 332
 product decline and import capacity, 319–21
 trade surplus, 331
 vent-for-surplus theory, 163
 see also Latin America
Asia
 European overseas banks, 212–13
 foreign investment in, 208
 integration into world economy, 61–89
 newly industrialising countries, 341–61
assignats in Atlantic trade, 93, 96, 102, 103, 148n
Atlantic trade during French Revolution, 91–150
Australia
 foreign investment and loans in, 207–8, 209
 transplantation of animals to, 160
 vent-for-surplus theory, 163
Austria
 financial crisis (1931), 252, 299, 310
 foreign investment, 206
Austria-Hungary
 foreign investment in, 205–6, 213
automobile production *see* car industry

Baker Plan, Latin American debt relief, 334
Balkans, foreign investment in, 205–6, 213
Bank of England
 currency convertibility, 260–84
 international role, 18, 19, 208
 in 1930s' financial crisis, 253–4
Bank for International Settlements (BIS), 264, 267–8, 308–9
banking system
 factor in development of trade, 19
 growth to 1914, 191–219
 in 1930s' financial crisis, 252–3
Banque de Paris et des Pays-Bas (Paribas), 203, 211, 214
barbasco plant, source of steroid hormones, 164
Baring family, merchant bankers, 101–3, 112–13, 116–19, 125–30, 195, 209
Basle protocol (1975), 311
Batavia, China seas trade, 65, 78, 81, 86

Belgium
  banks, 198–9, 213
  currency convertibility, 271–2
  effects of First World War, 240
  foreign investment, 206
Berlin, market for British coal, 183–5
biens nationaux, 130, 136
bills of exchange
  merchant banking, 194, 196
  US banking system, 213, 214
bimetallic monetary standards, 17
BIS (Bank for International
    Settlements), 264, 267–8, 308–9
Bolivia
  foreign debt, 252, 326, 334
  see also Latin America
botanical distribution, nineteenth-
    century changes, 160
Braudel, Fernand, 61–2, 63–4, 70, 72
Brazil
  economic growth, 224, 225, 226, 227,
    228–9
  rubber cultivation, 160
  see also Latin America; newly
    industrialising countries
Bretton Woods agreements, 20, 230,
    231, 264–6, 289, 301, 304, 311
Britain
  currency convertibility, 260–84
  currency stabilisation, 243
  exports, 275–8
    coal, 168–90
  foreign investment, 204–5, 206, 208
  free trade, 13–15
  monetary system, 17
  rearmament, pre-Second World
    War, 257
  recovery, inter-war period, 255
  share of world trade, 4–6
business cycle, relationship to
    commodity and price structure,
    7

Canada
  foreign investment in, 207–8
  grain trade, 9, 159
  staple theory, 38
  vent-for-surplus theory, 163

canal building, effect on trade, 16
Canton, centre for European trade, 84,
    85
capital-accumulation effect of trade, 44
capital flows
  maintenance by world economic
    leader, 289
  United States, 290, 303–7
capital stock
  effect of First World War, 240
  growth, 232
capitalism, relation to colonial system,
    161–2
car industry
  Germany, inter-war period, 256
  Japan, 11
cartelisation, German coal, 184, 186
centre and periphery
  twentieth-century world economy,
    285–365
  United States' position, 288
Ceylon, transplantation of tea to, 160
Chile *see* Latin America
China
  economic growth, 226, 227, 228, 231,
    233
  influence on Asian newly
    industrialising countries, 341–2
  tea transplantation, 160
  unequal treaties, 23
China seas, and world economy, 61–89
Chinese junk trade, 85–6
classical trade theory, 34–40
clothing industry, newly industrialising
    countries, 347
coal, British, in Continental markets,
    168–90
Cobden–Chevalier Treaty (1860), 13–
    14
Codman brothers, Atlantic trade
    merchants, 91–150
coffee
  Atlantic trade, 105–6, 107, 119, 142n
  European imports of stimulants, 157
'Collective Approach', 261–75, 282
Colombia *see* Latin America; newly
    industrialising countries
colonialism, effects, 161–2, 164–5

commodity composition of trade, effects of Industrial Revolution, 159–60
commodity markets, US role, 292–8
commodity structure, 6–9
communication costs, effect on trade, 16
comparative advantage theory, 34–5, 53, 153–4, 349
competitiveness, transitional economies, 357
Corn Laws, repeal, 13, 40
cotton, cotton materials
  Atlantic trade, 120, 122
  China seas trade, 75, 83
  Indian, effect of Industrial Revolution, 159
country substitution, developing countries, 349
Couteulx, Le see Le Couteulx et Cie
Crédit Mobilier, 199–201, 205, 211, 212, 214
crisis management, function of world economic leader, 289
currency
  convertibility, 260–84
  stabilisation, 242–3, 246–7
  see also monetary relations

d'Allarde, Pierre Le Roy, see Allarde, Pierre Le Roy d'
Dawes Plan and loan (1920s), 244–5, 304
debt see foreign debt; war debts
decision-making, Atlantic trade merchants, 116, 144n
decolonisation, effects, 161–2
Denmark see Scandinavia
Depression see Great Depression
Deutschmark, currency convertibility, 260–84
developing countries see newly industrialising countries
development
  theoretical issues, 31–57
  through trade, 41–54
development stages, theories, 287–8, 347–9

division of labour, international, 42, 340, 343
dual sector model of development, 37, 38–40
'Dutch disease', 362n
Dutch East India Company, 68, 69–70, 77–82, 84
dynamic efficiency, 51–3

early industrial trade, 59–150
East China Sea, 64–70
economic development, theoretical issues, 31–57
economic growth and stagnation, 221–84
  Latin America, 314–37
economic hegemony, 153–67, 282
'economic miracles', Europe, 6
'économie-monde, l'', 63–4
écu, 264
educative effect of trade, 43
energy sources, role in industrialisation and growth, 12, 168
'engine of growth', 34, 41, 344
English East India Company, 82–5
entrepreneurial skills
  newly industrialising countries, 355–6
  relation to export development, 45–6
EPU (European Payments Union), 263–5, 267, 268–72, 275, 276, 277–9, 281
EPZs (export processing zones), 341, 343, 347, 355
ES (export-led growth strategy), 340, 344, 346, 347
Europe
  currency convertibility, 260–82
  domination of world trade, 4–6, 11, 154–8
  industrialisation, 10–12
  international banking, 190–219
  trade in China seas, 61–89
  and world economy, 153–67, 239–59
European Monetary Agreement, 275–7
European Payments Union see EPU

European Recovery Program (Marshall Plan), 264, 266, 289, 301, 305, 309, 310, 311
exchange rates, 19–22, 242–3, 246–8, 298–303
see also currency
export-goods production function, 45
Export–Import Bank, 305, 311
export-led growth strategy (ES), 340, 344, 346, 347
export processing zones (EPZs), 341, 343, 347, 355
export stimuli, 44–8
exports per head of population, 235
'external sterling', 261
external war debts, effect of First World War, 244–5

factor-weight effect of trade, 44
FAO (Food and Agriculture Organization), 289
Federal Reserve System (US), 298, 306, 310
financial innovation, 11, 151–219
fiscal policy, US, 290–1, 307–10
Food and Agriculture Organization (FAO), 289
Fordney-McCumber tariff (1922), 244, 293
foreign capital, Latin America, 324–30
foreign debt
 Europe, 248–9
 Latin America, 232, 306, 315, 324–35
foreign exchange, US role, 290, 298–303
foreign investment, 204–8
Formosa
 East China Sea trade, 67, 77
 see also Taiwan
France
 banks, 197–204, 208–10, 212–13, 215
 effects of First World War, 240
 foreign investment, 205–6
 recovery, after 1930s' Depression, 256
 see also French Revolution

free trade, 12–15, 292–6
 see also classical trade theory
'free-trade imperialism', 296
freight rates
 coal shipments from Britain, 168–70, 177–8, 179, 180, 184, 186
 see also transport costs
French Revolution
 Atlantic trade, 91–150
 effect on international finance, 194

'Gang of Four' (G-4), 339, 341, 347
GATT (General Agreement on Tariffs and Trade), 15, 265, 339, 340
GDP (gross domestic product), 4, 223–33, 235, 236, 245, 314, 316
General Agreement on Tariffs and Trade *see* GATT
General System of Preferences (GSP), 340
Genoa Conference (1922), 247
Germany
 banks, 202, 204, 212–13
 currency convertibility, 260–84
 financial crisis (1931), 252, 299, 310
 foreign investment, 206
 market for British coal, 178–86
 recovery after 1930s' Depression, 256
 reparations after First World War, 244–5, 249, 250–1, 310, 328
gold standard, 17, 18, 19–21, 246–8, 255
'Golden Avalanche', 301
Gompertz curve of material transformation, 288
goods markets (commodity markets), US role, 292–8
grain trade, 9, 91, 159, 169
Great Depression (1873–96), 14, 16, 18, 19
Great Depression (1929–39), 249–57, 314–35
gross domestic product *see* GDP
growth
 economic, 221–84
 industrial, determinant of world trade, 10–12

INDEX

GSP (General System of Preferences), 340
guano, 166n

H–O (Heckscher–Ohlin) theory of trade, 53
habit-forming stimulants, European imports, 157
Hamburg
  commercial and financial centre, 104
  market for British coal, 179–80, 181
haute banque parisienne, 197, 211, 212
Hawley–Smoot tariff, 14, 251–2, 294, 295
Heckscher–Ohlin (H–O) theory of trade, 53
hegemony, economic, 153–67, 282
hevea brasiliensis seeds, smuggling and cultivation, 160
'hinterland relationships', newly industrialising countries, 349, 352–4
Hongkong *see* 'Gang of Four'
Hungary, Austrian investment in, 206

ideas, diffusion through international movements of capital, 216
ideologies, effect on integration of markets, 10
IET (Interest Equalization Tax), 305
IMF (International Monetary Fund), 264–5, 273, 301
impact effect of trade, 43–4
Imperial Preference system, 255
imperialism, 162, 296
import-substituting industrialisation (ISI), 40, 49–51
import substitution, 314, 324
  effect on development, 48–9, 358
income-distribution effect of trade, 44
increasing returns to scale, 10–12
indexation, effect on inflation, 332
India
  cotton industry, effect of Industrial Revolution, 159
  economic growth, 225, 226, 227, 228, 231, 233
  newly industrialising country, 357
  tea transplantation, 160
  vent-for-surplus theory, 163
Indonesia *see* newly industrialising countries
industrial growth, 2–4, 10–12
Industrial Revolution, effects, 158–9
industrialisation, 11, 12, 168, 176–7, 241
infant industry protection, 49–51
inflation
  Atlantic trade during French Revolution, 91–100
  after First World War, 242–3
  Latin America, 332–3
information, for Atlantic trade during French Revolution, 116–24
innovation, technological and financial, 11, 151–219
integration of markets, 10, 160
inter-war period
  Europe and world economy, 239–59
  United States, 289
Interest Equalization Tax (IET), 305
internal war debts, effect of First World War, 242–3
International Bank of Reconstruction and Development (World Bank), 304
international division of labour, 42, 340, 343
International Energy Agency, 297
international holding company, origin, 213
International Monetary Fund (IMF), 264–5, 273, 301
Intra-European Payments Scheme, 310
intra-industry trade, growth, 9
investment, international, 204–8
'invisible hand', 216
ISI (import-substituting industrialisation), 40, 49–51
Italian bankers, 191–2

Japan
  banking system, 215–16
  car industry, 11

Japan (*continued*)
  China seas trade, 64–6, 68–9
  status as industrialised country, 341
'Japan-bashing', 297
joint stock banks, 197–204, 208, 212–13, 214–15

Kondratieff model of recurring cycles, 288
Korea
  China seas trade, 68, 69
  newly industrialising country, 356
  see also 'Gang of Four'
'Kuwait effect', 362n

labour, in dual sector model, 38–40
labour skills, relation to exports, 45–6
labour unions, attitude to free trade, 29
laissez-faire, 12, 139n, 229
Latin America
  economic growth and decline, 229, 232–3, 314–37
  European overseas banks, 212–13
  financial crisis (1930s), 252
  foreign investment in, 208
Latin Monetary Union, 17
law *see* legal security
Le Couteulx et Cie, Atlantic trade, 92–100
leading-sector analysis, 37–8
legal security, determinant of world trade, 22–3
Lend-Lease, 289, 304, 311
lender of last resort, 18, 20, 289, 290, 299
  United States, 310–12
Locarno Pact (1925), 246
loi Dallarde, 139n
London, financial and banking centre, 18, 208, 247–8
Louvre agreement (1987), 303, 311

Macao
  China seas trade, 73, 75, 77
  see also newly industrialising countries

macro-economic policy, US, 290, 307–10
Magdeburg, market for British coal, 180–3
Malacca, China seas trade, 70, 75
Malaya, Malaysia,
  China seas trade, 71, 79
  rubber cultivation, 160
  see also newly industrialising countries
Manila, China seas trade, 73, 75, 77, 82, 86
maritime space, 61–2, 64–5
mark, German *see* Deutschmark
markets
  commodity, 290, 292–8
  effects of First World War, 241–2
  rationalisation and integration, 10, 160
Marshall Aid and Plan (European Recovery Program), 264, 266, 289, 301, 305, 309, 310, 311
Mediterranean sea, maritime space, 61–2
Méditerranée et le monde méditerranéen à l'époque de Philippe II, La, 61
mercantilism, 12–13
merchant banking, 194–7, 209–10
Mexico
  barbasco-based industry, 164
  US loans, 306
  see also Latin America; newly industrialising countries
Mill, John Stuart, 36, 42–3
monetary policy, US, 290, 307–10
monetary relations, determinant of world trade, 17–22
Multi-Fibre Arrangement, 347
multilateral treaties, 23
multinational firms, 164, 191, 347

Nagasaki, China seas trade, 66, 67, 73, 81, 86
Napoleonic Wars, effects, 4, 17, 194
National Monetary Commission (US), 307–8
Navigation Act, repeal, 13

NDCs (newly declining countries), 338, 339
NECs (newly exporting countries), 344–6
neo-protectionism, 347, 355
Netherlands
 banks, 198–9
 currency convertibility, 271, 272
 effect of OPEC oil embargo, 297
 foreign investment, 206
 market for British coal, 176–8
New York, financial centre, 248
New Zealand, foreign investment in, 207–8
newly declining countries (NDCs), 338, 339
newly exporting countries (NECs), 344–6
newly industrialising countries (NICs), 48, 338–65
Norway *see* Scandinavia
'nuclear group' of currencies, 266, 270

OECD countries
 economic performance, 223–37
 effect of newly industrialising countries, 343–4
OEEC, trade supervision, 263, 273
 see also EPU, OECD
oil
 importance for new industrial civilisation, 161
 see also OPEC
OMAs (orderly marketing agreements), 15
OPEC
 embargo and price increases (oil shocks), 9, 231, 239, 297, 306
 power strategy, 340
'Operation Robot', 261–5, 282
opium, China seas trade, 85, 157–8
opportunity and risk, Atlantic trade during French Revolution, 90–150
orderly marketing agreements (OMAs), 15
'organisational dualism', 52

Organization for Economic Co-operation and Development *see* OECD
Organization for European Economic Co-operation *see* OEEC
Organization of Petroleum Exporting Countries *see* OPEC

Pacific, newly industrialising countries, 361
Paribas (Banque de Paris et des Pays-Bas), 203, 211, 214
Patani (Malaya), China seas trade, 79
Payne-Aldrich tariff, 293
peasant export crops, 36
periphery and centre, twentieth-century world economy, 285–365
Peru *see* Latin America
pharmaceutical industry, Mexico, 164
Philippines
 China seas trade, 71, 72, 73
 see also Manila; newly industrialising countries
Plaza Agreement (1985), 303, 311
population increase, 6, 159, 234–5, 241
Portugal
 China seas trade, 65, 66, 68, 73, 74–6
 newly industrialising country, 343, 346, 352
 Ricardo's comparative cost theory, 34, 40
post-war reconstruction and recovery, Europe, 240–5
pound sterling
 currency convertibility, 260–84
 valuation and devaluation, inter-war period, 246–7, 253–4
power, as capacity to produce and move goods, 288
pre-industrial trade, 59–89
price structure, 6–9
primary goods, new sources, 159
primary products, share of world trade, 7
product substitution, developing countries, 349

productivity theory, 35, 42
protectionism, 12–15, 251, 295, 347, 352, 355
Prussia *see* Germany

'quota hopping', 347
'quota propelled growth', 347

railways
  effect on trade, 16
  Germany, 179, 180, 181–2, 186
  Netherlands, 177–8, 187n
  Russia, 207
  see also transport
Randall Commission, 267, 273
rational market behaviour, 163–4
raw materials, for industrial growth, 9, 12, 161
rearmament, Europe, 257
Reciprocal Trade Agreements Act (1934), 15, 289, 295
reconstruction, Europe, 240–5
recovery
  after Great Depression, 254–7
  post-war, 240–5
regional structure of world trade, 4–6
reparations after First World War, 244–5, 249, 250–1, 310, 328
Republican Party (US), attitude to free trade, 14, 293
Ricardo's comparative cost theory, 34–5, 40
rice, transplantation, 160
risk and opportunity, Atlantic trade during French Revolution, 90–150, 116
road building, effect on trade, 16, 256
Rothschild family, bankers, 194, 195–7, 198, 200–2, 203, 209
rubber cultivation, 160
Russia
  banking system, 215
  economic growth, 226, 227, 228–9
  foreign investment in, 207
  trade ventures to US, 124
  see also USSR

Ryukyu islands, China seas trade, 69, 71, 72, 73

S-curve of material transformation, 288
Saint-Simon, Count Henri de, 198
Scandinavia
  banking system, 214–15
  foreign investment in, 207
SDRs (Special Drawing Rights), 302
Seoul declaration on Third World debt, 292
Siam, China seas trade, 71, 72, 73, 76, 79
silk, China seas trade, 77, 78, 79, 80–1
silver
  China seas trade, 75–6, 78, 82–3
  coins and monetary standard, 17–18, 300
Singapore *see* 'Gang of Four'
Singer–Prebisch thesis, 7
skilled labour
  effect of First World War, 240
  relation to exports, 45
Smith, Adam, 11, 12, 35, 42, 216
Smithsonian agreement (1971), 302
Smoot–Hawley tariff *see* Hawley–Smoot tariff
Société Générale de Belgique, 198–9, 213
Société Générale de Crédit Mobilier *see* Crédit Mobilier
South China Sea, 70–3
Spain, China seas trade, 73, 75
Special Drawing Rights (SDRs), 302
spectacles, significance of invention, 166n
stages of development, theories, 287–8, 347–9
stagnation and growth, twentieth-century, 221–84
staple theory, 37–8, 163
statistics of world trade, 1–2
steam engine, effect on transport, 16
steamships, for coal transport, 170–1, 173, 179
sterling *see* pound sterling

INDEX 375

steroid hormone production, Mexico, 164
stimulants, European imports, 157
stock market crashes
  (1929), 249–50
  (1987), 239
substitution effect of trade, 44
Suez Canal, effect on trade, 16, 173
sugar, European imports, 157
supply-motored model of staple theory, 43–4
Sweden, banks, 215
  energy sources, 187n
  recovery, inter-war period, 255
  vent-for-surplus theory, 163
  see also Scandinavia
Switzerland
  energy sources, 168
  foreign investment, 206

Taiwan, 356
  see also Formosa; 'Gang of Four'
tariffs, 13, 14, 15, 251–2, 257, 292–6
tea
  China seas trade, 77, 84
  European imports of stimulants, 157
  transplantation, 160
technological innovation, 11, 151–219
technology
  diffusion with international movements of capital, 216
  effect of Industrial Revolution, 158–60
telegraph, effect on trade, 16
terms of trade, 79, 162–3, 316–17, 318, 319
TEs (transitional economies), 354–9
textile industry, newly industrialising countries, 346, 347
Thailand see newly industrialising countries
theoretical issues, trade and development, 31–57
Third World
  impoverishment, precondition for industrial growth in Europe, 11
  share of world trade, 6

source of raw materials, 161
  see also newly industrialising countries
tobacco, European imports of stimulants, 157
trade
  contribution to development, 33–58, 41–54
  pre-industrial and early industrial, 59–150
  theoretical issues, 31–57
  world
    evolution, 1–30
    increase after Industrial Revolution, 158–9
trade barriers, determinant of world trade, 12–15
  see also protectionism; tariffs
trade theory, classical, 34–40
trade treaties, 13–14
trade wars, 14, 254
trades unions, attitude to free trade, 296
transitional economies (TEs), 354–9
transport, effect of First World War, 240
transport costs, effect on world trade, 16, 158
  see also freight rates
treaties
  multilateral, 23
  trade, 13–14
Tripartite Monetary Agreement (1936), 20, 271, 289, 301, 310–11

United Kingdom see Britain
United Nations see UNRRA
United States of America
  Atlantic trade during French Revolution, 91–150
  banking system, 212, 213–14
  currency convertibility, 273–4
  economic growth, 226, 227, 228–9, 230, 241
  economic leader, 288

United States of America (*continued*)
  foreign investment in (1870–1914), 205–6
  Great Depression (1929–1939), 249–50
  industrialisation, 12
  investment abroad, 206–7
  recovery, after 1930s' Depression, 255
  share of world trade, 6
  trade policy, 14–15
  vent-for-surplus theory, 163
  in world economy, 288–313
Universal Postal Union, 23
UNRRA (United Nations Relief and Rehabilitation Agency), 289, 305
USSR
  economic growth, 226, 227, 229, 231, 233
  see also Russia

vent-for-surplus theory, 35, 163
VERs (voluntary export restraints), 15
Vietnam, China seas trade, 71–3, 80–1
Vietnam War (1960s), effect on US balance of payments, 302
Voluntary Credit Restraint Program (US), 305

voluntary export restraints (VERs), 15

war debts, effect of First World War 242–5, 310
war preparations (1930s), 257
water power, for industrialisation, 168, 186–7n
water transport, 16, 177, 178
Wealth of Nations see Smith, Adam
working population *see* skilled labour
World Bank (International Bank of Reconstruction and Development), 304
World Economic Conference (1927), 293
World Economic Conference (1933), 255, 294, 299, 334
world trade
  evolution, 1–30
  increase after Industrial Revolution, 158–9
World Wars
  effects, 6, 19, 239–45
  preparations, 257

Young Plan (1930s), 251, 308

zero-sum society, 288
zoological distribution, nineteenth-century changes, 160